CODE CALCULATIONS

Based on the 2020 *National Electrical Code*®

Code Calculations is intended to be an educational resource for the user and contains procedures commonly practiced in industry and the trade. Specific procedures vary with each task and must be performed by a qualified person. For maximum safety, always refer to specific manufacturer recommendations, insurance regulations, specific job site and plant procedures, applicable federal, state, and local regulations, and any authority having jurisdiction. The *electrical training ALLIANCE* assumes no responsibility or liability in connection with this material or its use by any individual or organization.

© 2020, 2017, 2014, 2011 *electrical training ALLIANCE*

This material is for the exclusive use by the IBEW-NECA JATCs and programs approved by the *electrical training ALLIANCE*. Possession and/or use by others is strictly prohibited as this proprietary material is for exclusive use by the *electrical training ALLIANCE* and programs approved by the *electrical training ALLIANCE*.

All rights reserved. No part of this material shall be reproduced, stored in a retrieval system, or transmitted by any means whether electronic, mechanical, photocopying, recording, or otherwise without the express written permission of the *electrical training ALLIANCE*.

1 2 3 4 5 6 7 8 9 – 20 – 9 8 7 6 5 4 3 2 1

Printed in the United States of America

TABLE OF CONTENTS

CHAPTER 1	**ELECTRICAL SYSTEMS**	XIV

1.1	GENERAL	2
1.2	SINGLE-PHASE 2-WIRE SYSTEMS	2
1.3	SINGLE-PHASE 3-WIRE SYSTEMS	3
1.4	3-PHASE 4-WIRE WYE SYSTEM	4
1.5	3-PHASE 4-WIRE DELTA SYSTEM	6
1.6	3-WIRE MULTIPHASE SYSTEMS	9
	DEFINITIONS AND TERMS	10
	SUMMARY	10
	REVIEW QUESTIONS	11

TABLE OF CONTENTS

CHAPTER 2 CONDUCTOR AMPACITY CALCULATIONS — 12

2.1	GENERAL	14
2.2	AMPACITY	14
2.3	TABLES	15
2.4	FACTORS AFFECTING AMPACITY	16
2.5	310.15 AMPACITY TABLES FOR CONDUCTORS RATED 0–2,000 VOLTS	17
2.6	PROBLEMS USING A TEMPERATURE CORRECTION FACTOR	21
2.7	PROBLEMS USING AN ADJUSTMENT FACTOR	22
2.8	AMPACITY OF BARE CONDUCTORS	28
2.9	THE NEUTRAL CONDUCTOR AND THE AMPACITY ADJUSTMENT FACTOR	28
2.10	COUNTING EQUIPMENT GROUNDING AND BONDING CONDUCTORS	30
2.11	APPLICATION OF 310.12 FOR SINGLE-PHASE DWELLING SERVICES AND FEEDERS	31
2.12	SPECIAL AMPACITY INFORMATION	34
	DEFINITIONS AND TERMS	38
	SUMMARY	38
	REVIEW QUESTIONS	39

TABLE OF CONTENTS

CHAPTER 3 CONDUCTOR AMPACITY CALCULATIONS II — 40

3.1	INTRODUCTION	42
3.2	TEMPERATURE LIMITATIONS OF EQUIPMENT	42
3.3	CONTINUOUS LOADS AND BRANCH CIRCUITS	47
3.4	CONTINUOUS LOADS AND FEEDERS	55
3.5	SERVICES WITH CONTINUOUS AND NONCONTINUOUS LOADS	58
	DEFINITIONS AND TERMS	59
	SUMMARY	60
	REVIEW QUESTIONS	61

CHAPTER 4 BOXES — 62

4.1	DETERMINING THE NUMBER OF CONDUCTORS IN A BOX	64
4.2	BOX FILL FOR STANDARD BOXES	64
4.3	EXAMPLES OF INDIVIDUAL VOLUME ALLOWANCES	67
4.4	USING TABLE 314.16(A) AND TABLE 314.16(B)	72
4.5	SIZING PULL AND JUNCTION BOXES FOR CONDUCTORS FOR SYSTEMS 1,000 VOLTS OR LESS	76
4.6	SIZING PULL AND JUNCTION BOXES FOR CONDUCTORS FOR SYSTEMS OVER 1,000 VOLTS	79
	DEFINITIONS AND TERMS	85
	SUMMARY	86
	REVIEW QUESTIONS	86

TABLE OF CONTENTS

CHAPTER 5 RACEWAY FILL — 88

- 5.1 CONDUIT AND TUBING FILLS — 90
- 5.2 USING TABLES 4 AND 5 OF CHAPTER 9 — 93
- 5.3 USING TABLES 4 AND 5A OF CHAPTER 9 — 98
- 5.4 USING TABLE 8 OF CHAPTER 9 FOR BARE CONDUCTORS — 98
- 5.5 SHORT NIPPLE FILL USING NOTE 4 TO TABLE 1 OF CHAPTER 9 — 101
- 5.6 USING NOTE 7 TO TABLE 1 OF CHAPTER 9 — 102
- 5.7 MULTICONDUCTOR CABLES IN CONDUIT OR TUBING — 102
- 5.8 ADDING CONDUCTORS TO EXISTING CONDUIT OR TUBING — 103
- 5.9 TABLES FOR $3/8$-INCH FLEXIBLE METAL CONDUIT — 103
- 5.10 UNDERFLOOR TYPE RACEWAYS — 104
- 5.11 METAL WIREWAYS, NONMETALLIC WIREWAYS, AND AUXILIARY GUTTERS — 107
- DEFINITIONS AND TERMS — 110
- SUMMARY — 110
- REVIEW QUESTIONS — 111

CHAPTER 6 MOTOR CALCULATIONS — 112

- 6.1 MOTOR BRANCH-CIRCUIT CONDUCTORS — 114
- 6.2 MOTOR BRANCH-CIRCUIT SHORT-CIRCUIT AND GROUND-FAULT PROTECTION — 123
- 6.3 MOTOR OVERLOAD PROTECTION — 136
- 6.4 MOTOR DISCONNECTING MEANS — 140
- 6.5 AIR-CONDITIONING AND REFRIGERATING EQUIPMENT MOTORS — 151
- DEFINITIONS AND TERMS — 155
- SUMMARY — 156
- REVIEW QUESTIONS — 156

TABLE OF CONTENTS

CHAPTER 7	VOLTAGE DROP	158

7.1	CHAPTER 9, TABLE 8 FOR RESISTANCE OF WIRE	160
7.2	RESISTANCE TEXTBOOK EQUATION: *CODE* BOOK EQUATION	160
7.3	RESISTANCE EQUATION BASED UPON *CODE* BOOK VALUES	161
7.4	RESISTANCE EQUATION CORRECTION FACTOR	161
7.5	EQUATION FOR CHANGING RESISTANCE FROM 75°C TO 60°C WIRE	162
7.6	DEVELOPING THE VOLTAGE DROP EQUATION	163
7.7	USING THE VOLTAGE DROP EQUATION	165
7.8	VOLTAGE DROP FOR FEEDERS AND BRANCH CIRCUITS	169
7.9	USING ALTERNATE METHODS TO SOLVE FOR VOLTAGE DROP	169
	DEFINITIONS AND TERMS	172
	SUMMARY	172
	REVIEW QUESTIONS	173

CHAPTER 8	APPLIANCES	174

8.1	RANGE LOADS—FEEDER DEMANDS—DWELLING UNITS WITH 120/240-VOLT, SINGLE-PHASE SERVICE	176
8.2	DEVELOPING AN EQUATION FOR SINGLE-PHASE RANGES ON A 3-PHASE SYSTEM	182
8.3	BRANCH-CIRCUITS FOR RANGE LOADS	185
8.4	RANGE LOADS—BRANCH-CIRCUIT CONDUCTORS	186
8.5	HOUSEHOLD COOKING EQUIPMENT IN SCHOOLS	189
8.6	COMMERCIAL COOKING APPLIANCES	189
8.7	BRANCH-CIRCUITS SERVING AN ELECTRIC CLOTHES DRYER	190
8.8	OTHER APPLIANCES	191
	DEFINITIONS AND TERMS	193
	SUMMARY	194
	REVIEW QUESTIONS	195

TABLE OF CONTENTS

CHAPTER 9 LOAD CALCULATIONS — 196

9.1	GENERAL REQUIREMENTS FOR RESIDENTIAL LOADS	198
9.2	DWELLING UNIT—STANDARD CALCULATION METHOD	198
9.3	MULTIFAMILY DWELLINGS	207
9.4	COMMERCIAL BUILDINGS	215
9.5	OFFICE BUILDINGS	221
	DEFINITIONS AND TERMS	225
	SUMMARY	226
	REVIEW QUESTIONS	227

CHAPTER 10 TRANSFORMER OVERCURRENT PROTECTION — 228

10.1	PROTECTING TRANSFORMER WINDINGS (1,000 VOLTS, NOMINAL, OR LESS)	230
10.2	240.21(B) FEEDER TAPS AND 240.21(C) TRANSFORMER SECONDARY CONDUCTORS	239
10.3	DEDICATED TRANSFORMERS USED IN FIRE PUMP CIRCUITS	248
	DEFINITIONS AND TERMS	249
	SUMMARY	250
	REVIEW QUESTIONS	250

TABLE OF CONTENTS

CHAPTER 11 CABLE TRAY	252

11.1	CABLE TRAY FILL CALCULATIONS FOR MULTICONDUCTOR INSTALLATIONS	254
11.2	CABLE TRAY FILL CALCULATIONS FOR SINGLE-CONDUCTOR INSTALLATIONS	264
11.3	AMPACITY OF MULTICONDUCTOR INSTALLATIONS	268
11.4	AMPACITY OF SINGLE-CONDUCTOR INSTALLATIONS	269
	DEFINITIONS AND TERMS	272
	SUMMARY	272
	REVIEW QUESTIONS	273

CHAPTER 12 ELECTRIC WELDERS	274

12.1	ARTICLE 630, ELECTRIC WELDERS	276
12.2	ARC WELDERS	277
12.3	RESISTANCE WELDERS	285
	DEFINITIONS AND TERMS	288
	SUMMARY	288
	REVIEW QUESTIONS	289

FEATURES

Problems provide application of *Code* requirements to real-world installations.

Figures, including photographs and artwork, clearly illustrate concepts from the text.

Code Excerpts are "ripped" from the 2020 *National Electrical Code*.

For additional information related to QR Codes, visit qr.njatcdb.org Item #1079

Quick Response Codes (QR Codes) create a link between the textbook and the Internet. They can be scanned using Smartphone applications to obtain additional information online. (To access the information without using a Smartphone, visit qr.njatcdb.org and enter the referenced Item #.)

FEATURES

Clear, easy-to-use **Contents** pages in the front of the textbook and inside each chapter enable the reader to quickly find important *Code Calculations* concepts.

An **Introduction** and **Objectives** at the beginning of each chapter introduce readers to the concepts to be learned in the chapter.

At the conclusion of each chapter, **Definitions and Terms,** a concise chapter **Summary,** and **Review Questions** reinforce the most important concepts included in the chapter.

INTRODUCTION

Code Calculations 2020 is developed by the *electrical training ALLIANCE* as a valuable resource for the electrical industry by the joint efforts of the International Brotherhood of Electrical Workers (IBEW) and the National Electrical Contractors Association (NECA). Based on the 2020 *National Electrical Code (NEC)*, it is revised and updated to be on the leading edge for performing *Code*-related calculations.

The 2020 edition of *Code Calculations* reflects the new changes in lighting load calculations, the importance of voltage drop calculations due to adoptions of energy codes, the new tables for cable tray fill, and other *NEC* changes. *Code Calculations* assists the *Code* user in understanding and applying the challenging aspects of calculations in the *Code*. It solves math-related *Code* topics such as ampacity, conductor terminations, continuous and noncontinuous loads, box size, voltage drop, tap rules, motor installations, transformers, building loads, and electrical systems.

The textbook is intended for a variety of *Code* users such as apprentices, Journeymen Electrical Workers, foremen, estimators, project managers, and electrical engineers. *Code Calculations* provides the necessary skills and knowledge to achieve adequate, safe, and *Code*-compliant installations, and is well-suited for *Code* examination preparation study material.

ABOUT THIS BOOK

Code Calculations begins with understanding the different types of electrical voltage systems. It then moves on to understanding ampacity with consideration of wiring methods and temperature rating of equipment from Chapter 3 of the *NEC* and Article 110 and voltage drop calculations. Calculations are performed for sizing circuits for noncontinuous and continuous loads as well as dwelling and non-dwelling load calculations. *Code* calculations as they relate to equipment such as boxes, enclosures, raceways, cable trays, appliances, motors, transformers, and welders are discussed and performed. The textbook is a valuable resource for any *Code* user desiring to understand and perform *Code*-related calculations as they impact real-world installations based upon the 2020 *NEC*.

ACKNOWLEDGMENTS

Technical information and assistance has been furnished by the following companies and organizations:

ABB	NECA
American Technical Publishers	Legrand/Cablofil
Baldor Electric Company	Legrand/Wiremold
Calculated Industries, Inc.	Philips Color Kinetics
Eaton's Bussmann Business	Rigid
Fluke	Raychem QuickNet, Tyco Thermal Controls
Honeywell/Salsibury	Schneider Electric
The Lincoln Electric Co.	

NFPA 70®, National Electrical Code and *NEC®* are registered trademarks of the National Fire Protection Association, Quincy, MA.

QR CODES

ABB	The Lincoln Electric Co.
AFC Cable Systems	National Fire Protection Association (NFPA)
Baldor Electric Company	Legrand/Cablofil
Eaton's Bussmann Business	Schneider Electric
General Electric Company	Southwire Company
IAEI Magazine	Web Restaurant Store

ABOUT THE SUBJECT MATTER EXPERT UPDATING THIS EDITION

Derrick Atkins is the training director at the Minneapolis Electrical JATC. He holds a Bachelor of Science degree in physics from the University of Minnesota and an associate of applied science degree in electrical construction and maintenance at Dunwoody College of Technology. He also holds a Class A Master Electrical license with the State of Minnesota.

Atkins joined the IBEW Local 292 as an apprentice electrician in 1996 and completed his apprenticeship in 2000. He has worked as a foreman and general foreman on a variety of industrial projects. In 2005, he taught full-time as an instructor for the Minneapolis Electrical JATC, and two years later worked as a project manager and estimator with his primary focus as design build of various industrial projects. He then returned to full-time teaching at the JATC and is now currently serving as the training director.

CHAPTER 1
ELECTRICAL SYSTEMS

A fundamental understanding of the various alternating current (AC) electrical systems encountered is required. An Electrical Worker needs to fully understand all aspects of an electrical system to properly apply the rules of the *National Electrical Code* and perform proper calculations. Different systems require different equations for calculations such as the amount of current on neutral conductors, differences of line and phase currents, and differences of voltages in the system. All aspects of the system need to be considered for an installation to be safe and effective. The analysis provided will cover the common electrical systems encountered and the properties associated with these systems.

OBJECTIVES

- Discuss the five most common electrical systems encountered.
- Calculate system voltages for each system.
- Calculate currents for ungrounded, grounded, and neutral conductors of each system.
- Calculate the high leg voltage for a delta system.
- Discuss the grounding of each system and the effects on voltage calculations.

TABLE OF CONTENTS

1.1	GENERAL	2
1.2	SINGLE-PHASE 2-WIRE SYSTEMS	2
1.3	SINGLE-PHASE 3-WIRE SYSTEMS	3
1.4	3-PHASE 4-WIRE WYE SYSTEM	4
1.5	3-PHASE 4-WIRE DELTA SYSTEM	6
1.6	3-WIRE MULTIPHASE SYSTEMS	9
DEFINITIONS AND TERMS		10
SUMMARY		10
REVIEW QUESTIONS		11

1.1 GENERAL

An electrical system consists of a source of power delivering voltage and current in a particular configuration to be distributed and used by electrical loads. Power sources can be anything from transformers, whether customer-owned or utility; generators; or any other separately derived system. The focus will be solely on alternating current (AC) systems, and not direct current (DC) systems as encountered in a typical solar or battery-powered production system. Single-phase and 3-phase systems are the backbone of power distribution systems used today. Discussion of each system, the number of wires, different configurations (wye versus delta), and calculations pertaining to each system will be covered. While 2-phase systems were used in the past, and while the *National Electrical Code (NEC)* still contains requirements for them, they are not common and need not be addressed. All system voltages are considered to be nominal, root-mean-square (rms), AC system voltages. See the *NEC* definition for voltage.

1.2 SINGLE-PHASE 2-WIRE SYSTEMS

The simplest of all electrical systems is the single-phase, 2-wire system. **See Figure 1-1**. Some applications for the system would include a control circuit for a doorbell in a house, a furnace control circuit, or a power supply in a building automation system. It should be noted that only one system voltage can be derived from conductors L1 to L2. Common system voltages would include 120 volts and 24 volts. Only one voltage can be obtained.

Since the *NEC* defines the neutral point as the midpoint of a single-phase 3-wire system, as there is no midpoint on a 2-wire system, there can be no neutral conductor. Any conductor that is grounded would be considered a grounded phase conductor and not a neutral conductor.

If the system operates at less than 50 volts, **Section 250.20(A)** requires the system to be grounded if the supply to the transformer is more than 150 volts to ground, the supply system to the transformer is ungrounded, or the 2-wire system is installed outside using overhead conductors. If the system operates between 50 to 1,000 volts, **250.20(B)(1)** would require the system to be grounded if the voltage from L1 to L2 is 150 volts or less. The *NEC*, in **250.26(1)**, permits either L1 or L2 to be grounded. The grounded conductor would have to be identified per **200.6**. It should be noted that the grounded conductor is a phase conductor. It is not a neutral conductor, as there is no neutral point with this system. Whether the system is grounded or ungrounded, the voltage to ground will be the same with only one potential difference between the two conductors. The current on the two conductors will be the same due to Kirchhoff's current law that the sum of the currents into a point has to equal the sum of the currents out of the same point. Additionally,

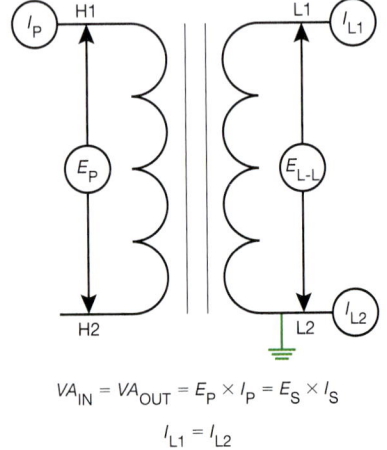

$$VA_{IN} = VA_{OUT} = E_P \times I_P = E_S \times I_S$$

$$I_{L1} = I_{L2}$$

Figure 1-1. Single-Phase, 2-Wire System. *The single-phase, 2-wire system provides two conductors, Line 1 (L1) and Line 2 (L2), with only one voltage potential provided.*

CHAPTER 1   ELECTRICAL SYSTEMS

power into the system is equal to power out of the system. **See Problem 1-1**.

PROBLEM 1-1

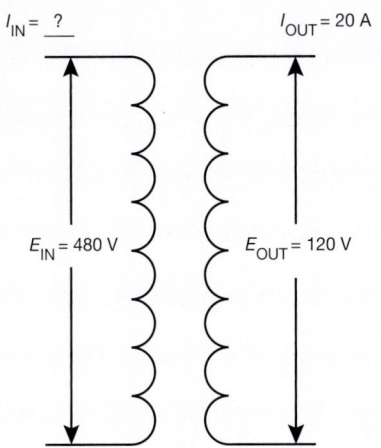

If the secondary voltage is 120 volts, the secondary current is 20 amperes, and the primary voltage is 480 volts, what is the primary current?

Solution

Since $E_{in} \times I_{in} = E_{out} \times I_{out}$
Then $480 \times I_{in} = 120 \times 20$
Answer: $I_{in} = (120 \times 20) \div 480 = 5$ A

1.3 SINGLE-PHASE 3-WIRE SYSTEMS

For a residential service or small commercial application, a single-phase, 3-wire system is commonly supplied by the utility to the premise. **See Figure 1-2**. The system provides two voltages, a line-to-neutral (L-N) voltage and a line-to-line (L-L) voltage. The line-to-neutral voltage is always half of the line-to-line voltage as the coil is center tapped. Typical system voltages would be listed as 120/240 volts or 110/220 volts with the lower voltage being the line-neutral voltage and the higher voltage being the line-line voltage.

Two system voltages will always be listed. This type of system is referred to as a 3-wire system with the first two wires, typically ungrounded conductors, being L1 and L2, and the third wire being the neutral conductor. **See Problem 1-2**.

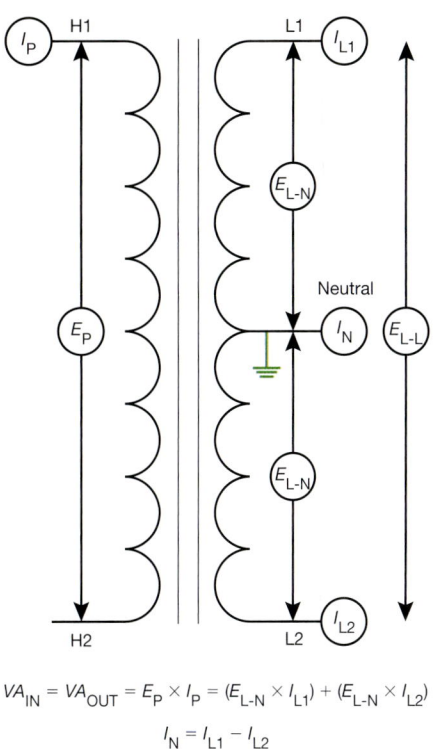

$VA_{IN} = VA_{OUT} = E_P \times I_P = (E_{L-N} \times I_{L1}) + (E_{L-N} \times I_{L2})$

$I_N = I_{L1} - I_{L2}$

Figure 1-2. Single-Phase, 3-Wire System. The single-phase, 3-wire system is commonly used for power distribution in dwelling units and provides two system voltages, typically 120/240 volts, where 120 volts is measured from Line 1 (L1) or Line 2 (L2) to the neutral conductor and 240 volts is measured between L1 and L2.

PROBLEM 1-2

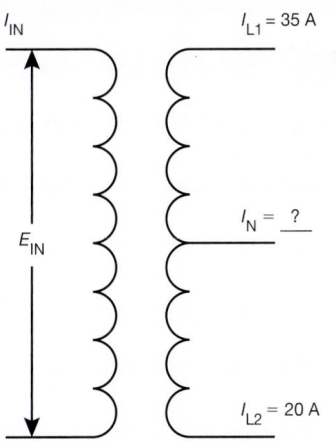

Given $I_{L1} = 35$ A and $I_{L2} = 20$ A, what is the neutral current?

Solution

Answer: $I_N = I_{L1} - I_{L2} = 35 - 20 = 15$ A

The neutral conductor will carry the current difference of the two line conductors. Just like the single-phase 2-wire system, power in is equal to power out. **See Figure 1-3**.

The center tap between L1 and L2 is a neutral point. Any circuit conductor connected to it would be a neutral conductor as defined by the *NEC*. **Section 250.26(2)** requires the neutral conductor to be the grounded conductor. **Section 250.20(B)(1)** requires systems operating between 50 and 1,000 volts to be grounded if the voltage to ground can be limited to not more than 150 volts. Any 3-wire system with a line-to-neutral voltage of 150 volts or less would be required to be grounded. A 120/240-volt system shall be grounded, but a 240/480-volt system would not be required to be grounded. The voltage to ground for the 120/240-volt system would be the same as the line-to-neutral voltage of 120 volts. **See Problem 1-3**.

PROBLEM 1-3

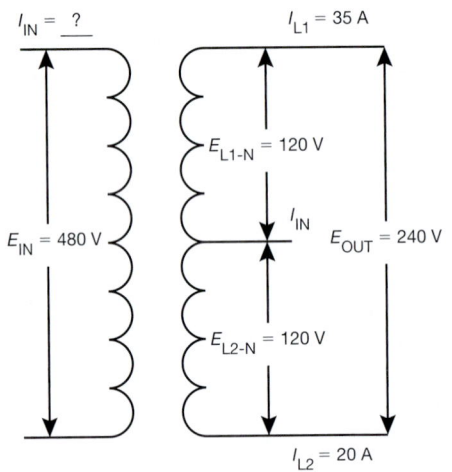

Given I_{L1} = 35 A and I_{L2} = 20 A, a primary voltage of 480 volts, and a secondary voltage of 120/240 volts, what is the primary current?

Solution

$$I_P \times E_P = I_{L1} \times E_{L-N} + I_{L2} \times E_{L-N} = E_{L-N} \times (I_{L1} + I_{L2})$$

$$I_P = \frac{E_{L-N} \times (I_{L1} + I_{L2})}{E_P}$$

$$= \frac{120 \times (35 + 20)}{480}$$

$$= \frac{120}{480} \times 55$$

$$= 13.75 \text{ A}$$

Answer: 13.75 A

Figure 1-3. Single-Phase, 3-Wire, Dwelling Unit Panelboard. Single-phase, 3-wire, 120/240-volt systems are the most common electrical supply to single-family dwelling units. The two ungrounded conductors supplying the main circuit breaker will have 240 volts measured between each other, and 120 volts from each measured to the grounded (neutral) conductor, identified with white marking tape.

1.4 3-PHASE 4-WIRE WYE SYSTEM

The most common multiphase system is a 3-phase, 4-wire, wye system. **See Figure 1-4**. The neutral point is common to all three phases (A, B, and

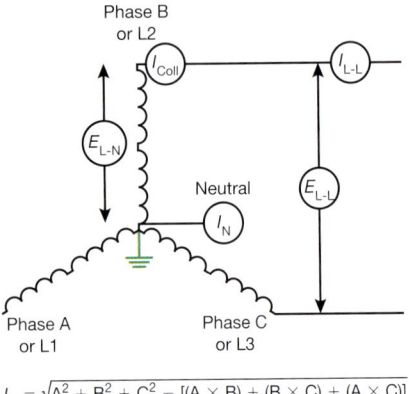

Figure 1-4. 3-Phase, 4-Wire, Wye System. The 3-phase, 4-wire, wye system is the most common commercial and industrial system and provides a line-to-neutral voltage measured from phase A, B, or C to the neutral conductor and a line-to-line voltage measured between any two phase conductors of phase A, B, or C.

C). Phases A, B, and C are conductors for L1, L2, and L3, and the neutral conductor connected to the midpoint or common point would be conductor 4, making this system a 4-wire system.

Section 250.26(3) describes a multiphase system with one wire common to the phases, and applies to the 3-phase, 4-wire, wye system by requiring the neutral conductor to be grounded. If the system is between 50 and 1,000 volts, **250.20(B)(2)** would require the system to be grounded when the neutral conductor is used as a circuit conductor.

Since a line conductor is connected directly in series to a phase winding, the line current and the phase current are equal to each other as given by the equation $I_{line} = I_{phase}$. With the phase coils being 120° out of phase with each other, the line-to-line voltage, or line voltage, will be equal to 1.732 multiplied by the phase or coil voltage, as given by the equation $E_{line} = 1.732 \times E_{phase}$. Typical system voltages will be listed as 208Y/120, 480Y/277, etc. The lower voltage is the line-to-neutral voltage and the higher voltage is the line-to-line voltage or line voltage. **See Problem 1-4**.

The unbalanced neutral current can be solved with the use of vectors, or can be determined algebraically by taking the square root of the sum of the phase currents squared minus the sum of the products of the phase currents, as given by the formula shown:

$$I_N = \sqrt{A^2 + B^2 + C^2 - ([A \times B] + [B \times C] + [A \times C])}$$

See Problem 1-5.

PROBLEM 1-4

Answer the following based on a 3-phase, 4-wire, wye system:

When the coil current is 30 A, what is the line current?

Since $I_{Coil} = I_{L-L}$, the line current is equal to 30 A

Solution

When the coil voltage is equal to 347 volts, what is the line voltage?

Since $E_{L-L} = 1.732 \times E_{L-N}$

Answer: Then $E_{L-L} = 1.732 \times 347$
$= 600$ V

PROBLEM 1-5

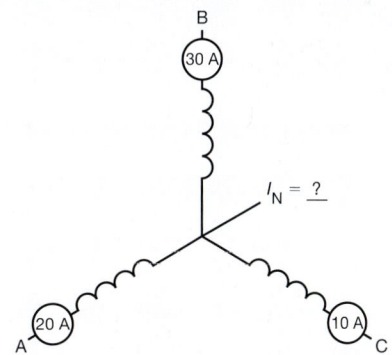

For a 3-phase, 4-wire, wye system, what is the neutral current when the current on phase A is 20 A, phase B is 30 A, and phase C is 10 A?

Solution

Since $I_N = \sqrt{A^2 + B^2 + C^2 - ([A \times B] + [B \times C] + [A \times C])}$

Then $I_N = \sqrt{20^2 + 30^2 + 10^2 - ([20 \times 30] + [30 \times 10] + [20 \times 10])}$

Answer: $I_N = \sqrt{[400 + 900 + 100 - (600 + 300 + 200)]}$
$= \sqrt{[1{,}400 - (1{,}100)]}$
$= \sqrt{[300]}$
$= 17.32$ A

PROBLEM 1-6

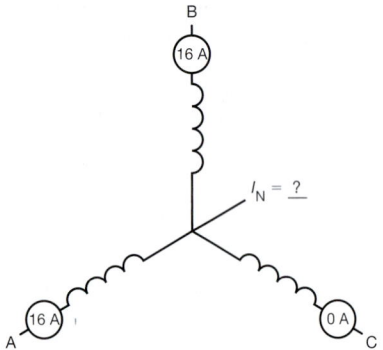

For a 3-phase, 4-wire, wye system, what is the neutral current when the current on phase A is 16 A, phase B is 16 A, and phase C is 0 A? [Note, this is essentially a 3-wire multi-wire circuit on a 3-phase, 4-wire, wye system; see **220.61(C)(1)** and **310.15(B)(5)(b)**.]

Solution

Since $I_N = \sqrt{A^2 + B^2 + C^2 - ([A \times B] + [B \times C] + [A \times C])}$

Then $I_N = \sqrt{16^2 + 16^2 + 0^2 - ([16 \times 16] + [16 \times 0] + [16 \times 0])}$

$I_N = \sqrt{16^2 + 16^2 - (16^2)}$

$= \sqrt{16^2}$

$= 16 \text{ A}$

Answer: 16 A

Figure 1-5. 3-Phase, 4-Wire, Wye Panelboard. Many commercial panelboards are supplied with 3-phase, 4-wire, wye systems such as 208/120 volts to provide power to 120-volt receptacles in a building.

Under normal operations, with an equal amount of current on all 3-phase conductors, the neutral will carry only the unbalanced current. If there are only two ungrounded conductors and the neutral conductor, forming a 3-wire multiwire circuit, the neutral conductor will carry approximately the same current as the two ungrounded conductors. See Problem 1-6. This is addressed in **220.61(C)(1)** and **310.15(E)(2)**. See Figure 1-5.

1.5 3-PHASE 4-WIRE DELTA SYSTEM

A system that may be encountered, but is not as common as the 3-phase, 4-wire, wye system, is the 3-phase, 4-wire, delta system. **See Figure 1-6**. With the line-to-line conductors connecting directly in parallel to the corners of the phase coils, the line-to-line voltage, or line voltage, is equal to the phase or coil voltage as given by the equation $E_{line} = E_{phase}$. **See Problem 1-7**. The line current will be equal to the phase or coil current multiplied by 1.732, as given by the equation $I_{line} = 1.732 \times I_{phase}$. The center point, or neutral point, between two phases is tapped to derive a neutral conductor. The neutral point is equal potential between the two phases, but the third phase is elevated in potential

Figure 1-6. 3-Phase, 4-Wire, Delta System. The 3-phase, 4-wire, delta system is not as common as the wye system, but provides a line-to-neutral voltage measured between phase A or C, the neutral voltage measured between phase A or C and the neutral conductor, and a line-to-line voltage measured between two conductors of phase A, B, or C.

above the neutral point and is referred to as the high leg voltage. **See Problem 1-8**. In **Section 408.3(E)**, the B phase is required to be the high leg, requiring the neutral point to be made between phase A and phase C. Line-to-neutral loads then can be supplied by phase A to neutral and by phase C to neutral. Since phase B to neutral becomes the high leg, the voltage can be found by multiplying the line-to-neutral voltage by 1.732, as given by the equation $E_{high\ leg} = 1.732 \times E_{line-to-neutral}$. **See Problem 1-9**. If supplying line-to-neutral loads, only phase A and phase C are permitted to be used. The coil between phase A and phase C is identical to the single-phase 3-wire system, so the neutral conductor will carry the unbalanced current of phase A and phase C as given by the equation $I_{neutral} = I_A - I_C$.

PROBLEM 1-8

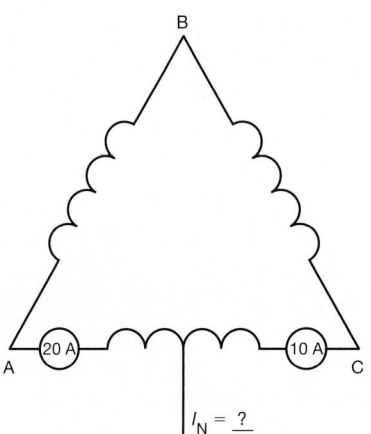

For a 3-phase, 4-wire, delta system, what is the neutral current when the current on phase A is 20 amperes, and the current on phase C is 10 amperes?

Solution

Since $I_N = I_A - I_C$
Answer: Then $I_N = 20\ A - 10\ A$
$= 10\ A$

PROBLEM 1-7

Answer the following based on a 3-phase, 4-wire, delta system:

If the coil voltage is 480 volts, what is the line voltage?

Solution

Since $E_{Coil} = E_{L-L}$, the line voltage is equal to 480 volts
Answer: $E_{coil} = 480\ V$

If the coil current is equal to 50 amperes, what is the line current?

Solution

Since $I_{L-L} = 1.732 \times I_{phase}$
Answer: Then $I_{L-L} = 1.732 \times 50\ A$
$= 86.6\ A$

PROBLEM 1-9

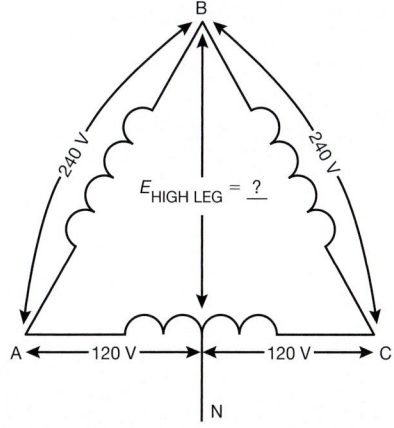

What is the high leg voltage of a 120/240-volt, 3-phase, 4-wire, delta system?

Solution

Since $E_{high\ leg} = 1.732 \times E_{line-to-neutral}$
Answer: Then $E_{high\ leg} = 1.732 \times 120\ V$
$= 207.84\ V$ or a nominal 208 V

Common system voltages will be 120/240-volt, 3-phase and 240/480-volt, 3-phase. The line-to-neutral voltage is always half of the line-to-line voltage. The high leg voltage, phase B to ground, is typically not listed on most equipment, and therefore is not a usable system voltage. The high leg conductor would have to be identified in accordance with **110.15**. **Section 250.20(B)(3)** requires a 3-phase, 4-wire, delta system operating between 50 and 1,000 volts to be grounded when the neutral is used as a circuit conductor. **Section 250.26(5)** describes a multiphase system where one phase is used similar to a single-phase, 3-wire system, which requires the neutral conductor to be the grounded conductor. **See Figure 1-7**.

A delta system can also be operated in an open delta configuration. **See Figure 1-8**. A common application would be to use three single-phase transformers in lieu of a single 3-phase transformer, such that if one transformer fails, the system can continue to supply the load. The only difference in properties is the reduction in power output of the system to that of 58% of a closed delta system. All other voltages remain the same as a closed delta system. Since one of the phase coils is removed, the line conductor is directly in series with the phase coil, and therefore the line current becomes equal to the coil current.

Figure 1-7. 3-Phase, 4-Wire, Delta Panelboard. Although not as common as wye systems, delta panelboards can supply 3-phase loads and line-to-neutral loads. Notice how every third breaker is missing due to the high leg voltage on phase B, as identified with orange marking tape.

$E_{L-L} = 2 \times E_{L-N}$ HIGH LEG $= 1.732 \times E_{L-N}$

$E_{L-L} = E_{Coil}$ $I_N = I_{L1} - I_{L3}$

Figure 1-8. 3-Phase, 4-Wire, Open Delta. The primary difference between a closed delta and open delta is the reduction of power to 58% of what the closed delta is capable of producing; in all other ways, system voltages remain unaffected.

1.6 3-WIRE MULTI-PHASE SYSTEMS

The last system to be discussed is the 3-phase, 3-wire system. It can be either wye or delta; however, the delta configuration is more common. **See Figure 1-9**.

With only three wires available (phases A, B, and C), only one system voltage is possible. Typical system voltages will be 240 volts, 400 volts, 480 volts, or 575 volts, but only one voltage is possible. With no center tap, there is not a neutral or common point in the 3-wire, 3-phase system. If the system is grounded as permitted in **250.21** or as required in **250.20(B)** to limit the voltage to ground to less than 150 volts, **Section 250.26(4)** requires any one phase conductor, either phase A, B, or C, to be grounded. The grounded conductor is not a neutral conductor, but rather a grounded phase conductor, and is required to be identified in accordance with **200.6**.

Section 404.2(B) prohibits a grounded conductor from being switched. An exception permits it to be switched if all conductors of the circuit are switched simultaneously. The system is permitted to be terminated with either a 3-pole disconnect switch or a 3-pole circuit breaker. **Section 240.22** requires no overcurrent protection device to be placed in series with a grounded conductor, and therefore, if a 3-pole fusible disconnect switch is used, it requires a neutral fuse to be placed in series with the grounded conductor. If the system is operated either grounded or ungrounded, the *Code* defines the voltage to ground as the line voltage in **Article 100**. For example, the voltage to ground on a 480-volt system, whether grounded or ungrounded, is 480 volts.

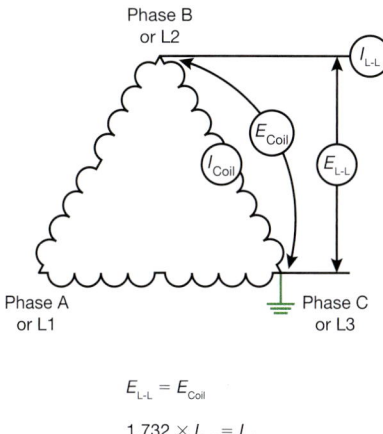

$E_{L\text{-}L} = E_{Coil}$

$1.732 \times I_{Coil} = I_{L\text{-}L}$

Figure 1-9. 3-Phase, 3-Wire, Multiphase System. Although multiphase systems can be either wye or delta, a delta system is able to provide only one system (line-to-line) voltage measured between any two conductors.

DEFINITIONS AND TERMS

Neutral Conductor - The conductor connected to the neutral point of a system that is intended to carry current under normal conditions. [**70**:100]

Neutral Point - The common point on a wye-connection in a polyphase system or midpoint on a single-phase, 3-wire system, or midpoint of a single-phase portion of a 3-phase delta system, or a midpoint of a 3-wire, direct-current system. [**70**:100]

Voltage (of a circuit) - The greatest root-mean-square (rms) (effective) difference of potential between any two conductors of the circuit concerned. [**70**:100]

Voltage, Nominal - A nominal value assigned to a circuit or system for the purpose of conveniently designating its voltage class (for example, 120/240 volts, 480Y/277 volts, 600 volts). [**70**:100]

Voltage to Ground - For grounded circuits, the voltage between the given conductor and that point or conductor of the circuit that is grounded; for ungrounded circuits, the greatest voltage between the given conductor and any other conductor of the circuit. [**70**:100]

Reproduced with permission of NFPA from NFPA 70®, *National Electrical Code*® (NEC®), 2020 edition. Copyright© 2019, National Fire Protection Association. For a full copy of the NEC®, please go to www.nfpa.org.

SUMMARY

A basic understanding of electrical systems is necessary to perform proper *Code* calculations. For example, in determining ampacities of conductors, the *Code* user needs to understand the electrical system to determine if the neutral is a current-carrying conductor or not. For determining load calculations, the *Code* user needs to know what the system voltages are, whether they are line-to-neutral values or line-to-line values, and which should be used in any given equation. Additionally, knowing the most common systems and where they are commonly used is imperative for a Qualified Electrical Worker to properly install, troubleshoot, and maintain electrical installations.

REVIEW QUESTIONS

1. What is the possible voltage for a single-phase, 2-wire system?
   a. 24 V
   b. 120/240 V
   c. 208Y/120 V
   d. 480/277 V

2. What is the possible voltage for a single-phase, 3-wire system?
   a. 24 V
   b. 120/240 V
   c. 208Y/120 V
   d. 480 V

3. What is the possible voltage for a 3-phase, 4-wire, wye system?
   a. 24 V
   b. 120/240 V
   c. 208Y/120 V
   d. 480 V

4. The possible voltage for a 3-phase, 4-wire, delta system is __?__.
   a. 24 V
   b. 120/240 V
   c. 208Y/120 V
   d. 480 V

5. The possible voltage for a 3-phase, 3-wire, delta system is __?__.
   a. 24/48 V
   b. 120/240 V
   c. 208Y/120 V
   d. 480 V

6. What is the phase current of a 3-phase, 480-volt, delta system when the line current is 42 amperes?
   a. 21 A
   b. 24 A
   c. 42 A
   d. 73 A

7. What is the line-to-neutral voltage of a 3-phase, 4-wire, wye system when the line voltage is 480 volts?
   a. 120 V
   b. 240 V
   c. 277 V
   d. 480 V

8. What is the high leg voltage of a 120/240-volt, 3-phase, delta system?
   a. 120 V
   b. 208 V
   c. 240 V
   d. 415 V

9. What is the neutral current of a single-phase, 3-wire system when the current on Line 1 is 11 amperes and the current on Line 2 is 14 amperes?
   a. 3 A
   b. 12.5 A
   c. 14 A
   d. 25 A

10. What is the neutral current on a 3-phase, 208Y/120-volt system when there are 15 amperes, 2 amperes, and 30 amperes of current on phases A, B, and C respectively?
    a. 13 A
    b. 17 A
    c. 24 A
    d. 47 A

CHAPTER 2
CONDUCTOR AMPACITY CALCULATIONS

Determining the *ampacity* of single insulated electrical conductors installed in raceways or cables or directly buried in the earth is the starting point of *Code* calculations. The word ampacity was created by the *National Electrical Code* Committee for use in the *NEC*. It is made up of two words: ampere and capacity. Ampere is the unit of measurement for electron flow; capacity indicates quantity. Thus, the term *ampacity* is a measurement of the electron capacity of a conductor, or the maximum number of electrons that can safely travel down a conductor at the same time. The official *NEC* definition for ampacity is found in **Article 100**, which defines ampacity as: "The maximum current, in amperes, that a conductor can carry continuously under the conditions of use without exceeding its temperature rating."

Conductor material, insulation, and size or AWG all require consideration when determining the ampacity of a conductor. Much information can be attained by paying particular attention to *NEC* table titles and headings. For example, a close reading of the ampacity table titles will show that heat dissipation plays a very large role in the ampacity of a conductor. The ampacity of a group of conductors enclosed in a raceway is less than that of single conductors in open air. This is because when conductors are contained in a raceway, the heat is contained within them, whereas when single conductors are installed in open air, the heat is easier to dissipate. Ampacity **Table 310.16** is the most frequently used table by Electrical Workers, as most installations are done in raceways and cables.

OBJECTIVES

- Discuss the effect of heat on a conductor's ampacity.
- Discuss heat containment and heat dissipation in accordance with the installation of the conductor.
- Use Ampacity **Table 310.16** to determine the conditions of use that affect conductor ampacities.
- Determine various adjustment and correction factors and apply those factors to calculate conductor ampacities.
- Calculate conductor ampacities under varying conditions of use.
- Calculate conductor sizes for dwelling services and feeders.
- Properly apply the specific ampacity restrictions to conductors of various wiring methods such as Type AC, MC, NM, SE, and UF cable, metal wireways, and auxiliary gutters.

TABLE OF CONTENTS

2.1	GENERAL	14
2.2	AMPACITY	14
2.3	TABLES	15
2.4	FACTORS AFFECTING AMPACITY	16
.1	Ambient Temperature Correction Factors	16
.2	General Application of Adjustment Factors	16
2.5	310.15 AMPACITY TABLES FOR CONDUCTORS RATED 0–2,000 VOLTS	17
.1	General	17
.2	General Requirements for Adjustment Factor Applications	18
.3	Specific Requirements for Adjustment Factor Applications	18
.4	Raceways and Cables Exposed to Sunlight on Rooftops	19
.5	Bare or Covered Conductors	19
.6	Neutral Conductor	19
.7	Grounding and Bonding Conductors	20
.8	120/240-Volt, 3-Wire, Single-Phase Dwelling Services and Feeders	20
.9	208Y/120-Volt, 3-Wire, Dwelling Feeders	20
2.6	PROBLEMS USING A TEMPERATURE CORRECTION FACTOR	21
2.7	PROBLEMS USING AN ADJUSTMENT FACTOR	22
.1	Ampacity Adjustment Factors Using Different Sized Conductors	23
.2	Ampacity Adjustment Factors Using Different Insulation Temperatures and Different Sized Conductors	23
.3	Applying Both Correction Factors and Adjustment Factors	24
.4	Applying Adjustment and Temperature Correction Factors to Cable Assemblies	25
.5	Applying Adjustment Factors	26
.6	Applying Adjustment Factors to Cables in Cable Tray	26
.7	Adjustment Factors to Current-Carrying Conductors in Limited Length Raceways	27
2.8	AMPACITY OF BARE CONDUCTORS	28
2.9	THE NEUTRAL CONDUCTOR AND THE AMPACITY ADJUSTMENT FACTOR	28
2.10	COUNTING EQUIPMENT GROUNDING AND BONDING CONDUCTORS	30
2.11	APPLICATION OF 310.12 FOR SINGLE-PHASE DWELLING SERVICES AND FEEDERS	31
2.12	SPECIAL AMPACITY INFORMATION	34
.1	Armored Cable	34
.2	Metal-Clad Cable	34
.3	Nonmetallic Sheathed Cable	35
.4	Service-Entrance Cable	36
.5	Metal Wireways and Sheet Metal Auxiliary Gutters	36
.6	Nonmetallic Wireways and Nonmetallic Auxiliary Gutters	37
	DEFINITIONS AND TERMS	38
	SUMMARY	38
	REVIEW QUESTIONS	39

2.1 GENERAL

Ampacities for conductors may be calculated by a complex mathematical formula or they may be determined using a combination of look-up tables and application factors. The calculation of ampacity in order to determine proper electrical conductor sizes for installation is a fundamental duty of a trained Electrical Worker. Frequently, the Electrical Worker is required to properly size conductors for installation, and so may benefit from an in-depth demonstration of using the *Code* to look up tables, applying the various application factors to those table values where necessary, and finally, determining the appropriate conductor insulation and size for a wide selection of practical applications.

Using table values and calculating the ampacity of a conductor is presented in **Parts II** and **III** of **Article 310**. Within these parts of **Article 310**, particular attention is directed to the general rules, temperature limitations of conductors, and the following:

- **310.4 Conductor Constructions and Applications**
  Table 310.4(A) Conductor Applications and Insulations Rated 600 Volts
- **310.12 Single-Phase Dwelling Services and Feeders**
  Table 310.12 Single-Phase Dwelling Services and Feeders
- **310.14 Ampacities for Conductors Rated 0 Volts – 2000 Volts, (A) General**
- **310.15 Ampacity Tables**
- **310.16 through 310.21 Ampacities for Various Conductors**

Do not be concerned with overcurrent protection for the conductors or the effects of connected loads at this time.

Before determining actual ampacities, it is imperative to have a clear understanding of the term ampacity, the different electrical conductor insulations, and the temperature limitations of those insulated conductors.

2.2 AMPACITY

The term *ampacity* means current-carrying capacity, and is a coined word built from two common words: *ampere* and *capacity*. **See Figure 2-1.**

AMPERE CAPACITY = AMPACITY

Figure 2-1. Ampacity. *Ampacity is derived from the words* ampere *and* capacity.

According to **Article 100, Definitions**, ampacity is defined as "the maximum current, in amperes, that a conductor can carry continuously under the conditions of use without exceeding its temperature rating." The four parts of this definition are:

- Maximum current, in amperes
- Able to carry continuously
- Under the conditions of use
- Without exceeding its temperature rating

Article 100, Definitions, identifies the *current-carrying capacity* of a conductor as the maximum amount of current that will raise the temperature of a particular conductor in a given environment to its rated temperature. Generally and unless otherwise stated, a conductor is assumed to be an insulated conductor.

Insulated current-carrying conductors have two basic parts: the inner conducting metal and the outer covering of electrical insulation. Remembering that plastic melts and degrades at a much lower temperature than metal, calculations should focus on the maximum operating temperature of electrical insulations as permitted in **Table 310.4(A)**. Therefore, the rated or maximum permitted temperature of a conductor is ultimately determined by the ability of the selected electrical insulating material (for example, conductor insulation) to withstand those temperatures along its entire length without significant degradation.

Conductor heating originates from many sources. These sources include:

1. *Area Heat.* Environment or ambient air temperature which may vary along the conductor's length or may vary during the time of day.
2. *Load Current Heat.* Heat generated by the load current flowing in the metal conductor material due to the natural resistance of the conductor. This heat includes the heat generated by ordinary or fundamental current, as well as any harmonic currents.
3. *Adjacent Conductor Heat.* Heat generated by current flowing through adjacent load-carrying conductors, which adds to the ambient heat and impedes the heat dissipation process within the conduit or cable assembly.
4. *Ability to Cool Down or Dissipate Heat.* Retained heat due to the inability of the surrounding media to dissipate heat. Surrounding media that may entrap heat includes additional conductor insulation, outer coverings or cable jackets, raceway or enclosure construction or placement, certain types of enclosures, soil temperature, wind velocity, and ambient air.

Therefore, the temperature of a conductor is reached by adding the four heat "sources." Since heat is the determining factor in the ampacity of a conductor, **310.14(A)(3)** clearly prohibits a conductor from being used if the maximum operating temperature for its particular insulation is exceeded anywhere along the length of the conductor. Thus, the most important statement regarding conductors is: Do not permit conductors to be heated beyond their limit.

2.3 TABLES

The ampacity tables needed for *Code* calculations are limited to **Table 310.16** and **Table 310.17**. Since conductors are placed in various applications and installed in various conditions, temperature corrections and adjustment factors may need to be applied to the ampacity of the selected conductor to ensure that the insulated conductor temperature is not exceeded. See **310.15(A)** through **(F)** and **310.12** for the exact text of these requirements and permissions. Other conditions (such as temperature rating of terminations and continuous duty loads) can be dealt with at a later stage.

The ampacity of current-carrying conductors given in the *NEC* tables does not consider conditions of use, as highlighted in the definition in **Article 100**. Rather, it is the ampacity allowed by the *Code* with established limiting parameters on the installation of conductors. Items of consideration when establishing the ampacity of a conductor are:

1. Temperature compatibility with connected equipment, especially at the connection point
2. Coordination with circuit and system overcurrent protection
3. Compliance with the requirements of product listings
4. Preservation of the safety benefits of established industry practices and standardized procedures

Where tables are used to determine ampacity, the table heading is used to determine whether the table applies in a certain situation or applies to specific conditions of use. The title of **Table 310.16** is as follows:

Ampacities of Insulated Conductors with Not More Than Three Current-Carrying Conductors in Raceway, Cable, or Earth (Directly Buried)

The two important installation parameters or "conditions of use" for determining the ampacity of the conductor are stated in the conditional rules of **310.16**. They are:

1. Wiring is installed in 30°C (86°F) ambient temperature
2. There are not more than three current-carrying conductors

Table 310.16 expresses the ampacity for a current-carrying conductor, provided there are not more than three conductors in the raceway or cable and provided that the ambient air temperature is 30°C. If either of these two basic factors is different, the ampacity of the current-carrying conductor shown in **Table 310.16** must be changed.

Table 310.17 changes the conditions of use from "…not more than three conductors in a raceway or cable" to "single-insulated conductors in free air." This is a major difference in the conditions of use. Therefore, the ampacities of **Table 310.16** are much different from the ampacities of **Table 310.17**. Make sure that the selected table matches the necessary conditions of use. For most work, the conditions of use will require **Table 310.16**.

There are many types of conductor insulation found in the headings of ampacity **Table 310.16** and **Table 310.17**. For an explanation of the type letters used in the tables and other important information concerning electrical conductor insulation, see **Table 310.4(A)**. Additional installation requirements are found in **310.10** through **310.14(A)(3)** and other articles of the *Code*. For the ampacities of flexible cords, see **Table 400.5(A)(a)**, and **Table 400.5(A)(b)**.

2.4 FACTORS AFFECTING AMPACITY

There are two important factors which directly affect the ampacity of an insulated conductor. These factors are ambient temperature correction factors and adjustment factors.

PROBLEM 2-1

Ambient Air 40°C

Three 6 AWG THW copper conductors are installed in electrical metallic tubing, Type EMT, in an ambient temperature of 40°C. What is the ampacity of each of the three current-carrying conductors?

Solution

Table 310.16 Ampacity
 6 AWG THW copper = 65 A
Table 310.4(A), THW = 75°C
Table 310.15(B)(1) Temperature Correction Factors
 75°C (THW) at 40°C ambient = 0.88
Ampacity at 40°C = Ampacity × Correction Factor
  = 65 × 0.88
  = 57.2
Answer: 57.2 A

2.4.1 Ambient Temperature Correction Factors

Both **310.16** and **310.17** stipulate that the fundamental ambient temperature is 30°C (86°F). This is clearly stated as one of the required conditions for use of the Table ampacities in both sections. An ambient temperature of 30°C (86°F) is considered to be one of the conditions of use.

Where project conditions have ambient temperatures other than 30°C (86°F), the ampacity table must be corrected from 30°C (86°F) to the ambient temperature for the expected job conditions. This correction is made using the correction factors found in **Table 310.15(B)(1)**. **See Problems 2-1 and 2-2.** Alternatively, the correction may be made by using a simple ratio formula. Further information about using this ratio formula may be found in **310.15(B)(1)**.

For example, where the basic conditions of use or the ambient temperature differ from that shown in the *Code* language of the section, additional correction is required to correct the ampacity.

Referring to **Table 310.16 Notes**, a correction factor must be used where the ambient air temperature is different from 30°C (86°F), as stated in the notes to the table. The correction factor is given as a percentage of the ampacity value selected from **Table 310.16**. The correction factors are found in **Table 310.15(B)(1)**. Correction factors, for the most part, are simple corrections for temperature once the ambient temperature is determined.

2.4.2 General Application of Adjustment Factors

Once the appropriate table is selected, other conditions of use may require adjustment. For example, again specifically referring to **Table 310.16**, an adjustment factor must be used where the number of current-carrying conductors in a raceway or cable exceeds three conductors, as stated in the notes to the table. The adjustment factor is given as a percentage of the ampacity value selected from **Table 310.16**. The adjustment factors for more than three current-carrying conductors in a raceway or cable are found in **Table 310.15(C)(1)**.

CHAPTER 2 CONDUCTOR AMPACITY CALCULATIONS

PROBLEM 2-2

Three 4 AWG THHN aluminum conductors are installed in an intermediate metal conduit, Type IMC, in an ambient temperature of 75°F. What is the ampacity of the current-carrying conductors?

Solution

Table 310.16 Ampacity
 4 AWG THHN aluminum = 75 A
Table 310.15(B)(1) Temperature Correction Factors
Table 310.4(A), THHN = 90°C
 90°C (THHN) at 75°F ambient = 1.04
 75 A × 1.04 = 78 A
Answer: 78 A

Another adjustment factor may need to be applied where raceways or cables are exposed to direct sunlight on rooftops if installed less than 23 millimeters (⅞ in.) from the roof. Again, the adjustment factor is determined by adding a temperature adder of 33°C (60°F) to the outdoor ambient temperature and selecting the appropriate adjustment factor percentage from **Table 310.15(B)(1)** or **Table 310.15(B)(2)**.

Adjustment factors to conductors are more difficult to determine, since many rules apply. For this reason, **310.15** contains many parts that come into play as adjustment factors may need to be applied.

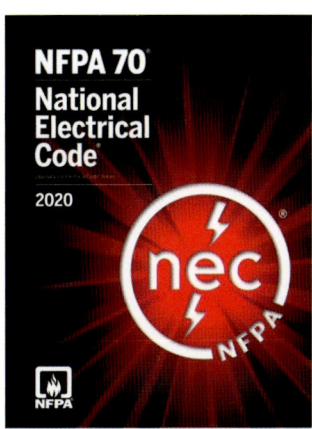

This is the 55th edition of the National Electrical Code. A total of 3,730 public inputs and 1,930 public comments were received to revise the 2017 NEC to the 2020 NEC.

2.5 310.15 AMPACITY TABLES FOR CONDUCTORS RATED 0–2,000 VOLTS

Section 310.15(A) through **(F)** applies to **Table 310.16** through **Table 310.21**. However, to see how it works, start out by applying it to **Table 310.16**. Ampacities found in **Table 310.16** are explained further in the following paragraphs.

2.5.1 General

Insulated conductors are defined in **Article 100** and recognized by **Section 310.4**. Therefore, only conductors described in **Table 310.4(A)** through **Table 310.4(B)** are considered insulated conductors suitable for general wiring. Notice that the subtle requirement of **Section 310.4** eliminates other insulated conductors for general wiring if they are not specifically recognized by this section and its tables.

Table 310.4(A) shows the physical properties of electrical insulation for general-use conductors specifically rated 600 volts or up to 1,000 volts if listed and marked. **Table 310.4(A)** is used to properly apply the insulations listed in the column headings of **Table 310.16**. For example, in **Table 310.16**, the insulation Type XHHW appears in both the 75°C and the 90°C columns for both copper and aluminum conductors. Depending upon whether the location for the XHHW conductor is a wet or a dry/damp location, the correct maximum operating temperature can be easily determined using **Table 310.4(A)**.

Specifically, **Table 310.4(A)** limits the maximum operating temperature of an XHHW conductor to the ampacity of the 75°C column where that conductor is used in a wet location. For a dry or damp location, **Table 310.4(A)** limits the maximum operating temperature of an XHHW conductor to the 90°C ampacity column. Notice that insulation Type XHHW-2 has the same maximum operating temperature of 90°C for both wet and dry/damp locations.

2.5.2 General Requirements for Adjustment Factor Applications

To apply adjustment factors correctly, one needs to have a thorough understanding of which conductors within a circuit create enough heat to be labeled as generating "load current heat." There are many sections within the *Code* which can assist in making this current-carrying or non–current-carrying determination. Some sections include conductors as always current-carrying, some sections specifically exclude certain conductors as current-carrying, and a few sections point out that a further determination must be made as to whether they are current-carrying or not.

To apply adjustment factors correctly, every current-carrying conductor needs to be counted accurately, and exempt conductors need to be eliminated from the count just as accurately.

Remember the spacing rule which permits raceways to adequately radiate some of their retained heat. **Section 310.15(C)(2)** requires that physical spacing be provided and maintained between all raceways. There are no exceptions to this rule, but no dimension is specifically stated either.

2.5.3 Specific Requirements for Adjustment Factor Applications

Some of the adjustment factor requirements specific to **310.15(C)(1)** are:

1. Where the number of current-carrying conductors in a raceway or cable exceeds three, or where a single conductor or multiconductor cable is installed without maintaining spacing for a continuous length longer than 24 inches and is not installed in a raceway, the ampacity of each conductor must be reduced by the factors of **Table 310.15(C)(1)**.
2. Where current-carrying conductors are assembled as a set of parallel conductors, each conductor is counted separately.
3. Where conductors of different systems, such as control circuits and power circuits, are installed in common raceways or cables, generally only the power and lighting conductors for branch circuits, feeders, and services need to be counted.

The footnote in **Table 310.15(C)(1)** further modifies the number of conductors required to be counted by including spare conductors in the raceway or cable, as they may be used in the future as current-carrying conductors and will affect the ampacity of the conductors. Neutral conductors and grounding or bonding conductors are omitted from the conductor count when meeting the provisions of **310.15(E)** and **310.15(F)**. Lastly, conductors that are connected to electrical components in such a way that they cannot be simultaneously energized are permitted to be omitted from the count. Conductors in a 3-way switching arrangement would be a common case in which this rule applies.

For example, if 30 or fewer current-carrying conductors are installed in a sheet metal auxiliary gutter or a metal wireway, the adjustment factors of **310.15(C)(1)** do not apply per **Sections 366.23(A)** and **376.22(B)**.

Short sections of wireways may also be used as junction boxes to supplement raceway wiring methods.

The following adjustment factors are not required to be used. Thus, the standard *NEC* permissive text of 90.5(B) "shall be permitted" is appropriate.

310.15(C)(1)

...

(a) Where conductors are installed in cable trays, the provisions of 392.80 shall apply.

(b) Adjustment factors shall not apply to conductors in raceways having a length not exceeding 600 mm (24 in.).

(c) Adjustment factors shall not apply to underground conductors entering or leaving an outdoor trench if those conductors have physical protection in the form of rigid metal conduit, intermediate metal conduit, rigid polyvinyl chloride conduit (PVC), or reinforced thermosetting resin conduit (RTRC) having a length not exceeding 3.05 m (10 ft), and if the number of conductors does not exceed four.

(d) Adjustment factors shall not apply to Type AC cable or to Type MC cable under the following conditions:

(1) The cables do not have an overall outer jacket.

(2) Each cable has not more than three current-carrying conductors.

(3) The conductors are 12 AWG copper.

(4) Not more than 20 current-carrying conductors are installed without maintaining spacing, are stacked, or are supported on "bridle rings."

Exception to (4): If cables meeting the requirements in 310.15(C)(1)(d)(1) through (C)(1)(d)(3) with more than 20 current-carrying conductors are installed longer than 600 mm (24 in.) without maintaining spacing, are stacked, or are supported on bridle rings, a 60 percent adjustment factor shall be applied.

2.5.4 Raceways and Cables Exposed to Sunlight on Rooftops

Where raceways and cables are exposed to direct sunlight on or above rooftops, **Section 310.15(B)(2)** in general requires the raceways and cables to be installed a minimum of 23 millimeters (⅞ in.) from the roof, measured from the bottom of the raceways or cables to the roof surface. When the raceways or cables are installed less than 23 millimeters (⅞ in.) from the roof, a temperature adder of 33°C (60°F) shall be added to the ambient temperature.

The informational note following the subsection points to one possible source of average warmest outdoor ambient temperature. The average warmest outdoor ambient temperature for a particular geographical area is also available from many sources in weather almanacs, as well as internet-based weather sites. However, the final selected average warmest outdoor ambient temperature will need to meet with the approval of the authority having jurisdiction for the area in question, since no specific data appears in the *NEC*. The **Exception to 310.15(B)(2)** does not require the temperature adder of 33°C (60°F) to apply when Type XHHW-2 conductors are installed closer than 23 millimeters (⅞ in.) from the roof.

2.5.5 Bare or Covered Conductors

Although bare and covered conductors have higher maximum operating temperatures than the insulated conductors of **Table 310.4(A)**, these conductors are not permitted to operate at a higher temperature than the adjacent insulated conductors. Bare and covered conductors operating at a higher temperature can cause irreparable harm to the insulated conductors if they are contained in the same raceway or cable. Therefore, the bare or covered conductor temperature may never exceed the lowest temperature rating of the adjacent insulated conductor for the purpose of determining ampacity.

2.5.6 Neutral Conductor

Both *neutral conductor* and *neutral point* are defined in **Article 100** of the *NEC*. The neutral conductor may count as a current-carrying conductor when applying the provisions of adjustment factors of **Table 310.15(C)(1)** according to the following statements:

1. A neutral that carries only the unbalanced current is not counted.
2. A neutral with two phases of a 3-phase wye system is counted.
3. Where the major portion of the load consists of nonlinear loads, harmonic currents are present

Code excerpts reproduced with permission of NFPA from NFPA 70®, *National Electrical Code*® (NEC®), 2020 edition. Copyright© 2019, National Fire Protection Association. For a full copy of the NEC®, please go to www.nfpa.org.

in the neutral conductor of a 3-phase, 4-wire, wye system. Therefore, the neutral conductor is counted.

2.5.7 Grounding and Bonding Conductors

Grounding and bonding conductors shall not be counted when applying the provisions of adjustment factors of **Table 310.15(C)(1)**.

2.5.8 120/240-Volt, 3-Wire, Single-Phase Dwelling Services and Feeders

Conductor sizing for 120/240-volt, single-phase dwelling services and feeders differs from the rules of **Table 310.16**, and conductors shall be permitted to be sized according to **310.12(A)** through **(D)**:

310.12

...

(A) Services. For a service rated 100 amperes through 400 amperes, the service conductors supplying the entire load associated with a one-family dwelling, or the service conductors supplying the entire load associated with an individual dwelling unit in a two-family or multifamily dwelling, shall be permitted to have an ampacity not less than 83 percent of the service rating. If no adjustment or correction factors are required, Table 310.12 shall be permitted to be applied.

(B) Feeders. For a feeder rated 100 amperes through 400 amperes, the feeder conductors supplying the entire load associated with a one-family dwelling, or the feeder conductors supplying the entire load associated with an individual dwelling unit in a two-family or multifamily dwelling, shall be permitted to have an ampacity not less than 83 percent of the feeder rating. If no adjustment or correction factors are required, Table 310.12 shall be permitted to be applied.

(C) Feeder Ampacities. In no case shall a feeder for an individual dwelling unit be required to have an ampacity greater than that specified in 310.12(A) or (B).

(D) Grounded Conductors. Grounded conductors shall be permitted to be sized smaller than the ungrounded conductors, if the requirements of 220.61 and 230.42 for service conductors or the requirements of 215.2 and 220.61 for feeder conductors are met.

It is important to note that the service and feeder conductors are sized with an ampacity of not less than 83% of the rating of the service or feeder, and not 83% of the load. As of the 2020 *NEC*, **Table 310.12** has been restored to **Article 310** and is permitted to be used for both services and feeders that supply the entire load associated with the dwelling unit provided no adjustment or correction factors are required. Additionally, since the Section applies to single-phase, 3-wire systems, the neutral conductor carries only the unbalanced load of the line conductors and is permitted to be reduced in size to carry the maximum unbalanced demand as permitted in **220.61**. However, it is still required to be large enough to handle the available ground-fault current as required by **230.42(C)** and **250.24(C)**.

2.5.9 208Y/120-Volt, 3-Wire, Dwelling Feeders

Conductor sizing for 208Y/120-volt, 3-wire dwelling feeders is similar to sizing for 120/240-volt, single-phase dwelling services and feeders, and requires a minimum ampacity or 83% of the rating of the feeder overcurrent protective device. The major difference between the 120/240-volt, single-phase service or feeder and the 208Y/120-volt, 3-wire dwelling feeder is the restriction of the neutral conductor from being permitted to be reduced in size based on the demand factor in **220.61(B)**. The grounded, or neutral, conductor on a 3-wire circuit from a 3-phase, 4-wire, wye system will carry the same amount of current as the two ungrounded conductors, and is prohibited to have any demand factors applied to it as determined by **Section 220.61(C)(1)**. Therefore, it is required not to be smaller than the ungrounded feeder conductors.

2.6 PROBLEMS USING A TEMPERATURE CORRECTION FACTOR

Any deviation from the 30°C ambient temperature designated for **Table 310.16** will cause a change in the ampacity of the conductor. The correction factor for changing the ampacity of the conductor is found in **Table 310.15(B)(1)**. When the ambient temperature is hotter than 30°C (86°F), the ampacity of the conductor will decrease. When the ambient temperature is cooler than 30°C or 86°F, the ampacity will increase. To use the temperature correction factor of **Table 310.15(B)(2)(a)** properly, the user must first determine the insulation type letters, such as THW, THWN, etc. The user then proceeds to **Table 310.4(A)** to determine the temperature rating associated with that particular type of insulation. The type of metal conductor (copper or aluminum) does not affect the temperature rating of a particular insulation. **See Problems 2-3 and 2-4.**

PROBLEM 2-3

A 2-conductor armored cable, Type AC, with 10 AWG 90°C insulated copper conductors, is installed in open bar joist areas having an ambient temperature of 105°F. What is the ampacity of the current-carrying conductors?

Solution

Table 310.16 Ampacity
  10 AWG 90°C insulated copper = 40 A
Table 310.15(B)(1) Temperature Correction Factors
  90°C insulation at 105°F ambient = 0.87
  40 A × 0.87 = 34.8 A
Answer: 34.8 A

PROBLEM 2-4

A 3-conductor metal-clad cable (with ground), Type MC, is installed in an area with an ambient temperature of 45°C. The conductors in the cable are 2 AWG copper with 90°C insulation. What is the ampacity of the current-carrying conductors?

Solution

Table 310.16 Ampacity
  2 AWG copper with 90°C insulation = 130 A
Table 310.15(B)(1) Temperature Correction Factors
  90°C conductor at 45°C ambient = 0.87
  130 A × 0.87 = 113.1 A
Answer: 113.1 A

Utility-owned drop conductors are not covered by the NEC according to **90.2(B)(5)**.

Type AC (armored) cable may include armor/bond wire ground. Courtesy of AFC Cable Systems®

For additional information, visit qr.njatcdb.org
Item #1024

2.7 PROBLEMS USING AN ADJUSTMENT FACTOR

The title of the ampacity **Table 310.16** indicates that the table applies only where not more than three current-carrying conductors are installed in any one raceway or cable. If there are more than three conductors in a raceway or cable, the ampacity changes. The heat problem caused by adjacent conductors comes into play very prominently when there are many current-carrying conductors in the same raceway. **Table 310.15(C)(1), Adjustment Factors for More Than Three Current-Carrying Conductors**, gives the adjustment factors as a percent and is to be used to reduce the allowable ampacity listed in **Table 310.16** and **Table 310.18**. See Problems 2-5, 2-6, and 2-7.

PROBLEM 2-5

Two 3-phase motors are fed with six 4 AWG THHN copper conductors in the same rigid metal conduit, Type RMC, in an ambient temperature of 30°C. What is the ampacity of each current-carrying conductor?

Solution

Table 310.16 Ampacity
  4 AWG THHN copper = 95 A
Table 310.15(C)(1) Adjustment Factors
  6 conductors = 80%
  95 × 0.80 = 76 A
Answer: 76 A

PROBLEM 2-6

Thirty 12 AWG THHW aluminum current-carrying conductors are installed in the same conduit in a wet location area with a 30°C ambient temperature. What is the ampacity of each conductor?

Solution

Table 310.4(A)
  Type THHW insulation used in a wet location is limited to 75°C
Table 310.16 Ampacity
  12 AWG THHW aluminum at 75°C = 20 A
Table 310.15(C)(1) Adjustment Factors
  30 conductors = 45%
  20 A × 0.45 = 9 A
Answer: 9 A

PROBLEM 2-7

Fifteen 10 AWG XHHW-2 copper current-carrying conductors are installed in the same conduit in an area with an ambient temperature of 30°C. What is the ampacity of each conductor?

Solution

Table 310.16 Ampacity
  10 AWG XHHW-2 copper = 40 A
Table 310.15(C)(1) Adjustment Factors
  15 conductors = 50%
  40 A × 0.50 = 20 A
Answer: 20 A

The basic application of the adjustment factor table will be illustrated first. Some other specific factors listed later in the subsection will be reviewed individually as they also affect the ampacity of the conductors.

Before continuing, refer back to **310.14(A), Ampacities for Conductors Rated 0 Volts – 2000 Volts**, and **310.15(A)** through **(F)** with an understanding that this text contains the practical physics of electrical power wiring and is of the utmost importance to electrical safety.

2.7.1 Ampacity Adjustment Factors Using Different Sized Conductors

For an installation where different sized conductors are installed in the same raceway, **Table 310.15(C)(1), Adjustment Factors**, is also applicable. **See Problem 2-8**.

PROBLEM 2-8

Three 2 AWG THWN, three 1 AWG THWN, and three 12 AWG THWN copper current-carrying conductors are installed in the same conduit in an area with an ambient temperature of 30°C. What is the ampacity of the 2 AWG, the 1 AWG, and the 12 AWG conductors?

Solution

Number of conductors 3 + 3 + 3 = 9
Table 310.15(C)(1) Adjustment Factors
 9 conductors = 70%
 Calculate conductors individually
Table 310.16 Ampacity
 2 AWG THWN copper; 115 A × 0.70 = 80.5 A
 1 AWG THWN copper; 130 A × 0.70 = 91.0 A
 12 AWG THWN copper; 25 A × 0.70 = 17.5 A
Answers: 2 AWG THWN = 80.5 A
  1 AWG THWN = 91.0 A
  12 AWG THWN = 17.5 A

2.7.2 Ampacity Adjustment Factors Using Different Insulation Temperatures and Different Sized Conductors

NEC **310.15(A) Informational Note No. 4** points to other sections of the *Code* that apply to conductors and the insulation placed on the conductors. In particular, **310.14(A)(3)** sets the requirements for the temperature limits for conductors. This section stipulates that "…no conductor can be installed such that its operating temperature exceeds that designated for the type of insulation involved." Where more than three current-carrying conductors are installed in the same raceway, **Table 310.15(C)(1)** is also applicable. **See Problem 2-9**.

PROBLEM 2-9

Two 8 AWG THHN and two 4 AWG TW copper current-carrying conductors are installed in the same rigid metal conduit, Type RMC, in an area with an ambient temperature of 30°C. Find the ampacities of the 8 AWG THHN and the 4 AWG TW conductors.

Solution

Number of conductors 2 + 2 = 4
Table 310.15(C)(1) Adjustment Factors
 4 conductors = 80%
Table 310.16 Ampacity
 4 AWG TW (using the 60°C column) = 70 A
 70 A × 0.80 = 56 A
 8 AWG THHN (using the 90°C column) = 55 A
 55 A × 0.80 = 44 A
 Check 44 A against 60°C column of Table 310.16.
 The 8 AWG (at 44 A) exceeds the 60°C column maximum ampacity of 40 A.
  The ampacity of 8 AWG must not exceed that of the 60°C column.
 Therefore, the 8 AWG THHN is limited to a maximum of 40 A.
Answers: 4 AWG TW = 56 A
  8 AWG THHN = 40 A

Comment: This problem contains two situations which require adjustment. First, there are more than three current-carrying conductors in a raceway, so each pair of example conductors must be adjusted to 80% of their table value. Second, since adjacent wires in a single conduit must not be subject to overheating, the lowest temperature insulation rating (60°C column ampacity from Table 310.16) must be applied to all conductors within a single conduit for this problem. Explaining it another way, since the most fragile insulation is the TW, the ampacity of THHN conductors must be reduced to the maximum operating temperature permitted for TW insulation, that is, the ampacity permitted in Table 310.16, using the 60°C column for copper conductors.

There is a potential danger in placing conductors with different temperature ratings within the same raceway. Where mixed, the ampacity of the higher-temperature conductors may have to be lowered in the event that the higher-temperature conductor overheats (and presents the risk of damaging) the adjacent lower-temperature conductors.

2.7.3 Applying Both Correction Factors and Adjustment Factors

The phrase used at the top of the percentage column of **Table 310.15(C)(1)**, "...as Adjusted for Ambient Temperature if Necessary," indicates that both the correction factor (temperature) and the adjustment factor (number of current-carrying conductors in a raceway or cable) must be applied whenever both are present. **See Problems 2-10, 2-11, and 2-12.**

PROBLEM 2-10

Nine 10 AWG THWN copper current-carrying conductors are installed in a one-inch conduit, Type RMC, in an area with an ambient temperature of 45°C. What is the ampacity of each conductor?

Solution

Table 310.16 Ampacity
 10 AWG THWN 75°C copper = 35 A
Table 310.15(B)(1) Correction Factors
 75°C conductor in a 45°C ambient = 0.82
Table 310.15(C)(1) Adjustment Factors
 9 current-carrying conductors = 70%
 35 A × 0.82 × 0.70 = 20.09 A
Answer: 20.09 A

Depending upon the location of the raceway or cable, adjustment and correction factors for more than three current-carrying conductors and ambient temperature other than 30°C (86°F) may both need to be applied.

PROBLEM 2-11

Twelve 8 AWG THHW copper current-carrying conductors are installed in a two-inch conduit, Type EMT, located in a dry location with an ambient temperature area of 128°F. What is the ampacity of each conductor?

Solution

Table 310.16 Ampacity
 8 AWG THHW 90°C copper = 55 A
Table 310.15(B)(1) Correction Factors
 90°C conductor at 128°F ambient = 0.76
Table 310.15(C)(1) Adjustment Factors
 12 conductors = 50%
 55 A × 0.76 × 0.50 = 20.9 A
Answer: 20.9 A

PROBLEM 2-12

Thirty-six 12 AWG THHN copper current-carrying conductors are installed in the same raceway located in an ambient temperature of 50°C. What is the ampacity of each conductor?

Solution

Table 310.16 Ampacity
 12 AWG THHN 90°C copper = 30 A
Table 310.15(B)(1) Correction Factors
 90°C conductor at 50°C ambient = 0.82
Table 310.15(C)(1) Adjustment Factors
 36 conductors = 40%
 30 A × 0.82 × 0.40 = 9.84 A
Answer: 9.84 A
Comment: Installations with this many current-carrying conductors in a raceway often waste a significant amount of copper and should be avoided wherever possible.

2.7.4 Applying Adjustment and Temperature Correction Factors to Cable Assemblies

Until now, only conductors installed in raceways have been considered. The ampacity tables, the ambient temperature correction factors, and the adjustment factors also apply to the installation of cable assemblies. **See Problems 2-13, 2-14, and 2-15.**

PROBLEM 2-13

MC Cable
Four 4/0 AWG
75°C Insulated Copper
Plus an Equipment
Grounding Conductor
Ambient Air 45°C

A 4-conductor, metal-clad cable is used as the feeder for a 120/208-volt panel supplying discharge lighting. The 4/0 AWG copper conductors have 75°C insulation and the cable is installed in an area with an ambient temperature of 45°C. What is the ampacity of each 4/0 AWG conductor? (The discharge lighting requires all four conductors to be counted as current-carrying conductors since the neutral conductor is considered a current-carrying conductor in accordance with 310.15(E)(4).)

Solution

Table 310.16 Ampacity
 4/0 AWG at 75°C copper = 230 A
Table 310.15(B)(1) Correction Factors
 75°C conductor in 45°C ambient = 0.82
Table 310.15(C)(1) Adjustment Factors
 4 current-carrying conductors = 80%
 230 A × 0.82 × 0.80 = 150.88 A
Answer: 150.88 A

Type MC cable is generally available in both solid and stranded conductors in sizes 12 and 10 AWG. Various insulation colors are also available for identification purposes for different phases and voltage systems.

PROBLEM 2-14

MC Cable
Six 12 AWG
90°C Copper
Plus an Equipment
Grounding Conductor
Ambient Air 40°C

A 6-conductor (three circuit), Type MC, metal-clad cable is used to supply three 20-ampere fluorescent lighting circuits within an office environment. The cable is comprised of three ungrounded conductors, three grounded conductors, and a green equipment grounding conductor. The 12 AWG copper conductors have 90°C insulation, and the cable is installed in an area with an ambient temperature of 40°C. What is the ampacity of each 12 AWG conductor?

Solution

Table 310.16 Ampacity
 12 AWG at 90°C copper = 30 A
Table 310.15(B)(1) Correction Factors
 90°C conductor in 40°C ambient = 0.91
Table 310.15(C)(1) Adjustment Factors
 6 current-carrying conductors = 80%
 30 A × 0.91 × 0.80 = 21.84 A
Answer: 21.84 A
Comment: This is a practical example which will be used later to determine a circuit final ampacity.

PROBLEM 2-15

PVC
8 AWG Copper
90°C Insulation
3/C Type TC Cable
Ambient Air 75°F

Two 3-conductor, Type TC cables are installed in a rigid PVC conduit in an area with an ambient temperature of 75°F. The conductors are 8 AWG copper with 90°C insulation. What is the ampacity of each current-carrying conductor?

Solution

Table 310.16 Ampacity
 8 AWG copper at 90°C = 55 A
Table 310.15(B)(1) Correction Factors
 90°C copper in 75°F ambient = 1.04
 2 cables × 3 = 6 conductors
Table 310.15(C)(1) Adjustment Factors
 6 conductors = 80%
 55 A × 1.04 × 0.80 = 45.76 A
Answer: 45.76 A

2.7.5 Applying Adjustment Factors

There is significant text contained in **310.15(C)(1), Adjustment Factors for More Than Three Current-Carrying Conductors**. The majority of these requirements are based on actual circuit properties and how heat is generated, dispersed, and not permitted to be retained within the circuit conductors, raceways, or cables or within surrounding circuits or raceways. Previously, fundamental methods of applying adjustment factors to correct circuit ampacity were presented; spare conductors and neutral conductors were also reviewed.

Within a raceway or cable, the actual conductor count may be adjusted or lowered by the number of neutral conductors which carry only the unbalanced current. Additionally, the actual count may be reduced by the number of grounding and bonding conductors. Generally, the actual power and lighting conductors (and the spare, if any) are considered current-carrying conductors. Other conductors could be control or signal conductors, which carry small amounts of current and may only last for short periods of time. Therefore, because they do not continuously carry current, they add little, if any, heat to the enclosure and are not counted as current-carrying conductors where **Table 310.15(C)(1)** is applied. **See Problem 2-16.**

Cable tray can be used to distribute multiconductor cables throughout an industrial plant.

PROBLEM 2-16

Two sets of 3-phase, 3-wire circuits, each comprised of 4 AWG THWN copper motor branch-circuit conductors, are installed in the same conduit with two 14 AWG THWN copper control circuit conductors in an ambient temperature of 30°C. What is the ampacity of only the six 4 AWG THWN copper motor branch-circuit conductors?

Solution

Table 310.16 Ampacity
  4 AWG THWN copper = 85 A
  Number of conductors 6 + 2 = 8
  Control circuit conductors do not count
  Number of current-carrying conductors = 6
Table 310.15(C)(1) Adjustment Factors
  6 conductors = 80%
  85 A × 0.80 = 68 A
Answer: 68 A

2.7.6 Applying Adjustment Factors to Cables in Cable Tray

NEC **310.15(C)(1)(a)** refers to **392.80**, which covers the ampacity of multiple conductor cables in cable trays. This section applies to multiconductor cables and requires the application of **Table 310.15(C)(1)** to multiple conductor cables with more than three current-carrying conductors installed in cable trays. The adjustment factor applies to each individual cable as if it were in a separate raceway and not to all of the conductors collectively contained within the tray. This method of calculation applies only where cables are installed without maintained spacing of one cable diameter between cables. For cables installed with maintained spacing of one cable diameter between cables in a single layer in an uncovered tray, the ampacity calculations for cables are much different. See **392.80(A)(1)(c)** for more details. **See Problem 2-17.**

PROBLEM 2-17

Three Multiconductor Tray Cables Installed in a Cable Tray Without Maintained Spacing

A 3-conductor, a 7-conductor, and a 15-conductor Type TC cable are all installed in a single uncovered cable tray without properly maintained cable diameter spacing. The installation area has an ambient temperature of 30°C. All of the individual conductors within the Type TC cables are 10 AWG 75°C insulated copper. What is the ampacity of each current-carrying conductor?

Solution

Calculation 1
The 3-conductor cable using 75°C copper conductors
Table 310.16 Ampacity
  10 AWG 75°C insulated copper = 35 A
392.80(A)(1)(a); adjustment factors do not apply
  No adjustment necessary
  3-conductor 10 AWG 75°C copper = 35 A
Answer: 35 A

Calculation 2
The 7-conductor cable
Table 310.16 Ampacity
  10 AWG 75°C insulated copper = 35 A
392.80(A)(1)(a) and Table 310.15(C)(1)
  Adjustment factor for 7 conductors = 70%
  35 A × 0.70 = 24.5 A
Answer: 24.5 A

Calculation 3
The 15-conductor cable
Table 310.16 Ampacity
  10 AWG 75°C insulated copper = 35 A
392.80(A)(1)(a) and Table 310.15(C)(1)
  Adjustment factor for 15 conductors = 50%
  35 A × 0.50 = 17.5 A
Answer: 17.5 A

Figure 2-2. Conductors in a Raceway Nipple. A 24-inch length of conduit or tubing is exempt from the adjustment factor requirements.

2.7.7 Adjustment Factors to Current-Carrying Conductors in Limited Length Raceways

NEC **310.15(C)(1)(b)** permits the installation of conductors in a raceway nipple, provided it is not over 24 inches in length, without applying any adjustment factor. **See Figure 2-2**.

NEC **310.15(C)(1)(c)** permits the installation of conductors in a conduit emerging from the ground without applying any adjustment factor, provided the rigid metal conduit, intermediate metal conduit, rigid polyvinyl chloride conduit (PVC), or reinforced thermosetting resin conduit (RTRC), is not over 10 feet long and there are not more than four conductors within the conduit. **See Figure 2-3**.

Figure 2-3. Conductors Emerging from the Ground. A 10-foot length of conduit is exempt from the adjustment factor requirements.

In addition, **310.15(C)(1)(d)** permits Type AC cable or Type MC cable under specific conditions to be exempt from the adjustment factor requirements. The following conditions are required to be met:

1. The cables are not permitted to have an overall outer jacket.
2. Each cable does not have more than three current-carrying conductors, allowing the cables to be only 2-conductor (plus ground), 3-conductor (plus ground), or 4-conductor (plus ground), if the neutral in the 4-conductor cable only carries (unbalanced without harmonics present) from a wye system.
3. The cables contain conductors that are only 12 AWG copper.
4. There is a maximum of 20 current-carrying conductors installed in the bundle without maintaining spacing, stacked, or supported on bridle rings.

The **Exception to 310.15(C)(1)(d)** contains mandatory language. If a bundle of MC or AC cables exceeds 20 current-carrying conductors, this exception requires a single adjustment factor of 60% to be applied to each current-carrying conductor within the bundle of cables.

> The most common form of wire stranding is a concentric-stranded conductor. Each layer of this stranding (after the initial core strand) has six more strands added, and each layer is applied in a direction opposite that of the layer under it. See the *NEC* **Chapter 9, Table 10** for more information on wire stranding.

2.8 AMPACITY OF BARE CONDUCTORS

The main rule of **Section 230.41** requires service entrance conductors to be insulated. The exception to this section permits the grounded conductor to be uninsulated or bare. For the purpose of determining ampacity, **310.15(D)** requires that bare and covered conductors installed with insulated conductors have temperature ratings equal to the lowest temperature rating of the (adjacent) insulated conductors. The easiest way to determine the ampacity of the bare or covered conductor where this mixture occurs is to consider the bare or covered conductor to have the same insulation as the ungrounded conductors and read the ampacity directly from the table. This will ensure temperature compatibility of all the conductors within the raceway and will prevent insulation damage to adjacent conductors. **See Problem 2-18**.

PROBLEM 2-18

Raceway — Two 500 kcmil THWN Copper
4/0 AWG Bare Copper

What is the ampacity of a 4/0 AWG bare copper grounded conductor run in the same raceway with two 500 kcmil THWN copper service conductors?

Solution

Table 310.16 Ampacity
  4/0 AWG THWN copper = 230 A
  4/0 AWG bare copper = 230 A
Answer: 230 A

2.9 THE NEUTRAL CONDUCTOR AND THE AMPACITY ADJUSTMENT FACTOR

NEC **310.15(E)** takes into consideration the three applications of a neutral conductor. Notice that when the neutral conductor is a current-carrying conductor, it counts when considering the application of the adjustment factors of **Table 310.15(C)(1)**. When the neutral conductor is not considered a current-carrying conductor, it is not counted.

NEC **310.15(E)(1)** covers the first application. The neutral conductor is treated as a non–current-carrying conductor and is not counted toward the adjustment factor. The neutral conductor of a 120/208-volt system supplying incandescent lighting will carry only the unbalanced current; should the load be perfectly balanced, theoretically the neutral conductor will carry no current. In multiwire branch circuits with a neutral conductor supplying only resistive loads (such as incandescent lighting and resistive heating), the neutral conductor is not counted. **See Problems 2-19, 2-20, 2-21, and 2-22.**

PROBLEM 2-19

A 3-phase, 4-wire, multiwire branch circuit is installed using 12 AWG THWN copper conductors in Type EMT as the branch circuits for incandescent lighting in an area of 30°C ambient temperature. What is the ampacity rating of each current-carrying conductor?

Solution

Table 310.16 Ampacity
  12 AWG THWN = 25 A
  Total number of conductors = 4
  310.15(E)(1), neutral conductor is not counted
  Number of current-carrying conductors = 3
  Adjustment factor is not applicable
Answer: 25 A

Power quality with lighting has been an ongoing issue for decades. Over the past number of years, harmonics produced by fluorescent lighting have been improved, however many fluorescent lights are being retrofitted and replaced with LED lighting. The U.S. Department of Energy projects lighting energy to be reduced by 75% by the year 2035 with the adoption of LEDs, compared to a no-LED scenario, translating to a total cumulative energy savings of nearly $630 billion in avoided energy costs.

PROBLEM 2-20

Two 3-phase, 4-wire, 120/208-volt multiwire branch circuits are installed using 14 AWG THWN copper conductors in Type EMT as the branch circuits for incandescent lighting in an area with an ambient temperature of 30°C. What is the ampacity of the current-carrying conductors?

Solution

Table 310.16 Ampacity
  14 AWG THWN copper = 20 A
  Total number of conductors = 8
  310.15(E)(1), neutral is not counted
  Number of current-carrying conductors = 6
Table 310.15(C)(1) Adjustment Factors
  6 conductors = 80%
  20 A × 0.80 = 16 A
Answer: 16 A

PROBLEM 2-21

Two phase "B" conductors, two phase "C" conductors, and two neutral conductors of a 120/208-volt system are installed in the same rigid metal conduit in an area with an ambient temperature of 30°C. The conductors are 10 AWG THHN aluminum. What is the ampacity of each current-carrying conductor? (Note: only one 3-wire multiwire branch circuit is shown in the graphic.)

Solution

Table 310.16 Ampacity
  10 AWG THHN Aluminum = 35 A
310.15(E)(2)
  All 6 conductors are current-carrying conductors
Table 310.15(C)(1) Adjustment Factors
  6 conductors = 80%
  35 A × 0.80 = 28 A
Answer: 28 A

Comment: 310.15(E)(2) covers the second application. This takes into consideration the installation of a neutral conductor with only two of the phase conductors of a 3-phase, 4-wire system. An example may be a 208Y/102-volt, 3-wire feeder to an apartment or condominium within a high-rise multifamily complex. In this situation, the neutral conductor will carry approximately the same current as the phase conductors and is counted as a current-carrying conductor.

PROBLEM 2-22

Multiwire Branch Circuit
All Conductors in Same Raceway

120/208 volts, or 277/480 volts
Neutral conductor is counted

A 277/480-volt, 3-phase, 4-wire multiwire branch circuit supplies a fluorescent lighting load. The branch circuit is installed in Type EMT using four 12 AWG THHN copper conductors in an area with an ambient temperature of 90°F. What is the ampacity of each of the current-carrying conductors?

Solution

Table 310.16 Ampacity
  12 AWG THHN copper = 30 A
Table 310.15(B)(1) Correction Factors
  90°C insulation in 90°F ambient = 0.96
Table 310.15(C)(1) Adjustment Factors
  All conductors count
  4 conductors = 80%
  30 A × 0.96 × 0.80 = 23.04 A

Answer: 23.04 A

Comment: 310.15(E)(3) covers the third application. This section requires the neutral conductor to be counted where the major portion of the load consists of nonlinear loads. Nonlinear loads cause harmonic currents in the neutral conductor. Electric discharge lighting, LED lighting, and data processing equipment are examples of nonlinear loads which may cause harmonic currents. Due to harmonic currents, the neutral conductor will often carry as much or sometimes even more, current than the line conductors. Therefore, the neutral conductors are counted as current-carrying conductors even where the load is balanced.

The illustrated *Code Calculations* problems are intended to show the basic ampacity only. No other factors, such as overcurrent protection, are taken into consideration at this time.

2.10 COUNTING EQUIPMENT GROUNDING AND BONDING CONDUCTORS

NEC **310.15(F)** covers the installation of the equipment grounding and bonding conductors. The equipment grounding and bonding conductors do not carry current during normal operation, but rather carry current only during fault conditions. Therefore, they are not counted during the application of adjustment factors according to the footnote of **Table 310.15(C)(1)**. **See Problem 2-23**.

PROBLEM 2-23

PVC
Current-Carrying Conductors
EGC Not Counted
IEGC Not Counted

EGC – Bare Equipment Grounding Conductor
IEGC – Insulated Equipment Grounding Conductor for Isolated Equipment Grounding

A 3-phase, 120/208-volt, 4-wire multiwire branch circuit supplies data processing equipment using isolated ground (Type IG) 120-volt receptacles in an area with an ambient temperature of 30°C. The rigid conduit contains four 12 AWG THHN copper branch-circuit conductors, one bare equipment grounding conductor, and one insulated equipment grounding conductor. What is the ampacity of the branch-circuit conductors?

Solution

Table 310.16 Ampacity
  12 AWG THHN copper = 30 A
  Total number of conductors = 6
  All three ungrounded conductors count
  The load is data processing equipment; one neutral conductor counts
  Neither of the two equipment grounding conductors counts
  Number of current-carrying conductors = 4
Table 310.15(C)(1) Adjustment Factors
  4 conductors = 80%
  30 A × 0.80 = 24 A

Answer: 24 A

2.11 APPLICATION OF 310.12 FOR SINGLE-PHASE DWELLING SERVICES AND FEEDERS

It is important to remember that, in general, conductor ampacities are determined from ampacity tables such as **Table 310.16**, unless modified by **310.15(A)** through **(F)**. **Section 310.12** is a conditional rule allowing dwelling unit service and feeder conductors to be used at an ampacity different than that permitted by the ampacity tables. **Table 310.12** provides conductor sizes for services or feeders rated from 100 amperes to 400 amperes. The note at the bottom of the table permits the usage of the table provided no adjustment or correction factors are required for the installation. Otherwise, the section permits sizing the dwelling unit service and feeder conductors to an ampacity of 83% of the service or feeder rating based upon the ampacities of **Table 310.16**. Two electrical system applications, 208Y/120-volt 3-wire feeders and 120/240-volt single-phase 3-wire services and feeders, are covered under the conditional rule. Note that 208Y/120-volt, 3-wire feeders are common for supplying the individual dwelling units of multifamily dwellings. Both systems are permitted to be sized in accordance with three requirements.

First, for a service rated 100 through 400 amperes, the service conductors supplying the entire load associated with a one-family dwelling or supplying the entire load associated with an individual dwelling unit in a two-family or multifamily dwelling are permitted to have an ampacity not less than 83% of the service rating. If no adjustment or correction factors are required, then **Table 310.12** is permitted to be used.

Second, for a feeder rated 100 through 400 amperes, the feeder conductors supplying the entire load associated with a one-family dwelling or supplying the entire load associated with an individual dwelling unit in a two-family or multifamily dwelling are permitted to have an ampacity not less than 83% of the feeder rating. If no adjustment or correction factors are required, then **Table 310.12** is permitted to be used.

Third, in no case could a feeder for an individual dwelling unit be required to have an ampacity greater than that specified in **310.12(A)** or **(B)**.

In **310.12(D)**, the permission to size grounded conductors smaller than the ungrounded conductors applies only for the 120/240-volt, single-phase service or feeder and not the 208Y/120-volt, 3-wire feeder. The 120/240-volt, single-phase, 3-wire service or feeder neutral conductor carries unbalanced current, and is therefore permitted to have demand factors applied in accordance with the requirements of **220.61** and as a ground fault conductor per **230.42(C)** and **250.24(C)** for service conductors, or in accordance with the requirements of **215.2** and **220.61** for feeder conductors. The 208Y/120-volt, 3-wire feeder neutral conductor carries approximately the same

Table 310.12 Single-Phase Dwelling Services and Feeders

Service or Feeder Rating (Amperes)	Conductor (AWG or kcmil) Copper	Conductor (AWG or kcmil) Aluminum or Copper-Clad Aluminum
100	4	2
110	3	1
125	2	1/0
150	1	2/0
175	1/0	3/0
200	2/0	4/0
225	3/0	250
250	4/0	300
300	250	350
350	350	500
400	400	600

Note: If no adjustment or correction factors are required, this table shall be permitted to be applied.

In the 2020 edition of the NEC, **Table 310.12** is returned to **Article 310** for sizing feeder and service conductors for dwelling units provided adjustment or correction factors are not required.

Reproduced with permission of NFPA from NFPA 70®, *National Electrical Code*® (NEC®), 2020 edition. Copyright© 2019, National Fire Protection Association. For a full copy of the NEC®, please go to www.nfpa.org.

amount of current as the two ungrounded conductors and is prohibited from having any demand factors applied per **220.61(C)(1)**. None of these permissive statements remove the requirements to apply ampacity correction or adjustment factors applicable to conductor installation(s) if necessary. However, it is important to remember that the grounded conductor is never *required* to be reduced in size; the *NEC* simply permits it in certain cases.

In addition, and where specifically permitted elsewhere in the *Code*, the grounded conductor is permitted to be smaller than the line conductors (ungrounded conductors). For any examples using **310.15(E)**, the grounded conductor could always be selected to equal the size of the ungrounded conductor. Sometimes the calculated load of the grounded conductor may be less than the calculated load of the ungrounded conductor. **See Problems 2-24, 2-25, and 2-26.**

PROBLEM 2-24

The load for a one-family dwelling unit is calculated to be 137 amperes line load and 81 amperes neutral load. The service is single-phase, 120/240-volt, 3-wire and is to be installed with THWN copper conductors.

1. What is the minimum size service-entrance ungrounded (line or phase) conductors?
2. What is the minimum size grounded (neutral) conductor?

Solution

Calculation 1
Ungrounded service-entrance conductors
  137A load requires a 150A service
Table 310.12 is permitted to be used as there are no adjustment or correction factors
Table 310.12 for 150A service permits 1 AWG THWN
Answer: Ungrounded Conductors = 1 AWG THWN

Calculation 2
Grounded service-entrance conductor (neutral)
  Neutral conductor load = 81 A
Table 310.16 Ampacity
  81 A = 4 AWG THWN copper
Not smaller than required by 250.24(C) and Table 250.102(C)(1)
  1 AWG copper ungrounded service-entrance conductor = 6 AWG
  But 6 AWG is not adequate for 81 A of load
Answer: Grounded Conductor = 4 AWG THWN

PROBLEM 2-25

An apartment complex is supplied by a 208Y/120-volt, 3-phase, 4-wire, wye service. A 3-wire, 208Y/120-volt, 125-ampere feeder supplies a 125-ampere rated panelboard installed in the apartment to supply the entire load of the apartment. The conductors are installed in a location with an ambient temperature of 120°F.

1. What is the minimum size THWN ungrounded feeder conductor required to supply the apartment?
2. What is the minimum size THWN grounded feeder conductor required to supply the apartment??

Solution

Calculation 1
Since correction factors apply, Table 310.12 is not permitted to be used and 310.12(B) permits the conductors to have an ampacity of not less than 83% of the feeder rating
  125 A × 0.83 = 104 A
Table 310.16 Ampacity and Table 310.15(B)(1) Correction Factors
  1 AWG THWN = 130 A × 0.75 = 97.5 A and is not adequate for 104 A
  1/0 AWG TWHN = 150 A × 0.75 = 112.5 A and is adequate for 104 A
Answer: Ungrounded THWN feeder conductors = 1/0 AWG THWN

Calculation 2
Since 310.12(D) does not apply and 220.61(C)(1) prohibits applying demand factors to the neutral of a 208Y/120-volt, 3-wire feeder, the grounded conductor is required to be the same size as the ungrounded feeder conductors.
Answer: Grounded THWN feeder conductor = 1/0 AWG THWN

PROBLEM 2-26

The single-phase, 120/240-volt, 3-wire, 400-ampere service for a multifamily dwelling is calculated to be 380 amperes on each ungrounded service entrance conductor and has a 120-ampere load on the grounded service entrance conductor with all the conductors being THWN copper.

1. What size of ungrounded (line or phase) service-entrance conductor is needed? (Hint: This service for this situation does not qualify under 310.12(A).)
2. What is the minimum size grounded neutral service-entrance conductor required?
3. What is the minimum size feeder conductor required for the 100-ampere panel located in each apartment all with a 120-volt connected load? (Hint: Although the branch-circuit loads in each apartment are limited to 120 volts, the maximum unbalanced load on the ungrounded conductor cannot be accurately determined from this given information.)
4. What is the minimum size feeder conductor required for the 200-ampere, 120/240-volt, single-phase house panel?

Solution

Calculation 1
Multifamily dwelling ungrounded service-entrance conductors
Since Table 310.12(A) does not apply
From Table 310.16 Ampacity
  380A THWN copper = 500 kcmil
Answer: 230.23(A) Load 380A THWN copper = 500 kcmil

Calculation 2
Multifamily dwelling grounded service-entrance conductor
Table 310.16 Ampacity
  120A THWN = 1 AWG
250.24(C)(1) Minimum Size
Table 250.102(C)(1), Grounded Conductor
  Service conductor of 500 kcmil = 1/0 AWG
  Grounded service conductor cannot be smaller than 1/0 AWG
Answer: 1/0 AWG

Calculation 3
Typical dwelling unit ungrounded feeder conductors
Since no adjustment or correction factors are required, Table 310.12 is permitted by 310.12(B).
  100 A = 4 AWG THWN
  Grounded (neutral) conductor current for this feeder is not reduced in problem
  Since Table 250.102(C)(1) does not apply, match the full-size ungrounded conductor = 4 AWG
Answer: Line and Neutral 4 AWG

Calculation 4
House panel feeder
310.12(A) does not apply
Table 310.16 Ampacity
  200 A THWN = 3/0 AWG copper
Answer: 3/0 AWG

A multiple-occupancy building has multiple sets of service-entrance conductors.

PROBLEM 2-27

What is the ampacity of 3-conductor, Type AC cable comprised of three 8 AWG, 90°C insulated copper conductors installed in thermal insulation?

Solution

Table 310.16 Ampacity
  60°C Column 8 AWG = 40 A
Answer: 40 A

PROBLEM 2-28

A 12-2 (plus ground) Type MC cable, with an overall PVC outer jacket, listed suitable for direct burial, is installed underground to supply parking lot lighting. The Type MC cable is constructed with THHN/THWN insulated power conductors. What is the ampacity of the cable?

Solution

Article 100 Definition of Wet Location defines the installation as wet
Table 310.4(A) requires THWN to be used at 75°C temperature rating in a wet location
  12 AWG THWN in the 75°C column is 25 A in Table 310.16
Answer: 25 A

2.12 SPECIAL AMPACITY INFORMATION

The following is specific ampacity information for particular wiring methods and/or conditions.

2.12.1 Armored Cable

The use of **310.15** for determination of ampacities for the conductors of armored cable (Type AC) is required by **320.80(A)**. Where the armored cable is installed in thermal-type insulation, only 90°C conductors are permitted to be used, and the ampacity of the 90°C conductor is limited to that of a 60°C rated conductor.

2.12.2 Metal-Clad Cable

In general, **Section 330.80** requires the ampacity of metal-clad cable (Type MC) with conductors 14 AWG and larger to be determined in accordance with **310.14**. **Section 330.112(A)** indicates the conductors used in MC cable larger than 16 AWG shall be of a type listed in **Table 310.4(A)** or of a type identified for use in MC cable. Typical insulation types used by manufacturers include THHN/THWN, XHHW, or XHHW-2. Due to differing types of insulation, when selecting the ampacity of the cable, it should first be determined if the location is dry or wet, which will determine the cable temperature rating of either 90°C or 75°C, respectively. In order to adjust the ampacity of the cable based on conditions of use, the insulation type must be known, and adjustment factors can then be based on the appropriate temperature rating of the insulation. **See Problems 2-27 and 2-28.**

2.12.3 Nonmetallic Sheathed Cable

Power conductors within nonmetallic sheathed cable, or Type NM cable (including NMC and NMS), are constructed with insulation rated at 90°C based on **Section 334.112**; however, the ampacity of the cable shall be selected in accordance with a 60°C rated conductor. The 90°C conductor rating is permitted to be used for temperature correction and ampacity adjustment calculations, but the final calculated ampacity of these 90°C conductors shall not exceed that of a 60°C rated conductor, according to **Section 334.80**. See Problems 2-29, 2-30, and 2-31.

PROBLEM 2-29

A 3-conductor, 12 AWG (with ground) copper Type NM cable is installed in an area with a 30°C ambient temperature. What is the ampacity of the circuit conductors?

Solution

Section 334.80 Ampacity
Table 310.16 Ampacity
  12 AWG copper at 90°C = 30 A
  Number of conductors = 4
  Equipment grounding conductor not counted
  Number of current-carrying conductors = 3
Table 310.15(C)(1) Adjustment Factor does not apply
Table 310.15(B)(1) Correction Factor does not apply
Table 310.16 Ampacity
  Final derated ampacity not to exceed 60°C
  12 AWG copper at 60°C = 20 A
Answer: 20 A

PROBLEM 2-30

Four 2-conductor, Type NM cables are installed in a rigid PVC conduit in an area with an ambient temperature of 45°C. Each current-carrying conductor in the NM cables is 10 AWG aluminum with 90°C insulation. What is the ampacity of each 10 AWG conductor?

Solution

Section 334.80 Ampacity
Table 310.16 Ampacity
  10 AWG aluminum NM at 90°C = 35 A
Table 310.15(B)(1) Correction Factors
  90°C insulation in 45°C ambient = 0.87
Table 310.15(C)(1) Adjustment Factors
  4 cables × 2 current-carrying conductors = 8
  8 current-carrying conductors = 70%
  35 A × 0.87 × 0.70 = 21.31 A
  10 AWG aluminum at 60°C = 25 A
  Calculated ampacity is less than at 60°C
  21.3 A maximum permitted
Answer: 21.3 A

PROBLEM 2-31

Two 2-conductor, 8 AWG copper Type NM cables are installed in electrical metallic tubing, Type EMT, in an area with an ambient temperature of 35°C. What is the ampacity of each conductor?

Solution

Section 334.80 Ampacity
Table 310.16 Ampacity
  8 AWG copper at 90°C = 55 A
Table 310.15(B)(1) Correction Factors
  90°C insulated conductors in 35°C ambient = 0.96
Table 310.15(C)(1) Adjustment Factors
  2 cables × 2 conductors = 4 conductors
  4 current-carrying conductors = 80%
  55 A × 0.96 × 0.80 = 42.24 A
  8 AWG copper at 60°C = 40 A
  42.24 A exceeds 60°C ampacity
  42.24 A is not permitted
Answer: 40 A

Ampacity adjustments of NM cables may also be necessary where two or more cables are installed (1) through firestopped openings in wood framing members, or (2) in direct contact with thermal insulation without maintaining spacing.

2.12.4 Service-Entrance Cable

Frequently, service-entrance (Type SE) cable is used as branch circuit or feeder wiring in the interior of dwelling units. **Section 338.10(B)(4)(a)(1)** requires the installation to comply with the requirements of **Part II of Article 334**, excluding **334.80**. The reason for the exclusion is that Type NM cable is permitted to have adjustment and correction factors applied based on 90°C rated conductors; however, per UL standards, Type SE cable is permitted to be constructed with either 75°C or 90°C rated conductors, and applying **334.80** would adjust the cable incorrectly if it contains 75°C rated conductors.

When more than two Type SE cables with two or more current-carrying conductors in each cable are installed in contact with thermal insulation, caulk, or sealing foam without maintaining spacing, the ampacities are required to be adjusted in accordance with **Table 310.15(C)(1)**. When SE cables with conductors 10 AWG and smaller are installed in contact with thermal insulation, the ampacity is required to be selected in accordance with 60°C temperature rating. Type SE cables with conductors larger than 10 AWG are permitted to have the allowable ampacity selected in accordance with the temperature rating permitted by the equipment terminations per **110.14(C)** based on either 75°C or 90°C rated conductors contained in the cable. **See Problem 2-32**.

PROBLEM 2-32

A 6-3 (plus ground) aluminum SE cable is installed to supply a 120/240-volt range receptacle in a dwelling unit. The cable is constructed with RHW insulation and is installed in direct contact with thermal insulation. What is the ampacity of the cable?

Solution

Since it is only one cable and with conductors larger than 10 AWG, the contact with thermal insulation does not require the ampacity to be determined by the 60°C temperature rating per 338.10(B).
Use the RHW insulation rating in the 75°C column for aluminum conductors in Table 310.16
Answer: 50 A

PROBLEM 2-33

Metal Wireway with Twenty-Four 10 AWG THWN

What is the ampacity of each of twenty-four 10 AWG THWN copper current-carrying conductors installed in a metal wireway, occupying 18% of the interior cross-sectional area of the wireway in an area with an ambient temperature of 30°C?

Solution

Table 310.16 Ampacity
10 AWG THWN copper = 35 A
  Metal wireway contains less than 30 conductors
  Metal wireway is less than 20% full
Table 310.15(C)(1) Adjustment Factors does not apply
Answer: 35 A
Comment: This situation limits the metal wireway cross-sectional area to 18% fill, thus complying with 376.22(A). No adjustment factors are necessary, because the problem is limited to 24 current-carrying conductors.

2.12.5 Metal Wireways and Sheet Metal Auxiliary Gutters

NEC **376.22(A)**, which covers metal wireways, and **366.22(A)**, which covers sheet metal auxiliary gutters, directly relate to the permitted area

If more than two SE cables are installed in contact with thermal insulation, caulk, or sealing foam without maintaining spacing, the ampacity is required to be adjusted based upon number of current-carrying conductors.

of conductor fill allowed for these raceways. The maximum permitted fill of all contained conductors in both wiring methods is limited to 20%. **Table 1 of Chapter 9** does not apply.

In addition, **376.22(A)** (covering metal wireways) and **366.22(A)** (covering sheet metal auxiliary gutters) require the application of adjustment factors according to **310.15(C)(1)** only if the number of current-carrying conductors exceeds 30. Non–current-carrying conductors such as control and starting-duty–only conductors are not counted as current-carrying conductors according to **376.22(B)** and **366.22(A)**. See Problems 2-33 and 2-34.

2.12.6 Nonmetallic Wireways and Nonmetallic Auxiliary Gutters

Section 378.22 addresses the ampacity and the number of conductors permitted in nonmetallic wireways:

1. The number of all contained conductors is limited to not more than 20% of the interior cross-sectional area of a nonmetallic wireway. **Table 1 of Chapter 9** does not apply.
2. The adjustment factors of **310.15(C)(1)** apply to all the current-carrying conductors in a nonmetallic wireway.
3. The adjustment factors of **310.15(C)(1)** do not apply to conductors for signaling circuits or to controller conductors between a motor and its starter and used only for starting duty.

NEC **366.22(B)** specifies the number of all contained conductors in a nonmetallic auxiliary gutter be limited to not more than 20% of the interior cross-sectional area of the gutter. There are no exceptions.

NEC **366.23(B)** requires the adjustment factors of **310.15(C)(1)** to be applied to the current-carrying conductors, but not to signaling or control conductors installed in a nonmetallic auxiliary gutter.

It is important to always remember that the temperature correction factors of **Table 310.15(B)(1)** apply to conductors installed in all (metal and nonmetallic) wireways or auxiliary gutters, regardless of the number of conductors. **See Problem 2-35**.

PROBLEM 2-34

Metal Wireway with Forty 12 AWG THWN

What is the ampacity of each of forty 12 AWG THWN current-carrying copper conductors installed in a metal wireway, occupying 19% of the interior cross-sectional area, installed in an area with an ambient temperature of 30°C?

Solution

Table 310.16 Ampacity
  12 AWG THWN copper = 25 A
Table 310.15(C)(1) Adjustment Factors
  40 conductor = 40%
  25 A × 0.40 = 10 A
Answer: 10 A
Comment: This situation limits the metal wireway cross-sectional area to 19% fill, thus complying with 376.22(A). However, according to 376.22(B), an adjustment factor is necessary because the number of current-carrying conductors exceeds thirty.

PROBLEM 2-35

Nonmetallic Wireway with Ten 6 AWG THWN Copper and Eight 4 AWG THWN Copper

Ten 6 AWG THWN and eight 4 AWG THWN copper current-carrying conductors occupy 16% of the cross-sectional area of a nonmetallic wireway in an area with an ambient temperature of 30°C. What is the ampacity of each 6 AWG and each 4 AWG conductor?

Solution

Table 310.16 Ampacity
  6 AWG THWN = 65 A
  4 AWG THWN = 85 A
Total number of conductors
  10 + 8 = 18 conductors
Table 310.15(C)(1) Adjustment Factors
  18 current-carrying conductors = 50%
  65 A × 0.50 = 32.5 A
  85 A × 0.50 = 42.5 A
Answers: 6 AWG = 32.5 A
          4 AWG = 42.5 A

DEFINITIONS AND TERMS

Ampacity - The maximum current, in amperes, that a conductor can carry continuously under conditions of use without exceeding its temperature rating. [**70**:100]

Ambient temperature - The temperature of the air surrounding electrical circuit conductors.

Conditions of Use - A set of conditions specifically listed in the sub-sections of **310.16** through **310.21** for parameters to use **Tables 310.16** through **310.21**.

Conductor, Bare - A conductor having no covering or electrical insulation whatsoever. [**70**:100]

Conductor, Covered - A conductor encased within material of composition or thickness that is not recognized by this *Code* as electrical insulation. [**70**:100] An example of a covered conductor is the green covered grounding conductor within a Type NM (Nonmetallic Sheathed) cable.

Conductor, Insulated - A conductor encased within material of composition and thickness that is recognized by the *Code* as electrical insulation. [**70**:100] Examples of insulation used with conductors are found in **Tables 310.4(A) and (B)**.

Conductor Material - Basic electrical conductors are constructed of materials including copper, aluminum, and copper-clad aluminum. Other conductor materials reserved for high-temperature applications include nickel and nickel-coated copper.

Grounding Conductor, Equipment (EGC) - The conductive path(s) that is part of an effective ground-fault current path and connects normally non–current-carrying metal parts of equipment together and to the system grounded conductor or to the grounding electrode conductor, or both. [**70**:100] The equipment grounding conductor also performs bonding. **Section 250.118** contains a list of acceptable equipment grounding conductors.

Grounded Conductor - A system or circuit conductor that is intentionally grounded. [**70**:100]

Neutral Conductor - The conductor connected to the neutral point of a system that is intended to carry current under normal conditions.[**70**:100]

Nonlinear Load - A load where the wave shape of the steady-state current does not follow the wave shape of the applied voltage. [**70**:100] Examples of nonlinear loads may include electronic equipment, electronic/electric-discharge lighting, adjustable speed drive systems, and similar equipment.

Temperature Rating - The highest temperature that an insulated conductor can withstand for a long period of time before damage to the insulation occurs.

Reproduced with permission of NFPA from NFPA 70®, *National Electrical Code*® (NEC®), 2020 edition. Copyright© 2019, National Fire Protection Association. For a full copy of the NEC®, please go to www.nfpa.org.

SUMMARY

In order to make proper electrical installations, accurate determination of a conductor's ampacity is essential. Insulated conductors consist of two parts: the inner conducting metal and the outer insulation covering. If the ampacity is not correctly determined, the conducting metal can overheat and damage the insulation covering, leading to damaging and destructive failure. The ampacities of conductors are provided in the ampacity tables of **310.16** through **310.21**. The ampacity is determined by applying conditions of use as required by **310.15(A)** through **(F)**; such conditions may include having more than three current-carrying conductors in the raceway or cable or having ambient temperatures other than 30°C (86°F).

Remember, the proper application of the *NEC* will result in an installation essentially free from hazard. Precisely following the calculation methods outlined will provide installation guidelines that are essentially free from hazard, albeit not necessarily the most efficient, convenient, or adequate for good service or future expansion of electrical use.

REVIEW QUESTIONS

1. **Table 310.16** assumes what maximum number of current-carrying conductors installed in a raceway or cable?
   a. 2
   b. 3
   c. 10
   d. The maximum permitted based on conduit fill calculations

2. What is the correction factor, as a percentage, for 15 current-carrying conductors installed in a raceway?
   a. 45%
   b. 50%
   c. 70%
   d. 80%

3. **Table 310.16** assumes an ambient temperature of what temperature in degrees Fahrenheit?
   a. 30°F
   b. 40°F
   c. 86°F
   d. 104°F

4. What is the correction factor, as a decimal, for a THHN insulated conductor installed in a raceway with an ambient temperature of 125°F?
   a. 0.082
   b. 0.67
   c. 0.75
   d. 0.76

5. A 12-2 (plus ground) Type MC cable is installed to supply a line-to-neutral load. What is the minimum number of current-carrying conductors required to be counted?
   a. 0
   b. 1
   c. 2
   d. 3

6. A 14-3 (plus ground) Type NM-B cable is installed to supply a multiwire branch circuit in a dwelling unit with a 120/240-volt, single-phase, 3-wire service. The circuit is supplied by circuit 1 and circuit 3 and supplies only line-to-neutral loads. What is the minimum number of current-carrying conductors in the cable?
   a. 0
   b. 2
   c. 3
   d. 4

7. A 12-4 (plus ground) Type MC cable is used to supply 277-volt fluorescent luminaires in a commercial office building supplied by a 480Y/277-volt, 3-phase, 4-wire, wye service. What is the minimum number of current-carrying conductors required to be counted in the cable?
   a. 0
   b. 3
   c. 4
   d. 5

8. What is the temperature rating for Type NM cable required to be used to determine the ampacity of the cable?
   a. 40°C
   b. 60°C
   c. 75°C
   d. 90°C

9. A 120/240-volt dwelling unit service conductor is permitted to be sized at what percentage of the service rating?
   a. 80%
   b. 83%
   c. 100%
   d. 125%

10. What is the maximum number of current-carrying conductors permitted to be installed in a metal wireway that does not require the application of **Table 310.15(C)(1)** adjustment factors?
    a. 0
    b. 3
    c. 20
    d. 30

CHAPTER 3
CONDUCTOR AMPACITY CALCULATIONS II

Determination of conductor ampacity and sizing includes conductor terminations, the length of time a load is on, and the effects of "load time" or nearly constant heat on specific electrical equipment. Each one of these issues is related to the transfer of heat and the lack of heat dissipation. In addition, these issues are equipment-related issues, which ultimately influences the selection of the ampacity and the required size of a circuit conductor.

The *National Electrical Code* contains requirements for insulated conductor terminations on equipment. **Article 110** termination provisions must be accurately applied for each and every power and lighting circuit. The *NEC* requirements concerning continuous and noncontinuous loads and the calculations involved will be studied in depth. Since the length of time a load is present affects the circuit parameters, numerous calculations will be performed to finalize the size of the conductor and the overcurrent protective device. Most branch-circuit and feeder loads within commercial and industrial facilities are continuous loads. Examples using 100% rated circuit breakers are addressed as well.

OBJECTIVES

- Understand and apply the termination temperature limitations.
- Understand and determine which loads are considered continuous loads.
- Apply continuous load factors to branch circuits, feeders, and services.
- Calculate conductor ampacities for continuous and noncontinuous loads.
- Calculate the proper size overcurrent protection for continuous and noncontinuous loads.
- Understand and properly calculate conductor size having both continuous and noncontinuous loads using 100% rated overcurrent protective devices.

TABLE OF CONTENTS

3.1 INTRODUCTION — 42

3.2 TEMPERATURE LIMITATIONS OF EQUIPMENT — 42
- .1 Circuits and Equipment Rated at 100 Amperes or Less — 43
- .2 Circuits and Equipment Rated Over 100 Amperes — 45
- .3 Advantages of Using 90°C Conductors — 46
- .4 The Practical Solution Using 110.14(C) — 47

3.3 CONTINUOUS LOADS AND BRANCH CIRCUITS — 47
- .1 Branch Circuits Using Standard Circuit Breakers — 48
- .2 Branch-Circuit Load Using a 100% Rated Circuit Breaker — 49
- .3 Understanding 240.4 — 49
- .4 Continuous and Noncontinuous Load — 51
- .5 Conductor Size and Continuous Load — 51
- .6 Putting It All Together: Load, Overcurrent Protection, and Conductors — 52

3.4 CONTINUOUS LOADS AND FEEDERS — 55
- .1 Continuous Loads Only — 56
- .2 Continuous and Noncontinuous Loads — 57
- .3 Continuous Loads in a 3-Phase Feeder — 57

3.5 SERVICES WITH CONTINUOUS AND NONCONTINUOUS LOADS — 58

DEFINITIONS AND TERMS — 59

SUMMARY — 60

REVIEW QUESTIONS — 61

3.1 INTRODUCTION

The study of ampacity is more related to electrical equipment connected to conductors than it is to the specifics of various conductor current-carrying capacities. The capacity of a conductor from a thermal point of view must be understood. The physical properties of various types of conductors, the different causes of heat within and around electrical conductors, and the properties of an insulated conductor in a wring method that allow it to manage and dissipate that heat into the surrounding atmosphere must also be understood in order to proceed.

Equipment-related issues can influence the selection of the proper *NEC* value for the ampacity of a circuit conductor. The transfer of heat and the lack of heat dissipation should be studied as well. However, the initial focus should be on the conductor terminations, the length of time a load is on, and the effects of constant heat upon specific electrical equipment such as overcurrent protective devices and their enclosures.

3.2 TEMPERATURE LIMITATIONS OF EQUIPMENT

Section 110.3(B) requires that electrical equipment be installed and used according to any instructions included with the equipment's listing or labeling. Written manufacturer requirements and instructions, as well as those found in the equipment listing and labeling information, may duplicate or be more restrictive than the *Code* requirements.

Electrical conductors, circuit breakers, fuses, connectors, panelboards, and other electrical equipment all have temperature ratings. These temperature ratings are most often the maximum operating temperature permitted or the temperature limitations of the equipment. Electrical conductors are terminated using connectors or lugs on circuit breakers, fused switches, and other electrical equipment that includes temperature ratings or temperature limitations. These temperature ratings, such as 75°C terminations, are maximum limits and may not be exceeded.

The safety requirements of **110.14(C), Temperature Limitations,** are a set of rules limiting the temperature of equipment terminations within various panelboards, disconnect switches, circuit breakers, and other related equipment. The basic rule states: "The temperature rating associated with the ampacity of a conductor shall be selected and coordinated so as not to exceed the lowest temperature rating of any connected termination, conductor, or device."

This basic rule is divided into two main parts:

- Part 1 deals with circuits and equipment rated 100 amperes or less, or conductors 14 AWG through 1 AWG.
- Part 2 deals with circuits and equipment rated over 100 amperes or conductors larger than 1 AWG.

Part 1, addressing circuits and equipment rated 100 amperes or less, is further divided into four subcategories of conductors and their terminations:

1. 60°C conductors connected to 60°C terminations of equipment
2. 75°C or 90°C conductors connected to 60°C terminations of equipment
3. 75°C or 90°C conductors connected to 75°C terminations of equipment
4. Design B, C, or D motors permitted to use 75°C or 90°C conductors connecting to 75°C terminations

Part 2, covering circuits and equipment rated over 100 amperes, is further divided into two subcategories of conductors and their terminations:

1. 75°C conductors connected to 75°C terminations of equipment
2. 90°C conductors connected to 75°C terminations of equipment

In order to simplify these rules, it is necessary to apply the weakest link principle, wherein a chain is only as strong as its weakest link. When this

CHAPTER 3 CONDUCTOR AMPACITY CALCULATIONS II

principle is applied to temperature limitations, the final ampacity of a circuit is based upon the lowest temperature rating of any one part of the circuit and its connections. The application of this principle to electrical circuits will simplify the problems and allow a more thorough understanding of the calculations.

3.2.1 Circuits and Equipment Rated at 100 Amperes or Less

Circuits and equipment rated 100 amperes or less are dealt with in **110.14(C)(1)(a)**. This section is further divided into four subcategories:

1. Conductors rated 60°C connected to equipment rated 60°C
2. Conductors with an insulation rating higher than 60°C connected to equipment rated 60°C
3. Conductors with an insulation rating higher than 60°C connected to equipment rated higher than 60°C, provided it is listed at a higher temperature rating
4. Design B, C, and D motors which are permitted to be considered 75°C

3.2.1.1 Using 60°C Insulated Conductors

In **110.14(C)(1)(a)(1)**, equipment for circuits rated 100 amperes or less or 14 AWG through 1 AWG conductors are required to be rated for at least 60°C. This is the first and easiest of the four cases to understand. The *Code* recognizes that a rating of 60°C should be the fundamental (and lowest) temperature rating applied to conductors and equipment. Equipment that is 100 amperes or less rated at 60°C is, therefore, permitted to supply conductors rated at 60°C. **See Figure 3-1**.

3.2.1.2 Using 75°C or 90°C Insulated Conductors

Moving to the second case, **110.14(C)(1)(a)(2)** permits a 75°C conductor to be used with devices marked (with temperature limitations) of 60°C, provided the ampacity of the 75°C conductor is taken from the 60°C column of **Table 310.16**. This is done by using the 75°C copper (or aluminum) column from the table; go down to the row opposite the correct AWG size, then, before selecting the ampacity of the circuit, move horizontally to the left (in the same row) and select the ampacity within the 60°C column.

Figure 3-1. 60°C Equipment and Conductors Rated 100 Amperes or Less. Where the conductor insulation temperature and the circuit breaker conductor terminations are individually rated for 60°C according to **110.14(C)(1)(a)(1)**, the equipment is permitted to supply conductors rated at 60°C.

In this case, **110.14(C)(1)(a)(2)** also permits 90°C conductors to be used with devices marked with temperature limitations of 60°C, provided the ampacity of the 90°C conductor is again taken from the 60°C column of **Table 310.16**. This is done by using the 90°C copper (or aluminum) column from the table; go down to the row opposite the correct AWG size, then, before selecting the ampacity of the circuit, move horizontally to the left two columns (in the same row) and select the ampacity within the 60°C column. **See Problems 3-1 and 3-2.**

PROBLEM 3-1

A 6 AWG THWN copper conductor is connected to a circuit breaker with a termination temperature limitation marked (not to exceed) 60°C. What is the ampacity of the 6 AWG THWN copper conductor now that it is connected to this circuit breaker?

Solution

110.14(C)(1)(a)(2) applies
 Circuit breaker terminations = 60°C
Table 310.16 Ampacity
 Limited by circuit breaker to 60°C
 THWN ampacity at 75°C not permitted
 Use ampacity of 6 AWG copper at 60°C
 6 AWG THWN copper limited to 60°C ampacity = 55 A
Answer: 55 A
Comment: Applying the weakest link principle, both temperature ratings are 60°C, so the weakest link is 60°C. Therefore, ampacity must be based upon the 60°C column of Table 310.16.

PROBLEM 3-2

A 2 AWG THHN aluminum conductor is connected to a circuit breaker with a termination temperature limitation marked (not to exceed) 60°C and marked for copper or aluminum conductors. What is the allowable ampacity of the 2 AWG THHN aluminum conductor now that it is connected to this circuit breaker?

Solution

110.14(C)(1)(a)(2) applies
   Circuit breaker terminations = 60°C
Table 310.16 Ampacity
   Limited by circuit breaker to 60°C
   THHN ampacity at 90°C not permitted
   Use ampacity of 2 AWG aluminum at 60°C
   2 AWG THHN aluminum = 75 A

Answer: 75 A

Comment: Applying the weakest link principle, the insulated conductor temperature rating is 90°C and the circuit breaker termination temperature rating is 60°C, so the weakest link is 60°C. Therefore, the ampacity of the circuit conductors must be based upon the 60°C column of Table 310.16.

A disconnect switch rated under 100 amperes can be dual rated for 60°C/75°C copper or aluminum wire. It will allow the use of 60°C insulated conductors at a 60°C ampacity or the use of 75°C or 90°C insulated conductors at a 75°C ampacity.

3.2.1.3 For 100 Ampere Terminations or Less, at 75°C

Moving to the third case, **110.14(C)(1)(a)(3)** permits devices marked with a temperature limitation of 75°C to be used with 75°C conductors operating at their ampacity. This applies to equipment for circuits rated 100 amperes or less, or marked for 14 AWG through 1 AWG. Use the 75°C column of **Table 310.16**. This case is common because new equipment is frequently marked as acceptable to receive conductors rated 75°C. Also, new equipment may be dual rated and marked as 60°C/75°C, thereby acceptable for 75°C conductor terminations as well. **See Figure 3-2**.

*Figure 3-2. 75°C Equipment and Conductors Rated 100 Amperes or Less. Where the conductor insulation temperature and the circuit breaker conductor terminations both are rated and marked for 75°C and where it is acceptable according to **110.14(C)(1)(a)(3)**, the equipment is permitted to supply conductors rated at 75°C.*

3.2.1.4 Termination Provisions for Design B, C, and D motors

The fourth subsection, **110.14(C)(1)(a)(4)**, addresses motor terminations. Not all motors are listed, and therefore the requirement of **110.14(C)(1)(a)(3)** does not apply to all motor installations, in which case motor circuit conductors are required to be sized in accordance with the 60°C ampacity. As motors are terminated with wire splicing devices typically rated higher than 90°C, it is permissible to consider the motor termination at a temperature rating of 75°C as compared to the 60°C rating required in general for terminations of 100 amperes or less.

An EVSE charging station, although with a current rating under 100 amperes, may prohibit the use of 60°C insulated conductors by omission in the installation instructions but requires 75°C or greater conductors and is required to be used at the 75°C ampacity.

3.2.2 Circuits and Equipment Rated Over 100 Amperes

Circuits and equipment rated over 100 amperes are dealt with in **110.14(C)(1)(b)**. This section is further divided into two subcategories:

1. Conductors rated 75°C connected to equipment rated 75°C
2. Conductors rated 90°C connected to equipment rated 75°C

For additional information, visit qr.njatcdb.org Item #1026

Figure 3-3. 75°C Equipment and Conductors Rated More Than 100 A. *A circuit breaker with conductor terminations rated at 75°C can be installed with conductors larger than 1 AWG with THWN insulation rated at 75°C, all in accordance with **110.14(C)(1)(b)(1)**.*

3.2.2.1 Conductors Rated 75°C Connected to Equipment Rated 75°C

NEC **110.14(C)(1)(b)(1)** states that using 75°C insulated conductors requires equipment for circuits to be rated more than 100 amperes, or conductors larger than 1 AWG, to have a minimum temperature limitation marked (not to exceed) 75°C. Larger equipment and more amperes creates greater heat, requiring higher temperature rated conductors than required for equipment listed at 100 amperes or less. **See Figure 3-3**.

3.2.2.2 Conductors Rated 90°C Connected to Equipment Rated 75°C

Finally, *NEC* **110.14(C)(1)(b)(2)** permits the use of 90°C conductors with terminations rated and marked at 75°C, provided the ampacity of the 90°C conductors is taken from the 75°C column of **Table 310.16**. **See Problem 3-3**.

PROBLEM 3-3

What is the allowable ampacity of a 4/0 AWG THWN copper conductor connected to a circuit breaker with a wire connection temperature limitation marked (not to exceed) 75°C?

Solution

110.14(C)(1)(b)(1) applies
  Circuit breaker terminations = 75°C
Table 310.16 Ampacity
  THWN ampacity at 75°C
  4/0 AWG THWN copper = 230 A
Answer: 230 A

PROBLEM 3-4

All Conductors in the Same Raceway

Breakers 60°C

Eight 6 AWG THHN copper current-carrying conductors are installed to replace existing wiring within an existing single rigid metal conduit, Type RMC. The area of installation has an ambient temperature of 30°C. The new eight 6 AWG THHN conductors are connected to existing 50-ampere 2-pole circuit breakers with a marked terminal temperature rating of 60°C. What is the ampacity of the conductors, and is this an acceptable installation?

Solution

Table 310.16 Ampacity
  6 AWG THHN at 90°C = 75 A
Table 310.15(C)(1) Adjustment Factors
  8 current-carrying conductors = 70%
  75 A × 0.70 = 52.5 A
  6 AWG in 60°C column = 55 A
  55 A is not permitted
  Ampacity = 52.5 A
Answer: 52.5 A

Comment: Although the heat developed by a 55A load on 60°C equipment terminals is the maximum heating permitted on these circuit breaker terminals, the existing circuit breaker is rated for 50 A, which is below the maximum ampacity of the circuit conductors. The current is limited by the 50A circuit breaker to a value less than the maximum circuit conductor ampacity. Therefore, the installation is acceptable.

Transformers create additional heat when in use and require the use of higher temperature wire as indicated by the need for 90°C insulated conductors. They may be used with a 75°C ampacity as indicated in installation notes.

3.2.3 Advantages of Using 90°C Conductors

In accordance with **110.14(C)**, conductors with higher temperature ratings are permitted to be corrected and adjusted based upon their temperature rating, often allowing for a higher ampacity. **See Problem 3-4.**

Q. What is the advantage of using 90°C conductors if they cannot be used at their full 90°C ampacity from the tables?

A. There is an advantage to using 90°C insulated conductors when the conditions of use as shown in the list of conditions of **310.16** are changed. One example is where there are more than three current-carrying conductors in a raceway or cable. Another example is when the ambient temperature is above 86°F. Each of these conditions increases conductor temperature. Using 90°C insulated conductors allows the accommodation of some derating while not increasing the actual conductor size.

Q. Is there any equipment currently manufactured with terminations rated at 90°C?

A. If there is an installation where all the components are rated 90°C, the full ampacity of a 90°C conductor is permitted to be selected. However, for 600 volts or less, equipment with 90°C rated terminations is generally unavailable. Large equipment rated over 600 volts with terminations rated 90°C is available and often used today.

3.2.4 The Practical Solution Using 110.14(C)

In practice, the actual *NEC* rules are handled a little more easily and made more user-friendly by equipment manufacturers and listing agencies. Listed circuit breakers rated 125 amperes or less are marked with wire temperature ratings using one of three basic methods:

1. Wire temperature rating of 60°C
2. Combination temperature rating of 60°C/75°C
3. Wire temperature rating of 75°C only

This means that the circuit breaker terminations are listed for electrical conductor connections using insulated conductors rated either 60°C or 75°C. Most 125 ampere or less circuit breakers today are rated and marked as 60°C/75°C. One advantage of this dual marking allows older 60°C wiring to be connected to more modern or replacement circuit breakers. Another advantage is that 90°C wiring can be used for derating, but still may qualify for the 75°C ampacity.

All listed circuit breakers rated over 125 amperes are suitable for 75°C conductor terminations. At the present time, there are no listed 600-volt circuit breakers with conductor terminations rated at 90°C.

Conductors rated for higher temperatures (such as 90°C THHN or XHHW) are most often installed today, but importantly, they must not be loaded to carry more current than that permitted by the 75°C or 60°C ampacity of that size of conductor. This is because the temperature rating of conductor terminations on electrical equipment is most often the limiting factor (per the weakest link principle).

However, when applying adjustment and temperature correction factors, provided the actual load never exceeds the lowest temperature rating of the circuit conductor(s), equipment, or overcurrent protective devices, the circuit and all its connections are in compliance with **110.14(C)**.

3.3 CONTINUOUS LOADS AND BRANCH CIRCUITS

Article 100 defines *continuous load* as "a load where the maximum current is expected to continue for 3 hours or more." Stores, offices, and show window lighting are normally considered continuous loads.

A continuous load should not be confused with a continuous duty motor (load). The duty of a motor is determined by the application of the motor as defined in **Article 100** under the definition of *duty* and is not related to continuous loads.

The general *Code* requirements for all branch circuits connected to continuous loads are found in **210.19(A)** and **210.20(A)**. Some of the specific *Code* requirements for equipment connected to branch circuits are found in **422.10(A)** for appliance branch circuits, **422.13** for storage-type water heaters, **424.4(B)** for fixed electric space-heating equipment, **426.4** for fixed outdoor electric deicing and snow-melting equipment, and **427.4** for fixed electric heating equipment for pipelines and vessels.

Other *Code* requirements for continuous loads are included in **215.2(A)** for feeders and **230.42(A)** for services.

All of these *Code* sections are based upon the electrical safety requirement that conductors and equipment should not be subjected to overheating. As equipment and conductors are analyzed for full load operation, the consistent trouble areas of a circuit are the overcurrent protective devices and the wire terminations at the overcurrent protective devices. Testing laboratories confirm that circuits loaded at 100% in a continuous load application can safely carry the load for three hours or more. However, this is only true if the test is conducted on overcurrent protective devices and conductors placed in "open air." Once the test is performed on circuit parts within enclosures, these same circuits clearly overheat and cannot safely handle the load.

The historical solution to prevent overheating in circuits which contain continuous loads has been to upsize both the conductors and the overcurrent protective devices.

The exact *NEC* language for the branch-circuit solution is:

210.20(A) Continuous and Noncontinuous Loads. Where a branch circuit supplies continuous loads or any combination of continuous and noncontinuous loads, the rating of the overcurrent device shall not be less than the noncontinuous load plus 125 percent of the continuous load.

210.19(A) Branch Circuits Not More Than 600 Volts.

…

210.19(A)(1) General. Branch-circuit conductors shall have an ampacity not less than the larger of 210.19(A)(1)(a) or (A)(1)(b) and comply with 110.14(C) for equipment terminations.

(a) Where a branch circuit supplies continuous loads or any combination of continuous and noncontinuous loads, the minimum branch-circuit conductor size shall have an ampacity not less than the noncontinuous load plus 125 percent of the continuous load in accordance with 310.14.

(b) The minimum branch-circuit conductor size shall have an ampacity not less than the maximum load to be served after the application of any adjustment or correction factors in accordance with 310.15.

There is another solution in the *Code* (stated as an exception to both **210.19(A)(1)** and to **210.20(A)**) which permits certain overcurrent protective devices provided they are listed to carry their rated ampacity continuously (for three hours or more). These circuit breakers are referred to as *100% rated circuit breakers*. Although not widely used, they are available from many manufacturers.

An electrical conductor, by definition, is capable of carrying its full ampacity rating continuously.

Therefore, where conductors are applied to 100% rated circuit breakers, the conductors do not require upsizing since they are already considered 100% rated.

Most branch-circuit overcurrent protective devices are not rated to carry their current rating continuously and are required to have an "80%" rule applied to them.

3.3.1 Branch Circuits Using Standard Circuit Breakers

NEC **210.19(A)(1)** requires the ampacity of the branch-circuit conductors to not be less than the noncontinuous load plus 125% of the continuous load. In addition, **210.20(A)** requires the branch-circuit overcurrent protection to be not less than the noncontinuous load plus 125% of the continuous load. Both requirements carry an exception allowing the use of listed 100% rated overcurrent protective devices.

By neglecting the exceptions, both the branch circuit and overcurrent protection requirements handle the upsizing requirements by using the same formula: 100% of the noncontinuous load plus 125% of the continuous load. **See Problem 3-5**.

PROBLEM 3-5

A 120-volt branch circuit supplies a continuous load (CL) of 21 amperes. The ambient temperature is 30°C, so temperature correction is unnecessary. What is the minimum standard size circuit breaker permitted for the branch-circuit overcurrent protection?

Solution

210.20(A) Overcurrent Protection
  Min. OCPD = CL × 125%
            = 21 × 125%
            = 26.25 A
240.6(A), next larger std rating
Next larger std rating = 30 A
Answer: 30A circuit breaker
Comment: This situation deals with continuous loads and sizing a standard inverse-time circuit breaker based upon 125% of the continuous loads. A 100% rated circuit breaker can be sized directly to the load and in this application would use a 25-ampere circuit breaker.

3.3.2 Branch-Circuit Load Using a 100% Rated Circuit Breaker

Applying 100% rated overcurrent protective devices to branch circuits is permitted by the exception to **210.20(A)**. However, in today's marketplace, 100% rated circuit breakers of the branch circuit variety are rare or nonexistent. Although understanding how to apply 100% rated device products at the branch circuit level is valuable information from a practical point of view, there seem to be few, if any, applications available at this time. **See Problem 3-6**.

Estimators use manual or electronic rotometers to measure raceways and cable lengths from blueprints.

A 1,600-ampere insulated case circuit breaker can be rated for 100% at continuous operation.

PROBLEM 3-6

A 480-volt, 2-wire branch circuit supplies a large electronic information roadway sign inside a tunnel. This lighting circuit has a continuous load (CL) of 47 amperes.

1. What is the minimum size circuit breaker using a standard inverse-time circuit breaker permitted for the branch-circuit overcurrent protection?
2. As an alternate solution, what is the minimum standard size 100% rated circuit breaker for this application?

Calculation 1
210.20(A)(1)
$$\text{Min. circuit breaker} = CL \times 125\%$$
$$= 47 \times 1.25$$
$$= 58.75 \text{ A}$$
240.6(A)
Next larger standard size = 60 A
Answer: 60A inverse-time circuit breaker

Calculation 2
210.20(A)(1), Exception
$$\text{Min. 100\% circuit breaker} = CL \times 100\%$$
$$= 47 \times 1.00$$
$$= 47 \text{ A}$$
240.6(A)
Next larger std size = 50 A
Answer: 50A 100% rated circuit breaker

3.3.3 Understanding 240.4

For the overcurrent protection portion, there are more rules and permissions which need to be understood and applied. First and foremost is **Section 240.4**, which states:

> **240.4 Protection of Conductors.** Conductors, other than flexible cords, flexible cables, and fixture wires, shall be protected against overcurrent in accordance with their ampacities specified in 310.14, unless otherwise permitted or required in 240.4(A) through (G).

This general rule indicates that a conductor with an ampacity of 65 amperes must be protected by an overcurrent protective device rated at a maximum of 65 amperes, requiring a maximum standard size of only 60 amperes. Due to the mismatch of the conductor ampacity to a standard size overcurrent protective device as listed in **240.6(A)**, **240.4(B)** permits using the next larger standard size overcurrent

For additional information, visit qr.njatcdb.org Item #2554

protective device as a permissive rule to the general rule of **240.4**. It requires three conditions to be met to protect a conductor with an overcurrent protective device higher than its ampacity:

1. The conductors being protected are not part of a branch circuit supplying more than one receptacle for cord-and-plug-connected portable loads.
2. The ampacity of the conductors does not correspond with the standard ampere rating of a fuse or a circuit breaker without overload trip adjustments above its rating (but shall be permitted to have other trip or rating adjustments).
3. The next higher standard rating selected does not exceed 800 amperes.

The first condition does not permit a branch circuit conductor supplying more than one receptacle to be protected at a rating above its ampacity as the load is not controlled, and the conductor could easily have too much load placed on it. The second condition requires a conductor with an ampacity that matches a standard size overcurrent protective device to be protected at that rating. The third condition restricts the permissive rule to 800 amperes or less. See **240.4(C)** for ratings above 800 amperes.

Figure 3-4. Coordination of Conductor Ampacity to Overcurrent Protective Device. *A flow chart can be used for the selection of conductors and overcurrent protective devices (OCPDs) when using* **240.4(B)**.

Returning to the conductor with the ampacity of 65 amperes, **240.4(B)** would permit the conductor to be protected with the 70-ampere overcurrent protective device provided the three conditions are met. Although the 65-ampere conductor is permitted to be protected by the 70-ampere overcurrent protective device, only a maximum of 65 amperes of load is permitted to be placed on the conductor, not up to 70 amperes of load. Note that the 70-ampere overcurrent protective device does not change the ampacity of the conductor, which remains at 65 amperes. **See Figure 3-4.**

Application of **240.4(B)** is simple when given a conductor ampacity. If it corresponds to a standard size, it must be protected at that standard size. If it does not correspond to a standard size, it is permitted to be protected by an overcurrent protective device higher than its ampacity. **See Problems 3-7 and 3-8.**

PROBLEM 3-7

What is the maximum standard size overcurrent protective device permitted to protect the following THWN conductors when they are not part of a branch circuit supplying more than one receptacle and are terminated to equipment rated 75°C?

8 AWG THWN
4 AWG THWN
1 AWG THWN
1/0 AWG THWN
500 kcmil THWN

Solution

Table 310.16

Conductor Size	Ampacity from 75°C Column	Next Higher Standard Size
8 AWG THWN	50 Amperes	50-Ampere
4 AWG THWN	85 Amperes	90-Ampere
1 AWG THWN	130 Amperes	150-Ampere
1/0 AWG THWN	150 Amperes	150-Ampere
500 kcmil THWN	380 Amperes	400-Ampere

Note: For both the 8 AWG and the 1/0 AWG conductors, their ampacities correspond to standard sizes, so their maximum standard size overcurrent protective device size is not permitted to be increased, but rather selected to protect at their ampacities.

3.3.4 Continuous and Noncontinuous Load

Whether determining the ampacity of the conductors or the rating of the overcurrent protective device, the language is the same. The *Code* requires that each shall have the capacity to handle "… not less than the noncontinuous load plus 125 percent of the continuous load."

From a practical point of view, after the continuous and noncontinuous loads are determined, the overcurrent protective device should be determined first, and then the size of the circuit conductors should be determined.

3.3.5 Conductor Size and Continuous Load

In **210.19(A)(1)**, branch-circuit conductors are required to be sized based upon two comparisons, and the largest conductor size is the minimum required. **See Figure 3-5.** First, in **210.19(A)(1)(a)**, before the application of adjustment or correction factors but while considering temperature ratings in compliance with **110.14(C)**, the branch-circuit conductors need to have an ampacity of not less than the sum of the noncontinuous load and 125% of the continuous load. The second comparison in **210.19(A)(1)(b)** requires the conductor ampacity after the application of any adjustment or correction factors to have an ampacity of not less than the actual load. The intent of this section is not to require the adjustment and correction factors to be applied to the ampacity of the conductors and the application of 125% of continuous loads to be compared simultaneously; instead, they are to be treated as separate comparisons.

PROBLEM 3-8

What is the minimum size THWN branch-circuit conductor permitted to be protected by the following overcurrent protective device (OCPD) when all equipment is listed at 75°C, and the conductors do not supply more than one receptacle?

OCPD:

30-ampere

60-ampere

100-ampere

200-ampere

225-ampere

300-ampere

400-ampere

Solution:

OCPD	Minimum size conductor from 75°C column Table 310.16
30-ampere	10 AWG THWN (See small conductor rule 240.4(D)
60-ampere	6 AWG THWN ampacity of 65 amperes
100-ampere	3 AWG THWN ampacity of 100 amperes
200-ampere	3/0 AWG THWN ampacity of 200 amperes
250-ampere	4/0 AWG THWN ampacity of 230 amperes
300-ampere	250 kcmil THWN ampacity of 255 amperes
400-ampere	500 kcmil THWN ampacity of 380 amperes

Comment: Keep in mind that, for example, a 250 kcmil THWN conductor with ampacity is permitted to be protected at 300 amperes as it is the next standard size overcurrent protective device above the ampacity of the conductor, but the load is still limited to no more than 255 amperes due to the ampacity of the conductor. Based on the size of the load, the minimum size conductor permitted by 240.4(B) may not be allowed. Each circuit requires coordination between the load, the overcurrent protective device, and the conductor size.

210.19(A)(1)
Select Larger of 210.19(A)(1)(a) or 210.19(A)(1)(b)
210.19(A)(1)(a)
Comparison 1
Ampacity (do not apply adjustment and correction factors. Do apply 110.14(c).) → Not less than noncontinuous and 125% of continuous load.
210.19(A)(1)(b)
Comparison 2
Ampacity (after application of adjustment and correction factors.) → Not less than max load (do not apply 125% to continuous load).

Figure 3-5. Considering Adjustment and Correction Factors and Continuous Load. A flow chart can be used to properly select branch-circuit conductors in accordance with **210.19(A)(1)**.

TEMPERATURE CONVERSION

FAHRENHEIT TO CELSIUS CONVERSION

Convert 82°F to Celsius.

$$°C = \frac{(°F - 32)}{1.8}$$

$$°C = \frac{(82 - 32)}{1.8}$$

$$°C = \frac{50}{1.8}$$

$$°C = 27.8°C$$

- 212°F — WATER BOILS — 100°C
- 180°F RANGE — 100°C RANGE
- 82°F = 27.8°C
- 18°C = 64.4°F
- 32°F — WATER FREEZES — 0°C

FAHRENHEIT SCALE — **CELSIUS SCALE**

CELSIUS TO FAHRENHEIT CONVERSION

Convert 18°C to Fahrenheit.

$$°F = (1.8 \times °C) + 32$$

$$°F = (1.8 \times 18) + 32$$

$$°F = 32.4 + 32$$

$$°F = 64.4°F$$

The most accurate way to convert temperature from one scale to another is by using visual adaptations and math. However, quick estimated conversions are possible by using NEC **Table 310.15(B)(1)** and going between columns one and five. For example, 11–15°C equals 51–59°F.

3.3.6 Putting It All Together: Load, Overcurrent Protection, and Conductors

Sizing a branch circuit is a three-step process that involves using **Sections 210.20**, **210.19**, and **240.4**. **See Figure 3-6**.

Step one sizes the overcurrent protection to a minimum of not less than the sum of 100% of the noncontinuous and 125% of the continuous load. If the calculation does not correspond to a standard rating of overcurrent protective device per **240.6**, then the next higher standard size would be selected. To reduce the size would not serve the load and would result in nuisance tripping of the overcurrent protective device.

Step two sizes the conductor to a minimum ampacity as required to serve the load and prevent overloading the conductor. In sizing the conductor, remember the two comparisons to be made in accordance with **210.19(A)(1)**.

Finally, step three is required to ensure coordination between the conductor ampacity and the rating of the overcurrent protective device to protect the conductor against overcurrent based on **240.4**. Remember to use the permissive rule of **240.4(B)** to prevent oversizing the conductor.

The three-step process can be applied not only to branch circuits, but to feeders and services as well. **See Problems 3-9, 3-10, 3-11, and 3-12.**

Straight Through

Through	2
Terminate	4
Total	6

Figure 3-6. Sizing Branch Circuits Based on a Given Load. Following the three steps listed and utilizing **Sections 210.19, 210.20, 215.2, 215.3, 230.42, 230.90, and 240.4** will accurately size any branch circuit, feeder, or service based on load.

CHAPTER 3 CONDUCTOR AMPACITY CALCULATIONS II

PROBLEM 3-9

A 277-volt, single-phase circuit supplies a 6 kW continuous load and a 4 kW noncontinuous load.

1. What is the minimum standard size inverse-time circuit breaker (with terminations dual rated and marked at 60°C/75°C)?
2. Determine the minimum size XHHW-2 copper circuit conductors for this branch circuit.

Solution

Calculation 1
Continuous load (CL):

$$\text{CL amperes} = \frac{\text{CL kW} \times 1{,}000}{277}$$
$$= \frac{6 \times 1{,}000}{277}$$
$$= 21.7 \text{ A}$$

Answer: 21.7 A

Calculation 2
Noncontinuous load (NCL):

$$\text{NCL amperes} = \frac{\text{NCL kW} \times 1{,}000}{277}$$
$$= \frac{4 \times 1{,}000}{277}$$
$$= 14.4 \text{ A}$$

Answer: 14.4 A

Calculation 3
Breaker rating:
210.20(A) Branch-circuit OCPD

$$\text{Min. OCPD} = (\text{CL} \times 125\%) + \text{NCL}$$
$$= (21.7 \times 125\%) + 14.4$$
$$= 41.5 \text{ A}$$

240.6(A), next larger std size
Next larger std size = 45 A

Answer: 45A circuit breaker (60°C/75°C rated)

Calculation 4
Conductor ampacity:
210.19(A)(1)

$$\text{Min. ampacity} = (\text{CL} \times 125\%) + \text{NCL}$$
$$= (21.7 \times 1.25) + 14.4 \text{ A}$$
$$= 41.5 \text{ A}$$

110.14(C)(1)(a)(3)
90°C rated wire connected to 60°C/75°C rated circuit breaker
Table 310.16 Ampacity using 75°C column
41.5 A requires 8 AWG XHHW-2

Answer: 8 AWG XHHW-2 copper

PROBLEM 3-10

A 120-volt circuit supplies a continuous load of 7.5 kW.

1. What is the minimum standard size inverse-time circuit breaker permitted for branch-circuit overcurrent protection with conductor terminations rated at 75°C?
2. What size THWN copper conductors are needed so that the overcurrent protective device will protect the load and the conductors?

Solution

Calculation 1
210.20(A) Circuit breaker rating

$$\text{CL amperes} = \frac{\text{kW} \times 1{,}000}{E}$$
$$= \frac{7.5 \times 1{,}000}{120}$$
$$= 62.5 \text{ A}$$

$$\text{Min. OCPD} = \text{CL} \times 125\%$$
$$= 62.5 \times 1.25$$
$$= 78.12 \text{ A}$$

240.6(A), next larger std size
Next larger std size = 80 A

Answer: 80A circuit breaker

Calculation 2
210.19(A)(1) Conductor Ampacity
Use 78.12 A from Calculation 1
Table 310.16 Ampacity, 75°C column
78.12 A requires 4 AWG THWN rated at 85 A
80A OCPD will protect conductors

Answer: 4 AWG THWN copper

PROBLEM 3-11

A 120-volt circuit supplies a continuous load of 10.5 kW.

1. What is the minimum standard size 100% rated circuit breaker permitted for branch-circuit overcurrent protection with conductor terminations rated at 75°C?
2. What size THWN copper conductors are needed so that the overcurrent protective device will protect the load and the conductors?

Solution

Calculation 1

210.20(A) Circuit breaker rating

Min. OCPD = CL × 100%

$$\text{CL amperes} = \frac{kW \times 1{,}000}{E}$$

$$= \frac{10.50 \times 1{,}000}{120}$$

$$= 87.5 \text{ A}$$

Min. OCPD = 87.5 × 100% = 87.5 A

240.6(A), next larger std size

Next larger std size = 90 A

Answer: 90A circuit breaker

Calculation 2

210.19(A)(1) Conductor Ampacity

Use 87.5 A from Calculation 1

Table 310.16 Ampacity, 75°C column

87.5 A requires 3 AWG THWN copper

4 AWG THWN copper is too small

90A OCPD will protect 3 AWG THWN conductors

Answer: 3 AWG THWN copper

PROBLEM 3-12

A 40-ampere, 3-pole circuit breaker with a temperature rating of 60°C/75°C supplies a 480-volt, 3-phase, 26 kW continuous load. What is the minimum required THHN branch-circuit conductor to supply the load when there are a total of nine current-carrying conductors in the raceway?

Solution

Determine the current rating of the load:

$$I = \frac{kW \times 1{,}000}{1.732 \times \text{Volts}}$$

$$= \frac{26 \times 1{,}000}{1.732 \times 480}$$

$$= 31.27 \text{ A}$$

For a 40-ampere branch circuit, check if an 8 AWG THHN would be adequate

Determine the ampacity of an 8 AWG THHN with nine current-carrying conductors:

From Table 310.16, the 90°C value is 55 A

From Table 310.15(C)(1), the correction factor is 70% for nine current-carrying conductors

Ampacity of 8 AWG THHN = 55 A × 0.7 = 38.5 A

Comparison 1:

Ampacity before adjustment correction factors is adequate for 125% of continuous load

Ampacity of 8 AWG THHN terminated to a 40A breaker with a temperature rating of 60°C/75°C from Table 310.16 is 50 A from the 75°C column

125% of continuous load is 1.25 × 31.27 A = 39.09 A

8 AWG THHN with an ampacity of 50 A is adequate for 39.09 A

Comparison 2:

Ampacity after application of adjustment and correction factors not less than maximum load

55 amperes × 0.7 = 38.5 A is adequate for maximum load of 31.27 A

8 AWG THHN is adequate for the load per 210.19(A)(1)

Note: It is important to verify that the conductor is protected by the overcurrent protective device in accordance with 240.4. Using the permissive rule of 240.4(B), the 8 AWG THHN conductor with an ampacity of 38.5 A is permitted to be protected by the next higher standard overcurrent protective device of 40 A.

3.4 CONTINUOUS LOADS AND FEEDERS

Section 215.3 requires feeder overcurrent protective devices to be rated not less than the noncontinuous load plus 125% of the continuous load. **See Problem 3-13**. Similar to the text in **210.19(A)(1)**, feeder conductors are required to be sized to the larger of either **215.2(A)(1)(a)** or **(b)** as follows:

215.2(A)(1) General. Feeder conductors shall have an ampacity not less than the larger of 215.2(A)(1)(a) or (A)(1)(b) and shall comply with 110.14(C).

(a) Where a feeder supplies continuous loads or any combination of continuous and noncontinuous loads, the minimum feeder conductor size shall have an ampacity not less than the noncontinuous load plus 125 percent of the continuous load.

…

(b) The minimum feeder conductor size shall have an ampacity not less than the maximum load to be served after the application of any adjustment or correction factors in accordance with 310.14.

Feeder conductors are required to be sized with two comparisons, and the largest conductor required is the minimum required. First, before the application of adjustment and correction factors and in compliance with **110.14(C)**, feeder conductors are to have an ampacity of not less than the sum of the noncontinuous load and 125% of the continuous load. Secondly, after application of adjustment and correction factors, feeder conductors are to have an ampacity of not less than the maximum load without applying 125% to the continuous load.

Remember, there are two separate comparisons, and the largest conductor required from the two comparisons is the minimum required feeder conductor.

PROBLEM 3-13

Two 4-wire multiwire branch circuits installed in the same raceway and supplied by a 480/277-volt, 3-phase system supply 277-volt hardwired LED lighting fixtures. The LED lights are operated continuously. Each of the six circuits has 15.5 amperes of load. What is the minimum size branch circuit and minimum size THHN conductor permitted when installed in an ambient of 120°F and all equipment is 75°C?

Solution

Calculation 1
Step 1: size the overcurrent protective device per 210.20
  125% of continuous load = 1.25 × 15.5 A = 19.38 A
  Select next larger standard size per 240.6
Answer: 20A overcurrent protective device, 20A branch circuit
Remember that a branch circuit is rated by its overcurrent protective device per 210.18.

Calculation 2
Step 2: size the conductor to the load
  Comparison 1: 210.19(A)(1)(a)
  The ampacity before adjustment and correction factors and considering temperature ratings of equipment is not less than noncontinuous plus 125% of continuous load
  12 AWG THHN has ampacity from Table 310.16 of 25 A based on 75°C equipment terminations
  (CL × 125% + NCL) = (15.5 A × 1.25) = 19.38 A
  12 AWG THHN has an adequate ampacity of 25 A for 19.38 A
  Comparison 2: 210.19(A)(1)(b)
  The branch-circuit conductor ampacity after the application of adjustment and correction factors is not less than maximum load
  For a 20A OCPD, a 12 AWG THHN is generally required by 240.4(D)
  The following correction factors are required to be applied:
  - For ambient temperature of 120°F and THHN insulation, the correction factor is 82% from Table 310.15(B)(1)
  - Since the lighting load is nonlinear, see the informational note for nonlinear loads in Article 100. The two neutrals of the two multiwire branch circuits need to be counted as current-carrying conductors in accordance with 310.15(E)(3). Therefore, having eight current-carrying conductors in the raceway requires a 70% correction factor from Table 310.15(C)(1)
  Ampacity of 12 AWG THHN = 30 A × 0.82 × 0.7 = 17.22 A
  Compare the adjusted ampacity to the ampacity based on the termination ratings of the equipment, which is 25 A. Selecting the lower of the two values to comply with 110.14(C) means that the ampacity of the 12 AWG THHN is therefore 17.22 A.
  12 AWG THHN with ampacity of 17.22 A is adequate for the maximum load of 15.5 A
Answer: 12 AWG THHN copper

Calculation 3
Step 3: ensure protection of conductor by overcurrent protective device
  240.4(B) permits the next standard size overcurrent protective device above the ampacity of the conductor provided three conditions are met:
  1. There are no more than one receptacles in the circuit.
  2. The ampacity of the conductor does not correspond to a standard rating.
  3. The overcurrent rating does not exceed 800 A.
  12 AWG THHN with ampacity of 17.22 A is permitted to be protected by a 20A overcurrent protective device as it meets the three requirements of 240.4(B)
Answer: 20A branch circuit with 12 THHN conductors

Code excerpts reproduced with permission of NFPA from NFPA 70®, *National Electrical Code*® (NEC®), 2020 edition. Copyright© 2019, National Fire Protection Association. For a full copy of the NEC®, please go to www.nfpa.org.

PROBLEM 3-14

What standard size feeder overcurrent protective device is needed on a 240-volt, single-phase feeder supplying a 175-ampere continuous load?

Solution

Section 215.3 Feeder OCPD

Min. OCPD = load amperes × 125%

= 175 × 1.25

= 218.75 A

240.6(A), next larger std size

Next larger std size = 225 A

Answer: 225A fuse or circuit breaker

In **215.2(A)(1)(a), Exception No. 1**, the use of an assembly with an overcurrent protective device listed for operation at 100% of its rating is permitted. Where breakers of this type are used for continuous loads, neither the overcurrent protective device nor the conductors are required to be increased by 125%. Either way, the selected overcurrent protective device must always protect the feeder conductors.

3.4.1 Continuous Loads Only

Sizing overcurrent protective devices and conductors for continuous loads only is simple and

PROBLEM 3-15

A feeder supplies a continuous load of 100 amperes and a noncontinuous load of 35 amperes.

1. What is the minimum standard rating of time-delay fuses used for the feeder overcurrent protection?
2. What size THWN copper conductors are needed?
3. What size THWN grounded copper conductor is needed?

Solution

Calculation 1

Section 215.3 OCPD selection

Not less than (CL × 125%) + NCL

Min. OCPD = (100 × 1.25) + 35

= 160 A

240.6(A), next larger std size

Next larger std size = 175 A

Answer: 175A time-delay fuses

Calculation 2

215.2(A)(1)(a)

The ampacity, before adjustment or correction factors and considering temperature ratings of equipment, is not less than noncontinuous plus 125% of continuous load

2/0 AWG THWN has an ampacity from Table 310.16 of 175 A

(CL × 125%) + NCL = (100 A × 1.25) + 35 A = 160 A

2/0 AWG THWN has an adequate ampacity for 160 A

215.2(A)(1)(b)

The ampacity after application of adjustment or correction factors is not less than the maximum load

Since there are no adjustment or correction factors, the ampacity of the 2/0 AWG THWN of 175 A is adequate for the maximum load of 135 A

Answer: 2/0 AWG THWN copper

Calculation 3

Grounded conductor (alternate solution)

Reduced size, 215.2(A)(1)(a), Exception No. 3

Min. amperes = Not less than 100% of CL + NCL

= 100 + 35

= 135 A

Table 310.16 Ampacity

135 A = 1/0 AWG THWN copper

Answer: 1/0 AWG THWN copper

straightforward from a *Code* calculation perspective. The overcurrent protective device and the conductor are sized at 125%. Any Electrical Worker performing maintenance on conductors and equipment operating 24 hours a day, seven days a week, knows that continuous operation causes additional stress on conductors and equipment due to the additional heat load and can be problematic. **See Problem 3-14**.

Equipment operating continuously-loaded 24/7 is most likely vital equipment, and therefore some engineers and designers will size feeders and transformers with continuous loads larger than the *Code* minimum of 125%.

3.4.2 Continuous and Noncontinuous Loads

Whenever feeders for continuous and noncontinuous loads are calculated, there is an exception which permits the grounded conductor of the feeder to be sized at only 100% of the continuous plus noncontinuous loads. Since the grounded conductor is not connected to the overcurrent protective device protecting the feeder, sizing the conductors 25% larger than the load is not required for sizing the grounded conductor. **See Problem 3-15**.

3.4.3 Continuous Loads in a 3-Phase Feeder

It is important to understand that a grounded conductor, with or without harmonic currents present, is permitted to be calculated according to **215.2(A)(1)(a) Exception No. 3. See Problem 3-16**.

Temperature limitations of the conductor terminations are marked on the inside of equipment.

PROBLEM 3-16

A 120/208-volt, 3-phase feeder supplies a continuous lighting load of 42,400 VA, with no harmonic currents considered.

1. What is the minimum overcurrent protection for this feeder?
2. What is the minimum size THWN copper conductors required for this feeder?
3. What is the minimum size THWN copper grounded conductor required?

Solution

Calculation 1
Section 215.3 Overcurrent protection

$$\text{CL amperes} = \frac{VA}{E \times 1.73}$$
$$= \frac{42{,}400}{208 \times 1.73}$$
$$= 117.8 \text{ A}$$

Min. OCPD = CL × 125%
   = 117.8 × 125%
   = 147.25 A

240.6(A), next larger std size
Next larger std size = 150 A
Answer: 150A circuit breaker or fuse

Calculation 2
215.2(A)(1)(a)

Feeder conductor ampacity, before adjustment or correction factors and considering temperature ratings of equipment, is not less than noncontinuous plus 125% of continuous load

CL × 125% = 117.8 A × 1.25 = 147.25 A
1/0 AWG THWN has an ampacity from Table 310.16 of 150 A
215.2(A)(1)(b)

The ampacity, after application of adjustment or correction factors, is not less than the maximum load.

For a 150A OCPD, 1 AWG THWN conductor has ampacity of 130 A from Table 310.16, and the maximum load is 117.8 A. Additionally, 240.4(B) would permit the 1 AWG THWN conductor to be supplied by the 150A OCPD; however, larger size conductors are permitted.

The feeder conductor is required to be sized to the larger of either 215.2(A)(1)(a) or (b). Since 215.2(A)(1)(a) requires a 1/0 AWG THWN, the correct answer is 1/0 AWG THWN.

Answer: 1/0 AWG THWN

Calculation 3
Grounded Conductor Size (minimum)
215.2(A)(1)(a), Exception No. 3
  Not less than 100% of the CL + NCL
  Min. amperes = 117.8 A
Table 310.16 Ampacity
  118 A = 1 AWG THWN copper
Answer: 1 AWG THWN copper

Grounded conductors with and without harmonic currents are covered further in **220.61(A)**.

3.5 SERVICES WITH CONTINUOUS AND NONCONTINUOUS LOADS

Service calculations according to **Section 230.42** are very similar to previous requirements for calculating sizes of overcurrent protective devices and conductors where continuous and noncontinuous loads are present. Service calculations are usually based upon anticipated loads calculated according to **Article 220**. In addition, **Part III** of **Article 220** permits the use of demand factors, which can be dealt with at a later stage.

To begin with, simply perform calculations using given loads, postponing the application of demand factors of **Article 220**. See Problem 3-17.

PROBLEM 3-17

A 277/480-volt, 3-phase, 4-wire service supplies a small retail commercial building. The calculated loads given are a continuous load of 75 kVA and a noncontinuous load of 60 kVA.

1. What is the minimum size THWN-2 copper conductors required for this service?
2. What is the minimum overcurrent protection for the service?

Solution

Calculation 1
Service size using THWN-2 copper
230.42(A)(1) Min. size

$$CL\ amperes = \frac{kVA \times 1{,}000}{E \times 1.73}$$
$$= \frac{75 \times 1{,}000}{480 \times 1.73}$$
$$= 90.3\ A$$

$$NCL\ amperes = \frac{VA}{E \times 1.73}$$
$$= \frac{60{,}000}{480 \times 1.73}$$
$$= 72.3\ A$$

Service amperes = (CL × 125%) + NCL
= (90.3 × 1.25) + 72.3
= 185 A

110.14(C)(1)(b)(2) Circuit Breaker Terminals
Use Table 310.16 75°C column
Table 310.16 Ampacity
185 A = 3/0 AWG
Answer: 3/0 THWN-2 copper

Calculation 2
Service overcurrent protective device, minimum
Min. OCPD size = 185 A
240.4(B) and 240.6(A), next larger std size
Next larger std size = 200 A
Answer: 200A circuit breaker or fuse

DEFINITIONS AND TERMS

Branch Circuit - The circuit conductors between the final overcurrent device protecting the circuit and the outlet(s). [**70**:100]

Overcurrent Protective Device, Branch-Circuit - A device capable of providing protection for service, feeder, and branch circuits and equipment over the full range of overcurrents between its rated current and its interrupting rating. Such devices are provided with interrupting ratings appropriate for the intended use, but no less than 5000 amperes. [**70**:100]

Continuous Load - A load where the maximum current is expected to continue for 3 hours or more. [**70**:100]

Device - A unit of an electrical system, other than a conductor, that carries or controls electric energy as its principal function. [**70**:100]

Equipment - A general term, including fittings, devices, appliances, luminaires, apparatus, machinery, and the like used as a part of, or in connection with, an electrical installation. [**70**:100]

Feeder - All circuit conductors between the service equipment, the source of a separately derived system, or other power supply source and the final branch-circuit overcurrent device. [**70**:100]

Interrupting Rating - The highest current at rated voltage that a device is identified to interrupt under standard test conditions. [**70**:100]

Listed - Equipment, materials, or services included in a list published by an organization that is acceptable to the authority having jurisdiction and concerned with evaluation of products or services, that maintains periodic inspection of production of listed equipment or materials or periodic evaluation of services, and whose listing states that either the equipment, material, or service meets appropriate designated standards or has been tested and found suitable for a specified purpose. [**70**:100]

Overcurrent - Any current in excess of the rated current of equipment or the ampacity of a conductor. It may result from overload, short circuit, or ground fault. [**70**:100]

Utilization Equipment - Equipment that utilizes electric energy for electronic, electromechanical, chemical, heating, lighting, or similar purposes. [**70**:100]

Abbreviations			
60°C/75°C	Dual-Rated Terminal Temperature Rating	NCL	Noncontinuous Load
CL	Continuous Load	OCPD	Overcurrent Protective Device
Max	Maximum	Std	Standard
Min	Minimum		

Reproduced with permission of NFPA from NFPA 70®, *National Electrical Code*® (NEC®), 2020 edition. Copyright© 2019, National Fire Protection Association. For a full copy of the NEC®, please go to www.nfpa.org.

SUMMARY

In **110.3(B)**, it is required that listed or labeled equipment be installed and used in accordance with any instructions included in the listing or labeling. One very common and important listing and labeling requirement of equipment is the temperature rating associated with equipment, as it directly impacts the ampacity of conductors. As it relates to the ampacity of conductors, **110.14(C)** is an extremely important *NEC* reference to understand. A conductor's ampacity is selected based on the lowest temperature rating of any device, equipment, or conductor associated with the conductor, and the temperature rating of the conductor is permitted to be used for ampacity adjustments and corrections, provided the final ampacity does not exceed the value permitted by the equipment termination temperature rating. Equipment rated 100 amperes or less is permitted to use 60°C conductors or conductors with higher temperature ratings, but with the ampacity selected at a 60°C ampacity. Equipment may also be listed, for example, at 75°C and use conductors with insulation ratings at 75°C or higher, but with the ampacity selected in accordance with 75°C. Equipment over 100 amperes, due to higher currents and more heat, requires the use of 75°C or higher temperature rated conductors with the ampacity selected in accordance with 75°C.

Sizing a branch circuit, a feeder, or a service to supply a load is a three-step process. First ensure the overcurrent protective device has a minimum rating of not less than 100% of the noncontinuous and 125% of the continuous load. See **Sections 210.20**, **215.3**, and **230.90**. Second, ensure the conductor has an ampacity after adjustment and correction factors of not less than the maximum load and an ampacity (before adjustment and correction factors) of not less than 100% of the noncontinuous and 125% of the continuous load. Remember to make two separate comparisons. See **Sections 210.19**, **215.2**, and **230.42**. Third, verify that the conductor, based on its ampacity, is protected by the overcurrent protective device in accordance with **240.4**. Following these three steps will ensure accurately sized circuits.

REVIEW QUESTIONS

1. What is the ampacity of an 8 AWG THHN conductor terminated to a 40-ampere circuit breaker which does not have a temperature rating marked on the breaker?
   a. 35 A
   b. 40 A
   c. 50 A
   d. 55 A

2. What is the ampacity of a 4 THHN conductor terminated to an 80-ampere circuit breaker which is marked for 60°C/75°C terminations?
   a. 70 A
   b. 80 A
   c. 85 A
   d. 95 A

3. What is the ampacity of a 300 kcmil THHN conductor terminated to a 250-ampere circuit breaker?
   a. 240 A
   b. 250 A
   c. 285 A
   d. 320 A

4. A 12 AWG THHN branch-circuit conductor is installed in a raceway with eight other current-carrying conductors. It is terminated to a 20-ampere circuit breaker and all terminations in the circuit are rated for 60°C. What is the ampacity of the 12 AWG THHN in the installation?
   a. 14 A
   b. 16 A
   c. 20 A
   d. 21 A

5. What is the maximum standard size overcurrent protective device permitted to protect a 4/0 AWG THWN conductor?
   a. 200 A
   b. 225 A
   c. 250 A
   d. 300 A

6. What is the maximum noncontinuous load, in amperes, permitted to be supplied by a 20-ampere branch circuit?
   a. 16 A
   b. 20 A
   c. 24 A
   d. 25 A

7. What minimum standard size branch circuit is required for a 208-volt, single-phase, 8-kW continuous load?
   a. 30 A
   b. 40 A
   c. 45 A
   d. 50 A

8. What is the maximum continuous load, in amperes, permitted to be supplied by a 225-ampere feeder overcurrent protective device?
   a. 180 A
   b. 200 A
   c. 225 A
   d. 281 A

9. What is the maximum amount of noncontinuous load that may be supplied by a 500 kcmil THWN feeder conductor that is supplied by a 400-ampere feeder overcurrent protective device?
   a. 304 A
   b. 320 A
   c. 380 A
   d. 400 A

10. What is the maximum amount of continuous load, in watts, that may be added to a 200-ampere, 480-volt, 3-phase feeder which already has 75 amperes of continuous load on it?
    a. 70,666 W
    b. 83,136 W
    c. 103,920 W
    d. 116,390 W

CHAPTER 4
BOXES

Electrical boxes are often used to begin, splice, and terminate various electrical wiring methods used for branch circuits and feeders. Boxes also play the same important role in low-voltage systems and communication circuits. Electrical boxes permit accessibility to circuit conductors, thereby allowing easy access for measurement, testing, and, where necessary, additions and replacements. Sometimes boxes and (accessible) fittings are simply used to permit raceways and cables to change direction or to bend around tight corners. Electrical boxes are constructed of metal or nonmetallic (composite) material.

Whatever a box's purpose and whatever its construction, the Electrical Worker must clearly understand the safety aspects of selecting the properly-sized box for the required conditions of use. This involves understanding the physical aspects of layout and placement, understanding the environment the box is placed in, and understanding how the conductors and other various devices or equipment within the enclosure will be protected from harsh environments outside of the enclosure. Calculations driven by **Article 314** can be used to determine the safe amount of physical space or volume within the box required for a particular set of installation conditions.

The title of **Article 314** is actually a description of the various boxes and associated items covered within the article. Included are outlet and device boxes, pull and junction boxes, conduit bodies, fittings, and handhole enclosures. Each box or enclosure installed is judged (and often inspected) for its ability to permit a quantity of conductors, splices, devices, and equipment to operate safely, thereby preventing shock or fire hazard to persons or property using these enclosures and the devices placed within them.

OBJECTIVES

- Identify and distinguish between a conduit fitting and a device.
- Recognize and describe standard outlet boxes.
- Determine and apply proper volume allowances for each type of box fill.
- Calculate the minimum outlet box sizes using both **Table 314.16(A)** and **Table 314.16(B)**.
- Compare and contrast the various methods of determining conductor fill for standard boxes.
- Calculate the minimum dimensions for pull and junction boxes for straight and angle pulls of conductors for systems 1,000 volts, nominal, or less.
- Calculate the minimum dimensions for pull and junction boxes for straight and angle pulls of conductors for systems over 1,000 volts.
- Calculate the minimum dimensions for handhole enclosures for conductors for systems 1,000 volts, nominal, or less.

TABLE OF CONTENTS

4.1	**DETERMINING THE NUMBER OF CONDUCTORS IN A BOX**	**64**
4.2	**BOX FILL FOR STANDARD BOXES**	**64**
.1	Conductors	64
.2	Equipment Grounding Conductors	65
.3	Clamps	66
.4	Support Fittings	66
.5	Device(s) or Equipment in a Box	66
4.3	**EXAMPLES OF INDIVIDUAL VOLUME ALLOWANCES**	**67**
.1	Counting Clamps and Fittings	67
.2	Counting Devices	67
.3	Counting Equipment Grounding Conductors	68
.4	Counting Terminated Conductors	69
.5	Counting Conductors Pulled Straight Through	69
.6	Counting Fixture Wires	69
.7	Counting Looped and Unbroken Conductors	69
.8	Counting Jumper Conductors	69
.9	Exceptions to Counting Conductors	70
.10	Determining Clamp Allowances	70
.11	Determining Fitting Allowances	71
.12	Determining Yoke or Strap Allowances	71
.13	Determining EGC Allowances	72
4.4	**USING TABLE 314.16(A) AND TABLE 314.16(B)**	**72**
.1	Conductors of Different Sizes	72
.2	Nonstandard Boxes	73
.3	Adding to an Existing Box	74
.4	Conduit Body	74
4.5	**SIZING PULL AND JUNCTION BOXES FOR CONDUCTORS FOR SYSTEMS 1,000 VOLTS OR LESS**	**76**
.1	Straight-Through Pull	76
.2	Angle Pull	76
.3	Dimensions Between Conduit Entries	77
.4	Raceways Entering Opposite a Removable Cover	78
.5	Combination Straight and Angle Pulls	79
4.6	**SIZING PULL AND JUNCTION BOXES FOR CONDUCTORS FOR SYSTEMS OVER 1,000 VOLTS**	**79**
.1	Straight-Through Pull Using Single Conductor Cables for Systems Over 1,000 Volts	80
.2	Straight-Through Pull Using Multiconductor Cables for Systems Rated Over 1,000 Volts	80
.3	Angle Pull and Conduit Entry Dimension Using Cables for Systems Rated Over 1,000 Volts	81
.4	Cable Entry Opposite Removable Cover	83
	DEFINITIONS AND TERMS	**85**
	SUMMARY	**86**
	REVIEW QUESTIONS	**86**

4.1 DETERMINING THE NUMBER OF CONDUCTORS IN A BOX

According to **Section 314.16**, boxes and conduit bodies must be an approved size to provide free space for all enclosed conductors. However, it does not apply to motor terminal housings. **Section 314.16** determines the maximum number of conductors allowed for wire sizes 18 AWG through 6 AWG based on volume calculations. For conductor sizes 4 AWG and larger, **Section 314.28** determines the minimum dimensions of enclosures based on multiplication factors of raceway sizes.

To determine the maximum number of conductors that may be placed within a box, the total space within an empty box, the space taken up by the conductors within the box, and the space taken up by various other devices, equipment, barriers, and fittings within the box must be determined. The fundamental equation used to determine the maximum number of conductors permitted inside a box is equal to the volume of space within the box minus the space required for the volume of conductors. Where the maximum number of conductors permitted inside a box is determined in accordance with **Section 314.16**, there will be sufficient free space for the enclosed conductors.

Figure 4-1. Device Box. A standard metal device box found in **Table 314.16(A)** has a minimum volume of 12.5 in.^{3}.

4.2 BOX FILL FOR STANDARD BOXES

Table 314.16(A) lists the maximum number of conductors permitted in a box, provided that all of the following are true:

- The box is a standard size
- There is nothing in the box except conductors
- All the conductors are the same AWG size
- No conductor is larger than 6 AWG

When equipment other than conductors (such as fittings, devices, and barriers) are installed in a standard box, adjustments have to be made for the number of conductors permitted. *NEC* **314.16(B)(1)** through **314.16(B)(5)** list the deductions from **Table 314.16(A)** that need to be made. Additionally, in **314.16(A)**, deductions for barriers within a box are required to be made for a metal barrier at a volume of 8.2 cubic centimeters ($^1/_2$ in.^{3}) and a nonmetallic barrier of 16.4 cubic centimeters (1.0 in.^{3}) unless the volume is marked on the barrier. Remember, where extension boxes, extension rings, and plaster frames are stacked on top of standard boxes, the total available box volume becomes the sum of the volumes of the items assembled together. **See Figure 4-1.**

4.2.1 Conductors

In order to calculate the amount of conductors permitted in a box, it must first be known what counts as a conductor for the purposes of these calculations.

1. Each conductor that originates outside the box and terminates within the box is counted as one conductor.
2. Each conductor that originates outside the box and is spliced within the box counts as one conductor. If a conductor enters a box and is spliced to another conductor leaving the box, then each conductor is counted, for a total conductor count of two.

3. Each conductor that passes through the box without a splice or termination counts as one conductor.
4. A conductor, where no part leaves the box, shall not be counted.

If the unbroken conductor is as long as or longer than twice the minimum length, the long conductor counts as two conductors. The minimum conductor length required within boxes for conductor terminations and splices is explained in **Section 300.14**. The minimum required length of the free conductor is six inches and is measured from where it emerges from the raceway or cable sheath. For boxes with small openings (an opening dimension less than eight inches), the minimum required length for each conductor is six inches, with at least three inches of the conductor outside the opening.

As an example, consider a four-inch metal box with an ungrounded and grounded conductor installed to supply power to a receptacle. Per **Section 300.14**, the minimum length of a free conductor is six inches. If the unspliced length of free conductor is 12 inches or more (twice the six-inch minimum length), the conductor is required to be counted as two conductors. **See Problems 4-1 and 4-2.**

4.2.2 Equipment Grounding Conductors

Equipment grounding conductors must also be counted when calculating the number of permitted conductors, though their requirements differ slightly. The requirements are modified for the 2020 *NEC*.

1. Where up to four bare, insulated, or covered equipment grounding conductors are present, they are counted as a single volume allowance based on the largest equipment grounding conductor present.
2. For each additional equipment grounding conductor present, a $1/4$ volume allowance needs to be made for each additional equipment grounding conductor based upon the largest equipment grounding conductor present.

PROBLEM 4-1

What is the minimum box volume needed for the installation of four 12 AWG THHN copper conductors and four 10 AWG THW aluminum conductors?

Solution

Table 314.16(B)
  12 AWG = 2.25 in.^{3}
  10 AWG = 2.50 in.^{3}
Total volume

12 AWG =	2.25 in.^{3} × 4	9 in.^{3}
10 AWG =	2.50 in.^{3} × 4	10 in.^{3}
Minimum volume required		19 in.^{3}

Answer: 19 in.^{3} min. volume

PROBLEM 4-2

Which of the following four boxes could be used for the installation shown in Problem 4-1?

  4 × 1 1/2 octagonal   4 × 2 1/8 octagonal
  4 × 1 1/2 square   4 11/16 × 1 1/4 square

Solution

Minimum cubic inch (in.^{3}) volume needed = 19 in.^{3}
Table 314.16(A): in.^{3} volume of boxes

4 × 1 1/2 octagonal =	15.5 in.^{3}	Not acceptable
4 × 2 1/8 octagonal =	21.5 in.^{3}	Acceptable
4 × 1 1/2 square =	21.0 in.^{3}	Acceptable
4 11/16 × 1 1/4 square =	25.5 in.^{3}	Acceptable

3. Isolated equipment grounding conductors are no longer required to be counted for box fill purposes. **See Problem 4-3**.

PROBLEM 4-3

What is the minimum box volume required for the illustration?

Solution

EGCs all count as one 12 AWG
Fixture stud counts the same as the largest conductor
Fixture wires count as two conductors
Table 314.16(A) and Table 314.16(B)
Cubic inch displacement from Table 314.16(B)

16 AWG =	1.75 in.³ × 2	3.50 in.³
12 AWG =	2.25 in.³ × 5	11.25 in.³
10 AWG =	2.50 in.³ × 2	5.00 in.³
8 AWG =	3.00 in.³ × 2	6.00 in.³
Fixture stud		
8 AWG =	3.00 in.³ × 1	3.00 in.³
Minimum box volume		28.75 in.³

Answer: 28.75 in.³ min. volume

Fixture Stud	Count 1 Conductor
Fixture Hickey	Count 1 Conductor
Cable Clamps 2	Count 1 Conductor
Total	3 Conductors

Figure 4-2. Round/Octagon Box and Fittings. *Counting conductors includes counting the fixture studs, hickeys, and clamps installed within a four-inch by three-inch by ½-inch round/octagonal standard metal box. See* **Table 314.16(A)**.

4.2.3 Clamps

Clamps installed inside the box, whether installed by the factory or installed in the field, are counted as one conductor. In both cases, the conductor size is based upon the largest conductor present in the box. No allowance is required for a cable connector if the clamping mechanism is outside the box. Clamp assemblies with cable terminations are not covered.

4.2.4 Support Fittings

Where one or more fixture studs and fixture hickeys are present, each type of fitting is counted as one conductor. Note that a single conductor allowance is made for each type of support fitting: a single volume allowance for the fixture stud(s), and a single volume allowance for the fixture hickey(s). In both cases, the conductor size is based upon the largest conductor present in the box.

4.2.5 Device(s) or Equipment in a Box

Various devices and fittings must also be counted, depending on their type.

1. A yoke or strap with a switch counts as two conductors.
2. A yoke or strap with a duplex receptacle counts as two conductors.
3. A yoke or strap with a triplex receptacle counts as two conductors.
4. A yoke or strap with a switch and light on the same yoke or strap counts as two conductors.
5. A yoke with any combination of three devices or equipment on the same yoke or strap counts as two conductors.
6. Where a device or utilization equipment is wider than that required for a single-gang device box (2 in.), each gang of width required for mounting must count as two conductors.

In all cases, the conductor size is based upon the conductor size connected to the device or equipment on the yoke or strap.

CHAPTER 4 BOXES 67

4.3 EXAMPLES OF INDIVIDUAL VOLUME ALLOWANCES

The following examples illustrate the individual volume allowances for various installations.

4.3.1 Counting Clamps and Fittings

Determining the volume allowances for clamps and fittings is covered in **314.16(B)(2)** and **314.16(B)(3)**. An example would include installing fixture studs, hickeys, and clamps within a standard octagonal metal box. **See Figure 4-2**.

4.3.2 Counting Devices

NEC **314.16(B)(4)** covers the requirements for device or equipment fill. The definition of utilization equipment, found in **Article 100**, includes modern devices which use or consume small amounts of energy. Box-mounted equipment is included as well.

For each yoke, mounting assembly, or strap containing one or more devices, a double volume (conductor) allowance is made in accordance with **Table 314.16(A)**, based upon the largest conductor connected to the device. Where a device or utilization equipment is wider than a standard device width box (2 in.), a double volume allowance shall be made for each standard device width. **See Figure 4-3**.

It is important to recognize the minimum volume required for each single-gang device based upon the size and the number of conductors represented. Also important is knowing the minimum volume required for extra-wide equipment, such as fire alarm horn/light (flush and semi-recessed) assemblies requiring standard two-gang boxes, as well as standard two-gang electrical devices, such as a 4-wire, 30-ampere electric dryer receptacle. For these types of devices or equipment, a double volume (conductor) allowance must be made for each gang or each two inches of width the device requires, in addition to the other fill requirements of **Section 314.16**. **See Figure 4-4**.

Figure 4-3. Devices in Boxes. *The conductor count must include devices which may be located within the standard metal box according to* **Table 310.16(A)**.

1 Yoke
2 Devices
Count as
2 Conductors

1 Yoke
1 Device
Count as
2 Conductors

1 Yoke
2 Devices
Count as
2 Conductors

1 Yoke
3 Devices
Count as
2 Conductors

Figure 4-4. 2-Gang Device. *A 4-wire, 125/250-volt, 30-ampere household dryer receptacle provides an example of using a double volume allowance for each gang device requiring mounting in a two-gang outlet.*

For additional information, visit qr.njatcdb.org
Item #1028

4.3.3 Counting Equipment Grounding Conductors

Two requirements for counting equipment grounding conductors are:

1. For up to four equipment grounding conductors (EGCs) used for general grounding of metal equipment and raceways, which can be insulated, covered, or bare, a single volume allowance is required based on the largest EGC present, including isolated equipment grounding conductors.

2. If more than four equipment grounding conductors are present, each additional equipment grounding conductor adds a $1/4$ volume allowance based on the largest EGC present. **See Figure 4-5.**

EGC	Up to 4 Equipment Grounding Conductors Including the Isolated Equipment Grounding Conductor	Count 1
EBJ	Bonding Jumper Installed from Metal Box to Receptacle, located within the Box	Count 0
Total Count for EGCs		**1**

EGC	First Four Equipment Grounding Conductors Based on Largest EGC Present	Count 1
EGC	Each Additional Equipment Grounding Conductor Present is a ¼ Volumne Allowance Based on Largest EGC Present (2 Additional Above 4)	Count 2 × ¼ = ½
EBJ	Bonding Jumper Installed from Metal Box to Receptacle, located within the Box	Count 0
Total Count for EGCs		**1 ½**

Figure 4-5. Equipment Grounding Conductors. Several equipment grounding conductors (EGCs) plus an isolated equipment grounding conductor (IEGC) can be housed in the same metal box.

Figure 4-6. Spliced Conductors. Each conductor terminated within a standard metal box is counted as one conductor.

Figure 4-7. Straight Through Conductors. "Straight through" conductors within a standard metal box are also counted as one conductor each.

4.3.4 Counting Terminated Conductors

Each conductor which terminates in the box is counted as a single conductor. **See Figure 4-6**.

4.3.5 Counting Conductors Pulled Straight Through

When an unspliced conductor is pulled straight through the box, it counts as one conductor. Often junction boxes are installed to limit the number of bends in the run to less than 360° of the bend, and conductors are pulled straight through the box without a splice. **See Figure 4-7**.

4.3.6 Counting Fixture Wires

When fixture wires are installed to connect to a fixture outside the box, they count as conductors inside the box. **See Figure 4-8**.

4.3.7 Counting Looped and Unbroken Conductors

When conductors are looped through the box in unbroken lengths but terminate on a device, they count as two conductors. An unbroken length is defined as "not less than twice the minimum length of free conductor as required by **Section 300.14**…" (usually two times six inches, or a 12-inch minimum length). For example, an unbroken looped conductor may pass through a box and be used to supply a device mounted within the metal box. **See Figure 4-9**.

4.3.8 Counting Jumper Conductors

Jumpers, sometimes called pigtails, that do not leave the box are not counted. Jumpers are usually connected to devices in the box, such as receptacles and switches. **See Figure 4-10**.

Through	1
Terminate	4
Fixture Wire	2
Total	7

Figure 4-8. Fixture Wires. Fixture wires that leave the metal box are still counted as conductors within the box.

Unbroken Loops for Receptacles or Switches Count as Terminations

4 Conductors

Figure 4-9. Looped Conductors. Unbroken looped conductors which will be connected to a device mounted within the metal box are counted as terminations within the box.

Conductors Terminating in Box	4
Pigtails Within Box (2)	0
Total Conductors	4

Figure 4-10. Jumpers/Pigtails. Jumpers or pigtails that are spliced in a box to supply a receptacle are not required to be counted for volume allowance requirements.

For additional information, visit qr.njatcdb.org Item #1029

Figure 4-11. Domed Luminaire. Some of the conductors within a domed cover are not required to be counted as fill within a box.

Equipment Grounding Conductors Terminate in Box	Count 1
2 Internal Cable Clamps	Count 8
	Count 1
Total Count	10

Figure 4-12. Factory-Installed Cable Clamps. The allowance of Type NM cable clamps used in a standard metal box must be determined.

2	8 AWG at	3.00 in.³	=	6 in.³
1	Fixture Stud at	3.00 in.³	=	3 in.³
4	12 AWG at	2.25 in.³	=	9 in.³
	Total			18 in.³

Figure 4-13. Various Conductor Sizes and Fittings in Enclosures. Different sized (AWG) conductors and a fixture stud support inside a standard metal box all have allowances which must be determined.

4.3.9 Exceptions to Counting Conductors

An exception is made for a dome-type canopy, such as one used with a combination fan/light fixture installation. **See Figure 4-11**.

Additionally, where either or both of the following terminate in the box, they are not counted in the box calculation:

1. Equipment grounding conductor
2. Not more than four 16 AWG or smaller fixture wires

Where there are more than four fixture wires, each fixture wire over four counts as one conductor.

4.3.10 Determining Clamp Allowances

According to **314.16(B)(2)**, where there are one or more factory-installed or field-installed internal clamps mounted within a box, all of the clamps count as only one single conductor. Where a cable connector has its clamping mechanism outside of the box, there is no conductor allowance necessary for the cable connector. Also, there is no allowance necessary for locknuts or bushings installed within a box. An example would include standard metallic or nonmetallic boxes using Type NM cable clamps. **See Figure 4-12**.

2	8 AWG at	3.00 in.³	=	6 in.³
4	12 AWG at	2.25 in.³	=	9 in.³
1	Yoke at (2x)	2.25 in.³	=	4.5 in.³
	Total			19.5 in.³

Figure 4-14. Yoke or Strap Allowance. Simple devices mounted in a box have their own allowances for counting.

4.3.11 Determining Fitting Allowances

Often different sized conductors and various devices and equipment are installed in the same enclosure. According to **314.16(B)(2)** and **314.16(B)(3)**, the actual conductor allowance varies where different sized conductors occupy the same box. Specifically, when calculating box size for mixed conductor sizes, the cubic inch area (or volume allowance) used for a fixture stud, a cable clamp, or a support hickey is the same as the cubic inch area of the largest conductor entering the box. **See Figure 4-13**.

4.3.12 Determining Yoke or Strap Allowances

A yoke or strap is counted as two conductors according to **314.16(B)(4)**. When calculating the box size for mixed sizes of conductors, the cubic inch area for the yoke or strap is the cubic inch area of the largest conductor connected to a device or equipment supported by the yoke or strap. **See Figure 4-14**.

Reproduced with permission of NFPA from NFPA 70®, *National Electrical Code*® (NEC®), 2020 edition. Copyright© 2019, National Fire Protection Association. For a full copy of the NEC®, please go to www.nfpa.org.

Table 110.28 Enclosure Selection

Provides a Degree of Protection Against the Following Environmental Conditions	For Outdoor Use — Enclosure Type Number									
	3	3R	3S	3X	3RX	3SX	4	4X	6	6P
Incidental contact with the enclosed equipment	X	X	X	X	X	X	X	X	X	X
Rain, snow, and sleet	X	X	X	X	X	X	X	X	X	X
Sleet*	—	—	X	—	—	X	—	—	—	—
Windblown dust	X	—	X	X	—	X	X	X	X	X
Hosedown	—	—	—	—	—	—	X	X	X	X
Corrosive agents	—	—	—	X	X	X	—	X	—	X
Temporary submersion	—	—	—	—	—	—	—	—	X	X
Prolonged submersion	—	—	—	—	—	—	—	—	—	X

Provides a Degree of Protection Against the Following Environmental Conditions	For Indoor Use — Enclosure Type Number									
	1	2	4	4X	5	6	6P	12	12K	13
Incidental contact with the enclosed equipment	X	X	X	X	X	X	X	X	X	X
Falling dirt	X	X	X	X	X	X	X	X	X	X
Falling liquids and light splashing	—	X	X	X	X	X	X	X	X	X
Circulating dust, lint, fibers, and flyings	—	—	X	X	—	X	X	X	X	X
Settling airborne dust, lint, fibers, and flyings	—	—	X	X	X	X	X	X	X	X
Hosedown and splashing water	—	—	X	X	—	X	X	—	—	—
Oil and coolant seepage	—	—	—	—	—	—	—	X	X	X
Oil or coolant spraying and splashing	—	—	—	—	—	—	—	—	—	X
Corrosive agents	—	—	—	X	—	—	X	—	—	—
Temporary submersion	—	—	—	—	—	X	X	—	—	—
Prolonged submersion	—	—	—	—	—	—	X	—	—	—

*Mechanism shall be operable when ice covered.

Informational Note No. 1: The term raintight is typically used in conjunction with Enclosure Types 3, 3S, 3SX, 3X, 4, 4X, 6, and 6P. The term *rainproof* is typically used in conjunction with Enclosure Types 3R and 3RX. The term watertight is typically used in conjunction with Enclosure Types 4, 4X, 6, and 6P. The term *driptight* is typically used in conjunction with Enclosure Types 2, 5, 12, 12K, and 13. The term dusttight is typically used in conjunction with Enclosure Types 3, 3S, 3SX, 3X, 4, 4X, 5, 6, 6P, 12, 12K, and 13.

Informational Note No. 2: Ingress protection (IP) ratings may be found in ANSI/IEC 60529, Degrees of Protection Provided by Enclosures. IP ratings are not a substitute for Enclosure Type ratings.

Informational Note No. 3: Dusttight enclosures are suitable for use in hazardous locations in accordance with 502.10(B)(4), 503.10(A)(2), and 506.15(C)(9).

Informational Note No. 4: Dusttight enclosures are suitable for use in unclassified locations and in Class II, Division 2; Class III; and Zone 22 hazardous (classified) locations.

Table 110.28 should be used for selecting the appropriate enclosure for the specific environment in which it will be installed.

Wire connectors and splicing devices do not count in volume allowance calculations.

Equipment Grounding Conductor
Use one 10 AWG at 2.5 in.³

Figure 4-15. Equipment Grounding Conductors. *EGC allowances are based on the largest EGC entering the box.*

Table 314.16(B) Volume Allowance Required per Conductor

Size of Conductor (AWG)	Free Space Within Box for Each Conductor	
	cm³	in.³
18	24.6	1.50
16	28.7	1.75
14	32.8	2.00
12	36.9	2.25
10	41.0	2.50
8	49.2	3.00
6	81.9	5.00

Figure 4-16. Table 314.16(B). *Table 314.16(B) lists conductor sizes 18 AWG through 6 AWG and the respective volume allowance required per conductor.*

Reproduced with permission of NFPA from NFPA 70®, *National Electrical Code*® (NEC®), 2020 edition. Copyright© 2019, National Fire Protection Association. For a full copy of the NEC®, please go to www.nfpa.org.

4.3.13 Determining EGC Allowances

If up to four equipment grounding conductors enter a box, according to **314.16(B)(5)**, they are counted as one conductor, including isolated equipment grounding conductors. If there are more than four equipment grounding conductors, each additional EGC is counted as a $1/4$ volume allowance.

When calculating the box size for mixed sizes of conductors, if there is more than one size equipment grounding conductor, the cubic inch area of the equipment grounding conductor is represented as that of the largest equipment grounding conductor entering the box. **See Figure 4-15.**

4.4 USING TABLE 314.16(A) AND TABLE 314.16(B)

Boxes and conduit bodies are required to have adequate space for enclosed conductors. **Table 314.16(A)** provides volumes of standard metal boxes, and **Table 314.16(B)** provides the minimum volume allowance for conductors 6 AWG and smaller.

4.4.1 Conductors of Different Sizes

When all the conductors in a box are not the same size, the maximum number of conductors is based upon the volume fill of the box. Volume is measured in cubic inches.

Table 314.16(B) lists the volume fill that shall be allowed for each conductor when a combination of sizes is installed. **See Figure 4-16.**

Table 314.16(A) has a column headed "Minimum Volume (in.³)" listing the cubic inch volume of each box. The type of insulation or conductor material is not considered when calculating box fill. **Table 314.16(A)** and **Table 314.16(B)** apply to both copper and aluminum conductors. **See Figure 4-17.**

CHAPTER 4 BOXES

Table 314.16(A) Metal Boxes

Box Trade Size (mm)	Box Trade Size (in.)		Minimum Volume cm³	Minimum Volume in.³	18	16	14	12	10	8	6
100 × 32	(4 × 1¼)	round/octagonal	205	12.5	8	7	6	5	5	5	2
100 × 38	(4 × 1½)	round/octagonal	254	15.5	10	8	7	6	6	5	3
100 × 54	(4 × 2⅛)	round/octagonal	353	21.5	14	12	10	9	8	7	4
100 × 32	(4 × 1¼)	square	295	18.0	12	10	9	8	7	6	3
100 × 38	(4 × 1½)	square	344	21.0	14	12	10	9	8	7	4
100 × 54	(4 × 2⅛)	square	497	30.3	20	17	15	13	12	10	6
120 × 32	(4¹¹⁄₁₆ × 1¼)	square	418	25.5	17	14	12	11	10	8	5
120 × 38	(4¹¹⁄₁₆ × 1½)	square	484	29.5	19	16	14	13	11	9	5
120 × 54	(4¹¹⁄₁₆ × 2⅛)	square	689	42.0	28	24	21	18	16	14	8
75 × 50 × 38	(3 × 2 × 1½)	device	123	7.5	5	4	3	3	3	2	1
75 × 50 × 50	(3 × 2 × 2)	device	164	10.0	6	5	5	4	4	3	2
75 × 50 × 57	(3 × 2 × 2¼)	device	172	10.5	7	6	5	4	4	3	2
75 × 50 × 65	(3 × 2 × 2½)	device	205	12.5	8	7	6	5	5	4	2
75 × 50 × 70	(3 × 2 × 2¾)	device	230	14.0	9	8	7	6	5	4	2
75 × 50 × 90	(3 × 2 × 3½)	device	295	18.0	12	10	9	8	7	6	3
100 × 54 × 38	(4 × 2⅛ × 1½)	device	169	10.3	6	5	5	4	4	3	2
100 × 54 × 48	(4 × 2⅛ × 1⅞)	device	213	13.0	8	7	6	5	5	4	2
100 × 54 × 54	(4 × 2⅛ × 2⅛)	device	238	14.5	9	8	7	6	5	4	2
95 × 50 × 65	(3¾ × 2 × 2½)	masonry box/gang	230	14.0	9	8	7	6	5	4	2
95 × 50 × 90	(3¾ × 2 × 3½)	masonry box/gang	344	21.0	14	12	10	9	8	7	4
min. 44.5 depth	FS — single cover/gang (1¾)		221	13.5	9	7	6	6	5	4	2
min. 60.3 depth	FD — single cover/gang (2⅜)		295	18.0	12	10	9	8	7	6	3
min. 44.5 depth	FS — multiple cover/gang (1¾)		295	18.0	12	10	9	8	7	6	3
min. 60.3 depth	FD — multiple cover/gang (2⅜)		395	24.0	16	13	12	10	9	8	4

*Where no volume allowances are required by 314.16(B)(2) through (B)(5).

Figure 4-17. Table 314.16(A). Table 314.16(A) is required to be used to determine the minimum volume and maximum number of conductors permitted for standard metal boxes.

Reproduced with permission of NFPA from NFPA 70®, *National Electrical Code®* (NEC®), 2020 edition. Copyright© 2019, National Fire Protection Association. For a full copy of the NEC®, please go to www.nfpa.org.

4.4.2 Nonstandard Boxes

"Nonstandard boxes" are boxes that do not appear in **Table 314.16(A)**. One significant group of nonstandard boxes are nonmetallic boxes, including round/octagonal boxes, square boxes, and device boxes. *NEC* **314.16(A)(2)** covers nonstandard boxes not found in **Table 314.16(A)** and boxes 100 cubic inches or less, and permits the volume to be marked on the box.

The volume of a box is determined by reading the volume stamped on the box, or in some cases, reviewing the manufacturer's data. Under no circumstance can the volume stamped on the box during manufacture [plus the volume(s) of any assembled section(s)] be less than the fill calculation in accordance with **314.16(B)**.

Up to four equipment grounding conductors count as a single volume allowance, and additional equipment grounding conductors are required to each be counted as a ¼ volume allowance based on the largest equipment grounding conductor present.

Volume calculations of listed nonmetallic boxes with marked clamp assemblies incorporating a cable termination for cable conductors do not require a cable-clamp allowance for the cable clamp(s) within the box, since the marked volume on the box has been adjusted by the manufacturer in accordance with **314.16(B)(2)**. **See Problem 4-4**.

PROBLEM 4-4

What is the maximum number of 12 AWG conductors that may be installed in a nonmetallic switch box with a marked volume of 18 in.^{3}?

Solution

Stamped volume = 18 in.^{3}
Table 314.16(B)
12 AWG = 2.25 in.^{3}

$$\text{Number of conductors} = \frac{\text{stamped box volume}}{\text{one conductor area}}$$
$$= \frac{18 \text{ in.}^3}{2.25 \text{ in.}^3}$$
$$= 8$$

Answer: Eight 12 AWG conductors

Table 314.16(A) is limited to only standard metal boxes.

4.4.3 Adding to an Existing Box

When conductors are added to existing boxes, the same calculations apply. **See Problem 4-5**.

PROBLEM 4-5

Assuming that the EMT is long enough, what is the maximum number of additional 14 AWG conductors that can be added and pulled directly through the box?

Solution

Table 314.16(A)
   Volume of a 4 × 1 1/2 square box = 21 in.^{3}
Table 314.16(B)
   Existing 12 AWG = 2.25 in.^{3}
   Total occupied space: 4 × 2.25 in.^{3} = 9 in.^{3}
   Unoccupied space: 21 − 9 = 12 in.^{3}
Table 314.16(B)
   14 AWG = 2 in.^{3}

$$\text{Number of conductors} = \frac{\text{unoccupied space}}{\text{one conductor volume}}$$
$$= \frac{12 \text{ in.}^3}{2 \text{ in.}^3}$$
$$= 6$$

Answer: 6 additional 14 AWG conductors

4.4.4 Conduit Body

NEC **314.16(C)** covers the requirements for conductor fill of sizes 6 AWG and smaller in conduit bodies. There are three subsections for requirements, and the first, in general, applies to the number of conductors permitted in a conduit body. **See Problem 4-6**. The maximum number of conductors is determined by the maximum number permitted by **Chapter 9, Table 1** for the

CHAPTER 4 BOXES
75

PROBLEM 4-6

1 in. RMC

1¼ in. Type LB conduit body

What is the maximum number of 8 AWG THWN copper conductors permitted in a 1 ¼-inch LB conduit body installed in a run of 1 inch rigid metal conduit (RMC)?

Solution

314.16(C)(1) requires the use of
 Chapter 9, Table 1, Note 1
 Note 1 refers to conduit and tubing fill tables in
 Annex C
 Annex C, Table C.8 is rigid metal conduit (RMC)
 8 AWG THWN in 1 in. RMC = 9 conductors max.
Answer: 9 conductors

conduit to which the conduit body is attached. **See Figure 4-18.** For example, the maximum number of conductors permitted in a two-inch Type LB conduit body connected to two-inch intermediate metal conduit (IMC) is determined by the allowable fill of the two-inch IMC as permitted by **Chapter 9, Table 1. See Problem 4-7.**

The second subsection, *NEC* **314.16(C)(2)**, permits splices, taps, or devices to be installed only in conduit bodies with their volumes clearly marked by the manufacturer. Conductor volumes are determined by **Table 314.16(B)**. The calculations are similar to that of a typical box fill.

The final subsection, *NEC* **314.16(C)(3)**, permits the use of short-radius conduit bodies, such as capped elbows, for the installation of the conduit and conductors provided they contain no splices, taps, or devices and are approved for the installation.

Figure 4-18. Various Conduit Bodies. Fill requirements for conductors pulled straight through conduit bodies are determined from **Chapter 9, Table 1**. When splices, taps, or devices are installed in conduit bodies, the volume shall be marked on the conduit body. See **314.16(C)**.

PROBLEM 4-7

10 AWG
1 in. RMC   1 in. RMC
1 in. RMC

A one-inch, form 7 TB (tee with entry into the back) conduit body is connected to three one-inch rigid metal conduits (RMC) with three 10 AWG conductors (hot, neutral, and equipment grounding) installed in each raceway. Are the nine conductors permitted to be spliced in the conduit body when it has a marked volume of 15 cubic inches?

Solution

From Table 314.16(B):
 10 AWG is 2.5 in.³

Three 10 AWG hot conductors is 3 × 2.5 in.³ =	7.5 in.³
Three 10 AWG neutral conductors is 3 × 2.5 in.³ =	7.5 in.³
Three 10 AWG equipment grounding conductors counts as 1 =	2.5 in.³
Total volume of conductors =	17.5 in.³

The conductor volume of 17.5 in.³ exceeds the volume of the TB, which is 15 in.³
Answer: This would be a violation; the installation is not permitted.

4.5 SIZING PULL AND JUNCTION BOXES FOR CONDUCTORS FOR SYSTEMS 1,000 VOLTS OR LESS

For conductors 4 AWG and larger, the size of the box is determined based upon multipliers of the raceway rather than volume calculations as required by **314.16**. *NEC* **314.28(A)(1)** is used for straight pull calculations, and **314.28(A)(2)** is used for angles or U-pulls and for splices.

4.5.1 Straight-Through Pull

The largest conductor listed in **Table 314.16(A)** is 6 AWG. For conductors 4 AWG or larger, **Section 314.28** is used for calculating the minimum box size needed.

The size of the box is based upon the trade size (standard trade diameter) of the largest raceway or cable assembly entering the box. According to **314.28(A)(1)**, for straight-through pulls where conductors are installed without splices, the minimum dimension for the length of the box must be at least eight times the raceway trade size. However, as stated in **314.28(A)(2)** for straight-through pulls where conductors are spliced, the minimum dimension is allowed to be reduced from eight times to six times the raceway trade size.

Where cables are used, the cable size should match the trade size raceway required for the same conductors.

For junction boxes for conductors for systems over 1,000 volts, nominal, a different set of measurements is used. Although the *Code* does not specify the depth or width of the box, it must be large enough to accommodate the largest raceway or cable fittings, such as locknuts and bushings, that will be used within the box. **See Problem 4-8**.

PROBLEM 4-8

What is the minimum length of a straight-through pull box for two sets of 480-volt feeders: one set is a 3-inch conduit and one set is a 2-inch conduit? Both feeders are unspliced.

Solution

Section 314.28(A)(1)
Min. length = 8 × largest raceway
= 8 × 3
= 24 in.
Answer: 24 in.

4.5.2 Angle Pull

NEC **314.28(A)(2)** covers splices, angles, and U-pulls. It requires a calculation of six times the diameter of the largest splice, angle, or U-pull raceway, plus the sum of the diameter of all additional raceways in the same row to determine the minimum distance from the side where the raceway enters the enclosure to the opposite wall of the enclosure. The distance between raceway entries shall not be less than six times the raceway trade size. **See Figure 4-19**.

Figure 4-19. Angles, U-Pulls, or Splices. NEC 314.28(A)(2) *requires a minimum distance of six times the diameter of the largest raceway used for an angle, U-pull, or splice, plus the sum of the diameter of all the raceways in the same row. When sizing the enclosure, enough space is needed between the raceway entry and the opposite wall of the enclosure to pull the conductors from the raceway, bend them, and reroute them into the other raceway.*

CHAPTER 4 BOXES

Figure 4-20. Multiple Rows for Angles, U-Pulls, or Splices. When multiple rows are encountered, calculate all rows to determine which row requires the largest distance from the raceway entries to the opposite wall. That dimension is to be used to determine the enclosure size.

At times, multiple raceway entries into the side of an enclosure are not able to fit in the same row; therefore, multiple rows are required. **See Figure 4-20.** In this situation, each row, as required by **314.28(A)(2)**, needs to be calculated separately, as if each row is in its own enclosure. The row yielding the largest dimension is used to calculate the minimum dimension for the enclosure from the side where the rows enter the enclosure to the opposite wall. **See Problem 4-9.**

4.5.3 Dimensions Between Conduit Entries

In addition to sizing the box according to the raceway or cable entries, the entrance and exit points of a cable must be taken into consideration so the cable is not required to be bent too short. **See Problem 4-10.**

PROBLEM 4-9

What is the length and width for the illustrated angle pull box?

Solution

Table 314.28(A)(2)
For any one side = (largest raceway in row × 6) + (sum of other raceway(s) in same row)
Repeat calculation for each side and use the greatest distance calculated for any one side
Row 1 (Dimension A)
  = (3 in. × 6) + (1 in.)
  = 19 in.
Row 2 (Dimension B)
  = (2 × 6) + (2 + 1 + 1)
  = 16 in.
Using only the minimum dimension = 19 in. × 16 in.
Answer: 19 in. × 16 in.

PROBLEM 4-10

What is the length and width of the box needed and what is the minimum distance between the entry and exit point for the conductors in the illustrated angle pull box?

Solution

Calculation 1
314.28(A)(2)
Overall box size
Length = (6 × largest raceway) + other raceways
  = (6 × 3 in.) + 2 in.
  = 20 in.
Answer: 20 in. for length (A) and width (B)

Calculation 2
314.18(A)(2)
Distance between raceways enclosing same conductors
Length (C) = 3 in. raceway × 6
  = 3 × 6
  = 18 in.
Length (D) = 2 in. raceway × 6
  = 2 × 6
  = 12 in.
Answer: (C) = 18 in. and (D) = 12 in.

*Pull and junction boxes located in hazardous locations must be identified as suitable according to **500.8(A)**.*

4.5.4 Raceways Entering Opposite a Removable Cover

The general rule of **314.28(A)(2)** requires the distance between the sides of the raceway entrance point and the opposite side to be six times the diameter of the raceway plus the sum of other raceway diameters in the same row. The purpose of this rule is to ensure that there is enough space between the raceway entry and the opposite wall of the enclosure to pull the conductors from the raceway, bend them, and reroute them into the other raceway. However, if a raceway enters a box on the side opposite a removable cover, such as the back of an enclosure, the wires can be easily drawn and rerouted when the cover is removed, so the depth required by this rule would be excessive.

As such, an exception for angle pulls entering the back of the enclosure (opposite the side of the removable cover) permits the depth of the box to be sized according to **Table 312.6(A)** based on

Figure 4-21. Removable Covers for Angle Pulls. *With a removable cover, the depth of the enclosure is determined by using the largest conductor in the raceway and using the dimension provided in **Table 312.6(A)** for one wire per terminal.*

the size of the wire in the raceway and for one wire per terminal. **Table 312.6(A)**, which is a minimum bending space table for conductors, makes the depth of the box dependent upon the size of the conductors entering the box. **See Figure 4-21**.

Note, however, that the length of the box is still calculated the same as for a standard angle pull. The distance from the bottom raceway entry to the furthest side is six times the trade size of the largest raceway, which requires a slightly larger enclosure than the calculation of six times the trade size of the raceway. The width of the enclosure is only required to be physically wide enough to accommodate the connector and locknut in the enclosure. **See Problem 4-11**.

PROBLEM 4-11

Three 4/0 AWG conductors in a 480-volt feeder circuit are pulled through an angle pull box with a removable cover directly opposite the raceway entry. Calculate the length and width of the box.

Solution

Calculation 1
314.28(A)(2) Exception and Table 312.6(A)
(A) dimension is based upon the conductor size entering through the raceway opposite the removable cover and it is based on one conductor termination from Table 312.6(A).
One 4/0 AWG termination = 4 in.
Answer: 4 in.

Calculation 2
314.28(A)(2)
Distance between raceway entries
(B) dimension = 6 × largest raceway
= 6 × 2
= 12 in.
Answer: 12 in.

CHAPTER 4 BOXES

4.5.5 Combination Straight and Angle Pulls

When there is a combination of a straight-through pull and an angle pull in the same pull box, both straight-through and angle calculations apply. Perform both calculations for the straight pull and angle pull for all sides, and the largest calculation for each side will determine the minimum dimensions for the enclosure. **See Problem 4-12**.

4.6 SIZING PULL AND JUNCTION BOXES FOR CONDUCTORS FOR SYSTEMS OVER 1,000 VOLTS

Part IV of **Article 314** deals with pull and junction boxes for use on systems over 1,000 volts. *NEC* **314.70(A)** sets the ground rules for all of the requirements within **Part IV**. *NEC* **314.70(A)** specifically omits any mention of **314.28(A)**, thereby omitting conduit size from the basic calculation of determining the final pull box size where conductors for systems over 1,000 volts are installed.

Section 314.71 covers the sizing of pull and junction boxes, conduit bodies, and handhole enclosures containing conductors or cables for systems over 1,000 volts, nominal (for example, a 4,160-volt feeder with conductor insulation rated 5,000 volts). The size of the pull or junction box depends upon the type of covering the higher-voltage conductors or cables have. Each type of covering requires a different bending radius and a different size pull or junction box.

Three types of conductor coverings are used for the higher voltage cables:

1. Shielded
2. Nonshielded
3. Lead-covered

PROBLEM 4-12

A pull box has a 3-inch conduit entering the box and a 2-inch conduit leaving the box for a straight-through pull and a 2-inch conduit leaving the box for an angle pull. Calculate the length and width for the pull box.

Solution

Calculation 1
314.28(A)(1)
Length
  Straight-through = 8 × straight pull raceway
                   = 8 × 3
                   = 24 in.
Answer: 24 in. length

Calculation 2
314.28(A)(2)
  Width
  Angle pull = 6 × angle pull raceway
             = 6 × 2
             = 12 in.
Answer: 12 in. width

Pull boxes are often installed in larger sizes than is required for a more efficient and convenient installation.

As pointed out in the second sentence of **311.44**, most cables above two kilovolts will be of the shielded variety; shielded cables are the most often used. Nonshielded cables are not as common and are generally used as jumpers or connecting cables within switchgear and equipment. Lead-covered or lead-sheathed cables are most often found in older underground distribution installations or in some utility underground installations. The installation of new lead-covered cables is rapidly diminishing in the electrical industry.

PROBLEM 4-13

Straight Pull
Length
3 Single Conductors OD 1 in. each

Perform three separate calculations to find the length and width of a straight-through pull box for three 5kV conductors with an outside diameter of 1 inch when all the conductors are either:

1. Shielded conductors
2. Nonshielded conductors
3. Lead-covered conductors

Solution

Calculation 1
314.71(A) Shielded conductors
Length = OD of conductor × 48
= 1 in. × 48
= 48 in.
Answer: 48 in. length

Calculation 2
314.71(A) Nonshielded conductors
Length = OD of conductor × 32
= 1 in. × 32
= 32 in.
Answer: 32 in. length

Calculation 3
314.71(A): Lead-covered conductors
Length = OD of conductor × 48
= 1 in. × 48
= 48 in.
Answer: 48 in. length

Comment: The problems associated with conductors for systems over 1,000 volts omit all references to conduit sizes to ensure the student understands that these pull boxes are not related to conduit sizes. Rather, the *Code* stipulates that only the diameter and type of cable determine the minimum pull or junction box size. The maximum size box or enclosure is not considered by the *NEC*.

Most often, many practical considerations force the increase of the box size above any minimum mandated by the *NEC*. These considerations are based on several factors, such as quantity, size, type of cable splices (if any), and whether cable racks or other supports are installed for conductor(s) supports within the box. For multiconductor cables, these factors require even more consideration. Consultation with the cable manufacturer is also critical for a satisfactory installation.

4.6.1 Straight-Through Pull Using Single Conductor Cables for Systems Over 1,000 Volts

The following problems for sizing pull and junction boxes, conduit bodies, and handhole enclosures for conductors or cables for systems over 1,000 volts, nominal, will illustrate the calculations for each type of conductor or cable covering. Use the largest outside diameter (OD) of any one conductor or cable. **See Problem 4-13**.

NEC **314.71(A)** requires the following minimum measurements for straight-through pull or junction boxes:

Minimum length (L) for shielded cables
= Largest cable OD × 48

Minimum length (L) for nonshielded cables
= Largest cable OD × 32

Minimum length (L) for lead-covered cables
= Largest cable OD × 48

4.6.2 Straight-Through Pull Using Multiconductor Cables for Systems Rated Over 1,000 Volts

For multiconductor cables for systems rated over 1,000 volts, **314.71(A)** is applicable. For shielded or lead-covered cables, the outside diameter of the cable is multiplied by 48 to determine the minimum length of the box. For nonshielded cables, the outside diameter of the cable is multiplied by 32 to determine the minimum length of the box. **See Problem 4-14**.

PROBLEM 4-14

Straight Pull
Length
Cable OD 1.25 in.

Perform two separate calculations to determine the length dimension of the junction box illustrated for a 1.25 in. diameter multiconductor cable when the single cable is either:

1. Shielded
2. Nonshielded

Solution

Calculation 1
314.71(A)
Shielded cable
Length = OD of cable × 48
= 1.25 × 48
= 60 in.

Answer: 60 in.

Calculation 2
314.71(A)
Nonshielded cable
Length = OD of cable × 32
= 1.25 × 32
= 40 in.

Answer: 40 in.

4.6.3 Angle Pull and Conduit Entry Dimension Using Cables for Systems Rated Over 1,000 Volts

Just as with lower-voltage cables, when an angle pull is made, the size of the box, the point of entry of the cable or conductors, and the exit angle are all considered.

Segmented bends, sometimes referred to as concentric bends, all have the same center point, but each has a different radius.

NEC **314.71(B)(1)** requires the following as minimum measurements for angle pull or junction boxes:

Minimum distance between entry and exit
= OD of largest cable × 36

Shielded single conductors
= (OD of largest cable × 36) + ODs of other cables

Shielded multiconductor cables
= (OD of largest cable × 36) + ODs of other cables

NEC **314.71(B)(1) Exception No. 2** covers the installation of nonshielded conductors and cables and requires the following as the minimum measurements for angle pull or junction boxes:

Minimum dimension for distance between entry and exit
= OD of largest cable × 24

Minimum distance from cable entry to the opposite wall of the box for nonshielded single cables
= (OD of largest cable × 24) + ODs of other cables

Minimum distance from cable entry to the opposite wall of the box for nonshielded multiconductor cables
= (OD of largest cable × 24) + ODs of other cables

See Problems 4-15 and 4-16.

PROBLEM 4-15

Angle Pull

OD = 1⅛ in.
OD = ¾ in.

1. Calculate the minimum size pull box measurements for dimensions A, B, C, and D using the following pull box containing only shielded single-conductor high-voltage cables.
2. Calculate the minimum size pull box measurements for dimensions A, B, C, and D using the following pull box containing only nonshielded single-conductor high-voltage cables.

Dimension (A) = Length
Dimension (B) = Width
Dimension (C) = Diagonal for large conductors
Dimension (D) = Diagonal for small conductors

Solution

Calculation 1 Shielded Conductors - 314.71(B)(1)
Find: Min. dimensions for (A) length and (B) width
Min. length of side = (OD of largest cable × 36) + OD of other cables

OD of largest cable =	1 ⅛ in. → 1.125 in.	
OD of smallest =	¾ in. → 0.75 in.	
OD of largest × 36 =	1.125 in. × 36	40.50 in.
OD of others =	2 × 1.125 in.	2.25 in.
	3 × 0.75 in.	2.25 in.
Total		45.00 in.

Answer: Both (A) length and (B) height = 45 in. min.

Shielded Conductors - 314.71(B)(1)
Find: Min. length of diagonal lines (C) and (D)
Min. length of diagonal = OD of cable × 36

OD of largest (C) =	1 ⅛ in. → 1.125 in.	
OD of smallest (D) =	¾ in. → 0.75 in.	
(C) diagonal length =	1.125 in. × 36	40.5 in.
(D) diagonal length =	0.75 in. × 36	27.0 in.

Answers: (C) diagonal = 40.5 in. min.
(D) diagonal = 27 in. min.

Calculation 2 Nonshielded Conductors - 314.71(B)(1) Ex. No. 2
Find: Min. dimensions for (A) length and (B) width
Min length of side = (OD of largest cable × 24) + OD of other cables

OD of largest cable =	1 ⅛ in. → 1.125 in.	
OD of smallest =	¾ in. → 0.75 in.	
OD of largest × 24 =	1.125 in × 24	27.00 in.
OD of others =	2 × 1.125 in.	2.25 in.
	3 × 0.75 in.	2.25 in.
Total		31.50 in.

Answer: 31.50 in. → 32 in. minimum length or width

Nonshielded Conductors
Find: Min. length of diagonal lines (C) and (D)
Min. length of diagonal = OD of largest × 24

OD of largest (C) =	1 ⅛ in. → 1.125 in.	
OD of smallest (D) =	¾ in. → 0.75 in.	
(C) diagonal length =	1.125 in. × 24	27 in.
(D) diagonal length =	0.75 in. × 24	18 in.

Answers: (C) diagonal = 27 in. min.
(D) diagonal = 18 in. min.

CHAPTER 4 BOXES

Back-to-back 90° bends consist of two 90° bends fabricated in the same length of conduit.

Power-driven threaders, often called "power ponies," are very similar to hand-driven threaders. However, power-driven threaders use a reversible electric motor to turn the die head. Power-driven threaders require the use of a hand oiler and can thread ½-inch to two-inch conduit. They are often used as the power supply for die heads directly mounted on large conduit.

4.6.4 Cable Entry Opposite Removable Cover

NEC 314.71(B)(1) Exception No. 1 gives permission to reduce the box dimension where a conductor or cable for a system rated over 1,000 volts enters from the wall of a box opposite a removable cover. Where this type of cable enters a box in this manner, the distance from the wall of the box to the cover is based on the diameter of the conductor or cable according to **Section 300.34**. **Section 300.34** requires the following minimum bending radius:

Single Conductor

Shielded	12 × overall diameter
Nonshielded	8 × overall diameter
Lead-covered	12 × overall diameter

PROBLEM 4-16

Calculate the dimensions A and B and the diagonal entry and exit measurements (C and D) for the illustrated junction box using multiple single-conductor neoprene jacketed cables for both a shielded and a nonshielded cable installation. Note that since both the entry side and exit side cables are the same, the box will be square, and therefore dimension A equals dimension B.

Solution

Calculation 1– Shielded Cable - 314.71(B)

Find: Min. dimensions for (A) length and (B) width

Length = (OD of largest cable × 36) + OD of other cables
= (1.75 in. × 36) + 1 in.
= 64 in.

Answer: (A) = 64 in. and (B) = 64 in.

Find: Min length of diagonal lines (C) and (D)
Min. length of diagonal = OD of cable × 36

(C) diagonal length = 1.75 in. × 36   63 in.
(D) diagonal length = 1.00 in. × 36   36 in.

Answers: (C) diagonal = 63 in. min.
(D) diagonal = 36 in. min.

Calculation 2– Nonshielded Conductors - 314.71(B), Ex. No. 2

Find: Min. dimensions for (A) length and (B) width
Length = (1.75 in. × 24) + 1 in.
= 42 in. + 1 in.
= 43 in.

Answer: (A) = 43 in. and (B) = 43 in.
Find: Min length of diagonal lines (C) and (D)
Min. length of diagonal = OD of cable × 24

(C) diagonal length = 1.75 in. × 24   42 in.
(D) diagonal length = 1.00 in. × 24   24 in.

Answers: (C) diagonal = 42 in. min.
(D) diagonal = 24 in. min.

For multiconductor or multiplexed single-conductors, having individually shielded conductors:

The greater of either:

| Individually shielded conductors | 12 × diameter |
| Overall diameter of cable | 7 × overall diameter |

See Problems 4-17 and 4-18.

PROBLEM 4-17

Three single-conductor 4/0 AWG shielded 5kV feeder conductors are pulled through an angle box with a removable cover directly opposite the raceway entry. Calculate the minimum depth of the box. (The OD for a single 4/0 AWG shielded 5kV cable is 0.825 in.)

Solution

314.71(B) Exception No.1 and 300.34

Depth = OD of cable × 12
= 0.825 × 12
= 9.9 → 10 in.

Answer: 10 in. minimum

PROBLEM 4-18

A multiconductor 5kV cable, consisting of four 2 AWG shielded conductors, is pulled through an angle box with a removable cover directly opposite the raceway entry. Calculate the minimum depth of the box. (The OD of each 2 AWG shielded 5kV conductor in the cable assembly is 0.572 in. The OD of the overall cable assembly is 1.28 in.)

Solution

314.71(B) Exception No. 1 and 300.34

Depth = OD of cable × 12
= 0.572 × 12
= 6.864 in.

Depth = OD of cable assembly × 7
= 1.28 × 7
= 8.96 in.

Use the greater of the two calculations

Answer: 8.96 in. → 9 in. minimum

DEFINITIONS AND TERMS

Conduit Body - A separate portion of a conduit or tubing system that provides access through a removable cover(s) to the interior of the system at a junction of two or more sections of the system or at a terminal point of the system. [**70**:100] Boxes such as FS and FD or larger cast or sheet metal boxes are not classified as conduit bodies.

Connector, Pressure (Solderless) - A device that establishes a connection between two or more conductors or between one or more conductors and a terminal by means of mechanical pressure and without the use of solder. [**70**:100]

Device - A unit of an electrical system that carries or controls electric energy as its principal function. [**70**:100]

Equipment - A general term, including fittings, devices, appliances, luminaires, apparatus, machinery, and the like used as a part of, or in connection with, an electrical installation. [**70**:100]

Fitting - An accessory such as a locknut, bushing, or other part of a wiring system that is intended primarily to perform a mechanical rather than an electrical function. [**70**:100]

Handhole Enclosure - An enclosure for use in underground systems, provided with an open or closed bottom, and sized to allow personnel to reach into, but not enter, for the purpose of installing, operating, or maintaining equipment or wiring or both. [**70**:100]

Lighting Outlet - An outlet intended for the direct connection of a lampholder or luminaire. [**70**:100]

Outlet - A point on the wiring system at which current is taken to supply utilization equipment. [**70**:100]

Receptacle - A contact device installed at the outlet for the connection of an attachment plug, or for the direct connection of electrical utilization equipment designed to mate with the corresponding contact device. A single receptacle is a single contact device with no other contact device on the same yoke or strap. A multiple receptacle is two or more contact devices on the same yoke or strap. [**70**:100]

Receptacle Outlet - An outlet where one or more receptacles are installed. [**70**:100]

Reproduced with permission of NFPA from NFPA 70®, *National Electrical Code*® (NEC®), 2020 edition. Copyright© 2019, National Fire Protection Association. For a full copy of the NEC®, please go to www.nfpa.org.

SUMMARY

For conductors 6 AWG and smaller, the minimum required enclosure is sized based on a volume calculation in accordance with **Section 314.16**. The installer should first determine the permitted volume of the box (and assembled sections such as plaster rings, extension rings, and so forth), and ensure the volumes of items installed in the box (such as conductors, devices, clamps, and so forth) do not exceed the volume of the box assembly. Sufficient space is necessary for the conductors to provide for an installation to be free of short-circuits, ground-faults, and other hazards.

For conductors 4 AWG and larger, the minimum enclosure is sized based on multiplication factors of the raceways in accordance with **Section 314.28**. For straight-pull installations, multiply the diameter of the largest straight pull raceway by eight. For angles, U-pulls, or splices, multiply the diameter of the largest angle, U-pull, or splice raceway by six and add the diameter(s) of all other raceways in the row to determine the distance from the raceway entry to the opposite wall. Adequate space is required to be able to pull and feed the conductors into the raceways without damaging the insulation of the conductors due to limited space. For pull and junction boxes used in systems over 1,000 volts, nominal, the calculations in **Section 314.71** are based upon multiplication factors of the largest outside diameter of shielded and nonshielded conductors or cables within each raceway.

REVIEW QUESTIONS

1. What is the proper method to determine the usable volume for a standard metal device box that is not marked by the manufacturer?
    a. Multiply the box dimensions of length, width, and depth
    b. Find the usable volume in **Table 314.16(A)**
    c. Look on the manufacturer's website
    d. Multiply the box dimensions of length and width

2. A four-inch square metal box that is 1½ inches deep is installed with a single-gang mudring with a volume marked on it of 3.5 cubic inches. What is the volume of the box assembly?
    a. 21.0 in.^{3}
    b. 24.5 in.^{3}
    c. 27.5 in.^{3}
    d. 33.8 in.^{3}

3. To determine conductor fill per **314.16(B)**, a conductor that originates outside of the box and passes straight through a box without splice or termination would be counted __?__.
    a. as 2.0 in.^{3}
    b. once
    c. twice
    d. It would not be counted.

4. When a 20-ampere, 125-volt duplex receptacle is installed in a box, the proper volume allowance for the device is __?__.
    a. a double volume allowance based on the largest conductor terminated to the device
    b. based on a single volume allowance of the largest conductor in the box
    c. based on the volume of the largest two conductors in the box
    d. not required to be counted if there are no internal cable clamps present

REVIEW QUESTIONS

5. Multiple equipment grounding conductors of various sizes, originating outside of the junction box, are installed and spliced inside the junction box. What is the minimum volume allowance required for the equipment grounding conductors?
   a. A single volume allowance is required based on the largest equipment grounding conductor present in the box.
   b. A single volume allowance is required for each different size equipment grounding conductor.
   c. A volume allowance is required for each equipment grounding conductor.
   d. No volume allowance is required if the equipment grounding conductors are bare.

6. What is the minimum volume allowance required for an 8 AWG conductor?
   a. 2.0 in.^{3}
   b. 2.5 in.^{3}
   c. 3.0 in.^{3}
   d. None of the above

7. What is the minimum required volume for a box with internal cable clamps that contains two 14-2 NM-B clamps with ground nonmetallic sheathed cables that originate outside of the box and supply a duplex receptacle in the box?
   a. 14 in.^{3}
   b. 16 in.^{3}
   c. 18 in.^{3}
   d. 20 in.^{3}

8. What is required to determine the minimum length of a straight-pull junction box for use with conductors 4 AWG and larger?
   a. Multiply the diameter of the largest raceway by 6
   b. Multiply the diameter of the largest raceway by 6 and add the diameter(s) of all other raceways in the row
   c. Multiply the diameter of the largest straight-pull raceway by 8
   d. Multiply the diameter of the largest straight-pull raceway by 8 and add the diameter(s) of all other raceways in the row

9. What is required to determine the minimum distance from the side the raceway enters to the opposite wall for an angle pull box with conductors 4 AWG and larger?
   a. Multiply the diameter of the largest angle-pull raceway by 6
   b. Multiply the diameter of the largest angle-pull raceway by 6 and add the diameter(s) of all other raceways in the row
   c. Multiply the diameter of the largest raceway by 8
   d. Multiply the diameter of the largest raceway by 8 and add the diameter(s) of all other raceways in the row

10. What is required to determine the minimum length of a straight-pull junction box that contains a 5,000-volt shielded cable?
    a. Multiply the diameter of the largest raceway by 6, and add the diameter(s) of all other raceways in the row
    b. Multiply the diameter of the largest raceway by 8
    c. Multiply the outside diameter of the cable by 32
    d. Multiply the outside diameter of the cable by 48

CHAPTER 5
RACEWAY FILL

Determining the number of conductors permitted to be installed in a raceway is one of the more common *Code* calculations performed by field installers, and can range from a simple to a complex calculation. In some instances, Electrical Workers are provided with detailed plans which make determining the number of conductors and the size of the raceway simple. In other cases, Electrical Workers are not provided with any prepared plans or specifications and are required to determine raceway fill calculations themselves, which may be challenging. With a proper understanding of the *National Electrical Code (NEC)* requirements of raceway fill calculations, and by breaking the operation down to simple steps, the process can be straightforward and organized.

Any *Code* user will benefit from a comprehensive review of the raceway fill calculation process using the **Chapter 3** wiring methods of the *NEC*. First, conduit and tubing wire fill calculations, including single and multiconductor cables, will be introduced using a step-by-step process to demonstrate the varied types of circular raceway fill calculations. Next, round and rectangular underfloor raceways must be considered, using the same step-by-step process. Square and rectangular raceways manufactured as metallic and nonmetallic wireways and auxiliary gutters must be considered separately, since calculating fill for these wiring methods uses a different process. Alternate raceways such as surface metal and nonmetallic raceways use manufacturer-specific look-up tables to determine specific conductor (and device) fill parameters.

OBJECTIVES

- Correctly apply the conductor fill requirements for raceways with one or more conductors installed.

- Calculate the maximum number of conductors permitted in specified raceways if all of the conductors are of the same size.

- Calculate the maximum number of conductors permitted in specified raceways if the conductors are of different sizes.

- Apply the **Notes to Chapter 9, Table 1**, as they relate to raceway fill.

- Determine, understand, and apply the different raceway-specific requirements as they apply to conductor fill calculations.

- Understand and apply manufacturer-specific conductor fill tables to specific surface raceways.

TABLE OF CONTENTS

5.1	**CONDUIT AND TUBING FILLS**	**90**
.1	Wiring Methods Covered	90
.2	Chapter 9, Table 1 and Accompanying Notes	90
.3	Annex C Tables	91
.4	Using Annex C Tables for Conduit and Tubing Fill	92
.5	Insulation Thickness	92
.6	Fixture Wires	93
5.2	**USING TABLES 4 AND 5 OF CHAPTER 9**	**93**
.1	Insulation Outer Covering	96
.2	Counting All Conductors	96
.3	Insulated and Bare Grounding and Bonding Conductors	97
5.3	**USING TABLES 4 AND 5A OF CHAPTER 9**	**98**
5.4	**USING TABLE 8 OF CHAPTER 9 FOR BARE CONDUCTORS**	**98**
5.5	**SHORT NIPPLE FILL USING NOTE 4 TO TABLE 1 OF CHAPTER 9**	**101**
5.6	**USING NOTE 7 TO TABLE 1 OF CHAPTER 9**	**102**
5.7	**MULTICONDUCTOR CABLES IN CONDUIT OR TUBING**	**102**
5.8	**ADDING CONDUCTORS TO EXISTING CONDUIT OR TUBING**	**103**
5.9	**TABLES FOR $3/8$-INCH FLEXIBLE METAL CONDUIT**	**103**
5.10	**UNDERFLOOR TYPE RACEWAYS**	**104**
.1	General	104
.2	Cross-Sectional Area Calculation for a Rectangular Underfloor Raceway	105
.3	Cross-Sectional Area Calculation for a Circular Underfloor Raceway	106
5.11	**METAL WIREWAYS, NONMETALLIC WIREWAYS, AND AUXILIARY GUTTERS**	**107**
.1	Article 376, Metal Wireways	107
.2	Article 378, Nonmetallic Wireways	108
.3	Article 366, Auxiliary Gutters	109
DEFINITIONS AND TERMS		**110**
SUMMARY		**110**
REVIEW QUESTIONS		**111**

5.1 CONDUIT AND TUBING FILLS

The *NEC* contains strict requirements to limit the number and size of conductors drawn into a conduit or tubing, but the *NEC* does not regulate the overall length of a conduit in most cases.

5.1.1 Wiring Methods Covered

The conduit and tubing wiring methods recognized in **Chapter 3** of the *NEC* refer to **Chapter 9, Table 1** for the maximum number of conductors permitted in the conduit or tubing. The following is a list of sections and wiring methods that refer to **Chapter 9, Table 1**:

342.22 Intermediate Metal Conduit: Type IMC
344.22 Rigid Metal Conduit: Type RMC
348.22* Flexible Metal Conduit: Type FMC
350.22(A)* Liquidtight Flexible Metal Conduit: Type LFMC
352.22 Rigid Polyvinyl Chloride Conduit: Type PVC
353.22 High Density Polyethylene Conduit: Type HDPE Conduit
354.22 Nonmetallic Underground Conduit with Conductors: Type NUCC
355.22 Reinforced Thermosetting Resin Conduit: Type RTRC
356.22 Liquidtight Flexible Nonmetallic Conduit: Type LFNC
358.22 Electrical Metallic Tubing: Type EMT
360.22(A)* Flexible Metallic Tubing: Type FMT
362.22 Electric Nonmetallic Tubing: Type ENT

*These wiring methods are also available in the trade size of ³/₈-inch, in which case the user should refer specifically to **Table 348.22** for insulated conductor fill.

For a more complete list, see **Section 300.17**.

In addition to conduit and tubing, other wiring methods such as underfloor raceways, auxiliary gutters, and wireways should be covered.

5.1.2 Chapter 9, Table 1 and Accompanying Notes

Chapter 9, Table 1 gives the maximum conduit and tubing fills permitted for any standard size conduit or tubing wiring method. It applies when all the conductors are the same size with the same insulation, and it applies when the conductor sizes and/or insulations are mixed.

For a single-conductor installation, **Table 1** permits a fill percentage of 53%, and for a two-conductor installation, a fill percentage of 31%. If there are three or more conductors in the conduit or tubing, **Table 1** limits the raceway or conduit fill to 40% of the internal cross-sectional area of all standard-sized conduit or tubing.

Note the reduction in fill percentage for the two-conductor installation. If two conductors are installed in a raceway, the outside diameters of the two conductors must be less than the internal diameter of the raceway, leaving excessive space in the raceway. With three or more conductors, the space in the raceway is more effectively utilized. See Figure 5-1.

When all of the conductors and/or fixture wires have the same insulation and are the same size, **Table 1, Note 1** refers the user to the tables in **Annex C** of the *Code*. The *Code* uses the annexes to present additional information. Because the tables in **Annex C** fulfill the correct fill requirements of **Chapter 9, Table 1**, the tables are often usable in the field. However, the tables are also based on conductors meeting all of the following requirements:

1. All the conductors are the same size.
2. All the conductors have the same insulation type.

1-Conductor 2-Conductors 3-Conductors

53% 31% 40%

Figure 5-1. Chapter 9, Table 1 Fill Percentages. Notice the excessive unfilled space for the two-conductor installation. Although three conductors or more may fill the raceway more effectively, with only three conductors installed, jamming in the raceway is a concern and is addressed in **Chapter 9, Table 1, Informational Note No. 2**.

Figure 5-2. Solid and Stranded Conductors. *Both copper and aluminum conductors are available in standard and compact wire stranding.*

The **Annex C** tables are titled **Conduit and Tubing Fill Tables for Conductors and Fixture Wires of the Same Size**. These tables are used for solid or stranded copper conductors. Some tables are reserved for "compact conductors" only. These are usable for all compact conductors, including both copper and aluminum. **See Figure 5-2**.

> Compact stranding is the result of a manufacturing process where the stranded conductor is compressed to the extent that the interstices (voids between strand wires) are virtually eliminated.

5.1.3 Annex C Tables

There are 33 separate fill tables in **Annex C**. Tables identified as "C" are for solid and concentric stranded conductors, while tables identified as "C(A)" are only for compact stranded conductors. New for the 2020 *NEC* are **Tables C.14** through **C.20** for permitted fill allowances in cable trays, which will be covered in more detail later.

The fills listed in **Tables C.1** through **C.13** are based on the fill limitation required in **Chapter 9, Table 1**. The calculations for the fill are already made in the tables for the various standard trade sizes. There are 13 tables that serve solid and stranded conductors and 13 tables that serve compact stranded conductors. The compact conductor tables are close to one page in length, whereas the solid and concentric (most common) stranded conductor tables are roughly four pages in length.

Because the inside cross-sectional areas of the various conduits and tubings are different, the actual fill will be different. Therefore, there is a separate table for almost every raceway containing standard conductors, and a separate table for almost every raceway containing compact conductors. (Note that reinforced thermosetting resin conduit (RTRC) continues to be omitted from **Table 4** and **Annex C**). The manufacturer should be contacted for appropriate technical dimensions to determine proper raceway fill.

There are two tables for each raceway type. The tables for standard solid and concentric stranded conductors are listed (note that these tables are listed in alphabetical order):

- **C.1 Electrical Metallic Tubing (EMT)**
- **C.2 Electrical Nonmetallic Tubing (ENT)**
- **C.3 Flexible Metal Conduit (FMC)**
- **C.4 Intermediate Metal Conduit (IMC)**
- **C.5 Liquidtight Flexible Nonmetallic Conduit (Type LFNC-A)**
- **C.6 Liquidtight Flexible Nonmetallic Conduit (Type LFNC-B)**
- **C.7 Liquidtight Flexible Nonmetallic Conduit (Type LFNC-C)**
- **C.8 Liquidtight Flexible Metal Conduit (LFMC)**
- **C.9 Rigid Metal Conduit (RMC)**
- **C.10 Rigid PVC Conduit, Schedule 80**
- **C.11 Rigid PVC Conduit, Schedule 40 and HDPE Conduit**
- **C.12 Type A, Rigid PVC Conduit**
- **C.13 Type EB, PVC Conduit**

Add an "A" to the above table numbers [for example: **C.1(A)**] and another complete set of tables is presented for compact conductors.

Notice that more compacted conductors of a corresponding size and insulation are permitted to be installed in the same standard size conduit than ordinary stranded copper conductors. For example, in a two-inch rigid metal conduit using 1 AWG THHN conductors, the maximum number of conductors permitted is:

C.9 1 AWG THHN (stranded) = 8 conductors
C.9(A) 1 AWG THHN (compact) = 10 conductors

See Figure 5-3. Compact conductor cables are available in either copper or aluminum construction, and the dimensions found in **Chapter 9, Table 5A** reflect both compact aluminum and compact copper building wire.

There are 10 notes and two informational notes to **Chapter 9, Table 1**. Many of these notes cover specific installations. For example, **Note 2** of this table indicates that when a conduit or tubing is used for physical protection of the conductors, the fill is not limited by **Table 1**. This includes such installations as cable sleeves and the supplemental protection of direct burial conductors emerging from the ground. However, the fundamental requirements of **Section 300.17** must be implemented to prevent cable or conductor damage.

5.1.4 Using Annex C Tables for Conduit and Tubing Fill

To avoid errors working with look-up tables in **Annex C**, use these steps:

1. Read the table header to make sure the correct tables are being used.
2. Based on raceway size, determine which column to use.
3. Select the proper row based on insulation type and conductor size.
4. Using a straight edge just below the selected row, follow the edge to the correct column and select the proper number.
5. Double-check the results.

See Problems 5-1 and 5-2.

5.1.5 Insulation Thickness

When determining the number of conductors permitted in a conduit or tubing, the thickness of the insulation and the jacket or outer covering, when present, is also taken into consideration. When an outer covering is added to the insulation of a conductor during manufacturing, it increases both the diameter and the cross-sectional area of the conductor. Therefore, it will, in turn, reduce the number of conductors permitted to be installed in a conduit or tubing without exceeding the 40% fill for three or more insulated conductors.

Some Type RHW, RHW-2, and RHH insulations do not require an outer covering and are marked with an asterisk in **Chapter 9, Table 5**, as well as in the **Annex C** tables. Other outer coverings are found in **Table 310.4(A)** and the

Raceway Fill Comparison
Maximum 8 AWG XHHW-2 within a 1 ½-inch Circular Raceway

Type of Raceway	Table No.	No. of Conductors	Compact Table No.	No. of Compact Conductors
EMT	C.1	18	C.1(A)	20
ENT	C.2	18	C.2(A)	20
FMC	C.3	17	C.3(A)	19
IMC	C.4	20	C.4(A)	22
LFNC-B	C.5	18	C.5(A)	20
LFMC	C.8	18	C.8(A)	20
RMC	C.9	19	C.9(A)	21
PVC Schedule 80	C.10	15	C.10(A)	17

Note: XHHW and not XHHW-2. Often XHHW and XHHW-2 use the same dimensions, as shown in Chapter 9, Table 5.

Figure 5-3. Concentric Lay Stranded versus Compact Stranded. A comparison of raceway fills using the maximum number of 8 AWG XHHW-2 in a 1 ½-inch circular raceway demonstrates the different fill requirements for concentric and compact conductors.

CHAPTER 5 RACEWAY FILL

PROBLEM 5-1

What is the maximum number of 4 AWG THHN copper conductors permitted in a 2-inch rigid metal conduit (RMC)?

Solution

Annex C Table of Contents points to Table C.8 for Rigid Metal Conduit (RMC)
Table C.8, Rigid Metal Conduit (RMC)
Max. 4 AWG THHN in 2 in. = 16 conductors
Answer: 16 conductors

PROBLEM 5-2

What is the maximum number of 4 AWG THHN compact aluminum conductors permitted in a 2-inch intermediate metal conduit (IMC)?

Solution

Annex C Table of Contents points to Table C.4(A) for Intermediate Metal Conduit (IMC)
Table C.4(A) Intermediate Metal Conduit (IMC)
Max. 4 AWG THHN in 2 in. = 20 conductors
Answer: 20 conductors

PROBLEM 5-3

1. What is the maximum number of 12 AWG RHW conductors without an outer covering that is permitted in a 1-inch rigid metal conduit (RMC)?
2. What is the maximum number of 12 AWG RHW conductors with an outer covering that is permitted in a 1-inch rigid metal conduit (RMC)?

Solution

Calculation 1
RHW without outer covering (RHW*)
Table C.8 Rigid Metal Conduit
  Max. 12 AWG RHW in 1-in. RMC = 13 conductors
Answer: 13 conductors

Calculation 2
RHW with outer covering (RHW)
Table C.8 Rigid Metal Conduit
  Max. 12 AWG RHW in 1-in. RMC = 10 conductors
Answer: 10 conductors

PROBLEM 5-4

What is the maximum number of 18 AWG, Type SFF-2 fixture wires permitted in a $^3/_4$-inch electrical metallic tubing (EMT)?

Solution

Table C.1 Electrical Metallic Tubing
  Max. 18 AWG SFF-2 in $^3/_4$-in. EMT = 18 conductors
Answer: 18 conductors

accompanying footnotes. For the purposes of calculation, include the outer covering dimensions only where an outer covering is specifically mentioned in the scenario. **See Problem 5-3**.

5.1.6 Fixture Wires

Although traditionally used for luminaire wiring, fixture wire is also permitted to be used for Class 1 circuits in **Section 725.49** and Class 2 and 3 circuits in **725.130(B)**, provided they are installed in and protected by a **Chapter 3** wiring method. For fire alarm circuit wiring, **Article 760** has similar permissions found in **760.49**. Another traditional use of fixture wire is for motor control circuits in compliance with **Section 430.72**.

  Section 402.7 refers to **Chapter 9, Table 1** for determining the maximum number of fixture wires that are permitted in a conduit or tubing. **Chapter 9, Table 1** refers to the fill tables in **Annex C**. Fixture wires are found in all of the **Annex C** tables, but fixture wires are not listed in the compact tables. **See Problem 5-4**.

5.2 USING TABLES 4 AND 5 OF CHAPTER 9

According to **Chapter 9, Table 1, Note 6**, where there is a combination of conductors with different sizes and/or insulations, **Tables 4**, **5**, and **5A** of **Chapter 9** are used for calculating the minimum size conduit or tubing. For calculating fills of combinations of conductors, the square inch area of a cross-section of a raceway is used. The **Table 4** charts contain the calculated square inch areas of a cross-section of standard size conduits and the permitted fill percentage. **Table 5** and **Table 5A** contain the square inch area of a cross-section of conductors including insulation and covering (if any).

Because each type of conduit and tubing has a different interior cross-sectional area, **Table 4** consists of 13 separate charts. There is one chart for each type of conduit or tubing. The fills listed in each chart of **Table 4** are based on **Table 1** fill percentages. **See Figure 5-4**. **Table 4** contains many other charts specific to other wiring methods. Each chart is laid out identically to the EMT chart. Note that each chart gives 100% of the cross-sectional area, in square inches, of each of the standard

Table 4 Dimensions and Percent Area of Conduit and Tubing (Areas of Conduit or Tubing for the Combinations of Wires Permitted in Table 1, Chapter 9)

Article 358 — Electrical Metallic Tubing (EMT)

Metric Designator	Trade Size	Over 2 Wires 40% mm²	in.²	60% mm²	in.²	1 Wire 53% mm²	in.²	2 Wires 31% mm²	in.²	Nominal Internal Diameter mm	in.	Total Area 100% mm²	in.²
16	½	78	0.122	118	0.182	104	0.161	61	0.094	15.8	0.622	196	0.304
21	¾	137	0.213	206	0.320	182	0.283	106	0.165	20.9	0.824	343	0.533
27	1	222	0.346	333	0.519	295	0.458	172	0.268	26.6	1.049	556	0.864
35	1¼	387	0.598	581	0.897	513	0.793	300	0.464	35.1	1.380	968	1.496
41	1½	526	0.814	788	1.221	696	1.079	407	0.631	40.9	1.610	1314	2.036
53	2	866	1.342	1299	2.013	1147	1.778	671	1.040	52.5	2.067	2165	3.356
63	2½	1513	2.343	2270	3.515	2005	3.105	1173	1.816	69.4	2.731	3783	5.858
78	3	2280	3.538	3421	5.307	3022	4.688	1767	2.742	85.2	3.356	5701	8.846
91	3½	2980	4.618	4471	6.927	3949	6.119	2310	3.579	97.4	3.834	7451	11.545
103	4	3808	5.901	5712	8.852	5046	7.819	2951	4.573	110.1	4.334	9521	14.753

Article 362 — Electrical Nonmetallic Tubing (ENT)

Metric Designator	Trade Size	Over 2 Wires 40% mm²	in.²	60% mm²	in.²	1 Wire 53% mm²	in.²	2 Wires 31% mm²	in.²	Nominal Internal Diameter mm	in.	Total Area 100% mm²	in.²
16	½	73	0.114	110	0.171	97	0.151	57	0.088	15.3	0.602	184	0.285
21	¾	131	0.203	197	0.305	174	0.269	102	0.157	20.4	0.804	328	0.508
27	1	215	0.333	322	0.499	284	0.441	166	0.258	26.1	1.029	537	0.832
35	1¼	375	0.581	562	0.872	497	0.770	291	0.450	34.5	1.36	937	1.453
41	1½	512	0.794	769	1.191	679	1.052	397	0.616	40.4	1.59	1281	1.986
53	2	849	1.316	1274	1.975	1125	1.744	658	1.020	52	2.047	2123	3.291
63	2½	—	—	—	—	—	—	—	—	—	—	—	—
78	3	—	—	—	—	—	—	—	—	—	—	—	—
91	3½	—	—	—	—	—	—	—	—	—	—	—	—

Article 348 — Flexible Metal Conduit (FMC)

Metric Designator	Trade Size	Over 2 Wires 40% mm²	in.²	60% mm²	in.²	1 Wire 53% mm²	in.²	2 Wires 31% mm²	in.²	Nominal Internal Diameter mm	in.	Total Area 100% mm²	in.²
12	⅜	30	0.046	44	0.069	39	0.061	23	0.036	9.7	0.384	74	0.116
16	½	81	0.127	122	0.190	108	0.168	63	0.098	16.1	0.635	204	0.317
21	¾	137	0.213	206	0.320	182	0.283	106	0.165	20.9	0.824	343	0.533
27	1	211	0.327	316	0.490	279	0.433	163	0.253	25.9	1.020	527	0.817
35	1¼	330	0.511	495	0.766	437	0.677	256	0.396	32.4	1.275	824	1.277
41	1½	480	0.743	720	1.115	636	0.985	372	0.576	39.1	1.538	1201	1.858
53	2	843	1.307	1264	1.961	1117	1.732	653	1.013	51.8	2.040	2107	3.269
63	2½	1267	1.963	1900	2.945	1678	2.602	982	1.522	63.5	2.500	3167	4.909
78	3	1824	2.827	2736	4.241	2417	3.746	1414	2.191	76.2	3.000	4560	7.069
91	3½	2483	3.848	3724	5.773	3290	5.099	1924	2.983	88.9	3.500	6207	9.621
103	4	3243	5.027	4864	7.540	4297	6.660	2513	3.896	101.6	4.000	8107	12.566

Article 342 — Intermediate Metal Conduit (IMC)

Metric Designator	Trade Size	Over 2 Wires 40% mm²	in.²	60% mm²	in.²	1 Wire 53% mm²	in.²	2 Wires 31% mm²	in.²	Nominal Internal Diameter mm	in.	Total Area 100% mm²	in.²
12	⅜	—	—	—	—	—	—	—	—	—	—	—	—
16	½	89	0.137	133	0.205	117	0.181	69	0.106	16.8	0.660	222	0.342
21	¾	151	0.235	226	0.352	200	0.311	117	0.182	21.9	0.864	377	0.586
27	1	248	0.384	372	0.575	329	0.508	192	0.297	28.1	1.105	620	0.959

Figure 5-4. Chapter 9, Table 4, EMT. The column for the most common fill percentage of 40% is located to the left in the table next to the column for raceway sizes to improve usability.

Reproduced with permission of NFPA from NFPA 70®, *National Electrical Code®* (NEC®), 2020 edition. Copyright© 2019, National Fire Protection Association. For a full copy of the NEC®, please go to www.nfpa.org.

size raceways in both metric and English units. The table also has a calculated 40% fill column, which is 40% of the 100% column. These two values may come in handy when calculating conduit and tubing fills. The column "Over 2 Wires, 40%" will be the most used column and is now located close to the trade size column to reduce "lookup errors."

Chapter 9, Table 5, is dedicated to conductors other than compact conductors. **See Figure 5-5**.

Table 5 Dimensions of Insulated Conductors and Fixture Wires

Type	Size (AWG or kcmil)	Approximate Area mm²	Approximate Area in.²	Approximate Diameter mm	Approximate Diameter in.
Type: FFH-2, RFH-1, RFH-2, RFHH-2, RHH*, RHW*, RHW-2*, RHH, RHW, RHW-2, SF-1, SF-2, SFF-1, SFF-2, TF, TFF, THHW, THW, THW-2, TW, XF, XFF					
RFH-2, FFH-2, RFHH-2	18	9.355	0.0145	3.454	0.136
	16	11.10	0.0172	3.759	0.148
RHH, RHW, RHW-2	14	18.90	0.0293	4.902	0.193
	12	22.77	0.0353	5.385	0.212
	10	28.19	0.0437	5.994	0.236
	8	53.87	0.0835	8.280	0.326
	6	67.16	0.1041	9.246	0.364
	4	86.00	0.1333	10.46	0.412
	3	98.13	0.1521	11.18	0.440
	2	112.9	0.1750	11.99	0.472
	1	171.6	0.2660	14.78	0.582
	1/0	196.1	0.3039	15.80	0.622
	2/0	226.1	0.3505	16.97	0.668
	3/0	262.7	0.4072	18.29	0.720
	4/0	306.7	0.4754	19.76	0.778
	250	405.9	0.6291	22.73	0.895
	300	457.3	0.7088	24.13	0.950
	350	507.7	0.7870	25.43	1.001
	400	556.5	0.8626	26.62	1.048
	500	650.5	1.0082	28.78	1.133
	600	782.9	1.2135	31.57	1.243
	700	874.9	1.3561	33.38	1.314
	750	920.8	1.4272	34.24	1.348
	800	965.0	1.4957	35.05	1.380
	900	1057	1.6377	36.68	1.444
	1000	1143	1.7719	38.15	1.502
	1250	1515	2.3479	43.92	1.729
	1500	1738	2.6938	47.04	1.852
	1750	1959	3.0357	49.94	1.966
	2000	2175	3.3719	52.63	2.072
SF-2, SFF-2	18	7.419	0.0115	3.073	0.121
	16	8.968	0.0139	3.378	0.133
	14	11.10	0.0172	3.759	0.148
SF-1, SFF-1	18	4.194	0.0065	2.311	0.091
RFH-1, TF, TFF, XF, XFF	18	5.161	0.0088	2.692	0.106
TF, TFF, XF, XFF	16	7.032	0.0109	2.997	0.118
TW, XF, XFF, THHW, THW, THW-2	14	8.968	0.0139	3.378	0.133
TW, THHW, THW, THW-2	12	11.68	0.0181	3.861	0.152
	10	15.68	0.0243	4.470	0.176
	8	28.19	0.0437	5.994	0.236
RHH*, RHW*, RHW-2*	14	13.48	0.0209	4.140	0.163
RHH*, RHW*, RHW-2*, XF, XFF	12	16.77	0.0260	4.623	0.182
Type: RHH*, RHW*, RHW-2*, THHN, THHW, THW, THW-2, TFN, TFFN, THWN, THWN-2, XF, XFF					
RHH,* RHW,* RHW-2,* XF, XFF	10	21.48	0.0333	5.232	0.206

(continues)

Figure 5-5. Chapter 9, Table 5. Table 5 of Chapter 9 shows the cross-sectional areas of conductors.

Reproduced with permission of NFPA from NFPA 70®, *National Electrical Code®* (NEC®), 2020 edition. Copyright© 2019, National Fire Protection Association. For a full copy of the NEC®, please go to www.nfpa.org.

Table 5 is applicable to solid and stranded copper and aluminum conductors and is based on "worst-case" scenario sizes. Each table lists a multitude of dimensions for insulated conductors and fixture wire. One column of the chart lists the square inch area of the conductor and is now located closer to the size column. **Note 10** applies to **Tables 5** and **5A** and indicates that where the actual values of conductor diameter and area are known, they are permitted to be used. **See Problem 5-5**.

PROBLEM 5-5

What minimum size electrical metallic tubing is needed for three 2/0 AWG XHHW-2 copper conductors and four 4/0 AWG XHHW-2 copper conductors?

Solution

Table 5
  Cross-sectional area of individual conductors
  2/0 AWG XHHW-2 = 0.2190 in.^{2}
  0.2190 × 3 =   0.6570
  4/0 AWG XHHW-2 = 0.3197 in.^{2}
  0.3197 × 4 =   1.2788
  Total square inch area: 1.9358

Table 4
  EMT chart, 40% fill column
  40% fill of 2 1/2-in. EMT = 2.343 in.^{2}
  1.9358 in.^{2} requires a 2 1/2-in. EMT
  Answer: 2 1/2-in. EMT

PROBLEM 5-6

What is the minimum size intermediate metal conduit (IMC) needed for the installation of four 14 AWG RHH copper conductors with outer coverings and six 12 AWG RHH copper conductors without outer coverings?

Solution

Table 5
  Cross-sectional area of individual conductors; first chart
  14 AWG RHH with outer covering = 0.0293 in.^{2}
  0.0293 × 4 =   0.1172
Table 5
  Second chart
  12 AWG RHH without outer covering = 0.0260 in.^{2}
  0.0260 × 6 =   0.1560
  Total square inch area: 0.2732

Table 4
  IMC chart; 40% fill column
  40% fill for 1-in. IMC = 0.384 in.^{2}
  0.2732 in.^{2} requires a 1-in. IMC
  Answer: 1-in. IMC

5.2.1 Insulation Outer Covering

It takes five charts in **Chapter 9, Table 5** and **5A** to list all of the various insulations and conductor sizes.

Note: The asterisk (*) note in **Table 5** refers to Type RHH, RHW, and RHW-2 insulation without an outer covering. There are two types of these conductors: one with an outer covering and one without an outer covering. **See Problem 5-6**.

5.2.2 Counting All Conductors

When calculating conduit and tubing fills, all conductors installed in the raceway contribute to the conductor-occupied space or conductor fill. This includes current-carrying conductors, non–current-carrying conductors, part-time current-carrying conductors, equipment bonding jumpers, and equipment grounding conductors. **See Problem 5-7**.

For additional information, visit qr.njatcdb.org Item #1031

PROBLEM 5-7

What is the minimum size intermediate metal conduit (IMC) required for the installation of three 2/0 AWG THWN copper conductors feeding a motor and three 12 AWG THHN copper conductors for the motor control circuit?

Solution

Table 5
  Cross-sectional area of individual conductors
  2/0 AWG THWN = 0.2223 in.^{2}
  0.2223 × 3 =   0.6669
  12 AWG THHN = 0.0133 in.^{2}
  0.0133 × 3 =   0.0399
  Total square inch area: 0.7068

Table 4
  IMC table; 40% fill column over 2 wires
  40% fill for 1 1/2-in. IMC = 0.890 in.^{2}
  0.7068 in.^{2} requires a 1 1/2-in. IMC
  Answer: 1 1/2-in. IMC

The NFPA standards development process encourages public participation in the development of its standards. All NFPA standards are revised and updated every three to five years in revision cycles that begin twice each year. Normally a standard's cycle takes approximately two years to complete. Each revision cycle proceeds according to a published schedule, which includes final dates for each stage in the standard's development process. The four fundamental steps in the NFPA standards development process are:

1. Public Input
2. Public Comment
3. NFPA Technical Meeting (Tech Session)
4. Standards Council Action (Appeals and Issuance of Standard)

5.2.3 Insulated and Bare Grounding and Bonding Conductors

Chapter 9, Table 1, Note 3 requires that equipment grounding or bonding conductors, where installed, shall be included in the conduit or tubing fill calculation. The actual dimensions of the equipment grounding or bonding conductor (insulated or bare) have to be used in this calculation.

Where a bare conductor is selected as the equipment grounding or bonding conductor, **Chapter 9, Table 8** is used to determine the conductor cross-sectional area. The column marked "Conductors, Overall Area, in.²" is used to determine the appropriate conductor area. The area is then added to the calculated area used by the other conductors to determine the total square inch area. **See Problem 5-8**.

PROBLEM 5-8

Four 3/0 AWG THHN copper conductors with a 6 AWG THHN copper equipment grounding conductor are to be installed in the same rigid PVC schedule 40 conduit. What is the minimum size PVC schedule 40 conduit required?

Solution

Table 5
   Cross-sectional area in square inches
   3/0 AWG THHN = 0.2679 in.²
   0.2679 × 4 =   1.0716
   6 AWG THHN = 0.0507 in.²
   0.0507 × 1 =   0.0507
   Total square inch area   1.1223

Table 4
   Rigid PVC Conduit, Schedule 40 chart
   40% fill column over 2 wires
   40% fill for 2 in. PVC = 1.316 in.²
   1.1223 in.² fill requires a 2-in. PVC, Schedule 40
   Answer: 2-in. Rigid PVC Conduit, Schedule 40

For additional information, visit qr.njatcdb.org Item #2561

5.3 USING TABLES 4 AND 5A OF CHAPTER 9

Table 5A lists the cross-sectional area in square inches for individual compact copper and aluminum conductors. See Figure 5-6.

PROBLEM 5-9

What minimum size rigid PVC schedule 80 conduit is needed for the installation of six 1 AWG XHHW compact aluminum conductors and four 6 AWG XHHW compact aluminum conductors?

Solution

Table 5A

Cross-sectional area in square inches

1 AWG XHHW = 0.1352 in.²

0.1352 × 6 =   0.8112

6 AWG XHHW = 0.0530 in.²

0.0530 × 4 =   0.2120

Total square inches   1.0232

Table 4

Rigid PVC Conduit, Schedule 80 chart

40% fill column for over 2 wires

40% fill for 2-in. PVC = 1.150 in.²

1.0232 in.² requires a 2-in. PVC

Answer: 2-in. Rigid PVC Conduit, Schedule 80

Industry sources have included compact building wire Types RHH, RHW, USE, THW, THHW, THHN, XHHW, and bare in sizes 8 AWG through 1,000 kcmil in **Table 5A**. It should be noted that XHHW-2 is not listed in **Table 5A** and may often have the same dimensions as XHHW; however, it may be necessary to consult the manufacturer's data sheets for actual dimensions.

The following is a comparison of the square inch area of a 1 AWG THHN concentric stranded conductor and a compact conductor:

Table 5 - Size 1 AWG THHN concentric stranded conductor = 0.1562 in.² area

Table 5A - Size 1 AWG THHN compact stranded conductor = 0.1352 in.² area

See Problem 5-9.

5.4 USING TABLE 8 OF CHAPTER 9 FOR BARE CONDUCTORS

A bare conductor is permitted according to two sections of the *NEC*:

- **250.118(1)** permits the use of a bare equipment grounding conductor.

Table 5A Compact Copper

Size (AWG or kcmil)	Bare Conductor Diameter mm	Bare Conductor Diameter in.	Type RHH* Approximate Diameter mm	Type RHH* Approximate Diameter in.	Type RHH* Approximate Area mm²	Type RHH* Approximate Area in.²	Types THW and THHW Approximate Diameter mm	Types THW and THHW Approximate Diameter in.	Types THW and THHW Approximate Area mm²	Types THW and THHW Approximate Area in.²	Type THHN Approximate Diameter mm	Type THHN Approximate Diameter in.	Type THHN Approximate Area mm²	Type THHN Approximate Area in.²	Type XHHW Approximate Diameter mm	Type XHHW Approximate Diameter in.	Type XHHW Approximate Area mm²	Type XHHW Approximate Area in.²	Size (AWG or kcmil)
8	3.404	0.134	6.604	0.260	34.25	0.0531	6.477	0.255	32.90	0.0510	—	—	—	—	5.690	0.224	25.42	0.0394	8
6	4.293	0.169	7.493	0.295	44.10	0.0683	7.366	0.290	42.58	0.0660	6.096	0.240	29.16	0.0452	6.604	0.260	34.19	0.0530	6
4	5.410	0.213	8.509	0.335	56.84	0.0881	8.509	0.335	56.84	0.0881	7.747	0.305	47.10	0.0730	7.747	0.305	47.10	0.0730	4
2	6.807	0.268	9.906	0.390	77.03	0.1194	9.906	0.390	77.03	0.1194	9.144	0.360	65.61	0.1017	9.144	0.360	65.61	0.1017	2
1	7.595	0.299	11.81	0.465	109.5	0.1698	11.81	0.465	109.5	0.1698	10.54	0.415	87.23	0.1352	10.54	0.415	87.23	0.1352	1
1/0	8.534	0.336	12.70	0.500	126.6	0.1963	12.70	0.500	126.6	0.1963	11.43	0.450	102.6	0.1590	11.43	0.450	102.6	0.1590	1/0
2/0	9.550	0.376	13.72	0.540	147.8	0.2290	13.84	0.545	150.5	0.2332	12.57	0.495	124.1	0.1924	12.45	0.490	121.6	0.1885	2/0
3/0	10.74	0.423	14.99	0.590	176.3	0.2733	14.99	0.590	176.3	0.2733	13.72	0.540	147.7	0.2290	13.72	0.540	147.7	0.2290	3/0
4/0	12.07	0.475	16.26	0.640	207.6	0.3217	16.38	0.645	210.8	0.3267	15.11	0.595	179.4	0.2780	14.99	0.590	176.3	0.2733	4/0
250	13.21	0.520	18.16	0.715	259.0	0.4015	18.42	0.725	266.3	0.4128	17.02	0.670	227.4	0.3525	16.76	0.660	220.7	0.3421	250
300	14.48	0.570	19.43	0.765	296.5	0.4596	19.69	0.775	304.3	0.4717	18.29	0.720	262.6	0.4071	18.16	0.715	259.0	0.4015	300
350	15.65	0.616	20.57	0.810	332.3	0.5153	20.83	0.820	340.7	0.5281	19.56	0.770	300.4	0.4656	19.30	0.760	292.6	0.4536	350
400	16.74	0.659	21.72	0.855	370.5	0.5741	21.97	0.865	379.1	0.5876	20.70	0.815	336.5	0.5216	20.32	0.800	324.3	0.5026	400
500	18.69	0.736	23.62	0.930	438.2	0.6793	23.88	0.940	447.7	0.6939	22.48	0.885	396.8	0.6151	22.35	0.880	392.4	0.6082	500
600	20.65	0.813	26.29	1.035	542.8	0.8413	26.67	1.050	558.6	0.8659	25.02	0.985	491.6	0.7620	24.89	0.980	486.6	0.7542	600
700	22.28	0.877	27.94	1.100	613.1	0.9503	28.19	1.110	624.3	0.9676	26.67	1.050	558.6	0.8659	26.67	1.050	558.6	0.8659	700
750	23.06	0.908	28.83	1.135	652.8	1.0118	29.21	1.150	670.1	1.0386	27.31	1.075	585.5	0.9076	27.69	1.090	602.0	0.9331	750
900	25.37	0.999	31.50	1.240	779.3	1.2076	31.09	1.224	759.1	1.1766	30.33	1.194	722.5	1.1196	29.69	1.169	692.3	1.0733	900
1000	26.92	1.060	32.64	1.285	836.6	1.2968	32.64	1.285	836.6	1.2968	31.88	1.255	798.1	1.2370	31.24	1.230	766.6	1.1882	1000

*Types RHH and RHW without outer coverings.

**Dimensions are from industry sources.

Figure 5-6. Chapter 9, Table 5A. An excerpt from **Table 5A** of **Chapter 9** shows the cross-sectional areas of compact copper and aluminum conductors.

Reproduced with permission of NFPA from NFPA 70®, *National Electrical Code*® (NEC®), 2020 edition. Copyright© 2019, National Fire Protection Association. For a full copy of the NEC®, please go to www.nfpa.org.

- **230.41 Exception** permits the use of a bare grounded conductor as a service-entrance conductor.

Where bare conductors are installed, **Chapter 9, Table 1, Note 8** permits the use of **Chapter 9, Table 8** for bare conductor dimensions. **Table 8, Conductor Properties**, gives various dimensions of uninsulated or bare conductors, including their cross-sectional square inch areas. **See Figure 5-7.**

Table 8 Conductor Properties

Size (AWG or kcmil)	Area mm²	Area Circular mils	Stranding Quantity	Stranding Diameter mm	Stranding Diameter in.	Overall Diameter mm	Overall Diameter in.	Overall Area mm²	Overall Area in.²	Copper Uncoated ohm/km	Copper Uncoated ohm/kFT	Copper Coated ohm/km	Copper Coated ohm/kFT	Aluminum ohm/km	Aluminum ohm/kFT
18	0.823	1620	1	—	—	1.02	0.040	0.823	0.001	25.5	7.77	26.5	8.08	42.0	12.8
18	0.823	1620	7	0.39	0.015	1.16	0.046	1.06	0.002	26.1	7.95	27.7	8.45	42.8	13.1
16	1.31	2580	1	—	—	1.29	0.051	1.31	0.002	16.0	4.89	16.7	5.08	26.4	8.05
16	1.31	2580	7	0.49	0.019	1.46	0.058	1.68	0.003	16.4	4.99	17.3	5.29	26.9	8.21
14	2.08	4110	1	—	—	1.63	0.064	2.08	0.003	10.1	3.07	10.4	3.19	16.6	5.06
14	2.08	4110	7	0.62	0.024	1.85	0.073	2.68	0.004	10.3	3.14	10.7	3.26	16.9	5.17
12	3.31	6530	1	—	—	2.05	0.081	3.31	0.005	6.34	1.93	6.57	2.01	10.45	3.18
12	3.31	6530	7	0.78	0.030	2.32	0.092	4.25	0.006	6.50	1.98	6.73	2.05	10.69	3.25
10	5.261	10380	1	—	—	2.588	0.102	5.26	0.008	3.984	1.21	4.148	1.26	6.561	2.00
10	5.261	10380	7	0.98	0.038	2.95	0.116	6.76	0.011	4.070	1.24	4.226	1.29	6.679	2.04
8	8.367	16510	1	—	—	3.264	0.128	8.37	0.013	2.506	0.764	2.579	0.786	4.125	1.26
8	8.367	16510	7	1.23	0.049	3.71	0.146	10.76	0.017	2.551	0.778	2.653	0.809	4.204	1.28
6	13.30	26240	7	1.56	0.061	4.67	0.184	17.09	0.027	1.608	0.491	1.671	0.510	2.652	0.808
4	21.15	41740	7	1.96	0.077	5.89	0.232	27.19	0.042	1.010	0.308	1.053	0.321	1.666	0.508
3	26.67	52620	7	2.20	0.087	6.60	0.260	34.28	0.053	0.802	0.245	0.833	0.254	1.320	0.403
2	33.62	66360	7	2.47	0.097	7.42	0.292	43.23	0.067	0.634	0.194	0.661	0.201	1.045	0.319
1	42.41	83690	19	1.69	0.066	8.43	0.332	55.80	0.087	0.505	0.154	0.524	0.160	0.829	0.253
1/0	53.49	105600	19	1.89	0.074	9.45	0.372	70.41	0.109	0.399	0.122	0.415	0.127	0.660	0.201
2/0	67.43	133100	19	2.13	0.084	10.62	0.418	88.74	0.137	0.3170	0.0967	0.329	0.101	0.523	0.159
3/0	85.01	167800	19	2.39	0.094	11.94	0.470	111.9	0.173	0.2512	0.0766	0.2610	0.0797	0.413	0.126
4/0	107.2	211600	19	2.68	0.106	13.41	0.528	141.1	0.219	0.1996	0.0608	0.2050	0.0626	0.328	0.100
250	127	—	37	2.09	0.082	14.61	0.575	168	0.260	0.1687	0.0515	0.1753	0.0535	0.2778	0.0847
300	152	—	37	2.29	0.090	16.00	0.630	201	0.312	0.1409	0.0429	0.1463	0.0446	0.2318	0.0707
350	177	—	37	2.47	0.097	17.30	0.681	235	0.364	0.1205	0.0367	0.1252	0.0382	0.1984	0.0605
400	203	—	37	2.64	0.104	18.49	0.728	268	0.416	0.1053	0.0321	0.1084	0.0331	0.1737	0.0529
500	253	—	37	2.95	0.116	20.65	0.813	336	0.519	0.0845	0.0258	0.0869	0.0265	0.1391	0.0424
600	304	—	61	2.52	0.099	22.68	0.893	404	0.626	0.0704	0.0214	0.0732	0.0223	0.1159	0.0353
700	355	—	61	2.72	0.107	24.49	0.964	471	0.730	0.0603	0.0184	0.0622	0.0189	0.0994	0.0303
750	380	—	61	2.82	0.111	25.35	0.998	505	0.782	0.0563	0.0171	0.0579	0.0176	0.0927	0.0282
800	405	—	61	2.91	0.114	26.16	1.030	538	0.834	0.0528	0.0161	0.0544	0.0166	0.0868	0.0265
900	456	—	61	3.09	0.122	27.79	1.094	606	0.940	0.0470	0.0143	0.0481	0.0147	0.0770	0.0235
1000	507	—	61	3.25	0.128	29.26	1.152	673	1.042	0.0423	0.0129	0.0434	0.0132	0.0695	0.0212
1250	633	—	91	2.98	0.117	32.74	1.289	842	1.305	0.0338	0.0103	0.0347	0.0106	0.0554	0.0169
1500	760	—	91	3.26	0.128	35.86	1.412	1011	1.566	0.02814	0.00858	0.02814	0.00883	0.0464	0.0141
1750	887	—	127	2.98	0.117	38.76	1.526	1180	1.829	0.02410	0.00735	0.02410	0.00756	0.0397	0.0121
2000	1013	—	127	3.19	0.126	41.45	1.632	1349	2.092	0.02109	0.00643	0.02109	0.00662	0.0348	0.0106

Notes:
1. These resistance values are valid only for the parameters as given. Using conductors having coated strands, different stranding type, and, especially, other temperatures changes the resistance.
2. Equation for temperature change: $R_2 = R_1 [1 + a (T_2 - 75)]$, where $a_{cu} = 0.00323$, $a_{AL} = 0.00330$ at 75°C.
3. Conductors with compact and compressed stranding have about 9 percent and 3 percent, respectively, smaller bare conductor diameters than those shown. See Table 5A for actual compact cable dimensions.
4. The IACS conductivities used: bare copper = 100%, aluminum = 61%.
5. Class B stranding is listed as well as solid for some sizes. Its overall diameter and area are those of its circumscribing circle.
Informational Note: The construction information is in accordance with NEMA WC/70-2009 or ANSI/UL 1581-2017. The resistance is calculated in accordance with *National Bureau of Standards Handbook 100*, dated 1966, and Handbook 109, dated 1972.

Figure 5-7. Chapter 9, Table 8 Conductor Properties. In addition to diameter and area dimensions of conductors, **Table 8** also provides information on the numbers of strands, circular mils area, and direct current resistance, which is all useful for a variety of Code calculations.

Reproduced with permission of NFPA from NFPA 70®, *National Electrical Code*® (NEC®), 2020 edition. Copyright© 2019, National Fire Protection Association. For a full copy of the NEC®, please go to www.nfpa.org.

Table 8 makes no distinction between the square inch area of a bare copper or a bare aluminum conductor. Therefore, the table is applicable to solid as well as concentric stranded copper and aluminum conductors. The insulated conductors are calculated according to **Table 5** or **5A**. For additional footnotes, refer to the actual **Chapter 9, Table 8** in the *NEC*. **See Problem 5-10**.

PROBLEM 5-10

Four 4/0 AWG THHN copper conductors and a 6 AWG bare copper equipment grounding conductor are to be installed in the same rigid PVC schedule 80 conduit. What minimum size conduit is needed?

Solution

Table 5
  Cross-sectional area of insulated conductors
Table 8
  Cross-sectional area of bare conductor
    4/0 AWG THHN = 0.3237 in.²
    0.3237 × 4 =   1.2948
    6 AWG bare = 0.0270 in.²
    0.0270 × 1 =   0.0270
    Total square inches   1.3218

Table 4
  Rigid PVC Conduit, Schedule 80 chart
  40% fill column for over 2 wires
  40% fill for 2 ½-in. PVC = 1.647 in.²
  1.3218 in.² requires a 2 ½-in. PVC
  Answer: 2 ½-in. Rigid PVC Conduit, Schedule 80

However, where bare conductors (aluminum or copper) of compact construction are used, the dimensions of **Table 5A** may be used in lieu of **Table 8**. **See Problems 5-11 and 5-12.**

Bare conductors can be used for services, feeders, or branch circuits. Grounded service-entrance conductors are permitted to be bare if they are used in a raceway or in an auxiliary gutter according to **Section 230.41**. An equipment grounding conductor may be bare when used in a feeder or branch circuit. It may be installed as a separate conductor where used in a metal raceway system and must be installed if used in nonmetallic raceway systems. Equipment grounding conductors are generally green or bare, in accordance with **250.119**. **See Problem 5-13.**

PROBLEM 5-11

A 3-phase, 4-wire, high-leg delta service is calculated to need one 4/0 AWG and two 250 kcmil phase THHW copper conductors and a bare 3/0 AWG grounded copper conductor as service entrance conductors. What is the minimum size rigid metal conduit required?

Solution

Table 5
  Cross-sectional area of insulated conductors
Table 8
  Cross-sectional area of bare conductor
    250 kcmil THHW = 0.4596 in.²
    0.4596 × 2 =   0.9192
    4/0 AWG THHW = 0.3718 in.²
    0.3718 × 1 =   0.3718
    3/0 AWG bare = 0.1730 in.²
    0.1730 in.² × 1 =   0.1730
    Total square inches   1.4640

Table 4
  Rigid Metal Conduit (RMC) chart
  40% fill for over two conductors
  40% fill for 2 ½-in. RMC = 1.946 in.²
  1.4640 in.² requires a 2 ½-in. RMC
  Answer: 2 ½-in. RMC

PROBLEM 5-12

A 3-phase, 4-wire, 120/208-volt service uses three 250-kcmil XHHW compact copper phase conductors and one bare concentric copper 4/0 AWG grounded conductor. What is the minimum conduit size required when using schedule 40 PVC conduit?

Solution

Table 5A
  Cross-sectional area of compact conductors
Table 8
  Cross-sectional area of bare conductor
    250 kcmil XHHW = 0.3421 in.²
    0.3421 × 3 =   1.0263
    4/0 AWG bare = 0.2190 in.²
    0.2190 × 1 =   0.2190
    Total square inches   1.2453

Table 4
  Rigid PVC Conduit, Schedule 40 chart
  40% fill for over 2 conductors
  40% fill for 2-in. PVC = 1.316 in.²
  1.2453 in.² requires a 2-in. PVC
  Answer: 2-in. Rigid PVC Conduit, Schedule 40

PROBLEM 5-13

A 3/0 AWG bare copper equipment bonding jumper is required to be installed in liquidtight flexible metal conduit (LFMC) with six 500 kcmil THHN copper conductors. What is the minimum size liquidtight flexible metal conduit needed between a current transformer (CT) cabinet and the service disconnecting means?

Solution

Table 5
  Cross-sectional area of insulated conductors
Table 8
  Cross-sectional area of bare conductor
    500 kcmil THHN = 0.7073 in.²
    0.7073 × 6 =   4.2438
    3/0 AWG bare = 0.1730 in.²
    0.1730 × 1 =   0.1730
    Total square inches   4.4168

Table 4
  Liquidtight Flexible Metal Conduit (LFMC) chart
  40% fill for over 2 conductors
  40% fill for 4-in. LFMC = 5.077 in.²
  4.4168 in.² requires a 4-in. LFMC

Answer: 4-in. LFMC

5.5 SHORT NIPPLE FILL USING NOTE 4 TO TABLE 1 OF CHAPTER 9

Chapter 9, Table 1, Note 4 permits nipples between boxes, cabinets, or the like, if not over 24 inches in length, to be filled to 60% of the cross-sectional area of the conduit or tubing. Each of the raceway tables within **Table 4** contains a 60% column. **See Figure 5-8**. Also, the adjustment factors of **310.15(C)(1)** need not apply where more than three current-carrying conductors are installed in a raceway. **See Problem 5-14**.

Figure 5-8. Conduit or Tubing Nipples. Each of the three conduit nipples may be filled to a maximum of 60% fill according to **Chapter 9, Table 1, Note 4**, as they are 24 inches or less in length.

PROBLEM 5-14

What is the maximum number of 1/0 AWG THWN-2 copper conductors permitted to be installed in a 3-inch intermediate metal conduit nipple, 18 inches in length, between an auxiliary gutter and a switchboard?

Solution

Nipple is less than 24 inches in length.
Table 1 Note 4
  Max. fill of 60% permitted
Table 4
  IMC chart; 60% fill column
  60% fill for a 3-in. IMC = 4.753 in.²
Table 5
  Cross-sectional area of conductors
  1/0 AWG THWN-2 = 0.1855 in.²

$$\text{Number of conductors} = \frac{60\% \text{ fill area}}{\text{single conductor in.}^2}$$
$$= \frac{4.753}{0.1855}$$
$$= 25.62 \text{ or } 25$$

Answer: 25 conductors

The electrical training ALLIANCE uses the industry's best subject matter experts for the development of their many textbooks on a wide variety of topics.

PROBLEM 5-15

What is the maximum number of 4 AWG XHHW copper conductors permitted in a ³/₄-inch electrical metallic tubing nipple, 20 inches in length?

Solution

Nipple is less than 24 inches in length
Table 1 Note 4
  Max. fill of 60% permitted
Table 4
  EMT chart; 60% fill column
  60% fill for a ³/₄-in. EMT = 0.320 in.²
Table 5
  Cross-sectional area conductor
  4 AWG XHHW copper = 0.0814 in.²

$$\text{Number of conductors} = \frac{60\% \text{ fill area}}{\text{single conductor in.}^2}$$
$$= \frac{0.320}{0.0814}$$
$$= 3.93$$

Table 1 Note 7
Next larger whole number permitted if the answer results in a decimal 0.8 or greater
0.93 is greater than 0.8; therefore, round up

Answer: 4 conductors

PROBLEM 5-16

What size electrical metallic tubing is needed for two 4/C 12 AWG with ground, Type NM cables measuring 0.72 inches in diameter?

Solution

$$r = \frac{D}{2}$$
$$= \frac{0.72}{2}$$
$$= 0.36 \text{ in.}$$

$$A = 3.1416 \times r^2 \times \text{number of cables}$$
$$= 3.1416 \times (0.36 \times 0.36) \times 2$$
$$= 0.814 \text{ in.}^2$$

Two cables = 2 conductors
Table 4
  EMT chart; 2 wires, 31% fill column
  31% fill for 2-in. EMT = 1.040 in.²
  0.814 in.² requires a 2-in. EMT

Answer: 2-in. EMT

5.6 USING NOTE 7 TO TABLE 1 OF CHAPTER 9

When calculating the fill of a single conductor or a number of conductors or cables in a conduit or tubing, where all of the conductors (including insulation) are the same size, if the decimal is equal to or greater than 0.8, **Note 7** to **Table 1** of **Chapter 9** permits the next higher number of conductors. See Problem 5-15.

5.7 MULTICONDUCTOR CABLES IN CONDUIT OR TUBING

Chapter 9, Table 1, Notes 5 and **9** set the method for calculating conduit or tubing size for multiconductor cables, optical fiber cables, and, where specifically permitted, flexible cords. The following factors are taken into consideration:

1. The actual diameter of the electrical cable, optical fiber cable, or flexible cord needs to be known or measured. From this equation, the area of a cable whose diameter is known is calculated as follows:

   r = radius of cable or flexible cord
   D = diameter of cable or flexible cord
   A = area of cable or flexible cord
   $$r = \frac{D}{2}$$
   $$A = \pi r^2$$
   $$= 3.1416 \times r^2$$

2. An elliptical shaped cable or cord is treated as a round cable and the largest diameter is used.
3. Each multiconductor electrical cable, optical fiber cable, or cord is treated as a single conductor.

See Problems 5-16 and 5-17.

5.8 ADDING CONDUCTORS TO EXISTING CONDUIT OR TUBING

Tables 4, **5**, and **5A** may also be used for calculating the number of conductors which are permitted to be added to an existing conduit without exceeding the fill limit. **See Problem 5-18**.

5.9 TABLES FOR ³⁄₈-INCH FLEXIBLE METAL CONDUIT

Table 348.22 is a special table for raceway fill where a ³⁄₈-inch flexible wiring method is used. The table is located in **Article 348, Flexible Metal Conduit: Type FMC**, but is referred to in other sections of the *Code* dealing with different types of raceways.

For example:

- **350.22(B)** - for ³⁄₈-inch liquidtight flexible metal conduit
- **360.22(B)** - for ³⁄₈-inch flexible metallic tubing

When a termination fitting, such as a box connector, is installed inside flexible metal conduit, it will decrease the internal cross-sectional area. Therefore, fewer conductors will be permitted in a flexible metal conduit with the fittings installed inside the conduit than if the fittings are installed outside the conduit.

Table 348.22 includes two columns for the two types, one for the fittings installed inside and one for fittings installed outside of the conduit, as well as a column for each of the four styles of conductors.

PROBLEM 5-17

A 6-foot length of 2-inch electrical metallic tubing is installed between a ceiling pull box and a lighting panel. How many runs of 3-conductor 12 AWG, Type NM cable with ground can be installed in the 2-inch EMT without exceeding the permitted fill? The diameter of the Type NM cable is 0.65 inches.

Solution

$$r = \frac{D}{2}$$
$$= \frac{0.65}{2}$$
$$= 0.325 \text{ in.}$$
$$A = 3.1416 \times r^2$$
$$= 3.1416 \times (0.325 \times 0.325)$$
$$= 0.3318 \text{ in.}^2$$

Table 4
EMT chart
40% fill column for (assumed) over 2 wires
40% fill for 2-in. EMT = 1.342 in.²

$$\text{Number of cables} = \frac{40\% \text{ fill area}}{\text{one cable area}}$$
$$= \frac{1.342}{0.3318}$$
$$= 4.04 \text{ or } 4 \text{ cables}$$

Answer: 4 cables in a 2-in. EMT

PROBLEM 5-18

An existing 1-inch electrical metallic tubing contains four 8 AWG THWN copper conductors. How many 10 AWG THWN copper conductors can be added without exceeding the 40% fill?

Solution

Table 4
 EMT chart; 40% fill column for over 2 wires
 40% fill for 1-in. EMT = 0.3460 in.²
Table 5
 Cross-sectional area for insulated conductors
 Space occupied by existing conductors
 8 AWG THWN = 0.0366 in.²
 0.0366 × 4 = 0.1464 in.²
 Space available = permitted space − occupied space
          = 0.3460 − 0.1464
          = 0.1996 in.²

10 AWG THWN = 0.0211 in.²

$$\text{Number permitted} = \frac{\text{space available}}{\text{conductor area}}$$
$$= \frac{0.1996}{0.0211}$$
$$= 9.46 \text{ or } 9$$

Answer: Permitted to add an additional nine 10 AWG THWN conductors

The footnote to the table indicates that an equipment grounding conductor of the same size is also permitted to be installed in the conduit with the other conductors. **See Problems 5-19 and 5-20.**

5.10 UNDERFLOOR TYPE RACEWAYS

NEC **Chapter 3, Wiring Methods and Materials**, contains three articles devoted to cellular and underfloor raceways. These raceways provide an economical method to deliver electricity, data, and communication circuits to office furniture while maintaining the "open space" design specified by many architects and designers.

PROBLEM 5-19

What is the maximum number of 16 AWG TFN conductors permitted in a ⅜-inch run of flexible metal conduit where fittings are installed inside the conduit? What is the maximum number of conductors permitted where the fittings are installed outside the conduit?

Solution

Calculation 1
Table 348.22
 16 AWG TFN with fittings inside = 4
Answer: 4 conductors and one equipment grounding conductor

Calculation 2
Table 348.22
 16 AWG TFN with fittings outside = 6
Answer: 6 conductors and one equipment grounding conductor

PROBLEM 5-20

What is the maximum number of 18 AWG FEP conductors permitted in a ⅜-inch run of liquidtight flexible metal conduit with fittings installed inside the conduit with an 18 AWG bare equipment grounding conductor?

Solution

350.22(B) refers to Table 348.22
 18 AWG FEP fittings inside = 5
 Table footnote permits one equipment grounding conductor to be added
Answer: 5 conductors and 1 equipment grounding conductor

5.10.1 General

The *Code* lists three types of raceways that are installed under the floor or as a part of the floor and are manufactured in a variety of cross-sectional areas. The maximum number of conductors permitted in these raceways is limited to 40% fill, just as conduits and tubing are limited to 40% fill for three or more conductors. Other than **Table 1**, there is no *Code* table set up for these various raceways. The manufacturer's data should be consulted in all cases.

Raceway fill is calculated using **Tables 5** and **5A** for the conductor areas:

- **372.22 Cellular Concrete Floor Raceway:** 40% fill
- **374.22 Cellular Metal Floor Raceway:** 40% fill
- **390.22 Underfloor Raceway:** 40% fill

These raceways are not standard sizes, and they do not have standard cross-sectional areas. In fact, some of these raceways have an irregular shape. In most, if not all, cases, the manufacturer's literature must be consulted to determine the actual cross-sectional area that is available for conductors or to determine the maximum number of conductors permitted within these specialty raceways.

Raceways are also limited to a maximum size conductor:

- **372.20 Cellular Concrete Floor Raceway:** no conductor larger than 1/0 AWG
- **374.20 Cellular Metal Floor Raceway:** no conductor larger than 1/0 AWG
- **390.20 Underfloor Raceway:** limited by manufacturer

The ampacity adjustment factors of **310.15(C)** must be applied to conductors installed in each of these raceways according to **Section 372.23**, **Section 374.23**, and **Section 390.23**.

5.10.2 Cross-Sectional Area Calculation for a Rectangular Underfloor Raceway

A rectangular underfloor raceway is designed and intended for installation beneath or flush with the surface of a floor. **See Figure 5-9**. Listed, labeled, or identified underfloor raceways often have installation instructions. Wire capacity charts and tables also accompany the installation instructions. If the raceways have wire capacity charts, those charts must be used as instructed.

Figure 5-9. Rectangular Underfloor Raceway. An isometric cross-sectional view of a common rectangular underfloor raceway reveals the typical dimensions and characteristics of this type of raceway.

Note that the referenced examples are meant to supplement and add to the learning process. However, only the internal cross-sectional areas and/or the wire charts supplied by the manufacturer are permitted to be used as the final determination of wire capacity for a given underfloor raceway.

To determine the 100% cross-sectional area available for conductors for this style of raceway, first calculate the area of the inside of the rectangle.

$Area$ (internal) $= Length \times Width$
$A = L \times W$
$\quad = 3 \times 2$
$\quad = 6$ in.^{2} (100% of the internal raceway area)

Since **Section 390.22** requires a maximum fill of 40%, the usable area for this raceway is:
$A = 6$ in.$^2 \times 0.4$
$\quad = 2.4$ in.^{2} (40% of internal usable area)
See Problems 5-21, 5-22, 5-23, and 5-24.

PROBLEM 5-21

What is the maximum number of 12 AWG THHW copper conductors permitted to be installed in a rectangular underfloor raceway with internal dimensions of 1 $\frac{1}{4}$ inches high and 3 inches wide where manufacturer data is not available?

Solution

$A = H \times W$
$\quad = 1.25 \times 3$
$\quad = 3.75$ in.^{2}

Section 390.6
$\quad$ Max. fill $=$ area $\times$ 40%
$\qquad = 3.75 \times 0.40$
$\qquad = 1.5$ in.^{2}

Table 5
$\quad$ 12 AWG THHW $= 0.0181$ in.^{2}

$\text{Number of conductors} = \dfrac{\text{max. fill}}{\text{one conductor area}}$

$\qquad = \dfrac{1.5}{0.0181}$

$\qquad = 82.87$ or 82

Answer: 82 conductors

Comment: In most cases, it is prudent to reduce this number because Table 310.15(C)(1) may need to be applied.

PROBLEM 5-22

What is the maximum number of 8 AWG THHW compact aluminum conductors permitted to be installed in a cell of a cellular metal underfloor raceway with a stated internal area of 2 square inches?

Solution

$A = 2.0$ in.^{2}

Section 374.5
$\quad$ Area max. fill $= A \times 40\%$
$\qquad = 2.0 \times 0.40$
$\qquad = 0.8$ in.^{2}

Table 5A
$\quad$ 8 AWG THHW $= 0.0510$ in.^{2}

$\text{Number of conductors} = \dfrac{\text{max. fill}}{\text{one conductor area}}$

$\qquad = \dfrac{0.8}{0.0510}$

$\qquad = 15.6$ or 15

Answer: 15 conductors

PROBLEM 5-23

What is the maximum number of 10 AWG THWN-2, solid copper conductors permitted to be installed in a cellular metal floor raceway with internal manufacturer's dimensions of 2 inches × 2 inches?

Solution

$A = L \times W$
$= 2 \times 2$
$= 4$ in.^{2}

Section 374.5
Area max. fill $= A \times 40\%$
$= 4 \times 0.40$
$= 1.6$ in.^{2}

Table 5
10 AWG THWN-2 $= 0.0211$ in.^{2}

$$\text{Number of conductors} = \frac{\text{max. fill}}{\text{one conductor area}}$$
$$= \frac{1.6}{0.0211}$$
$$= 75.8 \text{ or } 75$$

Answer: 75 conductors

Comment: Cellular metal floor raceway is covered by Article 374. Section 374.23 requires that the ampacity adjustments in 310.15(B)(3)(a) be applied to all current-carrying conductors installed in cellular metal floor raceways. For Problem 5-23, the current-carrying ampacity of the seventy-five 10 AWG THWN-2 conductors would be reduced to 35% of the original table ampacity.

PROBLEM 5-24

What is the maximum number of 10 AWG THWN copper conductors permitted to be installed in a cell of a cellular concrete underfloor raceway with an internal diameter of 2 inches? The manufacturer's data indicates that the 2-inch raceway has a usable total cross-sectional area of 2.057 square inches.

Solution

Section 372.11
Area max. fill $= A \times 40\%$
$= 2.057 \times 0.40$
$= 0.8228$ in.^{2}

Table 5
10 AWG THWN $= 0.0211$ in.^{2}

$$\text{Number of conductors} = \frac{\text{balance}}{\text{one conductor}}$$
$$= \frac{0.8228}{0.0211}$$
$$= 38.99$$

Chapter 9, Table 1, Note 7 does not apply to this raceway

Answer: 38 conductors

5.10.3 Cross-Sectional Area Calculation for a Circular Underfloor Raceway

A circular underfloor raceway may have an internal diameter of three inches. To determine the cross-sectional area available for conductors for this style of raceway, simply calculate the area of the inside of the circle.

$r = \dfrac{D}{2}$
$= \dfrac{3}{2}$
$= 1.5$

$\pi = 3.1416$
Area (internal) $= \pi r^2$
A $= 3.1416 \times 1.5^2$
$= 3.1416 \times (1.5 \times 1.5)$
$= 7.0686$ in.^{2} (100% of the internal raceway area)

See Problem 5-25.

PROBLEM 5-25

An existing underfloor raceway with an internal cross-sectional area of 3 square inches contains sixteen 8 AWG THW copper conductors. How many more 8 AWG THWN copper conductors are permitted to be installed in the same raceway?

Solution

Section 390.6
Area max. fill $= A \times 40\%$
$= 3 \times 0.40$
$= 1.2$ in.^{2}

Table 5
8 AWG THW $= 0.0437$ in.^{2}
Occupied space $= 16 \times 0.0437$
$= 0.6992$ in.^{2}

Space available $=$ permitted space − occupied space
$= 1.2 − 0.6992$
$= 0.5008$ in.^{2}

Table 5
8 AWG THWN $= 0.0366$ in.^{2}

$$\text{Number of conductors} = \frac{\text{space available}}{\text{one conductor}}$$
$$= \frac{0.5008}{0.0366}$$
$$= 13.68$$

Answer: 13 conductors

CHAPTER 5   RACEWAY FILL   107

*In offices, it is common to install a power and data under-floor raceway. **Section 390.15** has specific requirements for minimum concrete cover and the separation of raceways. Courtesy of Legrand/Wiremold.*

Requirements	Metal Wireways	Nonmetallic Wireways
Listing	No	Yes
Fill	20%	20%
Supports	5 ft.	3 or 4 ft.*
Ampacity Adjustment	Only over 30 conductors	Current-carrying conductors

*See 378.30(A) and (B).

Figure 5-10. Metal and Nonmetallic Wireway Comparison. Although both types of wireways permit only 20% conductor fill, nonmetallic wireways are required to be listed and require adjustment factors for all conductors in the wireway. See **378.6** and **378.22**.

5.11 METAL WIREWAYS, NONMETALLIC WIREWAYS, AND AUXILIARY GUTTERS

One of the basic differences between a metal wireway and an auxiliary gutter is that an auxiliary gutter is limited to 30 feet in length, while a wireway is not limited in length. Another basic difference between wireways and auxiliary gutters is that wireways are limited to a maximum size of a single conductor according to both **Section 376.21** and **Section 378.21**, while auxiliary gutters have no such limitation. The basic rules for the fill of a metal wireway or an auxiliary gutter are very much the same when it comes to the installation of electrical conductors other than busbars. **See Figure 5-10.** There is also a commonality between nonmetallic wireways and nonmetallic auxiliary gutters.

Section 376.21 indicates that "no conductor larger than that for which the wireway is designed shall be installed in any wireway." This statement leaves the user without an actual maximum wire size for a given size wireway. However, the largest wire permitted within a wireway or auxiliary gutter can be determined by using the wire size column and the "1 Wire per Terminal" column of **Table 312.6(A)**.

For example, a 500 kcmil conductor (one wire per terminal) requires at least a six-inch by six-inch wireway or auxiliary gutter. For a four-inch by four-inch wireway, the maximum size conductor permitted is 4/0 AWG. These maximum wire sizes may also be determined by using *ANSI/UL 870: Standard for Safety for Wireways, Auxiliary Gutters, and Associated Fittings*.

5.11.1 Article 376, Metal Wireways

Regarding metal wireways, *NEC* **376.22(A)** permits a maximum of 20% fill at any interior cross-sectional area, while *NEC* **376.22(B)** permits a maximum of 30 current-carrying conductors without applying adjustment factors. Note that signaling and motor conductors used only for starting are not counted as current-carrying conductors.

Splices and taps are permitted in wireways, provided they are accessible. Specifically, **376.56(A)** requires that splices and taps made in metal wireways must not exceed 75% of the cross-sectional area at the splice or tap location. **See Problems 5-26 and 5-27.**

PROBLEM 5-26

What is the maximum number of 1 AWG THWN copper conductors that are permitted to be installed in a metal wireway with internal dimensions of 3 inches × 4 inches?

Solution

$$A = L \times W$$
$$= 4 \times 3$$
$$= 12 \text{ in.}^2$$

376.22(A)

$$\text{Area max. fill} = A \times 20\%$$
$$= 12 \times 0.20$$
$$= 2.4 \text{ in.}^2$$

Table 5

1 AWG THWN = 0.1562 in.^{2}

$$\text{Number of conductors} = \frac{\text{max. fill}}{\text{one conductor}}$$
$$= \frac{2.4}{0.1562}$$
$$= 15.3$$

Answer: 15 conductors

PROBLEM 5-27

A metal wireway with inside dimensions of 3 inches × 3 inches contains twenty 12 AWG THWN and ten 10 AWG THWN current-carrying copper conductors. Is it permissible to add twelve more 10 AWG THWN current-carrying conductors in the wireway and stay within raceway fill limitations without applying the ampacity adjustment factors to the conductors?

Solution

Section 376.22
 Without applying adjustment factors, the maximum number of conductors permitted is 30
 Twenty (12 AWG) + ten (10 AWG) + twelve (10 AWG) = 42 conductors
 Max. number of conductors will be exceeded
 The cross-sectional area of 20% may not be exceeded, but the 30 conductor limitation would be exceeded.
Answer: No. Ampacity adjustment factors would need to be applied

PROBLEM 5-28

For the following, calculate the maximum number of conductors permitted in a 5-inch × 5-inch nonmetallic wireway for 350 kcmil where permitted by Section 378.21.

1. 350 kcmil THHW concentric stranded copper
2. 350 kcmil THHW compact stranded aluminum

Solution

Calculation 1
 Wireway area = 5 in. × 5 in.
  = 25 in.^{2}
Section 378.22
 Max. fill = A × 20%
  = 25 × 0.20
  = 5.0 in.^{2}
Table 5
 350 kcmil THHW = 0.5958 in.^{2}

$$\text{Number of conductors} = \frac{\text{max. fill}}{\text{one conductor}}$$
$$= \frac{5}{0.5958}$$
$$= 8.39 \text{ or } 8$$

Answer: Eight 350 kcmil THHW concentric copper conductors

Calculation 2
Table 5A
 350 kcmil THHW compact aluminum = 0.5281 in.^{2}

$$\text{Number of conductors} = \frac{\text{max. fill}}{\text{one conductor}}$$
$$= \frac{5}{0.5281}$$
$$= 9.47 \text{ or } 9$$

Answer: Nine 350 kcmil THHW compact aluminum conductors

5.11.2 Article 378, Nonmetallic Wireways

According to **Section 378.22** for nonmetallic wireways:

- A maximum of 20% fill at any interior cross-sectional area cannot be exceeded. There are no exceptions.
- The number of conductors is not limited.
- Adjustment factors apply to all current-carrying conductors.
- Signaling and motor conductors used for starting are not counted as current-carrying conductors.

Splices and taps are permitted in nonmetallic wireways, provided they are accessible. **Section 378.56** requires that splices and taps must not exceed 75% of the cross-sectional area at the splice or tap location. **See Problem 5-28**.

PROBLEM 5-29

A square sheet metal auxiliary gutter with internal dimensions of 3 inches × 3 inches contains six 1/0 AWG THW copper conductors. How many 4 AWG THHW copper conductors are permitted to be added without exceeding the maximum fill of the auxiliary gutter?

Solution

$A = L \times W$
 = 3 in. × 3 in.
 = 9 in.^{2}
366.22(A)
 Max. fill = $A \times 20\%$
  = 9 × 0.20
  = 1.8 in.^{2}
Table 5
 1/0 AWG THW copper = 0.2223 in.^{2}
 Occupied space = 0.2223 × 6 conductors
  = 1.3338 in.^{2}
 Space available = permitted space − occupied space
  = 1.8 − 1.3338
  = 0.4662 in.^{2}
Table 5
 4 AWG THHW = 0.0973 in.^{2}

$$\text{Number of conductors} = \frac{\text{space available}}{\text{one conductor}}$$
$$= \frac{0.4662}{0.0973}$$
$$= 4.79 \text{ or } 4$$

Answer: 4 conductors

5.11.3 Article 366, Auxiliary Gutters

According to **366.22(A)** and **366.23(A)** for sheet metallic auxiliary gutters:

- A maximum of 20% fill at any interior cross-sectional area is permitted.
- A maximum of 30 current-carrying conductors without ampacity adjustments is permitted.
- Signaling and motor conductors used for starting are not counted as current-carrying conductors.

Splices and taps are permitted in auxiliary gutters, provided they are accessible. The regulations are very much the same for wireways and auxiliary gutters. According to **366.56(A)**, splices and taps made in auxiliary gutters must not exceed 75% of the interior cross-sectional area at the tap or splice location. **See Problems 5-29, 5-30, and 5-31.**

PROBLEM 5-30

What is the maximum number of 10 AWG THHN current-carrying copper conductors permitted to be installed in a sheet metallic auxiliary gutter with a 4-inch × 4-inch internal area?

Solution

$A = L \times W$
$= 4 \text{ in.} \times 4 \text{ in.}$
$= 16 \text{ in.}^2$

366.22(A)
Max. fill $= A \times 20\%$
$= 16 \times 0.20$
$= 3.2 \text{ in.}^2$

Table 5
10 AWG THHN = 0.0211 in.²

$$\text{Number of conductors} = \frac{\text{max. fill}}{\text{one conductor}}$$
$$= \frac{3.2}{0.0211}$$
$$= 151.6 \text{ or } 151$$

Answer: 151 conductors

Comment: The 20% fill has not been exceeded, therefore, 151 conductors are permitted. However, when the 30-conductor limitation is exceeded, the ampacity adjustment factors of Table 310.15(C)(1) will apply and the conductors must be adjusted accordingly.

PROBLEM 5-31

Three 4/0 AWG THHN copper conductors are to be spliced in a sheet metallic auxiliary gutter with the splices staggered. Will an auxiliary gutter with inside dimensions of 2 ½ inches deep × 3 inches wide be large enough for the installation? (For this example only, assume the spliced cross-sectional area of any one conductor is three times the normal cross-sectional area of the conductor.)

Solution

$A = H \times W$
$= 2.5 \text{ in.} \times 3 \text{ in.}$
$= 7.5 \text{ in.}^2$

366.56(A)
Max. fill $= A \times 75\%$
$= 7.5 \times 0.75$
$= 5.625 \text{ in.}^2$

Table 5
Cross-sectional area of conductors
4/0 AWG THHN = 0.3237 in.²

Spliced conductor tripled = 0.3237 in.² × 3 =	0.9711
Remaining 2 conductors = 0.3237 in.² × 2 =	0.6474
Total	1.6185

Answer: Yes, the size given is sufficient and complies with *NEC* 366.56(A).

Comment: Since the splice plus the other two conductors occupies less than 5.625 in.², then the answer is yes, staggered splices are permitted.

The following definition from the NFPA Regulations governing the Development of NFPA Standards, Section 3.3.6.1, represents an official definition for all NFPA documents:

Approved. Acceptable to the authority having jurisdiction.

Note: The National Fire Protection Association does not approve, inspect, or certify any installations, procedures, equipment, or materials, nor does it approve or evaluate testing laboratories. In determining the acceptability of installations or procedures, equipment, or materials, the "authority having jurisdiction" may base acceptances on compliance with NFPA or other appropriate standards. In the absence of such standards, said authority may require evidence of proper installation, procedure, or use. The "authority having jurisdiction" may also refer to the listings or labeling practices of an organization that is concerned with product evaluations and is thus in a position to determine compliance with appropriate standards for the current production of listed items.

DEFINITIONS AND TERMS

Compact Stranding - The result of a manufacturing process where the standard conductor is compressed to the extent that the interstices (voids between strand wires) are virtually eliminated.

Conductor, Bare - A conductor having no covering or electrical insulation whatsoever. [**70**:100]

Conductor, Covered - A conductor encased within material of composition or thickness that is not recognized by this *Code* as electrical insulation. [**70**:100]

Conductor, Insulated - A conductor encased within material of composition and thickness that is recognized by this *Code* as electrical insulation. [**70**:100] Recognized insulation is found in Table 310.4(A).

Informative Annex - All Informative Annexes are not a part of the requirements of the *NEC*, but are included in the *NEC* for informational purposes only.

Nipple - A short piece of raceway usually, 24 inches or less in length.

Raceway - An enclosed channel designed expressly for holding wires, cables, or busbars, with additional functions as permitted in this *Code*. [**70**:100] A raceway is identified within specific article definitions.

Reproduced with permission of NFPA from NFPA 70®, *National Electrical Code*® (NEC®), 2020 edition. Copyright© 2019, National Fire Protection Association. For a full copy of the NEC®, please go to www.nfpa.org.

SUMMARY

The performance requirements for conduit fill are found in **Section 300.17**. Each specific *NEC* section containing fill requirements is found in the informational note following **Section 300.17**. Generally, most raceway articles in **Chapter 3** require the use of **Chapter 9, Table 1** to determine the maximum conduit and tubing fill permitted. Adhering to the conductor fill table requirements of **Chapter 9** allows conductors to safely dissipate heat, permits ease in conductor installation and removal, and prevents premature insulation failure due to shorts and grounds. Where all of the conductors are the same size and the same insulation, the look-up tables of **Annex C** are permitted to be used to determine the number of conductors permitted in a raceway. For specialized raceways, it is important to thoroughly review the manufacturer's literature to determine the maximum conductor size and the permitted conductor fill (tables) for their product. See **110.3(B)**.

REVIEW QUESTIONS

1. For a rigid metal conduit, if three or more conductors are installed, what is the maximum fill percentage permitted by the *Code*?
   a. 31%
   b. 40%
   c. 53%
   d. 60%

2. Which best describes the reason to limit the number of conductors in raceways?
   a. To dissipate heat and allow installation and withdrawal of conductors without damaging the conductors or insulation
   b. To provide physical protection of the conductors
   c. To provide physical protection to anyone contacting the conductors
   d. To allow for the future addition of conductors to the raceway

3. In order to use **Informative Annex C** to look up the maximum number of conductors in conduit or tubing, **Annex C** requires that __?__.
   a. all conductors must be copper
   b. all conductors must be smaller than 250 kcmil
   c. all conductors must be the same insulation type
   d. all conductors must be the same size (AWG) and the same insulation size

4. What is the main difference between **Chapter 9, Table 5** and **Chapter 9, Table 5A**?
   a. **Table 5** is for copper and aluminum conductors and **Table 5A** is only for aluminum.
   b. **Table 5** is for insulated conductors and **Table 5A** is for uninsulated conductors.
   c. **Table 5** is only for insulated copper conductors and **Table 5A** is only for compact aluminum conductors.
   d. **Table 5** is for solid or concentric lay stranded conductors and **Table 5A** is for compact stranded conductors.

5. What is the approximate area, in square inches, of a 12 AWG THHW copper conductor?
   a. 0.0181 in.^{2}
   b. 0.0260 in.^{2}
   c. 0.152 in.^{2}
   d. 0.182 in.^{2}

6. What is the maximum permitted fill area, in square inches, for a one-inch EMT nipple that is less than 24 inches in length?
   a. 0.346 in.^{2}
   b. 0.519 in.^{2}
   c. 0.864 in.^{2}
   d. 1.049 in.^{2}

7. In which case are equipment grounding conductors not required to be included in the conduit or tubing fill requirements?
   a. When the equipment grounding conductor is bare
   b. When the raceway is nonmetallic
   c. When there is only one equipment grounding conductor present
   d. There is no exception for fill requirements for equipment grounding conductors; they are always required to be included with the fill calculation

8. In which table would the dimensions for a bare conductor be found?
   a. **Chapter 9, Table 1**
   b. **Chapter 9, Table 4**
   c. **Chapter 9, Table 5**
   d. **Chapter 9, Table 8**

9. For a metal or nonmetallic wireway, what is the maximum fill percentage?
   a. 20%
   b. 31%
   c. 40%
   d. 60%

10. When calculating the maximum number of conductors, all of which have the same cross-sectional size including insulation, that are permitted to be installed in a conduit or tubing, what decimal is permitted to be rounded up to the next whole number of conductors to determine the maximum number of conductors permitted?
    a. 0.5
    b. 0.8
    c. 0.99
    d. No rounding is permitted; the decimal always needs to be dropped

CHAPTER 6
MOTOR CALCULATIONS

According to **Section 90.3**, **Article 430** contains the general rules for motors. These general requirements may be altered by the requirements of **Chapters 5**, **6**, or **7** for special occupancies, special equipment, or special conditions.

Article 430 is a large and complex group of electrical safety requirements for motors, and is organized in an orderly fashion. It covers all parts and components of the motor circuit, and there are 14 separate parts in **Article 430**, as shown in the *National Electrical Code* (*NEC*) table of contents. **Figure 430.1** at the beginning of the article provides an electrical single-line diagram providing a visual outline of the article as it relates to a motor circuit installation.

A thorough understanding of motor calculations and an understanding of the *NEC* requirements for all motor installations is essential for the knowledge and skills of a competent commercial and industrial Electrical Worker.

OBJECTIVES

- Calculate the ampacities of motor circuits and hermetically sealed air-conditioning motor branch circuits.
- Calculate and select the motor circuit copper conductor size using **Table 310.16**.
- Calculate and select the proper size branch-circuit short-circuit and ground-fault protection devices for motor circuits using **430.52** and **240.6(A)**.
- Calculate the size of the motor overload protection for motors in general.
- Using **430.7(B)**, **Table 430.251(A)**, and **Table 430.251(B)**, calculate the locked-rotor current for various motors.
- Calculate the minimum ampacity and horsepower rating necessary for a motor disconnecting means.

TABLE OF CONTENTS

6.1 MOTOR BRANCH-CIRCUIT CONDUCTORS ... 114
- .1 Introduction ... 114
- .2 General Application ... 114
- .3 Sizing Motor Branch-Circuit Conductors ... 115

6.2 MOTOR BRANCH-CIRCUIT SHORT-CIRCUIT AND GROUND-FAULT PROTECTION ... 123
- .1 General ... 123
- .2 Standard Sizes for Overcurrent Device Ratings (Basic Protection) ... 126
- .3 Calculations With and Without a Starting Current Problem ... 127

6.3 MOTOR OVERLOAD PROTECTION ... 136
- .1 General Requirements ... 136
- .2 Overload Protection With and Without Problem Starting Currents ... 137
- .3 Using Thermal Protectors ... 139
- .4 Using Fuses and Circuit Breakers as Motor Overload Protection ... 139
- .5 Overload Protection with Power Factor Corrected Motors ... 140

6.4 MOTOR DISCONNECTING MEANS ... 140
- .1 General Requirements ... 140
- .2 Locked-Rotor Current Calculations ... 141
- .3 Locked-Rotor Current Equations ... 143
- .4 Table 430.251(A) and Table 430.251(B), Conversion Tables for Locked-Rotor Current ... 143
- .5 Calculating Motor-Circuit Switch Horsepower for Motors Marked with Code Letters ... 144
- .6 Circuit Breaker as Motor Disconnecting Means for Other Than Design B Energy-Efficient Motors ... 148
- .7 Molded-Case Switch for Other than Design B Energy-Efficient Motors ... 150
- .8 Combination Ampere and Horsepower Rating for Other than Design B Energy-Efficient Motors ... 151

6.5 AIR-CONDITIONING AND REFRIGERATING EQUIPMENT MOTORS ... 151
- .1 Branch-Circuit Conductor Sizing ... 152
- .2 Overload Calculations ... 153
- .3 Motor Branch-Circuit Short-Circuit and Ground-Fault Protection ... 154

DEFINITIONS AND TERMS ... 155
SUMMARY ... 156
REVIEW QUESTIONS ... 156

6.1 MOTOR BRANCH-CIRCUIT CONDUCTORS

Motor branch-circuit conductors are covered in **Article 430, Part II, Motor Circuit Conductors**. Single motors are covered by **430.22** and multiple motors are covered by **430.24**.

6.1.1 Introduction

A branch circuit is the portion of the circuit that extends beyond the last overcurrent protective device. A motor branch circuit includes all conductors between the branch-circuit protection device and the motor. **See Figure 6-1**. Note that motor overload relays are intended for the running protection of the motor and are not considered the last or final overcurrent protective device.

NEC **430.6(A)(1)** gives some basic information for motor calculations. In particular, it identifies when the nameplate full-load current rating is to be used and when the ampacity values listed in the full-load current **Table 430.248**, **Table 430.249**, and **Table 430.250** are to be used.

6.1.2 General Application

1. Conductors shall be selected from the ampacity tables (primarily **Table 310.16** in accordance with **310.15**).
2. For motor circuits 100 amperes or less, *NEC* **110.14(C)(1)(a)(4)** permits the use of the temperature rating associated with the ampacity of the conductor for motors marked with design letters B, C, or D to have an insulation rating of 75°C (167°F) or higher, provided the ampacity of the conductor does not exceed the 75°C (167°F) ampacity.
3. *NEC* **240.4(D)** is a general overcurrent protection requirement for small conductors referenced at the bottom of **Table 310.16**. This general requirement is amended for motor and motor-control circuits by referencing specific overcurrent protection requirements identified in **Table 240.4(G)**. This table points directly to **Article 430, Parts III** and **IV**, which deal with motor branch-circuit overload protection and motor branch-circuit short-circuit and ground-fault protection. Therefore, the overcurrent protection requirements of **240.4(D)** do not apply to motor-circuit overcurrent protection. Instead, the user is directed to **Article 430** for this protection.
4. The ampacity values given in the motor full-load current tables are to be used to calculate the ampacity of motor branch-circuit conductors whether or not the full-load current is given on the nameplate.
5. The values given in **Table 430.248**, **Table 430.249**, and **Table 430.250** are the full-load currents (FLCs) for most motors of normal torque values and common speeds.

6.1.2.1 Low-Speed and Multispeed Motors
Low-speed and high-torque motors usually have higher full-load currents than those found in the tables, so the nameplate currents are required to be used for these types of motors. For multispeed motors, the full-load current will vary with the speed; again, the nameplate values are to be used.

6.1.2.2 Listed Appliances and Equipment of a Specific Type
According to **430.6(A)(1) Exceptions No. 2** and **3**, listed appliances and specific types of blower motors are allowed to use their equipment nameplate current ratings for calculating the ampacity of these branch-circuit conductors instead of the **Article 430** table values.

6.1.2.3 Torque Motors
According to **430.6(B)**, the motor rated current for torque motors is the locked-rotor current marked on the nameplate. This current is required to be used to calculate the ampacity of the branch-circuit conductors.

For additional information, visit qr.njatcdb.org Item #1033

Figure 6-1. Motor Branch Circuit. A complete branch circuit begins at the final overcurrent protective device and ends at the motor terminal box.

CHAPTER 6 MOTOR CALCULATIONS

6.1.2.4 Motors Used in AC Adjustable Voltage, Variable Torque Drive Systems

AC adjustable voltage motors and variable torque drive system conductors are covered in **430.6(C)**.

1. The maximum operating current given on the nameplate of the equipment controller or motor is required to be used to calculate the ampacity of the branch-circuit conductors.
2. Where the maximum operating current is not marked on the nameplate, 150% of the values given in **Table 430.249** and **Table 430.250** are required to be used.

The branch-circuit conductors supplying the conversion equipment for an adjustable-speed drive system are required to be 125% of the rated input current of the power conversion equipment according to **430.122(A)**.

6.1.3 Sizing Motor Branch-Circuit Conductors

Motors are often operated continuously in a wide variety of facilities. The requirements for sizing motor conductors are, therefore, similar to the requirements of **210.19** for continuously-loaded branch-circuit conductors with exceptions for special motor installations.

6.1.3.1 Continuous-Duty Motors

Section 430.22 requires the ampacity of motor branch-circuit conductors supplying a single motor used in a continuous duty application to be 125% of the motor full-load current (FLC). **See Problems 6-1, 6-2, and 6-3.**

*Due to the high full-load currents of motors rated more than 250 horsepower, paralleling conductors is often necessary to supply the motor. See NEC **310.10(G)** for parallel conductor requirements.*

PROBLEM 6-1

NAMEPLATE
25 HP 460 V 3 PH
FLC 32.5

What is the minimum ampacity of the branch-circuit conductors for a 25-horsepower, 460-volt, 3-phase squirrel-cage motor with a nameplate full-load current rating of 32.5 amperes?

Solution

Nameplate FLC is not used
430.6(A)(1)
Use table value for FLC
Table 430.250
25 hp at 460 V
Table value FLC = 34 A
Section 430.22
Ampacity = FLC × 125%
= 34 × 1.25
= 42.5 A

Answer: 42.5 A

PROBLEM 6-2

NAMEPLATE
10 HP 240 V 1 PH
FLC 44

What is the minimum size THHN copper conductors required for a 10-horsepower, 240-volt, single-phase Design B motor used in a continuous-duty application with a nameplate rating of 44 amperes?

Solution

Nameplate FLC is not used
430.6(A)
Use table value for FLC
Table 430.248
10 hp at 240 V
Table value FLC = 50 A
Section 430.22
Ampacity = FLC × 125%
= 50 × 1.25
= 62.5 A
Table 310.16
75°C column
62.5 A requires 6 AWG THHN

Answer: 6 AWG THHN

PROBLEM 6-3

What is the minimum ampacity of the branch-circuit conductors between the controller and the 3-phase, 460-volt multispeed motor for each of the following speeds and nameplate full-load currents?

50 hp	1,800 RPM	FLC = 65 A
40 hp	1,200 RPM	FLC = 52 A
15 hp	900 RPM	FLC = 21 A
10 hp	600 RPM	FLC = 15 A

Solution

430.22(B)

Use nameplate current ratings

Ampacity = FLC nameplate × 125%

1,800 RPM	= 65 × 1.25	= **81.25 A**
1,200 RPM	= 52 × 1.25	= **65 A**
900 RPM	= 21 × 1.25	= **26.25 A**
600 RPM	= 15 × 1.25	= **18.75 A**

NEC **430.22(B)** requires the ampacity of the branch-circuit conductors on the line side of a multispeed motor controller to be not less than 125% of the highest current rating of any one speed. **See Problem 6-4.**

PROBLEM 6-4

What is the ampacity of the branch-circuit conductors on the line side of the controller in Problem 6-3?

Solution

Highest nameplate FLC at any one speed = 65 A

Ampacity = FLC × 125%
= 65 × 1.25
= 81.25 A

Answer: 81.25 A

Comment: The branch-circuit conductors on the line side of the controller are the same ampacity as the conductors with the highest ampacity rating on the motor side of the controller.

6.1.3.3 Periodic and Varying Duty Motors

The ampacity of conductors for motors used for short-time, intermittent, periodic, or varying duty is permitted to have the branch-circuit conductor ampacity calculated using a special table, **Table 430.22(E), Duty-Cycle Service. See Problems 6-5, 6-6, and 6-7.**

PROBLEM 6-5

What is the minimum ampacity of the branch-circuit conductors for a 5-horsepower, single-phase, 230-volt motor with a nameplate current of 24.5 amperes, operating on a periodic duty cycle of 15 minutes?

Solution

Nameplate current rating is used

Table 430.22(E)

FLC 15 min. periodic duty = 90%

Ampacity = FLC (nameplate) × 90%
= 24.5 × 0.90
= 22.05 A

Answer: 22.05 A

PROBLEM 6-6

What is the minimum ampacity of the branch-circuit conductors for a continuous rated 15-horsepower, 230-volt, 3-phase varying duty type motor with a nameplate full-load current rating of 16.5 amperes?

Solution

Nameplate FLC is used

Table 430.22(E)

Continuous rated motor, varying duty = 200%

Ampacity = FLC (nameplate) × 200%
= 16.5 × 2.00
= 33 A

Answer: 33 A

CHAPTER 6 MOTOR CALCULATIONS

PROBLEM 6-7

What is the minimum size THWN copper conductors needed for the branch-circuit conductors in Problem 6-6?

Solution

Table 310.16
  THWN, 75°C copper column
  33A THWN requires 10 AWG copper
Answer: 10 AWG THWN copper

6.1.3.4 Torque Motor

Torque motors are designed for applications requiring high torque at a stall condition. Their size can range from small to large, and they utilize a direct drive application requiring no gearbox or belt connection to the load. One type of application would be a roll-winding of paper, film, or other type of material, allowing for varying and controlled take-up. The motor could be used in either a continuous or noncontinuous application. The term *locked-rotor current* (LRC) is used in conjunction with the torque motor. Locked-rotor current is the current a motor will draw with the shaft of the motor held stationary. A torque motor will drive the load until the shaft of the motor is stationary.

According to **430.6(B)**, when calculating the ampacity of the branch-circuit conductors for a torque motor, the nameplate locked-rotor current will be used. **See Problems 6-8 and 6-9.**

NEC **430.6(D)** clarifies that valve actuator motor assemblies are not torque motors and that the nameplate full-load current is the rated motor current to be used for calculations.

Two motors can be controlled from a common control system located in a single cabinet.

PROBLEM 6-8

What is the minimum ampacity of the branch-circuit conductors for a 230-volt, single-phase torque motor used in continuous-duty application with a nameplate locked-rotor current rating of 105 amperes?

Solution

430.6(B)
  Use nameplate locked-rotor current
430.22
  Ampacity = LRC (nameplate) × 125%
         = 105 × 1.25
         = 131.25 A
Answer: 131.25 A

PROBLEM 6-9

What is the minimum size XHHW branch-circuit copper conductors needed for the motor in Problem 6-8?

Solution

Table 310.16
  XHHW, 90°C column
110.14(C)(1)(b)(2)
  Limited to 75°C column
  131.25 A requires 1/0 AWG XHHW copper
Answer: 1/0 AWG XHHW copper

6.1.3.5 Wye-Start, Delta-Run Motor

The wye-start, delta-run motor is one technique used for reduced-voltage starting, resulting in a lower starting current. *NEC* **430.22(C)** requires the line conductors to the controller be calculated at 125% of the motor full-load current. This section also requires that the six (load) conductors between the controller and the motor be calculated at 72% of the motor full-load current. The informational note following **430.22(C)** explains that for a wye-start, delta-run connected motor, the motor circuit conductors carry 58% of the rated load current due to the delta configuration. The

72% is actually the product of 58% multiplied by 125%. **See Problem 6-10**.

6.1.3.6 Adjustable Speed Drive Motor - 430.122(A)

Circuit conductors supplying power conversion equipment included as part of an adjustable-speed drive system require the input conductors to be 125% of the input rating of the conversion unit. This compensates for the current used in the conversion unit.

6.1.3.7 Wound-Rotor Induction Motor

The wound-rotor induction motor is similar to a transformer with a primary and a secondary. The primary is the stationary or stator winding, and the secondary winding is wound on the rotor and allowed to turn. **See Problem 6-11**.

There are no line electrical connections to the secondary or rotor of a squirrel-cage induction motor. However, there are electrical control connections to the secondary (rotor) of the wound-rotor motor. These connections are used to connect resistance into the secondary circuit to control the starting and the speed of the motor. Therefore, there are two sets of conductors to calculate for the branch-circuit conductors of a wound-rotor motor. The branch-circuit conductors going to the motor, often referred to as the primary conductors, are connected to the stator. The leads used to connect the rotor, often referred to as the secondary conductors, are connected to a remote bank of resistors via slip rings. The resistance can be built into the controller, as for a drum controller, or the resistance can be a bank of resistors entirely separate or apart from the controller. **See Figure 6-2**.

Figure 6-2. Wound-Rotor Induction Motor. A wiring diagram of a wound-rotor induction motor includes the secondary winding and resistor bank.

Three different installation situations can affect the sizing of the secondary conductors:

1. Resistors within a controller rated as continuous duty
2. Resistors within a controller rated other than continuous duty (short-time, intermittent, periodic, or varying)
3. Resistors located apart from the controller

NEC **430.23(A)** covers **Problem 6-12**. For a continuous-duty motor with the resistors within the controller, the conductors connecting the

PROBLEM 6-10

Determine the minimum ampacity of the following branch-circuit conductors for a 20-horsepower, 3-phase, 440-volt, wye-start, delta-run motor.

1. Line conductors to controller
2. Conductors between controller and motor

Solution

Calculation 1
Line conductors to controller
Table 430.250
  20 hp at 440 V
  FLC = 27 A
430.22(C)
  Ampacity = FLC × 125%
         = 27 × 1.25
         = 33.75 A
Answer: 33.75 A

Calculation 2
All conductors between controller and motor
430.22(C)
  Ampacity = FLC × 72%
         = 27 × 0.72
         = 19.44 A
Answer: 19.44 A

PROBLEM 6-11

Determine the minimum size of the following THWN copper branch-circuit conductors for the installation of a 20-horsepower, 3-phase, 460-volt adjustable-speed Design B motor and a conversion unit with an input rating of 30 amperes. (All equipment is listed with 75°C temperature ratings.)

1. Input conductors to conversion unit
2. Conductors between conversion unit and motor

Solution

Calculation 1
Circuit conductors to drive unit
430.6(C) and 430.122(A)
  Ampacity = input current × 125%
       = 30 × 1.25
       = 37.5 A
Table 310.16 Ampacity
  THWN, 75°C copper column
  37.5 A requires 8 AWG THWN
Answer: 8 AWG THWN

Calculation 2
Conductors from drive unit to motor
Section 430.22
  Use table value
Table 430.250
  20 hp at 460 V
  FLC = 27 A
  Ampacity = FLC × 125%
       = 27 × 1.25
       = 33.75 A
Table 310.16 Ampacity
  THWN, 75°C copper column
  33.75 A requires 10 AWG THWN
Answer: 10 AWG THWN

PROBLEM 6-12

What is the minimum required ampacity of both the primary conductors and the secondary conductors of a continuous-duty, 50-horsepower, 460-volt, 3-phase, wound-rotor induction motor, with a full-load primary current of 62 amperes and a full-load secondary current of 102 amperes, when the secondary resistance is located within the controller?

Solution

Calculation 1
Primary branch-circuit conductors
  Nameplate FLC is not used
Table 430.250
  50 hp at 460 V
  FLC = 65 A
430.22
  Ampacity = FLC × 125%
       = 65 × 1.25
       = 81.25 A
Answer: 81.25 A

Calculation 2
Secondary conductors:
430.23(A)
  Ampacity = secondary nameplate FLC × 125%
       = 102 × 1.25
       = 127.5 A
Answer: 127.5 A

PROBLEM 6-13

What is the minimum ampacity of the primary branch-circuit conductors and secondary conductors for a continuous-duty, wound-rotor induction motor, with intermittent duty-rated secondary resistors that are installed within the controller and the following information on the nameplate: 75-horsepower, 460-volt, 3-phase, primary FLC 88 amperes and secondary FLC 150 amperes?

Solution

Calculation 1
Primary branch-circuit conductors
  Nameplate FLC not used
Table 430.250
  75 hp at 460 V
  FLC = 96 A
430.22(A)
  Use table value
  Ampacity = FLC × 125%
           = 96 × 1.25
           = 120 A
Answer: 120 A

Calculation 2
Secondary conductors
430.23(B)
  Use Table 430.22(E)
  Intermittent duty 15 min. = 85%
  Ampacity = secondary nameplate FLC × 85%
           = 150 × 0.85
           = 127.5 A
Answer: 127.5 A

PROBLEM 6-14

What is the ampacity of the primary and secondary conductors for a continuous-duty, wound-rotor induction motor with heavy intermittent-duty secondary resistors mounted in a separate enclosure from the controller with the following motor information on the nameplate: 25-horsepower, 3-phase, 208-volt, primary FLC 75 amperes and secondary FLC 142 amperes?

Solution

Calculation 1
Primary branch-circuit conductors
  Nameplate FLC not used
Table 430.250
  25 hp at 208 V
  FLC = 74.8 A
430.22(A)
  Ampacity = FLC × 125%
           = 74.8 × 1.25
           = 93.5 A
Answer: 93.5 A

Calculation 2
Secondary conductors
Table 430.23(C)
  Heavy intermittent duty = 85%
  Ampacity = secondary nameplate FLC × 85%
           = 142 × 0.85
           = 120.7 A
Answer: 120.7 A

---

secondary (rotor) to the controller are required to have an ampacity of not less than 125% of the nameplate full-load current of the motor secondary.

NEC **430.23(B)** covers the wound-rotor secondary conductors. For a wound-rotor motor with the resistor within the controller and a short-time, intermittent, periodic, or varying duty rating, the ampacity of the secondary conductors is required to be not less than the nameplate secondary current multiplied by the percentage given in **Table 430.22(E)**. Wound-rotor motors are used less today due to modern adjustable-speed drive AC motors. **See Problems 6-13 and 6-14.**

When the secondary resistor is separate from the controller, the ampacity of the conductors between the controller and resistor are required to be not less than the values given in **Table 430.23(C)**.

6.1.3.8 Circuit Conductors Supplying More Than One Motor

Section 430.24 covers the installation of two or more motors and other load(s) supplied by the same conductors. If only motor loads are installed, follow these three basic steps:

1. **Step 1:** Decide which motor has the largest FLC rating. (Note: largest horsepower may not be largest FLC)
2. **Step 2:** Multiply the largest FLC rating of one motor by 125%.
3. **Step 3:** Add FLC rating of all other motors.

If two motors of equal rating are installed on the same motor circuit conductors, the ampacity of the conductors is required to be 125% of the full-load current of one motor plus the full-load current of the second motor. Additionally, since **430.24** is in **Part II, Motor Circuit Conductors**, in addition to applying to branch-circuit conductors, it also applies to feeders and services as specified in **220.50**. **See Problem 6-15.**

PROBLEM 6-15

Two 5-horsepower, 208-volt, 3-phase squirrel-cage motors are to be installed on the same branch circuit. What is the minimum ampacity of the branch-circuit conductors?

Solution
Table 430.250
  5 hp at 208 V
  FLC = 16.7 A
430.24
  Ampacity = (FLC motor 1 × 125%) + FLC motor 2
           = (16.7 × 1.25) + 16.7
           = 37.575 A
Answer: 37.575 A

If two motors of unequal rating are installed on the same branch circuit, the ampacity of the branch-circuit conductors is required to be 125% of the full-load current of the largest motor plus the full-load current of the second motor. **See Problem 6-16**.

6.1.3.9 Circuit Conductors Combining Motors with Other Loads
Section 430.24 covers motor circuit conductors supplying both motor-operated and non–motor-operated equipment, such as lighting, heating, or appliances. For these circuits, the minimum ampacity of the motor circuit conductors must not be less than 125% of the full-load current of the largest motor, plus the full-load current(s) of the other motors, plus 100% of the noncontinuous load of the other equipment, plus 125% of the continuous load of the other equipment on the circuit. **See Problems 6-17 and 6-18**.

PROBLEM 6-16

What is the minimum ampacity of the branch-circuit conductors supplying two 230-volt, single-phase motors: one 5-horsepower and one 2-horsepower?

Solution
Table 430.248
  2 hp at 230 V
  FLC = 12 A
Table 430.248
  5 hp at 230 V
  FLC = 28 A
  28 A is largest FLC
  Ampacity = (largest FLC × 125%) + second motor FLC
           = (28 × 1.25) + 12
           = 47 A
Answer: 47 A

PROBLEM 6-17

What is the minimum ampacity of the branch-circuit conductors when the following 3-phase motors are installed on the same 460-volt branch circuit: one 10-horsepower squirrel-cage induction motor, one 25-horsepower squirrel-cage induction motor, and one 30-horsepower synchronous motor?

Solution
Table 430.250
  FLC, 3-phase, 460 V
  10hp squirrel-cage = 14 FLC
  25hp squirrel-cage = 34 FLC
  30hp synchronous = 32 FLC
  (Note the largest hp motor does not have the largest FLC)
  25 hp is largest FLC at 34 A
  Ampacity = (largest FLC × 125%) + FLC of others
           = (34 × 1.25) + (14 + 32)
           = 88.5 A
Answer: 88.5 A

PROBLEM 6-18

What is the minimum ampacity of the branch-circuit conductors supplying power to a 1-horsepower, 120-volt, single-phase, squirrel-cage motor and 600 watts of noncontinuous incandescent lighting load?

Solution

Table 430.248
1 hp at 120 V
FLC = 16 A
Lighting

$$I = \frac{P}{E}$$
$$= \frac{600}{120}$$
$$= 5 \text{ A}$$

430.24(1) and 430.24(3)
Ampacity = (motor FLC × 125%) + (lighting × 100%)
= (16 × 1.25) + (5 × 1)
= 20 + 5
= 25 A

Answer: 25 A

PROBLEM 6-20

A single-phase, 240-volt branch circuit consists of two 10-horsepower continuous-duty motors and one 5-horsepower, 15-minute periodic duty motor. The nameplate FLC for the 5-horsepower motor is 27 amperes. What is the minimum ampacity of the branch-circuit conductors?

Solution

Motor 1 and 2 = 10 hp
Table 430.248
10 hp at 240 V
FLC = 50 A
Motor 3 = 5 hp
430.24 Exception No. 1 and 430.22(E)
FLC - use nameplate value

Table 430.22(E)
Periodic duty 15 min. = 90%
5 hp ampacity = FLC × 90%
= 27 × 0.90
= 24.3 A
Total ampacity = (50 × 1.25) + (50 + 24.3)
= 62.5 + 74.3
= 136.8 A

Answer: 136.8 A

When a motor and fixed electrical space-heating equipment are installed on the same branch circuit, **Section 430.24 Exception No. 2** indicates that **424.4(B)** takes precedence. *NEC* **424.4(B), Branch-Circuit Sizing**, points out that these heater conductors are continuous-duty and require the branch-circuit conductors for the heater portion of the circuit to be increased to 125% of the heater ampacity. The result is that both the motor and heater require the common branch circuit to be sized at 125% of their combined full-load current. **See Problem 6-19**.

PROBLEM 6-19

A fixed electric space heater has 1,200 watts of resistance heating and an associated 3-horsepower, 240-volt, single-phase fan motor. The fixed space heater is to be installed on a single branch circuit. Calculate the minimum ampacity of the branch-circuit conductors.

Solution

Heater

$$I = \frac{P}{E}$$
$$= \frac{1,200}{240}$$
$$= 5 \text{ A}$$

Table 430.248
3 hp at 240 V
FLC = 17 A
430.24(1), 424.4(B), and 430.24(4)
I (total) = (17 × 125%) + (5 × 125%), or
Ampacity = I (total) × 125%
= 22 × 1.25
= 27.5 A

Answer: 27.5 A

When a group of motors is installed on the same circuit and one of the motors is short-time, intermittent, periodic, or varying duty, that motor's branch-circuit current is permitted to be calculated according to the table for duty-cycle service. **Section 430.24 Exception No. 1** references **430.22(E)** for these calculations. **See Problem 6-20**.

CHAPTER 6   MOTOR CALCULATIONS

When two motors, or one motor and other loads, are on the same branch circuit and are interlocked to prevent simultaneous operation, the branch-circuit conductors are permitted to be sized at 125% of the largest load (or total simultaneous load) according to **Section 430.24 Exception No. 3**. See **Problem 6-21**.

6.2 MOTOR BRANCH-CIRCUIT SHORT-CIRCUIT AND GROUND-FAULT PROTECTION

Motor branch-circuit short-circuit and ground-fault protection is covered by **Article 430, Part IV** as permitted by **240.4(G)**. Overcurrent protective devices sized to protect the motor circuit conductors in accordance with **240.4** will typically nuisance trip due to the inrush currents when the motor is starting. Higher sizes and ratings are therefore permitted in **Part IV** of **Article 430**.

6.2.1 General

The purpose of motor branch-circuit short-circuit and ground-fault protection is to protect the circuit conductors, motors, and motor-controller equipment against overcurrent due to short circuits or ground faults. **See Figure 6-3**.

Circuit breakers, fuses, and thermal protectors are permitted to be used as the overcurrent protective device (OCPD) for motor branch-circuit short-circuit and ground-fault protection.

Three types of fuses are used:

1. Non–time-delay fuses
2. Time-delay fuses
3. Class CC fuses

PROBLEM 6-21

A 20-horsepower and a 40-horsepower 3-phase, 460-volt motor are on the same branch circuit and are interlocked so that only one of the motors can operate at any given time. What is the minimum ampacity of the branch-circuit conductors?

Solution

430.24 Exception No. 3
  40 hp largest load operating at any given time
Table 430.250
  40 hp at 460 V
  FLC = 52 A
  Ampacity = FLC × 125%
    = 52 × 1.25
    = 65 A
Answer: 65 A

Figure 6-3. Motor One-Line Diagram. Circuit breakers or fuses serve as the motor branch-circuit short-circuit and ground-fault protection of a motor circuit as set forth in **Part IV** *of* **Article 430**.

Three types of circuit breakers (CBs) are used:

1. Fixed or inverse-time circuit breakers
2. Adjustable-trip circuit breakers
3. Instantaneous-trip circuit breakers, also known as motor circuit protectors (MCPs)

A more common term for *inverse-time circuit breaker* is *thermal-magnetic circuit breaker*.

Calculations for inverse-time and adjustable-trip circuit breakers use the same values.

6.2.1.1 Standard Size Ratings for Overcurrent Devices

The standard ampere ratings for fuses and fixed circuit breakers are listed in **240.6(A)**. The two types of fixed circuit breakers are the inverse-time circuit breaker and the nonadjustable circuit breaker.

The three parts to be looked at in **240.6(A)** are:

1. The standard ampere ratings for fuses and inverse-time circuit breakers are listed for 15 through 6,000 amperes. (Note: 15 amperes is the smallest standard rating listed for a circuit breaker.)
2. Special ampere ratings for fuses are additionally listed at 1, 3, 6, 10, and 601 amperes.
3. The use of nonstandard rated fuses or circuit breakers is permitted. Fuses are available in almost any size to fit the required installation.

NEC **430.6(A)** requires the use of the full-load currents in **Table 430.247**, **Table 430.248**, **Table 430.249**, and **Table 430.250**, as provided in the *Code*, for calculating the size of the motor branch-circuit short-circuit and ground-fault protection. The motor nameplate full-load current rating is generally not used. The values given in the tables are the full-load currents, which are suitable to be used for most motors running at usual speeds and with normal torque characteristics.

The calculations for the motor branch-circuit short-circuit and ground-fault protection for all squirrel-cage motors are the same when using a non–time-delay fuse, a time-delay fuse, an adjustable-trip circuit breaker, or an inverse-time circuit breaker. The percentages given in **Table 430.52** are the same for both types of alternating-current polyphase motors. The calculations differ only when an instantaneous-trip circuit breaker is used, because the percentage increases are different. The instantaneous-trip circuit breaker calculations should be looked at separately.

Table 430.52 Maximum Rating or Setting of Motor Branch-Circuit Short-Circuit and Ground-Fault Protective Devices

	Percentage of Full-Load Current			
Type of Motor	Nontime Delay Fuse[1]	Dual Element (Time-Delay) Fuse[1]	Instantaneous Trip Breaker	Inverse Time Breaker[2]
Single-phase motors	300	175	800	250
AC polyphase motors other than wound-rotor	300	175	800	250
Squirrel cage — other than Design B energy-efficient	300	175	800	250
Design B energy-efficient	300	175	1100	250
Synchronous[3]	300	175	800	250
Wound-rotor	150	150	800	150
DC (constant voltage)	150	150	250	150

Note: For certain exceptions to the values specified, see 430.54.
[1] The values in the Nontime Delay Fuse column apply to time-delay Class CC fuses.
[2] The values given in the last column also cover the ratings of nonadjustable inverse time types of circuit breakers that may be modified as in 430.52(C)(1), Exceptions No. 1 and No. 2.
[3] Synchronous motors of the low-torque, low-speed type (usually 450 rpm or lower), such as are used to drive reciprocating compressors, pumps, and so forth, that start unloaded, do not require a fuse rating or circuit-breaker setting in excess of 200 percent of full-load current.

Reproduced with permission of NFPA from NFPA 70®, *National Electrical Code*® (NEC®), 2020 edition. Copyright© 2019, National Fire Protection Association. For a full copy of the NEC®, please go to www.nfpa.org.

Figure 6-4. Table 430.52. *The percentages given in* **Table 430.52***, generally, are the maximum as permitted by the heading of the table.*

For a full-voltage, across-the-line start, starting current is effectively the same as the locked-rotor current of the motor, as full voltage is applied to the motor with little rotation. The locked-rotor current of a motor depends on the type and construction of the motor. When a motor is starting, the motor inrush current or motor starting current is much higher than the motor full-load current.

A general rule of thumb is to calculate the locked-rotor current for a motor (other than a Design B energy-efficient motor) at six times the motor full-load current. The starting current for a Design B energy-efficient motor will run eight or more times the full-load current of the motor.

6.2.1.2 Basic Protection

NEC **430.52(A)** sets the stage for providing a motor branch-circuit short-circuit and ground-fault overcurrent protective device.

NEC **430.52(B)** requires the motor branch-circuit short-circuit and ground-fault protective device to be able to carry the starting current.

NEC **430.52(C)** lists each of the various methods for calculating the rating or setting of the various overcurrent protective devices used for motor branch-circuit short-circuit and ground-fault protection.

The fundamental rule, found in **430.52(C)(1)**, requires that the maximum rating or setting of the protective device not exceed the values calculated according to **Table 430.52**. **See Figure 6-4**. As the calculation often results in a nonstandard size overcurrent protective device, and it is more desirable to use standard sizes, the general rule would require reducing the size from the maximum to a standard size. Since reducing the size to a standard rating may not be adequate to start the motor, **Exception No. 1** permits an increase from the maximum percentage to the next higher standard size overcurrent protective device. **See Figure 6-5**.

(C) Rating or Setting.

(1) In Accordance with Table 430.52. A protective device that has a rating or setting not exceeding the value calculated according to the values given in Table 430.52 shall be used.

Exception No. 1: Where the values for branch-circuit short-circuit and ground-fault protective devices determined by Table 430.52 do not correspond to the standard sizes or ratings of fuses, nonadjustable circuit breakers, thermal protective devices, or possible settings of adjustable circuit breakers, a higher size, rating, or possible setting that does not exceed the next higher standard ampere rating shall be permitted.

Figure 6-5. Exception No. 1 to Table 430.52. *If the calculation from* **Table 430.52** *does not correspond to a standard rating of an overcurrent protective device,* **Exception No. 1** *permits an increase to the next higher standard rating.*

NEC **430.52(C)(2)** requires the manufacturer's maximum rating not to be exceeded. Where maximum branch-circuit short-circuit and ground-fault protection ratings are shown in the manufacturer's overload relay table for use with a motor controller or otherwise marked on the equipment, the calculated standard size must not exceed the listed manufacturer's rating. This applies to all calculations when made with the basic rules or with the exceptions for starting current. This section also complies with the second sentence of **Section 110.9** such that the overload devices must be rated for not less than the current that must be interrupted.

6.2.1.3 Standard Example

To determine the maximum size branch-circuit short-circuit and ground-fault protective device, begin by looking up the motor full-load current rating from **Table 430.247**, **Table 430.248**, **Table 430.249**, or **Table 430.250**. Based upon the type of motor, and the type of overcurrent protective device, determine from **Table 430.52** the appropriate percentage. Multiply the percentage, in decimal form, by the motor full-load current to obtain the maximum rating. Often, the result will not correspond to a standard rating as specified in *NEC* **240.6(A)**; therefore, **430.52(C)(1) Exception No. 1** permits an increase in size to the next higher size. As "maximum" implies the largest possible, use **430.52(C)(1) Exception No. 1** to obtain the maximum size branch-circuit short-circuit and ground-fault protective device. **See Figure 6-6**.

6.2.2 Standard Sizes for Overcurrent Device Ratings (Basic Protection)

There are several necessary steps to determine the size of the maximum overcurrent protective device using time-delay fuses and non–time-delay fuses. In **Table 430.52(C)**, each type of overcurrent device is given a maximum rating or setting depending on the type of motor. For example, except for wound-rotor motors and direct current motors, the maximum rating of non–time-delay fuse values are 300% of the table value of the full-load current. For time-delay fuses, the maximum rating is 175% of the full-load current. After multiplying the appropriate percentage by the motor full-load current rating, **430.52(C)(1) Exception No. 1** is applied to obtain the maximum standard overcurrent device as specified in **240.6(A)**. It should be noted that the maximum standard size value is

For additional information, visit qr.njatcdb.org Item #1034

Dual element time-delay fuses and inverse-time circuit breakers are the most common form of motor branch-circuit short-circuit and ground-fault protective devices used today.

Solution

Calculation 1
Time-delay fuses (as shown)
Table 430.250
  20 hp at 460 V
  FLC = 27 A
Table 430.52
  Time-delay fuse = 175%
  OCPD = FLC x 175%
       = 27 × 1.75
       = 47.25 A
430.52(C)(1) Exception No. 1
  Next larger standard size permitted
240.6(A)
  Next larger size = 50 A
Answer: 50A time-delay fuses
Comment: 50 amperes is the maximum rating of the time-delay fuse for the 20-horsepower motor.

Calculation 2
Non–time-delay fuses (option 1)
Table 430.250
  20 hp at 460 V
  FLC = 27 A
Table 430.52
  Non–time-delay fuse = 300%
  OCPD = FLC x 300%
       = 27 × 3.00
       = 81 A
430.52(C)(1) Exception No. 1
  Next larger standard size permitted
240.6(A)
  Next larger size = 90 A
Answer: 90A non–time-delay fuses
Comment: 90 amperes is the maximum rating of the non–time-delay fuses for the 20-horsepower motor.

Calculation 3
Inverse-time circuit breaker (option 2)
Table 430.250
  20 hp at 460 V
  FLC = 27 A
Table 430.52
  Inverse time circuit breaker = 250%
  OCPD = FLC × 250%
       = 27 × 2.50
       = 67.5 A
430.52(C)(1) Exception No. 1
  Next larger standard size permitted
240.6(A)
  Next larger size = 70 A
Answer: 70A inverse-time circuit breaker
Comment: 70 amperes is the maximum rating of the inverse-time circuit breaker for the 20-horsepower motor.

Figure 6-6. Branch-Circuit Short-Circuit and Ground-Fault Protective Device Calculations. *This single-line drawing shows a time-delay fuse serving as the motor branch-circuit short-circuit and ground-fault protection for a 20-horsepower, 460-volt, 3-phase motor. Parallel calculations provide three different methods of protection.*

the same value as obtained when determining the maximum value in **6.2.1.3**. **See Problem 6-22**.

PROBLEM 6-22

Determine the maximum standard size time-delay fuses permitted for the motor branch-circuit short-circuit and ground-fault protection for a 25-horsepower, 240-volt, 3-phase, squirrel-cage motor with a nameplate full-load current of 64 amperes.

Solution

430.6(A)
  Use table value
Table 430.250
  25 hp at 240 V
  FLC = 68 A
430.52(C)(1)
  Time-delay fuse = 175%
  OCPD = FLC × 175%
        = 68 × 1.75
        = 119 A
430.52(C)(1) Exception No. 1
  Next larger standard size permitted
240.6(A)
  Next larger size = 125 A
Answer: 125A time-delay fuses

In practice, the maximum value stated in the *NEC* is not always desirable, but neither is the minimum value. The middle ground for motor protection most often is to avoid nuisance tripping during start-up of the motor while affording maximum protection. **See Problem 6-23**.

6.2.3 Calculations With and Without a Starting Current Problem

Due to the wide variety of motors and their given loads, sizing the branch-circuit short-circuit and ground-fault protection device correctly is important to ensure not only reliability for starting a motor, but the best protection for the motor and the motor circuit conductors.

6.2.3.1 The Basic Overcurrent Protection Rules

If starting current is not a problem, **430.52(C)(1) Exception No. 1** will result in the maximum motor branch-circuit short-circuit and ground-fault protection device. The non–time-delay fuse will result in the largest sized overcurrent protection compared to the inverse-time breaker, then the time-delay fuse, with varying equipment size. For a 40-horsepower, 460-volt, 3-phase, squirrel-cage motor, the

PROBLEM 6-23

Determine the maximum standard size non–time-delay fuses permitted for the motor branch-circuit short-circuit and ground-fault protection for a 25-horsepower, 240-volt, 3-phase, squirrel-cage, Design B energy-efficient motor.

Solution

Table 430.250
  25 hp at 240 V
  FLC = 68 A
430.52(C)(1)
  Non–time-delay fuses = 300%
  OCPD = FLC × 300%
        = 68 × 3.00
        = 204 A
430.52(C)(1) Exception No. 1
  Next larger standard size permitted
240.6(A)
  Next larger size = 225 A
Answer: 225A non–time-delay fuses
Comment: Take a practical look at Problem 6-23. The basic calculation of 204 amperes is permitted by the *Code* to go to the next higher size of 225 amperes. However, for some applications, it may be best practice to size the overcurrent protective device as close as possible to the equipment it is protecting. In this case, the best practical solution may be to select a 200-ampere fuse.

Type of OCPD	460-Volt 3-Phase FLC	Percentage of Full-Load Current Table 430.52	Next Higher Standard OCPD Rating
Non–Time-Delay Fuses	52	× 300% = 156 A	175 A
Time-Delay Fuses	52	× 175% = 91 A	100 A
Inverse-Time CB	52	× 250% = 130 A	150 A

Figure 6-7. Size Comparison of Overcurrent Protective Device Types. Dual element time-delay fuses were invented to help reduce the size of equipment needed to control motors. NEC 430.52(C)(1) Exception No. 1 was used to determine the maximum size overcurrent protective device.

sizes will vary from a 175-ampere non–time-delay fuse requiring a 200-ampere disconnect, to a 100-ampere time-delay fuse requiring only a 100-ampere disconnect. **See Figure 6-7**.

6.2.3.2 Exceptions to the Basic Overcurrent Protection Rules

If the previous calculated size from **430.52(C)(1) Exception No. 1** will not carry the starting current when attempting to start the motor, a different problem exists. The overcurrent protective device used is required to be able to carry the starting current in accordance with **430.52(B)**. NEC **430.52(C)(1) Exception No. 2** permits increasing the size of the overcurrent device if the starting current is excessive and nuisance trips the overcurrent protective device. A separate part of the exception applies to each type of overcurrent protective device. **See Figure 6-8**.

Type of OCPD	OCPD Rating Limit	Maximum Percent of FLC	430.52(C)(1) Exception
Non–Time-Delay Fuses	600 A or less	400%	Exception No. 2(a)
Non–Time-Delay Fuses (Type CC only)	None	400%	Exception No. 2(a)
Time-Delay Fuses	None	225%	Exception No. 2(b)
Large-Size Fuses	601-6,000 A	300%	Exception No. 2(d)
Inverse-Time CB	100 A or less	400%	Exception No. 2(c)
	Greater than 100 A	300%	Exception No. 2(c)

Figure 6-8. Summary of 430.52(C)(2) Exception No. 2. It is important to remember the percentages in 430.52(C)(2) Exception No. 2 are maximum values and should not be exceeded.

When referring to **430.52(C)(1) Exception No. 2**, it is important to note the phrase "shall in no case exceed…." This means that when calculations are made using this exception, the next smaller standard size overcurrent protective device must be selected. This is sometimes referred to as "rounding down." **See Problem 6-24**.

PROBLEM 6-24

Determine the maximum standard size time-delay fuses permitted for a 50-horsepower, 460-volt, 3-phase, squirrel-cage, Design B motor when the starting current is a problem.

Solution

Table 430.250
50 hp at 460 V
FLC = 65 A
430.52(C)(1) Exception No. 2(b)
Time-delay fuse = 225%
OCPD = FLC × 225%
   = 65 × 2.25
   = 146.25 A
This is a "not to exceed" value
240.6(A)
Next smaller size = 125 A
Answer: 125A time-delay fuse

The result of multiplying the given percentage by the motor full-load current will result in the maximum value; however, if a standard size is to be selected, the next lower standard size from **240.6(A)** is required to be selected. If starting current was not a problem, the maximum and maximum standard size yielded the same size in accordance with **430.52(C)(1) Exception No. 1**. If starting current is a problem, the maximum size is usually a nonstandard size, and the standard size is lower than the maximum value obtained from **430.52(C)(1) Exception No. 2**. **See Figure 6-9**.

CHAPTER 6 MOTOR CALCULATIONS

Type of OCPD	Section 430.52(C)(1) Exception	FLC	Percentage Table 430.52	Next Lower Standard OCPD Rating
Non–Time-Delay Fuses	Exception No. 2(a)	52	× 400% = 208 A	200 A
Class CC Fuses	Exception No. 2(a)	52	× 400% = 208 A	200 A
Time-Delay Fuses	Exception No. 2(b)	52	× 225% = 117 A	110 A
Inverse-Time CB	Exception No. 2(c)	52	× 400% = 208 A	200 A

Figure 6-9. Comparison of 430.52(C)(2) Exception No. 2. The use of the various overcurrent protective devices when starting current is a problem for a 40-horsepower, 460-volt, 3-phase, squirrel-cage motor should be considered. These values apply to Design B motors and Design B energy-efficient motors only when starting currents are a problem.

Problem 6-25 gives a comparison of the basic calculations and the calculations for starting current using **430.52(C)(1) Exception No. 2(a)** for non–time-delay fuses.

PROBLEM 6-25

Using the following methods, determine the maximum standard size non–time-delay fuses permitted for short-circuit and ground-fault protection for a 15-horsepower, 460-volt, 3-phase, squirrel-cage motor:

1. Basic calculation
2. Calculation with a starting current problem

Solution

Calculation 1
Basic calculation
Table 430.250
  15 hp at 460 V
  FLC = 21 A
Table 430.52
  Non–time-delay fuses = 300%
  OCPD = FLC × 300%
        = 21 × 3.00
        = 63 A
430.52(C)(1) Exception No. 1
  Next larger standard size permitted
240.6(A)
  Next larger size = 70 A
Answer: 70A non–time-delay fuses

Calculation 2
Calculation with a starting current problem
Table 430.250
  15 hp at 460 V
  FLC = 21 A
430.52(C)(1) Exception No. 2(a)
  Non–time-delay fuses = 400%
  OCPD = FLC × 400%
        = 21 × 4.00
        = 84 A
240.6(A)
  Next smaller size = 80 A
Answer: 80A non–time-delay fuses

Motor circuit overcurrent protective devices are typically located at the same location as the motor controller.

Type CC fuses are available in fractional sizes through 30 amperes in both time-delay and non–time-delay. The voltage rating is 600 volts AC. These fuses have an interrupting rating of 200,000 amperes rms symmetrical. Courtesy of Eaton.

Problem 6-26 compares the methods of basic calculation and calculation for starting current using **430.52(C)(1) Exception No. 2(b)** for time-delay fuses. Calculations using **430.52(C)(1) Exception No. 2(b)** with time-delay fuses are a reliable form of high-torque motor protection.

Problem 6-27 compares the basic calculation and the calculation for starting current using **Exception No. 2(c)** of **430.52(C)(1)** for an inverse-time circuit breaker. Calculations permitted by **430.52(C)(1) Exception No. 2(c)** using inverse-time circuit breakers are permitted.

PROBLEM 6-26

Using the following methods, determine the maximum standard size time-delay fuses permitted for branch-circuit short-circuit and ground-fault protection for a 25-horsepower, 440-volt, 3-phase squirrel-cage motor:

1. Basic protection
2. Absolute maximum under any possible condition

Solution

Calculation 1
Basic protection
Table 430.250
  25 hp at 440 V
  FLC = 34 A
Table 430.52
Time delay fuses = 175%
  OCPD = FLC × 175%
       = 34 × 1.75
       = 59.5 A
430.52(C)(1) Exception No. 1
  Next larger standard size permitted
240.6(A)
  Next larger size = 60 A
Answer: 60A time-delay fuse

Calculation 2
  Absolute maximum includes starting current
Table 430.250
  25 hp at 440 V
  FLC = 34 A
430.52(C)(1) Exception No. 2(a)
  Permits time-delay fuses up to 225%
  OCPD = FLC × 225%
       = 34 × 2.25
       = 76.5 A
240.6(A)
  Next smaller size = 70 A
Answer: 70A non–time-delay fuses

PROBLEM 6-27

Using the following methods, determine the maximum standard size inverse-time circuit breaker permitted for branch-circuit short-circuit and ground-fault protection for a 30-horsepower, 240-volt, 3-phase squirrel-cage motor:

1. Basic protection
2. Absolute maximum under any possible condition

Solution

Calculation 1
Basic protection
Table 430.250
  30 hp at 240 V
  FLC = 80 A
Table 430.52
  Inverse-time circuit breaker = 250%
  OCPD = FLC × 250%
       = 80 × 2.50
       = 200 A
240.6(A)
  200 A is a standard rating size
Answer: 200A inverse-time circuit breaker

Calculation 2
  Absolute maximum includes starting current
Table 430.250
  30 hp at 240 V
  FLC = 80 A
430.52(C)(1) Exception No. 2(c):
  Inverse-time circuit breakers (100 A or less) = 400%
  OCPD = FLC × 400%
       = 80 × 4.00
       = 320 A
240.6(A)
  Next smaller size = 300 A
Answer: 300A inverse-time circuit breaker

6.2.3.3 Single-Phase Motors

Table 430.52 provides a listing for single-phase motors. The calculations are also based upon **Section 430.52** and its exceptions. **See Problem 6-28**.

PROBLEM 6-28

Using the following methods, determine the maximum standard size time-delay fuses permitted for branch-circuit short-circuit and ground-fault protection for a 5-horsepower, 240-volt, single-phase capacitor-start motor.

1. Basic protection
2. Absolute maximum under any possible condition

Solution

Calculation 1
Basic protection
Table 430.248
  5 hp at 240 V
  FLC = 28 A
Table 430.52
  Time-delay fuse (single-phase) = 175%
  OCPD = FLC × 175%
       = 28 × 1.75
       = 49 A
430.52(C)(1) Exception No. 1
  Next larger standard size permitted
240.6(A)
  Next larger size = 50 A
Answer: 50A time-delay fuses

Calculation 2
  Absolute maximum includes starting current
Table 430.248
  5 hp at 240 V
  FLC = 28 A
430.52(C)(1) Exception No. 2(b)
  Time-delay fuses = 225%
  OCPD = FLC × 225%
       = 28 × 2.25
       = 63 A
240.6(A)
  Next smaller size = 60 A
Answer: 60A time-delay fuses

Five-horsepower, single-phase motors are hard to find and more costly as compared to 3-phase motors of the same size. Due to installation plus operating costs, alternative solutions should always be investigated.

6.2.3.4 Wound-Rotor Motors

Wound-rotor motors are also considered in **Table 430.52**. **See Problem 6-29**.

PROBLEM 6-29

Determine the maximum standard size permitted for the basic protection using an inverse-time circuit breaker for branch-circuit short-circuit and ground-fault protection for a 60-horsepower, 240-volt, 3-phase, wound-rotor induction motor.

Solution

Table 430.250
  60 hp at 240 V
  FLC = 154 A
Table 430.52
  Inverse-time circuit breaker (wound-rotor motor) = 150%
  OCPD = FLC × 150%
       = 154 × 1.50
       = 231 A
430.52(C)(1) Exception No. 1
  Next larger standard size permitted
240.6(A)
  Next larger size = 250 A
Answer: 250A inverse-time circuit breaker

6.2.3.5 Instantaneous-Trip Circuit Breakers

The instantaneous-trip circuit breaker (also known as a motor circuit protector, or MCP) is covered separately in **430.52(C)(3)**. The instantaneous-trip circuit breaker is adjustable and can be set to trip at any particular ampere rating within its range. Therefore, there is no need to round up, round down, or use the next larger or smaller standard size. The ampere rating calculated is the ampere setting for the instantaneous-trip circuit breaker.

NEC **430.52(C)(3)** puts several limitations on an instantaneous-trip circuit breaker. For example:

1. It must be part of a listed combination motor controller (such as a combination breaker and controller in the same enclosure).
2. There must be coordinated motor overload protection in each conductor.
3. There must be coordinated short-circuit and ground-fault protection in each conductor.
4. The instantaneous-trip circuit breaker must be adjustable.

PROBLEM 6-30

Using the following methods, determine the maximum motor branch-circuit short-circuit and ground-fault protection permitted for a 25-horsepower, 208-volt, 3-phase, squirrel-cage induction (other than Design B energy-efficient) motor using an instantaneous-trip circuit breaker.

1. Basic calculations
2. Absolute maximum under any possible conditions

Solution

Calculation 1
Basic protection
Table 430.250
  25 hp at 208 V
  FLC = 74.8 A
Table 430.52
  Other than Design B energy-efficient motors = 800%
  OCPD = FLC × 800%
       = 74.8 × 8.00
       = 598.4 A
Answer: 598.4A instantaneous-trip circuit breaker

Calculation 2
Absolute maximum includes starting current
Table 430.250
  25 hp at 208 V
  FLC = 74.8 A
430.52(C)(3) Exception No. 1
  Permits 1,300% of the FLC
  OCPD = FLC × 1,300%
       = 74.8 × 13.00
       = 972.4 A
Answer: 972.4A instantaneous-trip circuit breaker

Where instantaneous-trip circuit breakers are selected, there are two different basic values for the percentage of motor full-load current. Single-phase, synchronous, and squirrel-cage motors (other than Design B energy-efficient motors) are permitted to be rated up to 800% of the motor full-load current. Because the Design B energy-efficient motors have a much higher starting current, they are permitted to be rated up to 1,100% of the motor full-load current. The Design B high-efficiency motor is handled in the same way as the obsolete Design E energy-efficient motor of the past.

Where instantaneous-trip circuit breakers are used and there is a problem with starting currents, **430.52(C)(3) Exception No. 1** applies. The beginning portion of this exception permits two different values for the percentage of motor full-load current. Single-phase, synchronous, and squirrel-cage motors (other than Design B energy-efficient motors) are permitted to be rated up to 1,300% of the motor full-load current. Because Design B energy-efficient motors have a much higher starting current, they are permitted to be rated up to 1,700% of the motor full-load current.

The latter portion of **430.52(C)(3) Exception No. 1** provides that, when an engineering analysis is performed and a need is demonstrated, any values above the previously discussed 800% and 1,100% are allowed. Finally, this exception also permits the electrical engineer's evaluations to be used without actually trying the instantaneous-trip circuit breaker at a lower rating.

Basic Calculation
Table 430.52
Squirrel-cage motor
Other than Design B energy-efficient motors at 800% max
Design B energy-efficient motors at 1,100% max

Calculations when Starting Current is a Problem
430.52(C)(3) Exception No. 1
Other than Design B energy-efficient motors at 1,300% max
Design B energy-efficient motors at 1,700% max

See Problem 6-30.

6.2.3.6 Design B Energy-Efficient Motors

Problem 6-31 is unique to Design B energy-efficient motors. Although these rules are most often applied by electrical engineers, Electrical Workers need to be able to understand and apply these *Code* rules as well.

6.2.3.7 Synchronous Motors

Two things are common to the synchronous motor:

1. The power factor is considered in the calculations.
2. The percentages in **Table 430.52** are different.

The full-load current values given in **Table 430.250** are for the unity power factor. When no power factor is indicated, it is assumed to be the unity power factor, and the motor full-load current is read directly from **Table 430.250**. The footnote to **Table 430.250** calls attention to the fact that the motor full-load current must be increased using the power factor.

1. If the power factor is 90%, motor FLC = Table FLC × 1.10
2. If the power factor is 80%, motor FLC = Table FLC × 1.25

PROBLEM 6-31

Using the following methods, determine the maximum motor branch-circuit short-circuit and ground-fault protection permitted for a 25-horsepower, 460-volt, 3-phase, squirrel-cage induction, Design B energy-efficient motor using an instantaneous-trip circuit breaker.

1. Basic calculations
2. Absolute maximum under any possible conditions

Solution

Calculation 1
Basic protection
Table 430.250
　25 hp at 460 V
　FLC = 34 A
Table 430.52
　Design B energy-efficient motors = 1,100%
　OCPD = FLC × 1,100%
　　　　= 34 × 11.00
　　　　= 374 A
Answer: 374A instantaneous-trip circuit breaker

Calculation 2
　Absolute maximum includes starting current
Table 430.250
　25 hp at 460 V
　FLC = 34 A
430.52(C)(3) Exception No. 1
　Permits 1,700% of the FLC
　OCPD = FLC × 1,700%
　　　　= 34 × 17.00
　　　　= 578 A
Answer: 578A instantaneous-trip circuit breaker

The synchronous motor will have less full-load current than a squirrel-cage or wound-rotor induction motor, and the percentages permitted in **Table 430.52** can be different. The following problems are based upon the calculations for a synchronous motor. **See Problems 6-32 and 6-33.**

PROBLEM 6-32

Determine the motor branch-circuit short-circuit and ground-fault protection for a 50-horsepower, 460-volt, 3-phase synchronous motor using non–time-delay fuses. Note: the nameplate abbreviation for synchronous is SYN.

Solution

Table 430.250
   50 hp at 460 V
   FLC = 52 A
Table 430.52
   Synchronous motor, non–time-delay fuses = 300%
   OCPD = FLC × 300%
          = 52 × 3.00
          = 156 A
430.52(C)(1) Exception No. 1
   Next larger standard size permitted
240.6(A)
   Next larger size = 175 A
Answer: 175A non–time-delay fuses

6.2.3.8 Torque Motors

The motor branch-circuit short-circuit and ground-fault protection for a torque motor is based upon the size of the conductor used. The conductor size is based upon the nameplate full-load current of the motor, which is the locked-rotor current of the torque motor. For a continuous-duty application, the supply conductors would be sized at 125% of the LRC of the torque motor in accordance with **430.22**.

PROBLEM 6-33

Determine the motor branch-circuit short-circuit and ground-fault protection for a 60-horsepower, 460-volt, 3-phase synchronous motor with an 80% power factor using time-delay fuses. Note: the symbol for power factor is PF.

Solution

Table 430.250
   Synchronous-type unity power factor column
   60 hp at 460 V
   FLC = 61 A
   When 80% PF is required, multiply by 1.25
   FLC = 61 × 1.25
        = 76.25 A
Table 430.52
   Synchronous motor, time-delay fuses = 175%
   OCPD = FLC × 175%
          = 76.25 × 1.75
          = 133.43 A
430.52(C)(1) Exception No. 1
   Next larger standard size permitted
240.6(A)
   Next larger size = 150 A
Answer: 150A time-delay fuses

NEC **430.52(D)** applies to the rating or setting for torque motors and refers to **240.4(B)**. Once the supply conductors are determined using **430.22**, **240.4(B)** would be used to size the OCPD based upon the ampacity of the supply conductors.

When the conductor's ampacity does not correspond to standard size overcurrent devices, **240.4(B)(3)** permits the next higher overcurrent device for a conductor up to 800 amperes.

NEC **430.6(B)** requires that the nameplate full-load current rating be used for calculating the minimum size of the branch-circuit conductors. For a torque motor, the nameplate full-load current is the locked-rotor current (LRC). **See Problem 6-34.**

CHAPTER 6 MOTOR CALCULATIONS

PROBLEM 6-34

Time-Delay Fuses
Torque Motor
NAMEPLATE
5 HP 240 V 3 PH
LRC 91

Determine the maximum motor branch-circuit short-circuit and ground-fault protection for a 5-horsepower, 240-volt, 3-phase torque motor with a nameplate full-load current of 91 amperes, installed with THW copper conductors, using time-delay fuses, and used in a continuous-duty application.

Solution

430.6(B)
  Nameplate LRC = 91 A
430.22
  Ampacity = LRC × 125%
           = 91 × 1.25
           = 113.75 A
Table 310.16 Ampacity
  113.75 A = 2 AWG THW rated 115 A
240.4(B)
  Next larger standard size permitted
240.6(A)
  Next larger size = 125 A
Answer: 125A time-delay fuses

6.2.3.9 Basic Protection for Motor Circuits Containing Power Conversion Equipment

Adjustable-speed drives are covered by **Article 430**, **Parts I** through **IX**, unless modified or supplemented by **Part X**. Within **Part X** of **Article 430**, which covers branch-circuit short-circuit and ground-fault protection for single- and multiple-motor circuits containing power conversion equipment, there are special requirements related to overcurrent protective devices. **Sections 430.130** and **430.131** provide the user with the required overcurrent protection requirements for power conversion equipment such as adjustable-speed drive controllers.

In many cases, the proper type of overcurrent protective device, its rating, and its setting are marked on or provided within the installation instructions of the controller or equipment. If this information is provided with the power conversion equipment, it is required to be used per **110.3(B)**.

If detailed protection requirements are not provided with the equipment, **Sections 430.130** and **430.131** direct the user to follow specific protection requirements within **430.130**, which is based on specific equipment. The equipment protection is required to comply with the standard ratings and settings as specified within **430.52(C)(1)**, using **Table 430.52(C)(3)** for instantaneous-trip circuit breakers, **Table 430.52(C)(5)** for power electronic devices, and **Table 430.52(C)(6)** for self-protected combination controllers, all as determined by **430.6**.

In addition, if bypass circuits are incorporated, branch-circuit short-circuit and ground-fault protection is required to be incorporated to protect these additional circuits and added equipment. Be aware that specific limitations on the maximum permitted size of overcurrent protective devices used to protect power conversion are often specified or required.

Finally, should a single adjustable-speed drive be used to control several motors, this circuit is required to be protected by an overcurrent protective device in accordance with **430.131** and **430.53**.

Modern AC solid-state variable frequency drives (VFDs) are commonly used for commercial and industrial motor control.

6.3 MOTOR OVERLOAD PROTECTION

Both the motor and motor branch-circuit conductors must be protected against overload in accordance with **Part III** of **Article 430**.

6.3.1 General Requirements

The purpose of motor overload protection is to protect the motor, motor control apparatus, and motor branch-circuit conductors against excessive heating due to overloads. The overload current is a current that, when it persists for a sufficient length of time, can damage the equipment and/or the conductors. **See Figure 6-10**.

Overloads are caused by the following:

1. Failure to start
2. Excessive load on motor
3. Worn motor bearings
4. Other mechanical problems

Motor overloads cause a motor to draw more current. The added current produces more heat within the motor. The additional heat is often more than the motor was designed for, which reduces the life of the motor.

A motor branch-circuit short-circuit and ground-fault protection device protects the motor from short circuits and ground faults; it does not protect the motor from overloads.

Overload protection is designed to sense the current of the motor. When the setting of the overload device is exceeded, the device causes automatic disconnection of the motor. Overload protection can be accomplished by directly disconnecting line current or by causing the control circuit to stop the motor. Motor overload protection is often referred to as *motor running protection*.

Heaters installed in magnetic motor starters are the most common form of overload protection. Fuses, circuit breakers, and thermal protectors may also be used to provide overload protection, provided they fulfill the specific requirements for motor overload protection.

NEC **430.6(A)** and **430.32(A)(1)** both require the nameplate FLC be used when calculating motor overload protection. The overload calculations are the same for Design B, C, and D motors.

NEC **430.32(A)(1)** requires that overload protection devices for continuous-duty motors rated more than one horsepower be sized according to the motor nameplate FLC and the following motor nameplate information. These percentages are used for calculating the maximum overload protection.

Maximum overload protection (not to exceed):

1. Marked service factor: 125%
2. Marked temperature rise 40°C or less: 125%
3. All other motors: 115%

The service factor of 1.15 means that a motor is built to operate at 115% of its nameplate rating and may sustain this small overload without motor damage.

The 40°C temperature rise limit is rather common for most motors. The motor with a service factor of 1.15 or larger and a temperature rise of 40°C indicates a well-built motor, and the overload protection is permitted to be increased in size accordingly. Should the service factor or the temperature rise not be marked on the motor, or should a temperature rise be greater than

Figure 6-10. Motor Overloads. *Motor branch-circuit overload protection as covered in* **Part III** *of* **Article 430** *must be understood.*

40°C, the size of the motor overload protection should be reduced to a service factor of 1.15. **See Problem 6-35**.

PROBLEM 6-35

Determine the maximum overload protection (OL protection) for a 30-horsepower, 240-volt, 3-phase, squirrel-cage induction motor with a nameplate full-load current of 75 amperes, a service factor (SF) of 1.15, and a temperature rise of 40°C.

NAMEPLATE
30 HP 240 V 3 PH
SF 1.15
TEMP. RISE 40°C
FLC 75

Solution

430.32(A)(1)
  Max. OL protection
  Use nameplate FLC
  Service factor of 1.15, temperature rise of 40°C = 125%
  OL protection = FLC × 125%
               = 75 × 1.25
               = 93.75 A
Answer: 93.75 A

6.3.2 Overload Protection With and Without Problem Starting Currents

Excessive starting current can nuisance trip overload relays, and consideration for this is addressed in **430.32(C)**. Two items need to be considered: maximum overload protection, as previously discussed, and maximum overload protection if starting current is a problem. If the overload relays calculated by the percentages given in **430.32(A)(1)** do not permit the motor to start because of the starting current, **430.32(C)** permits the use of higher percentages. The values of **430.32(C)** allow about 15% more current before causing automatic disconnection of the motor.

One of the goals of overload protection is to protect a piece of electrical equipment as close to its rated full-load current as possible, while avoiding nuisance tripping during the starting current period.

NEC **430.32(C), Selection of Overload Relay**, is followed by an informational note. The informational note calls attention to the classification of motor overload relays. There are Class 10 and 10A, Class 20, and Class 30 overload relays. A Class 20 overload relay provides a longer motor acceleration time than a Class 10 or 10A overload relay. A Class 30 overload relay provides a longer motor acceleration time than a Class 20 overload relay. Therefore, selecting the higher class of overload relay may preclude the need for selecting a higher trip current. Once the motor has accelerated to full speed and current has reduced from starting current to full-load current, the optimal situation is to have the motor overload relay protecting the motor as close as practical.

Maximum overload protection where starting current is a problem:

1. Marked service factor of 1.15 or greater: 140%
2. Marked temperature rise to 40°C or less: 140%
3. All other motors: 130%

See Problem 6-36.

PROBLEM 6-36

Using the circuit diagram for Problem 6-35, determine the maximum overload protection, when the starting current is a problem, for a 30-horsepower, 240-volt, 3-phase, squirrel-cage induction motor with a nameplate full-load current of 75 amperes, a service factor of 1.15, and a temperature rise of 40°C.

Solution

Maximum protection with problem starting current:
430.32(C)
  Use nameplate FLC
  Service factor of 1.15, temperature rise of 40°C = 140%
  OL protection = FLC × 140%
               = 75 × 1.40
               = 105 A
Answer: 105 A

It is necessary to know when the starting current (or the motor acceleration time) is and is not considered a problem in order to calculate the maximum rating permitted for the overload protection device. The use of time-delay overload relays in some cases may preclude the need to select a higher overload trip setting of 130% or 140%. **See Problems 6-37 and 6-38.**

PROBLEM 6-37

Determine the overload rating of the overload relays for a 15-horsepower, 460-volt, 3-phase motor with a service factor (SF) of 1.15, a temperature rise of 40°C, and a nameplate current rating of 19 amperes.

1. What is the maximum overload protection?
2. What is the maximum overload protection with starting current?

Solution

Calculation 1
Max. OL protection
430.32(A)(1)
　Use nameplate FLC
　Service factor of 1.15, temperature rise of 40°C = 125%
　OL protection = FLC × 125%
　　　　　　　 = 19 × 1.25
　　　　　　　 = 23.75 A
Answer: 23.75 A

Calculation 2
Max. OL protection with problem starting current
430.32(C)
　Use nameplate FLC
　Service factor of 1.15, temperature rise of 40°C = 140%
　OL protection = FLC × 140%
　　　　　　　 = 19 × 1.40
　　　　　　　 = 26.6 A
Answer: 26.6 A

PROBLEM 6-38

Determine the rating of the motor overload relays for a 220-volt, 3-phase, 10-horsepower motor with a nameplate full-load current rating of 31.5 amperes.

1. What is the maximum overload protection?
2. What is the maximum overload protection with starting current?"

Solution

Calculation 1
Maximum OL protection
430.32(A)(1)
　Use nameplate FLC
　No service factor or temperature rise indicated
　All other motors = 115%
　OL protection = FLC × 115%
　　　　　　　 = 31.5 × 1.15
　　　　　　　 = 36.225 A
Answer: 36.225 A

Calculation 2
Maximum protection with problem starting current
430.32(C)
　Use nameplate FLC
　All other motors = 130%
　OL protection = FLC × 130%
　　　　　　　 = 31.5 × 1.30
　　　　　　　 = 40.95 A
Answer: 40.95 A

6.3.3 Using Thermal Protectors

When the overload protection is a thermal protector and it is an integral part of the motor, **430.32(A)(2)** gives a special percentage for it. Note that for these calculations, the motor full-load current table values are to be used. The larger the motor full-load current, the less the percentage of increase is for sizing thermal protectors:

1. Motor FLC 9 amperes or less: 170%
2. Motor FLC 9.1 through 20 amperes: 156%
3. Motor FLC greater than 20 amperes: 140%

See Problem 6-39.

PROBLEM 6-39

Determine the maximum ampere rating of a thermal protector used as the motor overload protection for a 5-horsepower, 440-volt, 3-phase motor with a nameplate rating of 8.6 amperes, a service factor of 1.15, and a temperature rise of 40°C.

Solution

Thermal protector, use table value for FLC
Table 430.250
  5 hp, 440 V, 3-phase
  FLC = 7.6 A
430.32(A)(2)
  Less than 9 A = 170%
  Thermal protector = FLC × 170%
                    = 7.6 A × 1.70
                    = 12.92 A
Answer: 12.92 A

6.3.4 Using Fuses and Circuit Breakers as Motor Overload Protection

NEC **430.32(A)** requires a separate overload device that is responsive to motor current. It could be a fuse or circuit breaker. A fuse may be used as the motor overload protection and as the motor branch-circuit short-circuit and ground-fault protection, provided it is sized for the overload protection as well. **See Problems 6-40 and 6-41.**

PROBLEM 6-40

Determine the largest time-delay fuse permitted for the overload protection, when the starting current is a problem, for a 3-horsepower, single-phase, 240-volt motor, with a service factor of 1.15, a temperature rise of 40°C, and a nameplate current rating of 15 amperes.

Solution

430.32(C)
  Service factor of 1.15, temperature rise of 40°C = 140%
  Maximum OL amperes not to exceed nameplate
  OL protection = FLC × 140%
                = 15 × 1.40
                = 21 A
  Not to exceed 21 A
240.6(A)
  Next smaller standard size = 20 A
Answer: 20A time-delay fuses

PROBLEM 6-41

Determine the maximum size inverse-time circuit breaker that is permitted to be used as the motor overload protection for a 20-horsepower, 460-volt, 3-phase motor with a nameplate full-load current rating of 25 amperes when the starting current is a problem.

Solution

430.32(C)
  All other motors = 130%
  OL protection = FLC × 130%
                = 25 A × 1.30
                = 32.5 A
  Not to exceed 32.5 A
240.6(A)
  Next smaller standard size = 30 A
Answer: 30A inverse-time circuit breaker

6.3.5 Overload Protection with Power Factor Corrected Motors

If a motor installation includes a capacitor connected on the load side of the motor overload device, the rating or setting of the motor overload device is required to be based upon the improved power factor of the motor circuit according to **Section 460.9**. **See Figure 6-11**. If a motor is power factor corrected, the voltage of the circuit remains the same. Since the motor is an inductive load but also consumes true power, the capacitor current is out of phase with the motor inductive current and causes a reduction in line current. The power factor is improved and moves closer to 100% as the circuit becomes less inductive. The motor current remains the same; however, due to the reduction in line current, the overloads see a reduced current and the overload protection needs to be resized due to the lower line current that is present through the overload relay. **See Problem 6-42**.

Figure 6-11. Power Factor Corrected Motor. Power factor correction for larger motors, such as 100 horsepower and larger, can easily be accomplished with a fixed capacitor bank mounted at the motor controller and on the load side of the controller. Therefore, the capacitor is only energized when the motor is running and will not cause a leading power factor when the motor is not running.

PROBLEM 6-42

Determine the maximum size overload protection for a 10-horsepower, 240-volt, 3-phase motor, with a full-load current rating of 33 amperes. It has a power factor of 85% and a service factor of 1.25 when capacitors are connected on the load side of the overload relays for power factor correction. The circuit also draws 29 amperes after the power factor correction.

Solution

460.9
  Nameplate full load current = 33 A
  Improved power factor corrected current = 29 A
  Use 29 A instead of 33 A
430.32(A)(1)
  Service factor = 125%
  OL protection = FLC (corrected) × 125%
      = 29 × 1.25
      = 36.25 A

Answer: 36.25 A

6.4 MOTOR DISCONNECTING MEANS

Disconnecting means are covered by **Part IX** of **Article 430**.

6.4.1 General Requirements

A motor disconnecting means, commonly referred to as the motor disconnect switch, has three responsibilities:

1. To safely carry the motor full-load current under normal operation
2. To be capable of being opened under load
3. To be capable of being opened under locked-rotor conditions

In general, a disconnect is required for both the controller and the motor and is required to be within sight. Under certain conditions, a single disconnect can serve both the controller and the motor and be located, for example, at a motor control center. **See Figure 6-12**.

To fulfill the first responsibility, the *Code* requires the motor disconnecting means to have an ampere rating. *NEC* **430.110(A)** requires the motor disconnecting means to have an ampere rating of at least 115% of the motor full-load current.

To fulfill the second and third responsibility, **Section 430.109** requires the motor-circuit switch to be horsepower-rated for the locked-rotor current and to be listed. The circuit breaker and molded-case switch are not horsepower-rated, but are tested and identified for interrupting locked-rotor current at six times their rated ampacity.

Section 430.109 permits the motor disconnecting switch to be one of the following "listed" pieces of equipment:

1. Motor-Circuit Switch: A motor-circuit switch is a fused switch rated in horsepower and used as a disconnecting means.
2. Molded-Case Circuit Breaker: A molded-case circuit breaker contains overcurrent protection and is used as a disconnecting means.
3. Molded-Case Switch: A molded-case switch has no overcurrent protection and serves as a disconnecting means.
4. Instantaneous-Trip Circuit Breaker: An instantaneous-trip circuit breaker is part of a listed combination motor controller.
5. Self-Protected Combination Controller: commonly referred to as a combination starter-disconnect; includes the overcurrent protection, disconnect, controller, and overloads all contained in one enclosure.
6. Manual Motor Controller: A manual motor controller is marked "Suitable as Motor Disconnect." It is installed between the motor branch-circuit short-circuit and ground-fault protection and the motor. It could be used as an isolating switch.
7. System Isolation Equipment: System isolation equipment shall be listed for disconnecting purposes. It shall be installed on the load side of the overcurrent protective device and its disconnecting means.

A motor disconnecting means is required to be capable of interrupting locked-rotor currents. The horsepower rating of a disconnecting means indicates the amount of locked-rotor current it is capable of interrupting. The motor-circuit switch is required to be horsepower rated.

Figure 6-12. Motor Disconnect. Motor disconnecting means are covered in **Part IX** of **Article 430**, and a disconnect for both the motor and the controller is required in accordance with **430.102**.

6.4.2 Locked-Rotor Current Calculations

Locked-rotor current is the amount of current a motor draws when the rotor of the motor is not rotating. No counter-electromotive force is developed in the motor rotor, and only the low resistance of the stator windings limits the line current. LRCs can take place at the time of starting as the motor rotor and the load are at rest, or when a fault takes place and the rotor is unable to turn. As a general rule of thumb, the locked-rotor current of a motor is equal to the starting current of the motor.

NEC 430.7(A)(8) requires motors to be marked with a code letter or else the locked-rotor amperes of the motor to be marked on the nameplate of the motor. The code letter indicates the range of the LRC for a particular motor and is usually found on Design B, C, and D motors, as well as Design B energy-efficient motors. (Do not confuse the design letter with the code letter, as they are two separate markings.) Additionally, remember that

Table 430.7(B) Locked-Rotor Indicating Code Letters

Code Letter	Kilovolt-Amperes per Horsepower with Locked Rotor
A	0–3.14
B	3.15–3.54
C	3.55–3.99
D	4.0–4.49
E	4.5–4.99
F	5.0–5.59
G	5.6–6.29
H	6.3–7.09
J	7.1–7.99
K	8.0–8.99
L	9.0–9.99
M	10.0–11.19
N	11.2–12.49
P	12.5–13.99
R	14.0–15.99
S	16.0–17.99
T	18.0–19.99
U	20.0–22.39
V	22.4 and up

Figure 6-13. Table 430.7(B). *The code letter provides a range of values for the locked-rotor current and is given in units of measurements of kilovolt-amperes per horsepower. A calculation must be performed to determine the LRC.*

Reproduced with permission of NFPA from NFPA 70®, *National Electrical Code*® (NEC®), 2020 edition. Copyright© 2019, National Fire Protection Association. For a full copy of the NEC®, please go to www.nfpa.org.

Design B energy-efficient motors typically have a very high starting current. **See Figure 6-13**.

NEC **Table 430.7(B)** lists a range of values for LRCs for motors marked with a particular code letter. For example, a motor marked with code letter F has a locked-rotor current ranging from 5.0 to 5.59 kVA per horsepower. This table can be used to calculate three values as illustrated in the following examples:

1. To calculate the lowest value, read directly from the table's lowest value listed.
   Example: Code letter C = 3.55 kVA
2. To calculate the maximum value, read directly from the table's highest value listed.
   Example: Code letter C = 3.99 kVA
3. To calculate the average value, add the lowest value and the highest value and divide by two.
   Example: Code letter C =
   $$\frac{(3.55 + 3.99)}{2} = 3.77 \text{ kVA}$$

PROBLEM 6-43

A 25-horsepower, 460-volt, 3-phase motor with a code letter K is to be installed.

1. What is the lowest LRC for the motor?
2. What is the average LRC for the motor?
3. What is the maximum LRC for the motor?

Solution

Calculation 1
Lowest LRC
Table 430.7(B)
Lowest kVA per hp
Code letter K = 8.0

$$LRC = \frac{(\text{kVA per hp} \times 1{,}000 \times \text{hp})}{(E \times 1.73)}$$

$$= \frac{(8 \times 1{,}000 \times 25)}{(460 \times 1.73)}$$

$$= 251.32 \text{ A}$$

Answer: 251.32 A lowest LRC

Calculation 2
Average LRC
Table 430.7(B)
Code letter K ranges 8.0 to 8.99
Lowest = 8.0 kVA per hp
Max = 8.99 kVA per hp

$$\text{Avg.} = \frac{(\text{max.} + \text{low})}{2}$$

$$= \frac{16.99}{2}$$

$$= 8.495 \text{ kVA per hp}$$

$$LRC = \frac{(\text{kVA per hp} \times 1{,}000 \times \text{hp})}{(E \times 1.73)}$$

$$= \frac{(8.495 \times 1{,}000 \times 25)}{(460 \times 1.73)}$$

$$= 266.87 \text{ A}$$

Answer: 266.87 A average LRC

Calculation 3
Max. LRC
Table 430.7(B)
Max. kVA per hp
Code letter K = 8.99

$$LRC = \frac{(\text{kVA per hp} \times 1{,}000 \times \text{hp})}{(E \times 1.73)}$$

$$= \frac{(8.99 \times 1{,}000 \times 25)}{(460 \times 1.73)}$$

$$= 282.42 \text{ A}$$

Answer: 282.42 A maximum LRC

6.4.3 Locked-Rotor Current Equations

The following equations are used for calculating the LRC for motors with a code letter. When working with LRC, do not round kVAs to whole numbers.

Single-Phase LRC

$$LRC = \frac{(\text{Locked-Rotor kVA per hp}) \times 1{,}000 \times hp}{E}$$

3-Phase LRC

$$LRC = \frac{(\text{Locked-Rotor kVA per hp}) \times 1{,}000 \times hp}{E \times 1.732}$$

Where:

LRC = locked-rotor current expressed in amperes (I)
Locked-rotor kVA per hp = value from **Table 430.7(B)**
$1{,}000$ = value used to convert kVA to volt amperes
hp = the horsepower of the motor under consideration
E = the voltage of the motor circuit under consideration

See Problem 6-43.

Once the horsepower rating of the motor is multiplied by the value in **Table 430.7(B)**, what remains is kVA. Note the similarity between the LRC equation and the following kVA power equation:

Single-Phase

$$I = \frac{kVA \times 1{,}000}{E}$$

Three-Phase

$$I = \frac{kVA \times 1{,}000}{E \times 1.732}$$

6.4.4 Table 430.251(A) and Table 430.251(B), Conversion Tables for Locked-Rotor Current

In the title of **Table 430.251(A)** and **Table 430.251(B)** is the term *Conversion Table*, which indicates that if the LRC is calculated, then the table can be used to convert the calculated LRC to the required horsepower-rated motor-circuit switch. **Table 430.251(A)** is used for single-phase motors and **Table 430.251(B)** is used for 3-phase motors. See **Figures 6-14 and 6-15**. **Section 430.109** requires a motor-circuit switch to be rated in horsepower, and many in the industry simply match the horsepower rating of the disconnect to the rating of the motor. Another method is to use the LRC conversion tables and the calculated LRC. After the calculations for LRC are made using **Table 430.7(B)**, the calculated LRC is converted to the horsepower rating needed for the motor disconnecting means by the use of **Table 430.251(A)** or **Table 430.251(B)**.

Table 430.251(A) Conversion Table of Single-Phase Locked-Rotor Currents for Selection of Disconnecting Means and Controllers as Determined from Horsepower and Voltage Rating
For use only with 430.110, 440.12, 440.41, and 455.8(C).

Rated Horsepower	Maximum Locked-Rotor Current in Amperes, Single Phase		
	115 Volts	208 Volts	230 Volts
½	58.8	32.5	29.4
¾	82.8	45.8	41.4
1	96	53	48
1½	120	66	60
2	144	80	72
3	204	113	102
5	336	186	168
7½	480	265	240
10	1000	332	300

Reproduced with permission of NFPA from NFPA 70®, *National Electrical Code*® (NEC®), 2020 edition. Copyright© 2019, National Fire Protection Association. For a full copy of the NEC®, please go to www.nfpa.org.

*Figure 6-14. Table 430.251(A). Table 430.251(A) converts LRC to horsepower and horsepower to LRC for single-phase motors and is required to be used in conjunction with **430.110**, **440.12**, **440.41**, and **455.8(C)**.*

Table 430.251(B) Conversion Table of Polyphase Design B, C, and D Maximum Locked-Rotor Currents for Selection of Disconnecting Means and Controllers as Determined from Horsepower and Voltage Rating and Design Letter
For use only with 430.110, 440.12, 440.41, and 455.8(C).

Rated Horsepower	115 Volts B, C, D	200 Volts B, C, D	208 Volts B, C, D	230 Volts B, C, D	460 Volts B, C, D	575 Volts B, C, D
½	40	23	22.1	20	10	8
¾	50	28.8	27.6	25	12.5	10
1	60	34.5	33	30	15	12
1½	80	46	44	40	20	16
2	100	57.5	55	50	25	20
3	—	73.6	71	64	32	25.6
5	—	105.8	102	92	46	36.8
7½	—	146	140	127	63.5	50.8
10	—	186.3	179	162	81	64.8
15	—	267	257	232	116	93
20	—	334	321	290	145	116
25	—	420	404	365	183	146
30	—	500	481	435	218	174
40	—	667	641	580	290	232
50	—	834	802	725	363	290
60	—	1001	962	870	435	348
75	—	1248	1200	1085	543	434
100	—	1668	1603	1450	725	580
125	—	2087	2007	1815	908	726
150	—	2496	2400	2170	1085	868
200	—	3335	3207	2900	1450	1160
250	—	—	—	—	1825	1460
300	—	—	—	—	2200	1760
350	—	—	—	—	2550	2040
400	—	—	—	—	2900	2320
450	—	—	—	—	3250	2600
500	—	—	—	—	3625	2900

Maximum Motor Locked-Rotor Current in Amperes, Two- and Three-Phase, Design B, C, and D*

*Design A motors are not limited to a maximum starting current or locked rotor current.

Figure 6-15. Table 430.251(B). Table 430.251(B) converts LRC to horsepower and horsepower to LRC for polyphase motors and is required to be used in conjunction with **430.110**, **440.12**, **440.41**, and **455.8(C)**.

Reproduced with permission of NFPA from NFPA 70®, *National Electrical Code*® (NEC®), 2020 edition. Copyright© 2019, National Fire Protection Association. For a full copy of the NEC®, please go to www.nfpa.org.

The starting current or LRC for a standard motor is generally six times or 600% of the full-load current. **Table 430.251(A)** for single-phase motors and **Table 430.251(B)** for polyphase motors with design letters B, C, and D are based upon the full-load current given in **Table 430.248** for single-phase motors and **Table 430.250** for 3-phase motors. The values listed are approximately six times the motor full-load current values given in the full-load current tables. The actual calculations show the values to be a little less than six times the full-load current. **See Problem 6-44**.

6.4.5 Calculating Motor-Circuit Switch Horsepower for Motors Marked with Code Letters

Although many designers, engineers, and installers match the horsepower rating of the motor disconnecting means to the horsepower rating of the motor based upon their code letters, some motors have a higher LRC than the matched horsepower-rated disconnect is capable of interrupting safely. Calculating the horsepower rating

A horsepower-rated disconnect switch indicates the amount of locked-rotor current it is capable of interrupting safely.

CHAPTER 6 MOTOR CALCULATIONS

145

PROBLEM 6-44

Using a 3-phase, 460-volt, 25-horsepower, squirrel-cage motor (other than a Design B energy-efficient motor) with a code letter F, determine the following:

1. What is the LRC rating of the motor using Table 430.251(B), Column 460 volts, B, C, D?
2. What is six times the FLC of Table 430.250?
3. What is the calculated maximum LRC using Table 430.7(B)?

Solution

Calculation 1
Table 430.251(B)
25 hp at 460 volts B, C, D column = 183 A
Answer: 183 A LRC

Calculation 2
Table 430.250, 25 hp at 460 V
FLC = 34 A
= 6 × FLC
= 6 × 34
Answer: 204 A LRC

Calculation 3
Table 430.7(B), Max. kVA per hp
Code letter F = 5.59 kVA per hp

$$LRC = \frac{(kVA\ per\ hp \times 1{,}000 \times hp)}{(E \times 1.73)}$$

$$= \frac{(5.59 \times 1{,}000 \times 25)}{(460 \times 1.73)}$$

$$= 175.61\ A$$

Answer: 175.61A maximum LRC

Comment: Selecting the horsepower rating of a switch from Table 430.251(B), using the calculated 175.61 amperes, a 25-horsepower switch is required.

of the motor-circuit switch based upon the code letter provides a safer installation.

6.4.5.1 General Information

As long as there is no code letter, or the code letter is between A and F, the horsepower rating of a listed motor disconnect switch is most often matched to the horsepower rating of the motor and used in accordance with its listing instructions per **110.3(B)**. For example, if the calculation is done to determine the horsepower rating for the motor-circuit switch for a motor with code letter A, a smaller horsepower rating may be determined, but it may not be suitable in accordance with its listing instructions per **110.3(B)**.

See Problem 6-45. For motors with code letters from G through V, the calculation may determine a higher horsepower rating for the disconnect switch than the rating of the motor. The motor disconnect switch is required to be used in accordance with its listing, and a higher horsepower-rated switch may be required. **See Problem 6-46**. Remember that **430.109(C)** requires the use of a listed motor circuit switch, and any listed equipment has to be used within its listing requirements.

PROBLEM 6-45

Determine the horsepower rating of a motor-circuit switch used as the disconnecting means for a 10-horsepower, 240-volt, 3-phase motor, code letter A, using the maximum LRC.

Solution

Table 430.7(B)
Max. kVA per hp
Code letter A = 3.14 kVA

$$LRC = \frac{(kVA\ per\ hp \times 1{,}000 \times hp)}{(E \times 1.73)}$$

$$= \frac{(3.14 \times 1{,}000 \times 10)}{(240 \times 1.73)}$$

$$= 75.63\ A$$

Table 430.251(B)
230 V column
75.63 A = 5 hp
Answer: 5hp motor-circuit switch

Comment: Although this proves that a 5-horsepower motor circuit switch can safely disconnect this specific 10-horsepower motor from the circuit, typically a 10-horsepower motor-circuit switch would be installed in accordance with 430.109(A)(1).

PROBLEM 6-46

Determine the horsepower rating of a motor-circuit switch used as a motor disconnecting means for a 10-horsepower, 240-volt, 3-phase motor, code letter F using maximum LRC.

Solution

Table 430.7(B)
 Max. kVA per hp
 Code letter F = 5.59 kVA

$$LRC = \frac{(\text{kVA per hp} \times 1{,}000 \times \text{hp})}{(E \times 1.73)}$$

$$= \frac{(5.59 \times 1{,}000 \times 10)}{(240 \times 1.73)}$$

$$= 134.63 \text{ A}$$

Table 430.251(B)
 230 V column
 134.63 A = 10 hp

Answer: 10hp motor-circuit switch

Comment: Notice that the calculated LRC requires a motor-circuit switch with the same horsepower rating as the motor when the code letter is F.

As the kVA per horsepower gets higher, it could result in a disconnecting means rated at a higher horsepower than the horsepower rating of the motor. This can be determined by the calculated LRC. **See Problem 6-47**.

PROBLEM 6-47

Determine the horsepower rating of a motor-circuit switch used as the disconnecting means for a 10-horsepower, 240-volt, 3-phase motor with code letter S using the maximum LRC.

Solution

Table 430.7(B)
 Max. kVA per hp
 Code letter S = 17.99 kVA

$$LRC = \frac{(\text{kVA per hp} \times 1{,}000 \times \text{hp})}{(E \times 1.73)}$$

$$= \frac{(17.99 \times 1{,}000 \times 10)}{(240 \times 1.73)}$$

$$= 433.28 \text{ A}$$

Table 430.251(B)
 230 V column
 433.28 A = 30 hp

Answer: 30hp motor-circuit switch

If one motor-circuit switch is used as the disconnecting means for two or more motors, **430.110(C)(1)** requires the horsepower rating of the motor disconnecting means to be determined by adding the sum of the LRCs of the motors as listed in **Table 430.251(A)** or **Table 430.251(B)** and treating the sum as a single motor. After determining the LRC sum total for the motors, apply that value using the applicable Table and convert to a horsepower rating for the single disconnecting means.

CHAPTER 6 MOTOR CALCULATIONS

It is important to ensure that the final horsepower rating has a current rating adequate for the FLC of all the motors. Add the FLCs, as taken from the FLC tables, of all the motors, and compare to the FLC of the horsepower rating of the switch by converting the horsepower rating of the switch to FLC using the FLC tables. **See Problem 6-48**.

6.4.5.2 Disconnecting Means for Combination Loads

If combination loads of motors and other than motor loads, such as a motor and a resistance heater load, are controlled by the same disconnecting means, **430.110(C)(1)** and **440.12(B)(1)** require the horsepower rating of the disconnecting means to be equal to the LRC of the motor plus the full-load current rating of the other loads.

Determine the LRCs of the motors from **Table 430.251(A)** or **Table 430.251(B)** and add the full-load currents of the other loads. Treat the sum as a single motor, and return to the LRC Tables to convert to a final horsepower rating. **See Problem 6-49**.

PROBLEM 6-48

Determine the maximum horsepower rating of a motor-circuit switch used as the disconnecting means for two 240-volt, 3-phase, simultaneously starting motors, if one motor is 15 horsepower and the other is 20 horsepower.

Solution

Calculation 1
430.110(C)(1)
Table 430.251(B)
230 V column
LRC of 15 hp = 232 A
LRC of 20 hp = 290 A
Total LRC = LRC #1 + LRC #2
   = 232 + 290
   = 522 A
Table 430.251(B)
230 V column
522 A = 40 hp
Answer: 40hp motor-circuit switch

Calculation 2
Table 430.250
FLC 15 hp = 42 A
FLC 20 hp = 54 A
Total FLC = 42 + 54 = 96 A
Table 430.250
FLC 40 hp = 104 A
104 A is adequate for 96 A
Answer: 40hp motor-circuit switch

PROBLEM 6-49

Determine the minimum horsepower rating of a motor-circuit switch used as the disconnecting means for a 5-horsepower, 240-volt, single-phase motor and 16,000 watts of resistance heat at 240 volts.

Solution

Table 430.251(A)
 230 V column
 Motor LRC = 168 A

Heater FLC $= \dfrac{W}{E}$
 $= \dfrac{16{,}000}{240}$
 $= 66.67$ A

430.110(C)(1)
 Disconnect rating = motor LRC + heater FLC
 $= 168 + 66.67$
 $= 234.67$ A

Table 430.251(A)
 Switch rating
 234.67 A = 7.5 hp

Answer: 7.5hp motor-circuit switch

PROBLEM 6-51

Determine the minimum ampacity of a circuit breaker used as the motor disconnecting means for a 5-horsepower, 240-volt, single-phase motor.

Solution

Table 430.248
 5 hp at 240 V
 FLC = 28 A
430.110(A)
 115% of motor FLC
 $I_{min.} = \text{FLC} \times 115\%$
  $= 28 \times 1.15$
  $= 32.2$ A
240.6(A)
 Next larger standard size = 35 A

Answer: 35A minimum circuit breaker rating

6.4.6 Circuit Breaker as Motor Disconnecting Means for Other Than Design B Energy-Efficient Motors

Circuit breakers and molded-case switches are not required to be horsepower rated. The reason is that LRC is considered to be six times the full-load current rating of the motor. Circuit breakers and molded-case switches are listed in the UL Product iQ as having been tested for six times the device's rating and identified for motor disconnecting means use as required by **Section 430.109**. See **Problem 6-50**.

PROBLEM 6-50

Determine the minimum ampacity of a circuit breaker used as a motor disconnecting means for a 20-horsepower, 460-volt, 3-phase motor.

Solution

Table 430.250
 20 hp at 460 V
 FLC = 27 A
430.110(A)
 115% of motor FLC
 $I_{min.} = \text{FLC} \times 115\%$
  $= 27 \times 1.15$
  $= 31.05$ A

Answer: 31.05A minimum circuit breaker rating
Comment: According to 240.6(A), the next standard size circuit breaker for 31.05 A is 35 A.

See **Problem 6-51**. *NEC* **430.110(A)** requires the motor disconnecting means to have an ampacity of at least 115% of the motor full-load current and is used for calculating the required ampere rating of the circuit breaker or the molded-case switch. **See Figure 6-16**.

CHAPTER 6 MOTOR CALCULATIONS

Given Information:

Using a 40hp, 460-volt, 3-phase squirrel-cage motor (other than Design B energy-efficient motors)
430.110(A)
Motor-circuit disconnecting means required to be not less than 115% of motor full-load current.
Table 430.250
40 hp at 460 V
FLC = 52 A
I rating switch = FLC × 115%
$\quad\quad\quad\quad\quad$ = 52 × 1.15
$\quad\quad\quad\quad\quad$ = 59.8 A
240.6(A)
Next larger standard size = 60 A

Table 430.251(B)
Motor-Locked Rotor Current
40 hp at 460 V
LRC = 290 A

UL Test
Circuit breaker interrupting ability = circuit breaker rating × 6
(same required for molded-case switches)
Interrupting ability = 60 × 6
$\quad\quad\quad\quad\quad\quad\quad$ = 360 A
Circuit Breaker LRC = 360 A
Comment: Circuit breaker is capable of interrupting LRC.

Figure 6-16. Circuit Breaker used as Motor Disconnect. The required horsepower rating for a motor disconnecting means for a circuit breaker or molded case switch is inherently built into the device due to the testing and listing requirements of the device.

If two or more motors are installed on the same branch circuit, **430.110(C)(1)** and **430.110(C)(2)** require the minimum ampacity of the motor disconnecting means to be 115% of the total of the motor full-load currents. The full-load motor currents are not determined by using the motor nameplate information; rather, the full-load current of each motor is determined using **Table 430.248** through **Table 430.250**. **See Problem 6-52.**

PROBLEM 6-52

Determine the minimum ampacity of a circuit breaker used as the motor disconnecting means for a 10-horsepower, 460-volt motor and a 15-horsepower, 460-volt motor on the same motor branch circuit.

Solution

Table 430.250
$\quad$ 10 hp at 460 V
$\quad$ FLC = 14 A
$\quad$ 15 hp at 460 V
$\quad$ FLC = 21 A

430.110(C)(2)
$\quad I_{min.}$ = (FLC #1 + FLC #2) × 115%
$\quad\quad\quad$ = (14 + 21) × 1.15
$\quad\quad\quad$ = 40.25 A
240.6(A)
$\quad$ Next larger standard size = 45 A
Answer: 45A minimum circuit breaker rating

When the same circuit breaker is used as the disconnecting means for motor(s) and heating or other load types, the disconnecting means is required to be 115% of the full-load current of the motor(s) plus full-load current of the heating or other load. **See Problem 6-53.**

PROBLEM 6-53

Determine the minimum ampacity of a circuit breaker used as the disconnecting means for a 5-horsepower, 240-volt, single-phase motor and a 5,000-watt resistance heating load installed on the same branch circuit.

Solution

Table 430.248
5 hp at 240 V
FLC = 28 A

$$\text{Heater FLC} = \frac{W}{E}$$
$$= \frac{5{,}000}{240}$$
$$= 20.83 \text{ A}$$

430.110(C)(2)

$I_{min.}$ = (motor FLC + heater FLC) × 115%
   = (28 + 20.83) × 1.15
   = 56.15 A

240.6(A)
Next larger standard size = 60 A
Answer: 56.15A minimum circuit breaker rating

6.4.7 Molded-Case Switch for Other than Design B Energy-Efficient Motors

A molded-case switch looks like a circuit breaker and is similarly rated in amperes, but there is no overcurrent protection built into it. It is tested by UL for six times its ampacity rating. Therefore, it is identified to be used as a disconnecting means for motor circuits. **See Problem 6-54.**

PROBLEM 6-54

Determine the minimum ampacity rating for a molded-case switch used as a motor disconnecting means for a 25-horsepower, 240-volt, 3-phase motor.

Solution

Table 430.250
25 hp at 240 V
FLC = 68 A

430.110(A)
115% of motor FLC
$I_{min.}$ = FLC × 115%
   = 68 × 1.15
   = 78.2 A

Answer: 78.2A minimum molded-case switch rating

Table 430.248 contains full-load current values for single-phase AC motors running at usual speeds and with normal torque characteristics.

6.4.8 Combination Ampere and Horsepower Rating for Other than Design B Energy-Efficient Motors

Section 430.109 requires a motor disconnect switch to have a horsepower rating capable of interrupting the LRC. **Section 430.110** requires the motor disconnect switch to have an ampere rating adequate to carry the full-load current of the motor. Both requirements must be satisfied for the disconnect switch to be *Code*-compliant. Each disconnecting device is also required to be "listed." Provided the motor code letter is not an issue, a listed disconnecting means with adequate current rating that is rated and marked for the horsepower and voltage of a motor is all that is necessary for sizing the motor disconnect. **See Problem 6-55**.

PROBLEM 6-55

Motor Circuit Switch

NAMEPLATE
30 HP 240 V 3 PH

Determine the minimum ampacity and minimum horsepower rating for a motor-circuit switch used for the disconnecting means for a 30-horsepower, 240-volt, 3-phase motor.

Solution

Table 430.250
  30 hp at 240 V
  FLC = 80 A
430.110(A)
  115% of FLC
  $I_{min.}$ = FLC × 115%
    = 80 × 1.15
    = 92 A
No code letter
Switch hp = Motor hp
Switch hp = 30 hp
Answer: 92A and 30hp minimum

Remember, a motor disconnecting means has three responsibilities:

1. To safely carry the motor full-load current under normal operation
2. To be capable of being opened under load
3. To be capable of being opened under locked-rotor conditions

6.5 AIR-CONDITIONING AND REFRIGERATING EQUIPMENT MOTORS

A hermetic refrigerant motor-compressor is a combination of a motor and a compressor enclosed in the same housing, where the shaft is sealed and the motor operates in a refrigerant. **See Figure 6-17**. Therefore, hermetically-sealed motors have different operating characteristics. These characteristics vary with the manufacturer. The manufacturer establishes the rated-load current (RLC) and the branch-circuit selection current (BCSC) for their particular motor.

Figure 6-17. Hermetic Refrigerant Motor-Compressor. Both the compressor mounted above the motor rotor and the motor are designed to be enclosed in the housing and operated in the refrigerant. As the refrigerant more effectively cools the motor than the air used by a typical motor, more load can be placed on the motor-compressor.

The RLC is the current resulting from the operation of the hermetically-sealed motor at its rated load, rated voltage, and rated frequency for the load served. The BCSC is always equal to or greater than the RLC. Therefore, it is used in calculations for selecting the motor branch-circuit conductors, short-circuit and ground-fault protection, overload protection, controller, and disconnecting means size.

Normally, the nameplate of a compressor-type motor includes the minimum branch-circuit amperes, maximum branch-circuit fuse rating, circuit-breaker rating, voltage rating, number of phases, rated-load current, and locked-rotor current. As such, there is seldom a need for these calculations in the field.

6.5.1 Branch-Circuit Conductor Sizing

Section 440.32 requires the conductors supplying a motor compressor to be 125% of the RLC or the BCSC, whichever is larger. In accordance with the definitions of RLC and BCSC in **440.2**, it is easiest to think of the RLC as the current at 100% operation, and the BCSC rating at a higher rating such as 115% or 125% as allowed by the overload setting of the motor-compressor. **See Problems 6-56 and 6-57.**

If two or more hermetically-sealed motors are on the same branch circuit, the branch-circuit conductors are required to be 125% of the largest motor BCSC or RLC, whichever is higher, plus the BCSC of the remaining motors in accordance with **440.33**.

PROBLEM 6-56

Determine the minimum branch-circuit conductor ampacity and size (THWN copper) for a single-phase, 240-volt compressor motor with a branch-circuit selection current (BCSC) of 25 amperes. Select conductors based upon Table 310.16, 75°C, copper in accordance with 110.14(C)(1)(a)(4).

Solution

Calculation 1
Branch-circuit conductor ampacity
440.32
   Ampacity = BCSC × 125%
   = 25 × 1.25
   = 31.25 A
Answer: 31.25 A

Calculation 2
Branch-circuit conductor size
Table 310.16
   75°C, copper column
   31.25 A = 10 AWG
Answer: 10 AWG THWN copper

PROBLEM 6-57

Determine the minimum branch-circuit conductor ampacity and size for a 3-phase, 460-volt compressor motor with a branch-circuit selection current of 43 amperes. Select conductors based upon Table 310.16, 75°C, copper in accordance with 110.14(C)(1)(a)(4).

Solution

Calculation 1
Branch-circuit conductor ampacity
440.32
   Ampacity = BCSC × 125%
   = 43 × 1.25
   = 53.75 A
Answer: 53.75 A

Calculation 2
Branch-circuit conductor size
Table 310.16
   75°C, copper column
   53.75 A = 6 AWG
Answer: 6 AWG THWN copper

For a combination of motor compressors and other equipment installed on the same branch circuit, the branch-circuit conductors are required to be 125% of the largest motor BCSC or RLC, whichever is higher, plus the BCSC of other compressors, the full-load currents of other motors, and the full-load currents of the other loads, in accordance with **440.34**. **See Problem 6-58**.

Section 440.35 is often used, as many motor compressors are installed in combination equipment.

The manufacturer is required to have the minimum circuit ampacity (MCA) marked on the equipment in accordance with **440.4(B)**. The branch-circuit conductors are required to have an ampacity sufficient for the MCA. According to **440.4(B)**, the MCA is calculated in accordance with **Part IV** of **Article 440**, which includes **440.32**, **440.33**, and **440.34**, so there is no need to multiply the MCA by 125%.

6.5.2 Overload Calculations

NEC **440.52(A)** covers the calculations for sizing the motor overload protection. This calculation uses the RLC of the compressor. Where overload relays are applied, the RLC is multiplied by 140%. If fuses or inverse-time circuit breakers are used, the RLC is multiplied by 125%. The sizing provides sufficient time delay to permit normal starting of the compressor. **See Problem 6-59**.

PROBLEM 6-58

Determine the motor branch-circuit conductor ampacity and size when two 240-volt, 3-phase, hermetically-sealed motors with branch-circuit selection currents of 56 amperes are installed on the same branch circuit. Select conductors based upon Table 310.16, 75°C, copper, XHHW-2 in accordance with 110.14(C)(1)(a)(4).

Solution

Calculation 1
Branch circuit conductor ampacity
440.33
Ampacity = (largest BCSC ×125%) + others
= (56 × 1.25) + 56
= 126 A
Answer: 126 A

Calculation 2
Branch circuit conductor size
Table 310.16
75°C, copper column
126 A = 1 AWG
Answer: 1 AWG XHHW-2 copper

PROBLEM 6-59

Determine the maximum overload relay protection permitted for a 240-volt, 3-phase hermetically-sealed compressor-type motor with a rated-load current of 27 amperes.

Solution

440.52(A)(1)
OL relay protection = RLC × 140%
= 27 × 1.40
= 37.8 A
Answer: 37.8 A

6.5.3 Motor Branch-Circuit Short-Circuit and Ground-Fault Protection

The basic requirement of **440.22(A)** requires the branch-circuit short-circuit and ground-fault protection not to exceed 175% of the hermetically-sealed motor RLC or BCSC, whichever is larger.

When starting current is a problem, the branch-circuit short-circuit and ground-fault protection must not exceed 225% of the hermetically-sealed motor RLC or BCSC, whichever is greater.

For combination equipment, **440.22(B)** requires the maximum value determined in **440.22(A)** to be added with the other loads of the combination equipment. The final value obtained by **440.22(B)** cannot be exceeded, so reduce the value to the next lower standard size from the maximum calculated value. Manufacturers are required to have the maximum branch-circuit short-circuit and ground-fault protective device marked on the combination equipment in accordance with **440.4(B)**. **See Problems 6-60 and 6-61.**

PROBLEM 6-60

Determine the maximum overload protection for a 240-volt, 3-phase, hermetically-sealed compressor-type motor with a rated-load current of 27 amperes using time-delay fuses.

Solution

440.52(B)(3)
  Not to exceed 125%
  OL protection (fuse) = RLC × 125%
                      = 27 × 1.25
                      = 33.75 A
240.6(A)
  Next smaller standard size = 30 A
Answer: 30 A

PROBLEM 6-61

Using the following methods, determine the maximum standard size non–time-delay fuses permitted for a 240-volt, 3-phase, hermetically-sealed motor with a branch-circuit selection current of 56 amperes:

1. Basic calculation
2. With starting current problem

Solution

Calculation 1
Basic calculation
440.22(A)
  Not to exceed 175%
  OCPD rating = BCSC × 175%
              = 56 × 1.75
              = 98 A
240.6(A)
  Next smaller size = 90 A
Answer: 90A non–time-delay fuses

Calculation 2
With problem starting current
440.22(A)
  Not to exceed 225%
  OCPD rating = BCSC × 225%
              = 56 × 2.25
              = 126 A
240.6(A)
  Next smaller size = 125 A
Answer: 125A non–time-delay fuses

The provisions of **Article 440** *apply to electric motor-driven air conditioning and refrigeration equipment and their related branch circuits and controllers.*

DEFINITIONS AND TERMS

Duty, Continuous - Operation at a substantially constant load for an indefinitely long time. [**70**:100]

Continuous Duty (Motor) - A motor that can continue to operate within the temperature limits after it has reached normal operating temperature.

Control Circuit - The circuit of a control apparatus or system that carries the electrical signals directing the performance of the controller but does not carry the main power current. [**70**:100]

Feeder - All circuit conductors between the service equipment, the source of a separately derived system, or other power supply source and the final branch-circuit overcurrent device. [**70**:100]

Full-Load Current (Motor) (FLC) - The current drawn from the line when the motor is operating at full-load torque and full-load speed at rated frequency and voltage. The *Code* specifies when the table value is used and when the motor nameplate value is used.

Locked-Rotor Current (LRC) - Measured current with the rotor locked and with the rated voltage and frequency applied to the motor. This is the current seen when starting the motor and load.

Motor Branch Circuit - The circuit conductors between the final overcurrent device protecting the circuit and the motor.

Motor Circuit Switch - A switch rated in horsepower, capable of interrupting the maximum operating overload current of a motor of the same horsepower rating as the switch at the rated voltage.

Motor Controller - Any switch or device that is normally used to start and stop a motor by making and breaking the motor circuit current.

Overcurrent - Any current in excess of the rated current of equipment or the ampacity of a conductor. It may result from overload, short circuit, or ground fault. [**70**:100]

Overload - Operation of equipment in excess of the normal, full-load rating, or of a conductor in excess of rated ampacity that, when it persists for a sufficient length of time, would cause damage or dangerous overheating. A fault, such as a short circuit or ground fault, is not an overload. [**70**:100]

Service Factor (SF) - A measure of the reserve margin built into a motor. Motors rated over 1.0 square feet have more than a normal margin, and are used where unusual conditions such as occasional high or low voltage or momentary overloads are likely to occur.

Temperature Rise - The amount by which a motor, operating under rated conditions, is hotter than its surroundings. On most motors, manufacturers have replaced the temperature rise rating on the motor nameplate with a listing of the ambient temperature rating, insulation class, and service factor.

Thermal Protector (as applied to motors) - A protective device for assembly as an integral part of a motor or motor-compressor that, when properly applied, protects the motor against dangerous overheating due to overload and failure to start. [**70**:100] This protection is available with either manual reset or automatic reset.

Reproduced with permission of NFPA from NFPA 70®, *National Electrical Code*® (NEC®), 2020 edition. Copyright© 2019, National Fire Protection Association. For a full copy of the NEC®, please go to www.nfpa.org.

SUMMARY

Although **Article 430** contains many requirements for motor installations, the *Code* user can make a proper installation by using **430.6** for full-load current rating, **430.22** for conductors, **430.32** for overload protection, **430.52** for overcurrent protection, and **430.110** for disconnecting means. Generally, the table full-load currents are used to size branch-circuit conductors, motor overcurrent protection, and disconnects. The nameplate full-load current is used to size individual motor overload protection as it is specific to the motor. The ampacity of both continuously-operated motors and motor compressors are sized at 125% of the full-load current or branch-circuit selection current. Overload protection is sized at 115% or 125%, depending upon the temperature rise or service factor of the motor. Branch-circuit short-circuit and ground-fault protective devices provide circuit and equipment protection from abnormally high values of current and are sized at 175% for time-delay fuses and 250% for circuit breakers. Motor-circuit switches are sized to handle the full-load current of the motor continuously at 115% and to have a horsepower rating capable of interrupting the motor current in a locked-rotor condition. Motor compressors are covered by **Article 440**, and manufacturers of combination equipment are required to have the minimum circuit ampacity and maximum overcurrent protection device marked on the equipment.

REVIEW QUESTIONS

1. For sizing motor branch-circuit conductors, branch-circuit short-circuit and ground-fault protection, and disconnecting means, the full-load current of the motor should be determined by __?__ .
   a. locating the full-load current rating as provided on the blueprints of the job
   b. locating the full-load current rating as determined by **Tables 430.247** through **430.250**
   c. locating the full-load current rating as marked on the motor
   d. multiplying the horsepower rating by 746 and dividing by the voltage

2. For sizing motor overload protection, the full-load current of the motor should be determined by __?__ .
   a. locating the full-load current rating as determined by **Tables 430.247** through **430.250**
   b. locating the full-load current rating as marked on the motor
   c. locating the full-load current rating as provided on the blueprints of the job
   d. multiplying the horsepower rating by 746 and dividing by the voltage

REVIEW QUESTIONS

3. For a continuously-operated motor, the motor circuit conductors are required to have an ampacity of not less than __?__ of the motor full-load current.
   a. 80%
   b. 100%
   c. 115%
   d. 125%

4. What is the maximum percentage of motor full-load current permitted for a polyphase motor for branch-circuit short-circuit and ground-fault protection if using a dual-element time-delay fuse?
   a. 175%
   b. 225%
   c. 250%
   d. 300%

5. What is the maximum standard size inverse-time circuit breaker permitted for a 20-horsepower, 460-volt, 3-phase motor with a full-load current rating of 27 amperes from **Table 430.250** when the starting current is a problem?
   a. 70 A
   b. 90 A
   c. 100 A
   d. 110 A

6. Which is not a reason to cause a motor to overload?
   a. Excessive load
   b. Failure of motor to start
   c. Lack of load
   d. Worn motor bearings

7. The horsepower rating required for a motor circuit switch used as the disconnecting means for the motor is required to __?__ .
   a. break available fault current to the motor in a ground-fault situation
   b. break the locked-rotor current of the motor
   c. handle the continuous full-load current of the motor
   d. start and stop the motor as a controller

8. If a power factor correction capacitor is added to the load side of a motor overload device, the line current through the motor overload device will __?__ .
   a. decrease
   b. increase
   c. increase, but very minimally
   d. remain the same

9. When two or more motors are supplied by the same motor circuit conductors, how is the minimum required ampacity for the conductors determined?
   a. Add all motor FLCs
   b. Add all motor FLCs and multiply by 125%
   c. Multiply any motor's FLC by 125% and add all other motor FLCs
   d. Multiply the largest motor FLC by 125% and add all other motor FLCs

10. For a combination piece of equipment employing multiple compressors and motors, what is the required minimum ampacity for the conductors supplying the equipment?
    a. The minimum circuit ampacity marked on the equipment
    b. The minimum circuit ampacity marked on the equipment and multiplied by 125%
    c. The sum of all branch circuit selection currents and full-load currents multiplied by 125%
    d. The sum of all rated load currents and full-load currents

CHAPTER 7
VOLTAGE DROP

Voltage drop calculations are based upon Ohm's Law and the resistance values as determined from **Chapter 9, Table 8** of the *National Electrical Code® (NEC)*. Many theory textbooks cover the subjects of wire resistance and voltage drop using various conductor temperature ratings, but few focus on the same conductor temperature ratings as **Table 310.16** and **Table 310.4(A)** of the *NEC*. The specific conductor temperature focus is 75°C; other temperatures require the use of specific voltage drop adjustment factors.

Most voltage drop calculations in the trade are made simple by using only DC values. However, it is also important to understand how to use AC circuit voltage equations related to **Chapter 9, Table 9** impedance values.

OBJECTIVES

- Calculate the resistance of various lengths of wire based upon the values from Chapter 9, Table 8 of the *Code*.
- Calculate the voltage drop on a branch circuit using the values from **Chapter 9, Table 8** of the *Code*.
- Adjust voltage drop calculations for use with other than 75°C insulated conductors.
- Make calculations based upon the voltage drop equation when the wire size, ampacity, or length of a circuit is unknown.
- Apply various voltage drop equations to both single-phase and 3-phase circuits.
- Calculate the AC voltage drop of branch circuits and motor circuits using the values from **Chapter 9, Table 9** of the *Code*.

TABLE OF CONTENTS

7.1	CHAPTER 9, TABLE 8 FOR RESISTANCE OF WIRE	160
7.2	RESISTANCE TEXTBOOK EQUATION: *CODE* BOOK EQUATION	160
7.3	RESISTANCE EQUATION BASED UPON *CODE* BOOK VALUES	161
7.4	RESISTANCE EQUATION CORRECTION FACTOR	161
7.5	EQUATION FOR CHANGING RESISTANCE FROM 75°C TO 60°C WIRE	162
7.6	DEVELOPING THE VOLTAGE DROP EQUATION	163
	.1 Voltage Drop Equation	164
	.2 Voltage Drop and Line Loss	164
	.3 Voltage Drop in Aluminum Conductors	165
	.4 Voltage Drop and Temperature Correction Factor	165
7.7	USING THE VOLTAGE DROP EQUATION	165
	.1 Equations for Selecting Wire Size	165
	.2 Developing the Values of *k* for Use with Table 8	166
	.3 Solving for Length *(L)*	167
	.4 Solving for Current *(I)*	168
7.8	VOLTAGE DROP FOR FEEDERS AND BRANCH CIRCUITS	169
7.9	USING ALTERNATE METHODS TO SOLVE FOR VOLTAGE DROP	169
	.1 Varying the Value of *k*	169
	.2 Using Chapter 9, Table 9	170
DEFINITIONS AND TERMS		172
SUMMARY		172
REVIEW QUESTIONS		173

7.1 CHAPTER 9, TABLE 8 FOR RESISTANCE OF WIRE

The voltage drop in an electrical circuit depends on the resistance that an electrical conductor offers to the flow of current in the circuit. The resistance of wire will change according to the temperature.

Ampacity **Table 310.16** lists three insulation temperatures: 60°C, 75°C, and 90°C. These are the insulation temperature ratings recognized by the *Code* for conductors rated 0–2,000 volts. **Chapter 9, Table 8** lists the DC resistance of wire at 75°C, which only applies to those conductors listed in the 75°C column of **Table 310.16**. **Chapter 9, Table 8** is the key for *Code* calculations of wire resistance and voltage drop. The resistance values in **Table 8** are given as DC resistance values. For all practical purposes, these same values are used for AC conductors and will give a reasonably accurate calculation of the voltage drop. **Chapter 9, Table 9** gives AC resistance and reactance for AC circuits with a power factor of 85%. The values in this table are based upon the Neher-McGrath conductor resistance calculations.

Table 9 is one source for computer-based electrical calculation programs used by design engineers for commercial and industrial installations where a conservative calculation is desired. **Table 8**, on the other hand, is generally used for field-based calculations to determine the approximate voltage drop in AC circuits.

The heading for the right-hand column of **Table 8** is "Direct-Current Resistance at 75°C (167°F)." The subheadings list copper and aluminum, with copper having two subheadings: uncoated and coated. When electrical conductors are insulated with natural rubber, as was once common, a reaction occurs between the sulfur in the vulcanized rubber and the copper. Electrical conductors are coated with tin to protect against that reaction. Wire using other types of insulation are not coated, since there is no reaction between the insulation and copper or aluminum. All 600-volt building wire installed today has non-rubber based insulation and is uncoated.

Note the number of decimal places used to indicate the ohms per thousand feet. It indicates that decimals for ohms per thousand feet should not be rounded off when calculating voltage drop. Conversely, volts, current, and length round off to the second decimal place, and circular mils round off to whole numbers.

7.2 RESISTANCE TEXTBOOK EQUATION: *CODE* BOOK EQUATION

The theory textbook equation for resistance is:

$$R = \frac{k \times L}{A}$$

or:

$$R = \frac{k \times L}{\text{cmil}}$$

Where:

R = resistance of the wire
k = resistance per mil foot of the material under consideration at a given temperature; usually based on 20°C
L = length of the wire
A = area of the wire expressed in circular mils
cmil = circular mil area of the wire

When the textbook equation is converted to *Code* book values, the following apply:

1. The resistance of the wire will increase as k is increased because the temperature of the conductor under consideration is increased from 20°C to 75°C. The temperature used is different. **Note 2** in **Chapter 9, Table 8** provides the formula for the adjustment of resistance based upon temperature.

CHAPTER 7 VOLTAGE DROP

2. The resistance of the wire will decrease as the circular mil area is increased. The constant k remains the same.
3. The resistance of the wire is increased as the length of the conductor increases. The constant k remains the same.

7.3 RESISTANCE EQUATION BASED UPON *CODE* BOOK VALUES

The following equation is used for calculating the resistance of wire using the *Code* resistance values given in **Chapter 9, Table 8**:

$$R = \frac{\text{DC resistance} \times L}{1{,}000}$$

Where:

R = resistance of the wire
DC = direct current
DC resistance = resistance per thousand feet of wire (as given in **Chapter 9, Table 8**)
L = length of the wire in feet
1,000 = converting ohms per thousand feet to ohms per foot

Direct-current resistance in the equation contains the k and the circular mil area expressed in the theory textbook equation and is based upon a temperature of 75°C. **See Problems 7-1 and 7-2.**

7.4 RESISTANCE EQUATION CORRECTION FACTOR

The resistance of wire is directly proportional to the ambient temperature. As the maximum operating temperature decreases, the resistance of a conductor will decrease. The resistance of fully heated 60°C conductors will be less than the resistance of fully heated 75°C conductors.

Knowledge of and experience with each tool enables the user to select the correct tool and use the proper procedure for determining a power quality source or event.

PROBLEM 7-1

What is the resistance of 175 feet of 14 AWG solid, uncoated copper conductor wire at 75°C?

Solution

Table 8
  75°C copper, uncoated column
  14 AWG solid = 3.07 Ω per 1,000 feet

$$R = \frac{\text{DC Resistance} \times L}{1{,}000}$$
$$= \frac{3.07 \times 175}{1{,}000}$$
$$= 0.53725 \ \Omega$$

Answer: 0.53725 Ω

PROBLEM 7-2

What is the resistance of 200 feet of 14 AWG THWN solid copper conductor wire?

Solution

Table 310.4(A) or Table 310.16
  THWN = 75°C wire
  THWN indicates thermoplastic insulation; therefore, it is uncoated.
Table 8
  75°C copper, uncoated column
  14 AWG solid = 3.07 Ω per 1,000 feet

$$R = \frac{\text{DC Resistance} \times L}{1{,}000}$$
$$= \frac{3.07 \times 200}{1{,}000}$$
$$= 0.614 \ \Omega$$

Answer: 0.614 Ω

PROBLEM 7-3

What is the resistance of 1,000 feet of 4 AWG uncoated copper conductor wire with 60°C insulation?

Solution

Table 8
75°C copper, uncoated column
1,000 feet of 4 AWG = 0.308 Ω
60°C is less than 75°C; resistance will decrease, so divide

$$\text{DC Resistance at }60°C = \frac{\text{DC Resistance at }75°C}{\text{correction factor}}$$
$$= \frac{0.308}{1.05}$$
$$= 0.2933\ \Omega$$

Answer: 0.2933 Ω

PROBLEM 7-4

What is the resistance of 1,000 feet of 2 AWG aluminum conductor wire with 90°C insulation?

Solution

Table 8
75°C aluminum column
1,000 feet of 2 AWG = 0.319 Ω
90°C is more than 75°C; resistance will increase, so multiply
DC resistance at 90°C = DC resistance at 75°C × 1.05
$$= 0.319 \times 1.05$$
$$= 0.33495\ \Omega$$

Answer: 0.33495 Ω

Table 8 is based upon the maximum operating temperature of conductors rated at 75°C and correlates with the *NEC* 75°C insulated conductors of **Table 310.4(A)**. Note the differences among 60°C, 75°C, and 90°C insulation ratings; there is a 15° change each time. Therefore, a correction factor can be used for the 15° change in temperature, which is 1.05 for either copper or aluminum. **See Problems 7-3 and 7-4.** When applying the calculation from the equation provided in **Note 2 of Chapter 9, Table 8**, the correction factor is evident. If the conductor is operating at a temperature other than 60°C, 75°C, or 90°C, the formula in **Note 2** should be used to adjust the resistance value of the conductor.

7.5 EQUATION FOR CHANGING RESISTANCE FROM 75°C TO 60°C WIRE

When the temperature drops, the resistance drops. Therefore, the 75°C equation is divided by the correction factor of 1.05.

$$R = \frac{\text{DC resistance} \times L}{1,000 \times 1.05}$$

See Problem 7-5.

EXAMPLE

Using Note 2 of Chapter 9, Table 8, show the approximate correction factor of 1.05 for resistance of a conductor operating at 60°C or 90°C instead of 75°C.

Solution

$R_2 = R_1 \times [1 + a(T2 - 75)]$ where $a_{cu} = 0.00323$, and $a_{AL} = 0.00330$ at 75°C
Select any size conductor, for example a 6 AWG copper conductor:
For 60°C and R_1 value of 6 AWG of 0.491 ohms per thousand feet (Ω/kft) from Chapter 9, Table 8
$R_2 = 0.491 \times [1 + 0.00323(60 - 75)]$
$\quad = 0.491 \times [1 + 0.00323(-15)]$
$\quad = 0.491 \times [1 - 0.0485]$
$\quad = 0.491 \times [0.9515]$
$\quad = 0.467\ \Omega/\text{kft}$

In comparison, $R_2 = \dfrac{R_1}{1.05}$
$\quad = \dfrac{0.491}{1.05}$
$\quad = 0.468\ \Omega/\text{kft}$

For 90°C and R_1 value of 6 AWG of 0.491 Ω/kft from Chapter 9, Table 8
$R_2 = 0.491 \times [1 + 0.00323(90 - 75)]$
$\quad = 0.491 \times [1 + 0.00323(15)]$
$\quad = 0.491 \times [1 + 0.0485]$
$\quad = 0.491 \times [1.0485]$
$\quad = 0.515\ \Omega/\text{kft}$

In comparison, $R_2 = R_1 \times 1.05 = 0.491 \times 1.05 = 0.516\ \Omega/\text{kft}$

Notice that in both approximations, utilizing the simplified correction factor of 1.05 differs by a factor of $1/1{,}000$ from the formula as provided in Note 2 of Table 8 and is adequate for adjustments for operating temperatures for field calculations.

PROBLEM 7-5

What is the resistance of 400 feet of 90°C insulated, uncoated 6 AWG copper wire?

Solution

Table 8
75°C copper, uncoated column
1,000 ft of 6 AWG = 0.491 Ω

$$R = \frac{\text{DC Resistance} \times L \times 1.05}{1,000}$$

$$= \frac{0.491 \times 400 \times 1.05}{1,000}$$

$$= 0.20622 \; \Omega$$

Answer: 0.20622 Ω

When the temperature increases, the resistance will increase. Therefore, the 75°C equation is multiplied by the correction factor of 1.05.

$$R = \frac{\text{DC resistance} \times L \times 1.05}{1,000}$$

See Problem 7-6.

PROBLEM 7-6

What is the resistance of 300 feet of 4 AWG THHN aluminum wire?

Solution

Table 310.4(A) or Table 310.16
THHN = 90°C wire
Table 8
75°C aluminum column
1,000 ft of 4 AWG = 0.508 Ω

$$R = \frac{\text{DC Resistance} \times L \times 1.05}{1,000}$$

$$= \frac{0.508 \times 300 \times 1.05}{1,000}$$

$$= 0.16002 \; \Omega$$

Answer: 0.16002 Ω

7.6 DEVELOPING THE VOLTAGE DROP EQUATION

Voltage is the amount of pressure necessary to force a given amount of current through the circuit conductor's resistance, although no productive work is done. It is measured in volts and identified with the symbol E_d or V_d.

The following is the development of the voltage drop equation using resistance values given in **Chapter 9, Table 8**:

Basic Ohm's Law Equation:

$$E_d = I \times R$$

Resistance Equation:

$$R = \frac{\text{DC resistance} \times L}{1,000}$$

R in both equations stands for resistance. Therefore, the R equation can be substituted for the R in the basic Ohm's Law equation (substituting equal for equal).

Substitute the resistance equation for the R in the basic Ohm's Law equation to solve for voltage drop.

$$E_d = \frac{I \times \text{DC resistance} \times L}{1,000}$$

Because two conductors are needed to power an electrical load, the distance to the load is doubled. Hence, the length (L) is multiplied by two in the equation for single-phase circuits, and by 1.73 for 3-phase circuits.

Appropriate lockout or tagout devices need to be applied to equipment in order to properly isolate all energy sources.

7.6.1 Voltage Drop Equation

Single-Phase:

$$V_d = \frac{\text{DC resistance} \times I \times 2L}{1{,}000}$$

3-Phase:

$$V_d = \frac{\text{DC resistance} \times I \times 1.73L}{1{,}000}$$

Where:

V_d = voltage drop expressed in volts
I = current in the conductor
DC resistance = resistance value per thousand feet as listed in **Table 8**
$2L$ = twice the length of the circuit from the supply point to the single-phase load
$1.73L$ = 1.73 times the length of the circuit from the supply point to the 3-phase load
$1{,}000$ = converting the ohms per thousand feet to ohms per foot

The difference between these two formulas is that single-phase uses $2L$, whereas 3-phase uses $1.73L$. **See Problem 7-7.**

PROBLEM 7-7

Calculate the voltage drop on a 60-foot, 120-volt, single-phase branch circuit of 14 AWG THWN uncoated solid copper conductor wire carrying 12 amperes.

Solution

Table 310.4(A) or Table 310.16
 THWN = 75°C
Table 8
 75°C copper, uncoated column
 14 AWG = 3.07 Ω/kft

$$V_d = \frac{\text{DC Resistance} \times I \times 2L}{1{,}000}$$
$$= \frac{3.07 \times 12 \times 2 \times 60}{1{,}000}$$
$$= 4.42 \text{ V}$$

Answer: 4.42 V

7.6.2 Voltage Drop and Line Loss

Voltage drop results in a loss of power in the line called "line loss" because it does no useful work. It is expressed in watts (W).

Single-Phase:

$$W = V_d \times I$$

3-Phase:

$$W = V_d \times I \times 1.73$$

See Problems 7-8, 7-9, and 7-10.

PROBLEM 7-8

Calculate the line loss for the branch circuit given in Problem 7-7.

Solution

$W = V_d \times I$
$= 4.42 \times 12$
$= 53.04 \text{ W}$

Answer: 53.04 W

PROBLEM 7-9

Calculate the voltage drop on a 100-foot, 480-volt, 3-phase branch circuit carrying 60 amperes and using 6 AWG THWN copper conductors.

Solution

Table 310.4(A) or Table 310.16
 THWN = 75°C uncoated
Table 8
 75°C copper uncoated
 6 AWG = 0.491 Ω/kft

$$V_d = \frac{\text{DC Resistance} \times I \times 1.73L}{1{,}000}$$
$$= \frac{0.491 \times 60 \times 1.73 \times 100}{1{,}000}$$
$$= 5.097 \text{ V}$$

Answer: 5.097 V

PROBLEM 7-10

Calculate the line loss for the branch circuit given in Problem 7-9.

Solution

$W = V_d \times I \times 1.73$
$= 5.097 \times 60 \times 1.73$
$= 529.07 \text{ W}$

Answer: 529.07 W

CHAPTER 7   VOLTAGE DROP

7.6.3 Voltage Drop in Aluminum Conductors

The basic voltage drop equation applies to copper or aluminum. The DC resistance per thousand feet changes, but the equation remains the same. **See Problem 7-11**.

7.6.4 Voltage Drop and Temperature Correction Factor

Table 310.16 has three temperature ratings and **Table 8** has one 75°C rating. Therefore, the temperature correction factor is also used in conjunction with the voltage drop equation.

For 60°C wire:

$$V_d = \frac{\text{DC resistance} \times I \times 2L}{1{,}000 \times 1.05}$$

See Problem 7-12.

For 90°C wire:

$$V_d = \frac{\text{DC resistance} \times I \times 2L \times 1.05}{1{,}000}$$

For 3-phase, $2L$ is changed to $1.73L$ in both equations.

7.7 USING THE VOLTAGE DROP EQUATION

NEC **210.19(A), Informational Note No. 3** states that voltage drop for branch circuits is recommended not to exceed 3% where reasonable efficiency is expected. This requires calculating the wire size in circular mil area in order to limit the voltage drop.

7.7.1 Equations for Selecting Wire Size

When the ampacity, length, and desired voltage drop are known, the equation is transposed to solve for the minimum circular mil area of the wire.

PROBLEM 7-11

Calculate the voltage drop on a 3-phase, 240-volt branch circuit of 1 AWG THWN aluminum carrying 90 amperes at a distance of 150 feet.

Solution

Table 310.4(A) or Table 310.16
THWN = 75°C
75°C aluminum column
1 AWG = 0.253 Ω/kft

$$V_d = \frac{\text{DC Resistance} \times I \times 1.73L}{1{,}000}$$

$$= \frac{0.253 \times 90 \times 1.73 \times 150}{1{,}000}$$

$$= 5.91 \text{ V}$$

Answer: 5.91 V

PROBLEM 7-12

Calculate the voltage drop on 2 AWG THHN copper conductor supplying a 125-ampere, single-phase load at a distance of 160 feet.

Solution

Table 310.4(A) or Table 310.16
THHN = 90°C plastic insulation, uncoated wire
Calculations increased by 1.05
Table 8
75°C copper uncoated
2 AWG = 0.194 Ω/kft

$$V_d = \frac{\text{DC Resistance} \times I \times 2L \times 1.05}{1{,}000}$$

$$= \frac{0.194 \times 125 \times 2 \times 160 \times 1.05}{1{,}000}$$

$$= 8.148 \text{ V}$$

Answer: 8.148 V

Single-Phase:

$$\text{cmil} = \frac{k \times I \times 2L}{V_d}$$

3-Phase:

$$\text{cmil} = \frac{k \times I \times 1.73L}{V_d}$$

Where:

cmil = circular mil area of 75°C wire as listed in Table 8
k = approximate resistance value per mil foot
I = line current

$2L$ = twice the length of a single-phase circuit
$1.73L$ = 1.73 times the length of a 3-phase circuit
V_d = desired voltage drop

If equipment instructions include a minimum voltage, voltage drop calculations should always be done to ensure compliance with **110.3(B)**.

7.7.2 Developing the Values of *k* for Use with Table 8

The approximate value of *k* is used when calculating wire size, length of conductor, or maximum amperes when trying to remain within the *Code*-recommended voltage drop percentage.

The approximate value of *k* used in the theory textbook equation is 10.4 for copper and 17 for aluminum at 20°C. **Table 8** is set up for 75°C; therefore, *k* must be a different value. The following *k* values are applicable to **Table 8** based upon 75°C.

For copper:

k for 75°C = 12.9

For aluminum:

k for 75°C = 21.2

For additional information, visit qr.njatcdb.org Item #1036

The following illustrates how to determine *k*:

EXAMPLES

How to determine *k*

Since

$$V_d = \frac{\text{DC resistance} \times I \times 2L}{1{,}000}$$

and

$$V_d = \frac{k \times I \times 2L}{\text{cmil}}$$

then

$$\frac{\text{DC Resistance} \times I \times 2L}{1{,}000} = \frac{k \times I \times 2L}{\text{cmil}}$$

$$\frac{\text{DC Resistance} \times \cancel{I} \times \cancel{2L}}{1{,}000} = \frac{k \times \cancel{I} \times \cancel{2L}}{\text{cmil}}$$

$$\frac{\text{DC Resistance}}{1{,}000} = \frac{k}{\text{cmil}}$$

$$k = \frac{\text{DC Resistance} \times \text{cmil}}{1{,}000}$$

Select 1,000 kcmil conductor and DC resistance

$$k = \frac{0.0129 \times 1{,}000{,}000}{1{,}000}$$
$$= 12.9 \text{ for copper}$$

$$k = \frac{0.0212 \times 1{,}000{,}000}{1{,}000}$$
$$= 21.2 \text{ for aluminum}$$

See Problems 7-13 and 7-14.

PROBLEM 7-13

Determine the size of THWN copper conductors needed for a branch circuit supplying a 200-ampere, single-phase, 240-volt load at a distance of 150 feet, with the voltage drop held within the recommended *Code* limits where reasonable efficiency is expected. Does this wire size comply with Table 310.16?

Solution

210.19(A) Informational Note No. 3

3% V_d recommended

$V_d = V_{\text{supply}} \times 3\%$
$= 240 \times 0.03$
$= 7.2$ V

$\text{cmil} = \dfrac{k \times I \times 2L}{V_d}$
$= \dfrac{12.9 \times 200 \times 2 \times 150}{7.2}$
$= 107{,}500$ cmil minimum

Table 8

Select next larger wire size

133,100 cmils = 2/0 AWG copper

Table 310.16 at 200 A requires 3/0 AWG THWN copper

Answer: 3/0 AWG THWN copper

PROBLEM 7-14

Determine the THWN aluminum wire size needed for branch-circuit conductors supplying a 115-ampere, 208-volt, 3-phase load at a distance of 130 feet with the voltage drop held within the *Code* recommendations where reasonable efficiency is expected.

Solution

210.19(A) Informational Note No. 3

3% V_d recommended

$V_d = V_{supply} \times 3\%$
$= 208 \times 0.03$
$= 6.24$ V

$$cmil = \frac{k \times I \times 1.73 L}{V_d}$$
$$= \frac{21.2 \times 115 \times 1.73 \times 130}{7.24}$$
$$= 87,870 \text{ cmil}$$

Table 8

87,870 cmil = 1/0 AWG aluminum

Answer: 1/0 AWG aluminum

7.7.3 Solving for Length (L)

When the wire size, voltage drop, and ampacity are known, the equation can be transposed to solve for length (L).

Single-Phase:
$$L = \frac{cmil \times V_d}{2k \times I}$$

3-Phase:
$$L = \frac{cmil \times V_d}{1.73 k \times I}$$

See Problems 7-15 and 7-16.

PROBLEM 7-15

A 120-volt branch circuit is to be installed with two 6 AWG THWN aluminum conductors serving a load with 50 amperes of current. Determine the maximum length of the conductors when the voltage drop is held within a 3% limit.

Solution

210.19(A) Informational Note No. 3

3% V_d recommended

$V_d = V_{supply} \times 3\%$
$= 120 \times 0.03$
$= 3.6$ V

Table 8

cmil column

6 AWG aluminum = 26,240 cmil

$$L = \frac{cmil \times V_d}{2k \times I}$$
$$= \frac{26,240 \times 3.6}{2 \times 21.2 \times 50}$$
$$= 44.56 \text{ ft}$$

Answer: 44.56 ft

PROBLEM 7-16

A 480-volt branch circuit is to be installed with three 1/0 AWG THWN copper conductors serving a 140-ampere, 3-phase load. Determine the maximum length of the conductors, with the voltage drop not exceeding 3%.

Solution

210.19(A) Informational Note No. 3

3% V_d recommended

$V_d = V_{supply} \times 3\%$
$= 480 \times 0.03$
$= 14.4$ V

Table 8

cmil column

1/0 AWG copper = 105,600 cmil

$$L = \frac{cmil \times V_d}{1.73 k \times I}$$
$$= \frac{105,600 \times 14.4}{1.73 \times 12.9 \times 140}$$
$$= 487 \text{ ft}$$

Answer: 487 ft

7.7.4 Solving for Current (I)

The same equation can be transposed to solve for the maximum current when the wire size, length, and desired voltage drop are known.

Single-Phase:

$$I = \frac{\text{cmil} \times V_d}{k \times 2L}$$

3-Phase:

$$I = \frac{\text{cmil} \times V_d}{k \times 1.73L}$$

See Problems 7-17 and 7-18.

PROBLEM 7-17

Determine the maximum load for a 220-volt, 3-phase circuit with 10 AWG THWN stranded copper conductors installed at a distance of 160 feet with the voltage drop held within *Code* recommendations.

Solution

210.19(A) Informational Note No. 3
3% V_d recommended
$V_d = V_{\text{supply}} \times 3\%$
$= 220 \times 0.03$
$= 6.6$ V
Table 8
cmil column
10 AWG copper stranded = 10,380 cmil

$$I = \frac{\text{cmil} \times V_d}{k \times 1.73L}$$
$$= \frac{10,380 \times 6.6}{12.9 \times 1.73 \times 160}$$
$$= 19.19 \text{ A}$$

Answer: 19.19 A

PROBLEM 7-18

Determine the maximum load for a 115-volt, single-phase circuit with 8 AWG THWN solid aluminum conductors installed at a distance of 120 feet, with the voltage drop not exceeding 3%.

Solution

210.19(A) Informational Note No. 3
3% V_d recommended
$V_d = V_{\text{supply}} \times 3\%$
$= 115 \times 0.03$
$= 3.45$ V
Table 8
cmil column
8 AWG aluminum = 16,510 cmil

$$I = \frac{\text{cmil} \times V_d}{k \times 2L}$$
$$= \frac{16,510 \times 3.45}{21.2 \times 2 \times 120}$$
$$= 11.19487 \text{ A}$$

Answer: 11.19 A

The PPE requirements of NFPA 70E do not address protection from physical trauma other than exposure to the thermal effects of arc flash. These circles identify the different types of trauma that result from injuries related to arc flash and arc blast.

In summary, the voltage drop equation can be used to select the wire size, determine *k*, and, using **Table 8**, calculate the circuit length and find the current amperes.

An arc flash protection boundary may be a greater distance from the exposed energized electrical conductors or circuit parts than the limited approach boundary.

7.8 VOLTAGE DROP FOR FEEDERS AND BRANCH CIRCUITS

According to **210.19(A) Informational Note No. 3**, the total voltage drop on a branch circuit and feeder is recommended not to exceed 5% where reasonable efficiency is expected. A similar recommendation is found in **215.2(A)(1) Informational Note No. 2** for feeders. **See Problem 7-19**.

While the federal government does not have a national energy code, state and local governmental authorities do adopt energy codes. Two energy codes are the *ASHRAE 90.1* and the *International Energy Conservation Code* (IECC). These codes both specify that the voltage drop for the combination of both the feeder and branch circuit conductors should not exceed 5%. Check with the local authority having jurisdiction (AHJ) on enforcement requirements.

7.9 USING ALTERNATE METHODS TO SOLVE FOR VOLTAGE DROP

An alternate method can also be used for calculating voltage drop.

7.9.1 Varying the Value of *k*

Instead of using the correction factor of 1.05, the value of *k* is given. The given value will take into consideration the material of the conductor and the temperature.

For example: *k* for copper could possibly be any number between 12.0 and 14.0; *k* for aluminum

PROBLEM 7-19

An installation on a 480-volt, 3-phase system consists of a 4/0 AWG THWN copper feeder supplying 225 amperes to a control center located 300 feet from the service. A 3-phase branch circuit of 2 AWG THWN copper carries 105 amperes to a 3-phase load located 125 feet from the control center.

1. What is the voltage drop on the feeder?
2. What is the voltage drop on the branch circuit?
3. What is the total voltage drop to the load?
4. What is the voltage drop percentage for feeder and branch circuit?

Solution

Calculation 1
Feeder voltage drop
Table 8
cmil column
4/0 AWG = 211,600 cmil

$$V_d = \frac{k \times I \times 1.73 L}{cmil}$$
$$= \frac{12.9 \times 225 \times 1.73 \times 300}{211,600}$$
$$= 7.12 \text{ V}$$

Answer: 7.12V feeder voltage drop

Calculation 2
Branch circuit voltage
Table 8
cmil column
2 AWG = 66,360

$$V_d = \frac{k \times I \times 1.73 L}{cmil}$$
$$= \frac{12.9 \times 105 \times 1.73 \times 125}{66,360}$$
$$= 4.41 \text{ V}$$

Answer: 4.41 V

Calculation 3
Total circuit voltage
$V_d = V_d$ (feeder) + V_d (branch circuit)
$= 7.12 + 4.41$
$= 11.53$ V
Answer = 11.53 V

Calculation 4
Percent for total circuit

$$V_d = \frac{V_d}{V_{supply}}$$
$$= \frac{11.53}{480}$$
$$= 0.024 \text{ or } 2.4\%$$

Answer: 2.4% for the total circuit

could possibly be between 20.0 and 23.0. **See Problems 7-20 and 7-21.**

PROBLEM 7-20

What is the voltage drop on a single-phase, 240-volt circuit carrying 80 amperes on a 4 AWG copper conductor at a distance of 200 feet? ($k = 13.0$)

Solution

Table 8
cmil column
4 AWG = 41,740 cmil

$$V_d = \frac{k \times I \times 2L}{cmil}$$

$$= \frac{13.0 \times 80 \times 2 \times 200}{41,740}$$

$$= 9.96 \text{ V}$$

Answer: 9.96 V

PROBLEM 7-21

What is the voltage drop on a 3-phase, 240-volt circuit carrying 45 amperes on an 8 AWG aluminum conductor at a distance of 175 feet? ($k = 21.2$)

Solution

Table 8
cmil column
8 AWG = 16,510 cmil

$$V_d = \frac{k \times I \times 1.73 L}{cmil}$$

$$= \frac{21.2 \times 45 \times 1.73 \times 175}{16,510}$$

$$= 17.49 \text{ V}$$

Answer: 17.49 V

When *k* has a given value, the equation can be transposed to solve for conductor size, maximum current, or length for a given or recommended voltage drop.

Single-Phase:

$$cmil = \frac{k \times I \times 2L}{V_d}$$

3-Phase:

$$cmil = \frac{k \times I \times 1.73L}{V_d}$$

See Problem 7-22.

PROBLEM 7-22

Determine the correct wire size for a THWN copper conductor needed to carry a single-phase, 60-ampere load a distance of 200 feet without exceeding a 3% drop for a 240-volt circuit. ($k = 12.8$)

Solution

$$V_d = 240 \times 3\%$$
$$= 240 \times 0.03$$
$$= 7.2 \text{ V}$$

$$cmil = \frac{k \times I \times 2L}{V_d}$$

$$= \frac{12.8 \times 60 \times 2 \times 200}{7.2}$$

$$= 42,667 \text{ cmil}$$

Table 8
42,667 cmil = 3 AWG

Answer: 3 AWG THWN copper

7.9.2 Using Chapter 9, Table 9

Chapter 9, Table 9 may also be used to perform AC voltage drop calculations. This table provides a comprehensive list of impedance (Z) values for AC circuits at an 85% power factor using 75°C insulated copper or aluminum conductors installed in PVC, steel, or aluminum conduits. According to the table footnote, adjustments may be made for different power factors as well. The final voltage drop calculated values results are approximate, as are most previous voltage drop calculations.

Note that the header of **Table 9** indicates that the values given are either ohms to neutral per kilometer or ohms to neutral per thousand feet. Care must be exercised to use consistent units of measure. English units (feet) are the choice for *Code* calculations.

To find the impedance of a circuit whose length is known in feet, use:

$$Z = \frac{\text{length (ft)} \times \text{table value}}{1{,}000 \text{ ft}}$$

See Problems 7-23 and 7-24.

Voltage drop is calculated with Ohm's Law:

$$V_d = I \times Z$$

CHAPTER 7 VOLTAGE DROP

PROBLEM 7-23

A feeder has a 320-ampere continuous load. The system source is 480 volts, 3-phase at the supply 400-ampere circuit breaker. The feeder is a three-inch steel conduit with three 500 kcmil THWN copper conductors operating at their rating of 75°C. The circuit length is 300 feet, and the power factor is 85%. Using Table 9, determine the approximate voltage drop of this circuit.

Solution

Calculation 1
Line-to-neutral circuit impedance (Z)
Table 9
  Effective Z at 0.85 PF for uncoated copper wires
  Steel conduit column
  500 kcmil copper wire = 0.050 Ω/kft

$$Z = \frac{\text{circuit length (ft)} \times \text{table value }(\Omega)}{1{,}000 \text{ ft}}$$

$$= \frac{300 \times 0.050}{1{,}000}$$

$$= 0.015 \ \Omega \text{ (line-to-neutral)}$$

Answer: 0.015 Ω line-to-neutral circuit impedance (Z)

Calculation 2
Line-to-neutral voltage drop (V_d)

$$V_d = I \times Z$$
$$= 320 \times 0.015$$
$$= 4.8 \text{ V}$$

Answer: 4.8 V line-to-neutral voltage drop

Calculation 3
Line-to-line voltage drop (V_d)

V_d (line-to-line) = V_d (line-to-neutral) × 1.732
$$= 4.80 \times 1.732$$
$$= 8.31 \ V_d \text{ (line-to-line)}$$

Answer: 8.31 V line-to-line voltage drop

Calculation 4
Voltage drop as a percentage of the circuit voltage

$$V_d\% = \frac{V_d}{\text{circuit voltage}} \times 100$$

$$= \frac{8.31}{480} \times 100$$

$$= 1.73\%$$

Answer: 1.73% voltage drop

Calculation 5
Actual voltage present at the load
Voltage at load = source voltage − voltage drop
$$= 480 - 8.31$$
$$= 471.69 \text{ V}$$

Answer: 471.69 V

PROBLEM 7-24

A motor circuit supplies a 50-horsepower, 208-volt, 3-phase motor with an 85% power factor and draws a 143-ampere load. The system source is 208 volts, 3-phase at the motor control center and the motor circuit is protected by a 300-ampere circuit breaker. The feeder is a two-inch steel conduit with three 3/0 AWG THWN copper conductors operating at their rating of 75°C. The circuit length is 150 feet. Using Table 9, determine the approximate voltage drop of this circuit.

Solution

Calculation 1
Line-to-neutral circuit impedance (Z)
Table 9
  Effective Z at 0.85 PF for uncoated copper wires
  Steel conduit column
  3/0 AWG copper wire = 0.094 Ω/kft

$$Z = \frac{\text{circuit length (ft)} \times \text{table value }(\Omega)}{1{,}000 \text{ ft}}$$

$$= \frac{150 \times 0.094}{1{,}000}$$

$$= 0.0141 \ \Omega \text{ (line-to-neutral)}$$

Answer: 0.0141 Ω line-to-neutral circuit impedance (Z)

Calculation 2
Line-to-neutral voltage drop (V_d)

$$V_d = I \times Z$$
$$= 143 \text{ A} \times 0.0141 \ \Omega$$
$$= 2.016 \text{ V}$$

Answer: 2.016 V line-to-neutral voltage drop

Calculation 3
Line-to-line voltage drop (V_d)

V_d (line-to-line) = V_d (line to neutral) × 1.732
$$= 2.016 \text{ V} \times 1.732$$
$$= 3.49 \text{ V}$$

Answer: 3.49 V line-to-line voltage drop

Calculation 4
Voltage drop as a percentage of the circuit voltage

$$V_d\% = \frac{V_d}{\text{circuit voltage}} \times 100$$

$$= \frac{3.49}{208} \times 100$$

$$= 1.68\%$$

Answer: 1.68% voltage drop

Calculation 5
Actual voltage present at the motor
Voltage at motor = source voltage − voltage drop
$$= 208 - 3.49$$
$$= 204.51 \text{ V}$$

Answer: 204.51 V

Most applications will require a calculation of voltage drop using phase-to-phase voltage. To do so, multiply the phase-to-neutral voltage drop by the square root of three (rounded to 1.732 in Problem 7-23 and Problem 7-24).

DEFINITIONS AND TERMS

Conductor, Aluminum - According to **310.3(B)**, both solid and stranded aluminum conductors in sizes 12 AWG through 1,000 kcmil are required to be composed of AA-8000 series electrical grade aluminum alloy.

Conductor, Copper - Annealed copper is the material generally used as a conductor in insulated wire and cable. Only soft drawn copper is used for general inside wiring.

Conductor, Copper Coated - When annealed copper is directly covered by rubber insulation, the copper is coated and usually covered with tin or a lead alloy, which is done for the mutual protection of the copper and the rubber. The manufacture of rubber-insulated conductors is generally considered obsolete today. Rubber insulated (with coated) conductors are limited to existing installations only.

Voltage Drop - The difference between the value of source voltage and load voltage.

SUMMARY

Voltage drop is nothing more than a straightforward Ohm's Law calculation of the voltage drop due to the resistance of the circuit conductors and the load current. Most field calculations use direct current resistive values as given in **Chapter 9, Table 8**. It is important to remember that the values given in **Chapter 9, Table 8** are based on a 75°C temperature rating. As temperature increases, resistance also increases. Although the difference in resistance between solid and stranded wires is negligible for field calculations, there is a large difference in resistance between copper and aluminum conductors. The primary difference between single-phase and 3-phase voltage drop equations is a factor of two for single-phase to account for the supply and return conductor, and a factor of 1.73, or the square root of three, to account for three conductors in a 3-phase circuit, with all other factors remaining the same.

In general, the *NEC* does not require a specific voltage drop percentage unless it is part of the equipment listing requirements. However, it does recommend a 3% voltage drop for the branch circuit and 3% for the feeder with a total voltage drop not to exceed 5% for the combination of the branch circuit and feeder. It is important to remember that although this recommendation is located in an informational note in the *NEC* and is therefore not mandatory; the electrical installer needs to ensure a safe, reliable, and quality installation with voltage drop always being an important consideration.

REVIEW QUESTIONS

1. For the majority of voltage drop calculations performed in the field by Electrical Workers to determine the resistance of conductors, which value, as provided by the *NEC*, is most commonly used?
   a. **Chapter 9, Table 5**, based on the insulation of the conductor
   b. **Chapter 9, Table 8**, DC Resistance based on 75°C
   c. **Chapter 9, Table 9**, AC Resistance and Reactance based on 90% power factor
   d. **Table 310.4(A)**

2. When using **Chapter 9, Table 8** to determine the DC resistance of a copper conductor with a thermoplastic insulation coating, which column should be used?
   a. Area as given in circular mil
   b. Coated
   c. Overall area
   d. Uncoated

3. As the operating temperature of the conductor increases, and the ambient temperature increases, the resistance of the conductor will __?__.
   a. change unpredictably
   b. decrease
   c. increase
   d. remain the same

4. Which is not a correct formula for voltage drop?
   a. $V_d = (1.732 \times k \times I \times L) \div cmil$
   b. $V_d = (1.732 \times L \times I \times R) \div 1{,}000$
   c. $V_d = (2 \times k \times I \times L) \div cmil$
   d. $V_d = (2 \times L \times I \times R) \div cmil$

5. The correct value for k for a THW copper conductor operating at its maximum temperature rating is __?__.
   a. 10.4
   b. 11.0
   c. 12.9
   d. 21.2

6. The amount of voltage drop in a given circuit is not dependent upon __?__.
   a. the amount of current
   b. the length of the circuit
   c. the size of the conductor
   d. whether the circuit is in conduit or a cable

7. The *NEC*-recommended voltage drop percentage for a branch circuit is __?__.
   a. 2%
   b. 3%
   c. 5%
   d. 3% is a requirement, not a recommendation

8. In the single-phase voltage drop formula, the purpose of the factor of two in the formula is __?__.
   a. to account for 180° phase shifting in single-phase line and neutral conductors
   b. to adjust the resistance value from **Chapter 9, Table 8** due to units of measurement
   c. to double the current for worst-case scenario
   d. to double the length of the conductor to account for the supply and return conductor from the point of supply to the load

9. When solving for a given circuit conductor to maintain no more than a 3% voltage drop in a branch circuit and using the voltage drop formula solving for circular mil, the circular mil value is __?__.
   a. a maximum cmil value
   b. a minimum cmil value
   c. required to be changed to a DC resistive value that is a minimum value
   d. the cmil value in **Chapter 9, Table 8**; select the conductor that is the next size conductor with a lower cmil value

10. Given a 480-volt, 172-ampere, 3-phase circuit that uses 350 kcmil THW aluminum conductors and has a distance of 525 feet from the supply to the load, what is the voltage drop of the circuit?
    a. 5.68 V
    b. 5.76 V
    c. 9.47 V
    d. 10.94 V

CHAPTER 8
APPLIANCES

The fundamental calculation methods of **Article 220** are used in determining branch-circuit, feeder, and service loads as they relate to appliances. Specific calculation requirements of **Article 422** should also be used as necessary. Largely, most of the calculations deal with household-type appliances, but some calculations may be applied to commercial appliances.

Specific appliance calculations include electric ranges, electric ovens, counter-mounted cooking units, household electric clothes dryers, storage-type electric water heaters, and a few other basic appliances. **Section 220.3** and **Table 220.3** of the *Code* provide a more detailed list of specialized applications that are additions to or modifications of those within **Article 220**.

Branch circuits for household ranges are required to comply with **210.19(A)(3)**. Load calculations for household ranges are permitted according to **Table 220.55** and the accompanying **Note 4**. Load calculations for household dryers must comply with **Section 220.54**, but are permitted to use the demand factors of **Table 220.54**. When dealing with appliances other than household kitchen equipment, the requirements of **Section 220.56** apply to commercial kitchen equipment, and the demand factors of **Table 220.56** are also permitted to be used for these calculations. Feeder and service neutral loads related to appliances are permitted to be reduced in accordance with **Section 220.61**.

Both single-phase and 3-phase feeder demand calculations are demonstrated. Most feeder calculations are 120/240-volt single-phase, 3-wire, unless they are specifically noted to be 3-phase.

OBJECTIVES

- Calculate branch-circuit loads for household appliances such as ranges, wall-mounted ovens, counter-mounted cooking units, clothes dryers, storage-type water heaters, and kitchen waste disposers.

- Determine the proper size branch-circuit conductor for an individual appliance branch circuit.

- Determine the proper size overcurrent protective device for an individual appliance branch circuit.

- Calculate feeder demand loads and ampacities for appliance loads.

- Calculate neutral loads and conductor sizes for appliance loads.

- Calculate appliance service and feeder demand loads for one-family and multifamily dwelling units.

- Calculate appliance loads, branch-circuit conductor sizes, and overcurrent protective device sizes for commercial appliances.

TABLE OF CONTENTS

8.1 RANGE LOADS—FEEDER DEMANDS—DWELLING UNITS WITH 120/240-VOLT, SINGLE-PHASE SERVICE 176
- .1 Ranges Not over 12 kW and of Unequal Rating 177
- .2 All Household Cooking Appliances over $1\frac{3}{4}$ kW through $8\frac{3}{4}$ kW 178
- .3 Ranges in Multifamily Dwellings 178
- .4 Ranges Rated over 12 kW and Less Than 27 kW 181

8.2 DEVELOPING AN EQUATION FOR SINGLE-PHASE RANGES ON A 3-PHASE SYSTEM 182

8.3 BRANCH-CIRCUITS FOR RANGE LOADS 185

8.4 RANGE LOADS—BRANCH-CIRCUIT CONDUCTORS 186

8.5 HOUSEHOLD COOKING EQUIPMENT IN SCHOOLS 189

8.6 COMMERCIAL COOKING APPLIANCES 189

8.7 BRANCH-CIRCUITS SERVING AN ELECTRIC CLOTHES DRYER 190

8.8 OTHER APPLIANCES 191
- .1 Branch Circuits Serving an Electric Water Heater 191
- .2 Branch Circuits Serving a Kitchen In-Sink Waste Disposer 192
- .3 Branch Circuits Serving a Unit Electric Heater 192

DEFINITIONS AND TERMS 193
SUMMARY 194
REVIEW QUESTIONS 195

8.1 RANGE LOADS—FEEDER DEMANDS—DWELLING UNITS WITH 120/240-VOLT, SINGLE-PHASE SERVICE

Section 220.55 and **Table 220.55** are used for calculating loads for household electric ranges and other cooking appliances installed in dwelling units. This section and table cover the installation of any of the following household cooking appliances having a rating of over $1^3/_4$ kilowatts (kW):

1. Household electric ranges
2. Wall-mounted electric ovens
3. Counter-mounted cooking units

A rating of $1^3/_4$ kW or less would be considered an electrical appliance and is not subject to **Section 220.55** or **Table 220.55**. Other household cooking appliances rated $1^3/_4$ kW or over include warming ovens, broilers, microwave ovens, and similar cooking appliances.

The calculations derived from the use of **Table 220.55** are generally reserved for feeder loads. However, per **220.14(B)**, it is permissible to calculate the branch-circuit load of one range according to **Table 220.55 Note 4**. Additional permissions are contained in **Note 4** as well.

NEC **220.61(B)(1)** permits the feeder demand on the neutral to be 70% of the feeder demand on the ungrounded conductors (line or phase conductors).

For range load calculations, kilovolt-amperes (kVA) and kilowatts (kW) are considered to be the same. All feeder demands will be calculated for line and neutral conductors and will be given in volt-amperes (VA).

The title of **Table 220.55** contains one instruction regarding the use of the table: Column C is to be used in all cases except as otherwise permitted in **Note 3**.

Assume the service is 120/240 volts, 3-wire, single-phase, unless otherwise noted.

PROBLEM 8-1

What is the feeder demand for one 10-kW range installed in a dwelling unit?

Solution

Calculation 1
Line load
Table 220.55
  Column C
  1 Range = 8 kW or 8,000 VA
Answer: 8,000 VA line

Calculation 2
Neutral load
220.61(B)(1)
  Neutral = line VA × 70%
         = 8,000 × 0.70
         = 5,600 VA
Answer: 5,600 VA neutral

Comment: According to Table 220.55 Note 4, this calculation is not limited to a feeder calculation. Rather, this calculation may also serve as the branch-circuit load calculation.

Range 10 kW

8.1.1 Ranges Not over 12 kW and of Unequal Rating

When the ranges are of unequal rating and no range is rated over 12 kW, the number of ranges can be counted and read from Column C. This is permitted by **Table 220.55 Note 2**. **Note 2** requires that when certain ranges of unequal ratings are installed, all ranges less than 12 kW are required to be counted as 12-kW ranges. **See Problems 8-1, 8-2, and 8-3.**

PROBLEM 8-2

What is the feeder demand for two identical 10-kW electric ranges installed in a dwelling unit?

Solution

Calculation 1
Line load
Table 220.55
  Column C
  2 ranges = 11 kW or 11,000 VA
Answer: 11,000 VA line

Calculation 2
Neutral load
220.61(B)(1)
  Neutral = line VA × 70%
         = 11,000 × 0.70
         = 7,700 VA
Answer: 7,700 VA neutral

PROBLEM 8-3

What is the feeder demand for one 10-kW range and one 12-kW range installed in a dwelling unit?

Solution

Calculation 1
Line load
Table 220.55 Note 2
  Two ranges unequal
  Both between $8^{3}/_{4}$ kW and 12 kW
  Treat as equal ranges
Table 220.55
  Column C
  2 ranges = 11 kW or 11,000 VA
Answer: 11,000 VA line

Calculation 2
Neutral load
220.61(B)(1)
  Neutral = line VA × 70%
         = 11,000 × 0.70
         = 7,700 VA
Answer: 7,700 VA neutral

8.1.2 All Household Cooking Appliances over 1³/₄ kW through 8³/₄ kW

Table 220.55 Note 3 contains four instructions:

1. **Note 3** may be used in lieu of Column C. The word "*may*" means that Column C does not have to be used (although both methods must be checked when trying to establish the smallest demand).
2. Add nameplate ratings of all cooking appliances rated between 1³/₄ kW and less than 3¹/₂ kW and multiply by the percentage in Column A.
3. Add nameplate ratings of all cooking appliances rated from 3¹/₂ kW through 8³/₄ kW and multiply by the percentage in Column B.
4. When the ranges are of unequal rating, and no range is rated over 12 kW, the number of ranges can be counted and read from Column C, as **Note 2** requires that when ranges of unequal rating are installed, all ranges less than 12 kW are required to be counted as 12-kW ranges. **See Problem 8-4**.

An option given by **Note 3** permits the use of either Column B or Column C. When the minimum answer is requested, both options must be calculated, and whichever calculation gives the smaller value should be used. **See Problem 8-5**.

Where the rating of the cooking appliances falls under both Columns A and B for a given number of appliances, calculate the demand factors for each column, then add them together.

8.1.3 Ranges in Multifamily Dwellings

Table 220.55 is applicable to range loads installed in multifamily dwellings. **See Problems 8-6, 8-7, and 8-8.**

PROBLEM 8-4

What is the feeder demand for two electric wall-mounted ovens installed in a dwelling unit, one at 2¹/₂ kW and the other at 3 kW?

Solution

Calculation 1
Line load
Table 220.55 Note 3
  Establish smallest demand
  Column A calculation
  Add nameplate ratings
  2.5 + 3 = 5.5 kW
Table 220.55
  Column A
  2 units = 75%
  5.5 kW × 0.75 = 4.125 kW
  Column C calculation
Table 220.55
  Column C
  2 units = 11 kW
4.125 kW is smaller than 11 kW; use smallest demand
Line = 4.125 kW or 4,125 VA
Answer: 4,125 VA line

Calculation 2
Neutral load
220.61(B)(1)
  Neutral = line VA × 70%
         = 4,125 × 0.70
         = 2,888 VA
Answer: 2,888 VA neutral

CHAPTER 8 APPLIANCES

PROBLEM 8-5

What is the feeder demand for three 8-kW electric ranges installed in a dwelling unit?

Solution

Calculation 1
Line load
Table 220.55 Note 3
  Establish smallest demand
  Column B calculation
  Add nameplate ratings
  8 + 8 + 8 = 24 kW
Table 220.55
  Column B
  3 ranges = 55%
  24 kW × 0.55 = 13.2 kW or 13,200 VA
  Column C calculation
Table 220.55
  Column C
  3 ranges under 12 kW = 14 kW
  13.2 kW is smaller than 14 kW; use smallest demand
Answer: 13,200 VA line

Calculation 2
Neutral load
220.61(B)(1)
  Neutral = line VA × 70%
         = 13,200 × 0.70
         = 9,240 VA
Answer: 9,240 VA neutral

Comment: Note 3 is permitted in lieu of Column C. As a comparison, if the three ranges had been read from Column C, the feeder demand would have been 14 kW. A lower demand load would be calculated by the use of Columns A or B when Note 3 is applied.

PROBLEM 8-6

What are the line and neutral feeder demands for three 3-kW ovens and three 8-kW ranges on the same feeder?

Solution

Calculation 1
3 kW oven line load
Table 220.55
  Column A
  3 units = 70%
  3 × 3 kW × 0.70 = 6.3 kW
8 kW range line load
Table 220.55
  Column B
  3 units = 55%
  3 × 8 kW × 0.55 = 13.2 kW
  Line = 6.3 + 13.2
       = 19.5 kW or 19,500 VA
Answer: 19,500 VA line

Calculation 2
Neutral load
220.61(B)(1)
  Neutral = line VA × 70%
         = 19,500 × 0.70
         = 13,650 VA
Answer: 13,650 VA neutral

Comment: The use of Note 3 and Columns A and B is used for a multifamily dwelling where a large number of electrical cooking appliances rated 1 3/4 kW through 8 3/4 kW are to be installed.

PROBLEM 8-7

A 28-unit multifamily dwelling has one 10-kW range installed in each unit. What is the feeder demand for the complex?

Solution

Calculation 1
Line load
Table 220.55
  Column C
  26–30 ranges = 15 kW + 1 kW for each range
  Total kW = 15 kW + (28 × 1)
         = 43 kW or 43,000 VA
Answer: 43,000 VA line

Calculation 2
Neutral load
220.61(B)(1)
  Neutral = line VA × 70%
        = 43,000 × 0.70
        = 30,100 VA
Answer: 30,100 VA neutral

PROBLEM 8-8

A 48-unit multifamily dwelling has a 12-kW range installed in each apartment. What is the feeder demand for the complex?

Solution

Calculation 1
Line load
Table 220.55
  Column C
  41–50 ranges = 25 kW + ³/₄ kW for each range

  Total kW = 25 kW + (48 × 0.75)
         = 25 + 36
         = 61 kW or 61,000 VA
Answer: 61,000 VA line

Calculation 2
Neutral load
220.61(B)(1)
  Neutral = line VA × 70%
        = 61,000 × 0.70
        = 42,700 VA
Answer: 42,700 VA neutral

8.1.4 Ranges Rated over 12 kW and Less Than 27 kW

Table 220.55 Note 1 covers individual ranges and ranges over 12 kW and less than 27 kW. The demand in Column C for the number of ranges is increased by 5% for each kilowatt over 12 kW. According to **220.5(B)**, calculations are permitted to be rounded to the nearest whole ampere, with decimal fractions smaller than 0.5 dropped. Generally, these solutions do not round or drop fractions less than 0.5 until the end of the calculation. **See Problems 8-9 and 8-10.**

PROBLEM 8-9

What is the feeder demand for a 15-kW range installed in a dwelling unit?

Solution

Calculation 1
Line Load
Table 220.55
  Column C
  One range = 8 kW
Table 220.55 Note 1
  5% increase for each kW over 12
  15 kW − 12 = 3 kW
  3 kW × 5% = 15% increase
  8 kW must be increased by 15% or 115% of Column C
  kW = 8 × 1.15
     = 9.2 kW or 9,200 VA
Answer: 9,200 VA line

Calculation 2
Neutral Load
220.61(B)(1)
  Neutral = line VA × 70%
         = 9,200 × 0.70
         = 6,440 VA
Answer: 6,440 VA neutral

PROBLEM 8-10

A multifamily dwelling consists of 24 units with a 15.8-kW range installed in each unit. What is the range feeder demand for the complex?

Solution

Calculation 1
Line Load
Table 220.55
  Column C
  24 ranges = 39 kW
Table 220.55 Note 1
  5% increase for each kW (or major fraction) over 12
  15.8 kW − 12 = 3.8 kW
  3.8 = 4.0
  4.0 × 5% = 20% increase
  39 kW must be increased by 20%, or
    120% of Column C
  kW = 39 × 1.20
     = 46.8 kW or 46,800 VA
Answer: 46,800 VA line

Calculation 2
Neutral Load
220.61(B)(1)
  Neutral = line VA × 70%
         = 46,800 × 0.70
         = 32,760 VA
Answer: 32,760 VA neutral

PROBLEM 8-11

A 12-unit multifamily installation consists of four 10-kW ranges, four 14-kW ranges, and four 16-kW ranges. What is the feeder demand for the complex?

Solution

Calculation 1
Line Load
Table 220.55
  Column C
  12 ranges = 27 kW
Table 220.55, Note 2
  Use 12 kW for the 10 kW ranges

  4 × 12 kW = 48
  4 × 14 kW = 56
  4 × 16 kW = 64
  12 ranges = 168 kW

$$\text{Average} = \frac{168 \text{ kW}}{12 \text{ ranges}}$$
$$= 14 \text{ kW}$$

Table 220.55 Note 1
  5% increase for each kW over 12
  14 kW – 12 = 2 kW
  2 kW × 5% = 10% increase
  27 kW must be increased by 10%, or 110% of Column C
  Total kW = Column C × 110%
       = 27 × 1.10
       = 29.7 kW or 29,700 VA
Answer: 29,700 VA line

Calculation 2
Neutral Load
220.61(B)(1)
  Neutral = line VA × 70%
       = 29,700 × 0.70
       = 20,790 VA
Answer: 20,790 VA neutral

Table 220.55 Note 2 covers the installation of a number of ranges with unequal ratings of 8 3/4 kW to 27 kW. An average value of kilowatt ratings is calculated. Use 12 kW for any range less than 12 kW. Read the demand for the total number of ranges in Column C. When the average value exceeds 12 kW, increase the Column C demand by 5% for each kilowatt or major fraction thereof. See Problem 8-11.

8.2 DEVELOPING AN EQUATION FOR SINGLE-PHASE RANGES ON A 3-PHASE SYSTEM

Many multifamily dwelling units are provided with a 208Y/120-volt, 3-phase, 4-wire service to supply the entire complex, with 3-wire feeders consisting of two ungrounded conductors and a grounded (neutral) conductor supplying each individual dwelling unit. As **Table 220.55** was created based upon demand for 120/240-volt, single-phase, 3-wire household ranges, if single-phase household ranges are supplied by a 3-phase, 4-wire system, a different method of calculating the demand for the ranges is required.

As stated in the last paragraph of **220.55**:

Where two or more single-phase ranges are supplied by a 3-phase, 4-wire feeder or service, the total load shall be calculated on the basis of twice the maximum number connected between any two phases.

Notice that the calculation is required to be done on the basis, not the results, of the calculation based on twice the maximum number between two phases.

CHAPTER 8 APPLIANCES

Figure 8-1. Three Household Ranges on 3-Phase Systems. *The demand for the ranges is to be determined on the basis of twice the maximum number on any two phases. In the diagram, the maximum number between two phases is one range; therefore, the calculation would be based on two times one range, or two ranges. The calculation is based on two ranges, but the demand for two ranges does not determine the final load.*

If, for example, there were three ranges, they would evenly distribute on the three phases, so twice the maximum number would be two times one range, or two ranges. **See Figure 8-1**. If there was an unbalanced number of ranges, such as four, it would be noted that two phases, such as A phase and B phase, would have two ranges connected, while A to C phases would only have one range, and B to C phase would only have one range. Therefore, the maximum number between two phases is two, and the calculation would be based on twice the maximum number, or two times two ranges, or four ranges. **See Figure 8-2**. The demand determined, based on twice the maximum number between two phases, would only be for two of the three phases, or two-thirds of the total demand, so another step is required.

Once twice the maximum number of ranges between two phases has been determined, it is required to determine the demand from Column C, applying **Note 1** or **Note 2** if applicable. The demand so obtained is based on demand for two phases and not all three. Therefore, it is required to take the demand based on two phases and divide by two to obtain the per-phase demand, then multiply the per-phase demand by three to obtain the equivalent 3-phase demand. **See Figure 8-3**.

Annex D, Example D5(a) performs a similar calculation. **See Problem 8-12**.

Figure 8-2. Four Household Ranges on 3-Phase Systems. *The maximum number of ranges between two phases is two as there are two ranges across A and B phases. The calculation is to be based on twice the maximum number: two times two ranges, or four ranges. Four ranges is the basis for the calculation.*

Figure 8-3. Final Determination of Load for Household Ranges on 3-Phase Systems. *With the calculation to be based on four ranges which would be equivalent to the demand for two of the three phases, the final demand is determined by dividing the demand of the four ranges by two to obtain a per phase demand. The per phase demand is then multiplied by three to obtain the equivalent 3-phase demand.*

PROBLEM 8-12

Calculate the line and neutral loads for thirty 12-kW ranges installed on a 120/208-volt, 3-phase, 4-wire system.

Solution

Calculation 1
Line Load
  Evenly divide the number of ranges
  30 ranges ÷ 3 = 10 ranges per phase
  Calculation to be based on twice the maximum number between two phases
  2 × 10 ranges = 20 ranges
  Demand from Table 220.55 Column C
  20 ranges = 35 kW

  Per phase demand = two phase demand ÷ 2
  35 ÷ 2 = 17.5 kW

  Equivalent 3-phase demand = per phase demand × 3
  17.5 × 3 = 52.5 kW or 52,500 VA
Answer: 52,500 VA line

Calculation 2
Neutral load
220.61(B)(1)
  Neutral = line VA × 70%
         = 52,500 × 0.70
         = 36,750 VA
Answer: 36,750 VA neutral

PROBLEM 8-13

What is the branch-circuit load for one 16-kW range installed in a one-family dwelling unit?

Solution

Calculation 1
Branch-circuit conductor load
Table 220.55 Note 4
  Use Table 220.55 for branch-circuit loads
Table 220.55
  Column C
  1 range = 8 kW
Table 220.55 Note 1
  5% increase for each kW over 12
  16 kW – 12 = 4 kW
  4 kW × 5% = 20% increase
  4 kW must be increased by 20%, or 120% of Column C
  Total kW = Column C × 120%
           = 8 × 1.20
           = 9.6 kW or 9,600 VA
Answer: 9,600 VA line

Calculation 2
Neutral conductor load
210.19(A)(3) Exception No. 2
  Range size exceeds 8,750 VA
  Neutral = line VA × 70%
         = 9,600 × 0.70
         = 6,720 VA
Answer: 6,720 VA neutral

8.3 BRANCH-CIRCUITS FOR RANGE LOADS

Up to this point, all calculations have been directed at feeders. **Table 220.55 Note 4** permits the use of **Table 220.55** for calculating branch-circuit loads for household electrical cooking appliances. **Note 4** covers several installations:

1. For the branch-circuit load for one range, use **Table 220.55**.
2. The branch-circuit load for one wall-mounted oven is the nameplate rating of the oven.
3. The branch-circuit load for one counter-mounted cooking unit is the nameplate rating of the cooking unit.
4. For the branch-circuit load for a counter-mounted cooking unit and not more than two wall-mounted ovens, all on the same branch circuit and located in the same room, add the nameplate ratings and calculate as one range, using **Table 220.55**.

See Problems 8-13, 8-14, and 8-15.

PROBLEM 8-14

What is the branch-circuit load for one 5-kW counter-mounted cooking unit?

Solution

Calculation 1
Branch-circuit conductor load
Table 220.55 Note 4
  Use nameplate rating
  Line = 5 kW or 5,000 VA
Answer: 5,000 VA line

Calculation 2
Neutral conductor load
210.19(A)(3) Exception No. 2
  Does not apply since 5,000 VA is less than 8,750 VA
  Neutral conductor load = 5,000 VA
Answer: 5,000 VA neutral

PROBLEM 8-15

What is the branch-circuit load for two 4-kW wall-mounted ovens and a 5-kW counter-mounted cooking unit installed on the same branch circuit in the same room of a one-family dwelling unit?

Solution

Calculation 1
Branch-circuit conductor load
Table 220.55 Note 4
  Same circuit, same room, not over 2 ovens
  Add and calculate as one range
  4 kW + 4 kW + 5 kW = 13 kW
Table 220.55
  Column C
  One range = 8 kW
Table 220.55 Note 1
  5% increase for each kW over 12
  13 kW − 12 = 1 kW
  1 kW × 5% = 5% increase
  1 kW must be increased by 5%, or 105% of Column C
  Total kW = Column C × 105%
           = 8 × 105%
           = 8.4 kW or 8,400 VA
Answer: 8,400 VA line

Calculation 2
Neutral conductor load
210.19(A)(3) Exception No. 2
  Does not apply since 8,400 VA is less than 8,750 VA
  Neutral conductor load = 8,400 VA
Answer: 8,400 VA neutral

8.4 RANGE LOADS–BRANCH-CIRCUIT CONDUCTORS

Section 210.19 sets the minimum ampacity and size of a branch circuit, and **210.19(A)(3)**, in turn, establishes the minimum conductor size permitted for branch-circuit conductors supplying household ranges and cooking appliances.

NEC **210.19(A)(3)** sets the minimum branch-circuit rating for an $8\,^3/_4$-kW or larger range at not less than 40 amperes. Therefore, the overcurrent protective device is required to be a minimum of 40 amperes and the branch-circuit conductors are required to have an ampacity of at least 40 amperes.

PROBLEM 8-16

What is the minimum size of THWN copper branch-circuit conductors and neutral conductor permitted for one 120/240-volt, 10-kW electric range installed in a one-family dwelling unit? What is the matching size circuit breaker for the conductors selected? What is the minimum size copper equipment grounding conductor?

Solution

Calculation 1
Branch-circuit conductors
Table 220.55 Note 4
  Use Table 220.55 for branch-circuit loads
Table 220.55
  One Range = 8 kW
Table 310.16
  75°C copper THWN column
  33.33 A = 10 AWG THWN
240.4(D)(7)
  Maximum overcurrent for 10 AWG = 30 A
210.19(A)(3)
  Does not meet minimum of 40 A
  Next larger standard size conductor = 8 AWG THWN
Table 310.16
  8 AWG THWN = 50 A
Answer: 8 AWG THWN minimum branch-circuit conductors

Calculation 2
Neutral conductor
220.61(B)(1)
  Neutral = line VA × 70%
         = 33.33 × 0.70
         = 23.33 A
Table 310.16
  75°C copper THWN column
  23.33 A = 12 AWG THWN
210.19(A)(3) Exception No. 2
  Does not meet minimum of 10 AWG for neutral
  Next larger standard size conductor = 10 AWG neutral
Answer: 10 AWG THWN minimum neutral conductor

Calculation 3
Circuit breaker
210.19(A)(3)
  Minimum rating of 40 A
Answer: 40A 2-pole circuit breaker

Calculation 4
Equipment Grounding Conductor
250.122 and Table 250.122
  40A circuit breaker = 10 AWG copper
Answer: 10 AWG copper

CHAPTER 8 APPLIANCES

NEC **210.19(A)(3) Exception No. 2** permits the neutral of a 3-wire branch circuit for 8 $^{3}/_{4}$-kW or larger household cooking appliances to be 70% of the branch circuit rating. However, it also limits the neutral to not be smaller than a 10 AWG wire. **See Problems 8-16 and 8-17.**

PROBLEM 8-17

What is the minimum ampacity and size of THHN copper branch-circuit and neutral conductors permitted for one 120/240-volt, 17.6-kW range installed in a one-family dwelling unit? Assume all equipment is listed at 75°C.

Range 17.6 kW

Solution

Calculation 1
Branch-circuit conductors
Table 220.55 Note 4
  Use Table 220.55 for branch-circuit loads
Table 220.55
  One range = 8 kW
Table 220.55 Note 1
  5% increase for each kW over 12
  17.6 kW − 12 = 5.6 kW
220.5(B)
  Round to the nearest whole number
  5.6 = 6 kW
  6 kW × 5% = 30% increase
  8 kW must be increased by 30% or 130% of Column C
  kW = 8 × 1.30
     = 10.4 kW or 10,400 VA

$$I = \frac{kW \times 1{,}000}{E}$$
$$= \frac{10.4 \times 1{,}000}{240}$$
$$= 43.33 \text{ A}$$

110.14(C)(1)
  Not to exceed Table 310.16
Table 310.16
  75°C copper THHN column
  43.33 A = 8 AWG THHN
210.19(A)(3)
  Fulfills minimum requirement of 40 A
Answer: 8 AWG THHN minimum branch-circuit conductors

Calculation 2
Neutral conductor
220.61(B)(1)
  Neutral = line VA × 70%
         = 43.33 × 0.70
         = 30.33 A
Table 310.16
  30.33 A = 10 AWG THHN
210.19(A)(3) Exception No. 2
  Fulfills minimum requirement of 10 AWG for neutral
Answer: 10 AWG THHN minimum neutral conductor

PROBLEM 8-18

Calculate the feeder demand for six 16-kW household electric ranges to be installed in a high school for instructional programs.

Solution

Calculation 1
Line load
Table 220.55 Note 1
  5% increase for each kW over 12
  16 kW − 12 = 4 kW
  4 kW × 5% = 20% increase
  4 kW must be increased by 20% or 120% of Column C
Table 220.55
  Column C
  6 ranges = 21 kW
  Total kW = 21 × 1.20
           = 25.2 kW or 25,200 VA
Answer: 25,200 VA line

Calculation 2
Neutral load
  The ranges are household electric ranges, so 220.61(B)(1) applies
220.61(B)(1)
  Neutral = line VA × 70%
         = 25,200 × 0.70
         = 17,640 VA
Answer: 17,640 VA neutral

PROBLEM 8-19

Calculate the lower feeder demand for four 12-kW ranges and four 4-kW wall-mounted ovens to be installed in a high school cooking lab for instructional programs.

Solution

Calculation 1
Lowest feeder demand
  Using Note 3
Table 220.55 Note 3
  4 ovens × 4 kW = 16 kW
Table 220.55
  Column B calculation
  4 units = 50% demand
  16 kW × 0.50 = 8 kW
Table 220.55
  Column C
  4 ranges = 17 kW
  8 kW oven load + 17 kW range = 25 kW
  Column C calculation
  4 ovens + 4 ranges = 8 units under 12 kW
Table 220.55
  Column C
  8 units = 23 kW
  23 kW is less than 25 kW; use lower demand
Answer: 23,000 VA line

Calculation 2
Neutral load
220.61(B)(1)
  Neutral = line VA × 70%
         = 23,000 × 0.70
         = 16,100 VA
Answer: 16,100 VA neutral

Comment: Note 3 is permitted to be used in lieu of Column C. Therefore, to calculate the lowest feeder demand, calculate both with and without Column C and use the lowest demand. *In lieu of* indicates a choice.

8.5 HOUSEHOLD COOKING EQUIPMENT IN SCHOOLS

Table 220.55 Note 5 permits the use of **Table 220.55** and its notes to be used for calculating feeder loads for household cooking appliances installed and used for instructional programs. **See Problems 8-18 and 8-19.**

8.6 COMMERCIAL COOKING APPLIANCES

Commercial cooking appliances are covered by **Section 220.56** and **Table 220.56**.

Included in commercial cooking appliances are the following:

- Electrical cooking equipment
- Dishwashers
- Booster heaters
- Water heaters
- Other kitchen equipment, including warming ovens, mixing machines, food processors, etc.

Section 220.56 applies to all the preceding kitchen equipment, provided it is controlled by a thermostat or is used in an intermittent duty fashion. However, **Section 220.56** does not apply to space heating, ventilating, and air-conditioning equipment.

The feeder demand is not permitted to be less than the sum of the two largest kitchen equipment loads.

NEC **220.61(B)(1)** permits the 70% derating factor for the neutral and applies to household electric ranges only. It does not apply to commercial cooking equipment. **See Problems 8-20 and 8-21.**

For additional information, visit qr.njatcdb.org Item #1037

PROBLEM 8-20

Calculate the feeder load for three 16-kW ranges, one 7.5-kW water heater, and one 4-kW dishwasher installed in a restaurant kitchen.

Solution

Section 220.56 and Table 220.56

3 × 16 kW range	= 48.0
1 × 7.5 kW range	= 7.5
1 × 4 kW dishwasher	= 4.0
Total load of 5 units	= 59.5 kW

Table 220.56
 5 units = 70% demand
 59.5 × 0.70 = 41.65 kW
Section 220.56
 Demand not to be less than the sum of the two largest loads
 Two largest = 16 + 16
  = 32 kW
 41.65 kW is larger than 32 kW; use largest load
 Answer: 41.6 kW or 41,650 VA for line and neutral feeder demand

RESTAURANT:
Three 16-kW Ranges
One 7.5-kW Water Heater
One 4 kW Dishwasher

PROBLEM 8-21

Calculate the feeder load for two 24-kW ranges, one 10-kW water heater, one 3-kW dishwasher with a 2-kW booster heater, and two 2-kW warming ovens to be installed in a restaurant kitchen.

RESTAURANT:
Two 24-kW Ranges
One 10-kW Water Heater
One 3-kW Dishwasher
One 2-kW Booster Heater
Two 2-kW Warming Ovens

Solution

Section 220.56 and Table 220.56

2 × 24 kW ranges	= 48
1 × 10 kW water heater	= 10
1 × 3 kW dishwasher	= 3
1 × 2 kW booster heater	= 2
2 × 2 kW warming oven	= 4
Total load of 7 units	= 67 kW

Table 220.56
  6 units and more = 65% demand
  67 kW × 0.65 = 43.55 kW
Section 220.56
  Demand not to be less than the sum of the two largest loads
  Two largest loads = 48 kW
  Calculated 43.55 kW is less than 48 kW; use largest load
  Answer: 48 kW or 48,000 VA for line and neutral feeder demands

8.7 BRANCH-CIRCUITS SERVING AN ELECTRIC CLOTHES DRYER

The branch-circuit loads for an electric clothes dryer are covered by **Part II** of **Article 220**. *NEC* **220.14(B)** permits a dryer load to be calculated according to **Section 220.54** (located in **Part III, Feeders**). The branch-circuit load shall be either 5,000 volt-amperes or the nameplate rating, whichever is larger. This is the basic method used for the following calculation.

Electric clothes dryers are not considered continuous loads. **See Problem 8-22**.

PROBLEM 8-22

What is the minimum size of Type MC cable with 90°C copper conductors permitted to supply a 4.5-kW, 120/240-volt, single-phase, 3-wire electric dryer installed in a one-family dwelling unit? What size overcurrent protective device using 75°C wire terminations will protect this circuit?

Solution

Calculation 1
Circuit conductors
220.14(B)
  Load to be calculated using Section 220.54
Section 220.54
  4.5 kW dryer must be calculated at 5 kW

$$I = \frac{kW \times 1{,}000}{E}$$
$$= \frac{5 \times 1{,}000}{240}$$
$$= 20.83 \text{ A}$$

220.5(B)
  Round to the nearest whole
  20.83 A = 21 A
110.14(C)(1)(a)(3)
  Use higher 75°C temperature conductor to match circuit breaker temperature rating of 75°C
Table 310.16
  75°C copper column
  **Note: use 240.4(D)(7)
240.4(D)(7)
  21 A = 10 AWG copper
Answer: 10-3 Type MC Cable (copper) with ground

Calculation 2
Overcurrent protective device
240.4(D)(7)
  10 AWG = 30 A
Answer: 30A 2-pole overcurrent protective device

8.8 OTHER APPLIANCES

The fundamental requirement for appliance branch circuits is that they carry the appliance current without overheating under their conditions of use. In addition, the branch-circuit rating for individual appliances cannot be less than the rating marked on the appliance.

Article 422 covers appliances used in any occupancy. For motor-operated appliances, **Article 430, Motors**, is to be used to determine the branch-circuit rating unless there are specific requirements for motor-operated appliances within **Article 422**.

8.8.1 Branch Circuits Serving an Electric Water Heater

Section 422.13 covers storage-type water heaters. This section requires that these water heaters be considered a continuous load for sizing the branch-circuit conductors and overcurrent protection. *NEC* **210.19(A)** for conductor sizing and **210.20(A)** for overcurrent protection are used for sizing these branch circuits. **See Problem 8-23**.

PROBLEM 8-23

What is the minimum size of Type NM, nonmetallic sheathed cable using copper branch-circuit conductors to supply a 50-gallon storage-type water heater? This water heater is furnished with standard 240-volt AC, single-phase non-simultaneous wiring, with separate 4,500-watt upper and lower heating elements. What size circuit breaker with 60/75°C wire terminations will protect this circuit?

Solution

Calculation 1
Type NM cable size

$$I = \frac{W}{E}$$
$$= \frac{4,500}{240}$$
$$= 18.75 \text{ A}$$

Section 422.13
  Considered a continuous load
210.19(A)(1)
  $I = continuous\ load \times 125\%$
  $= 18.75 \times 1.25$
  $= 23.44 \text{ A}$
Section 334.80
  NM cable not to exceed ampacity of 60°C rated conductor
Table 310.16
  60°C copper column
  **Note: use 240.4(D)(7)
240.4(D)(7)
  23.44 A = 10 AWG
Answer: 10-2 Type NM cable (copper) with ground

Calculation 2
Circuit breaker
240.4(D)(7)
  10 AWG = 30 A
Answer: 30A 2-pole circuit breaker
Comment: *Non-simultaneous* means these elements are NOT operating at the same time, and therefore only one 4,500 watt element is the actual load at any given time.

PROBLEM 8-24

A household kitchen waste disposer is supplied by an individual branch circuit. The waste disposer nameplate indicates it is a single-phase, ³/₄-horsepower, 120-volt, 8.1-ampere, intermittent-time rated motor equipped with manual reset overload protection. It does not have a recommended wire size or overcurrent protective device rating on the nameplate or in the product specification sheet. What is the minimum size of nonmetallic sheathed cable using copper branch-circuit conductors to supply this kitchen waste disposer? What size circuit breaker with 60/75°C wire terminations will protect this circuit? What is the minimum size AC general-use snap switch permitted to be used to disconnect the waste disposer?

Solution

Calculation 1
Type NM cable size
422.11(A)
  Use appliance marked rating
  Nameplate = 8.1 A
334.80
  NM cable not to exceed ampacity of 60°C rated conductor
210.18
  Minimum branch-circuit rating
  Minimum conductor size = 15 A
Table 310.16
  60°C copper column
  **Note: use 240.4(D)(3)
240.4(D)(3)
  15 A = 14 AWG copper
Answer: 14-2 Type NM cable (copper) with ground

Calculation 2
Circuit breaker
240.4(D)(3)
  14 AWG copper = 15A circuit breaker
Answer: 15A 1-pole circuit breaker

Calculation 3
Disposer disconnect switch using an AC general-use snap switch
404.14(A)(3)
  Motor load not to exceed 80% rating of switch
  Verify 15 A switch rating is sufficient
  Motor Load = switch rating × 80%
           = 15 × 0.8
           = 12 A
  12 A = max. motor load for 15A switch
  8.1 A is less than 12 A; use 15A switch
Answer: 15 A, 120 V general-use snap switch

8.8.2 Branch Circuits Serving a Kitchen In-Sink Waste Disposer

According to **422.60**, the voltage and current ratings are marked on the in-sink waste disposer. These ratings are permitted to be used to select the conductor size and the overcurrent protection. Also, **422.11(G)** requires an in-sink waste disposal motor to be equipped with an overload protective device, usually of the integral type. See **430.32(A)(2)**.

Since the overcurrent protective device size for the motor of the waste disposer is sometimes not marked on the product nameplate, **422.11(A)** is used for this calculation. This section requires the use of **Section 240.4**. Therefore, **240.4(D), Small Conductors**, is used to "match" the ampacity of the conductor size to the selected overcurrent protective device. **See Problem 8-24**.

8.8.3 Branch Circuits Serving a Unit Electric Heater

Article 424 covers fixed electric space-heating equipment, such as heating cable, unit heaters, boilers, central systems, etc. Fixed electric space-heating equipment is required to be considered a continuous load for determining the branch-circuit conductors and overcurrent protection. **See Problem 8-25**.

PROBLEM 8-25

What is the minimum size of THWN copper branch-circuit conductors permitted for one 3-kW, 120-volt, ceiling-mounted unit electric heater installed in a one-family attached garage with a nameplate full load current of 26.5 amperes? What size overcurrent protective device with 60/75°C wire terminations will protect this circuit? What is the minimum size copper equipment grounding conductor?

Solution

Calculation 1
Circuit conductors
424.4(B)
  Circuit conductors are to be sized at 125% of the load
210.19(A)(1)
  $I = continuous\ load \times 125\%$
     $= 26.5 \times 1.25$
     $= 34.125$ A
Table 310.16,
  75°C THWN copper column
  35 A = 10 AWG
240.4(D)(7)
  Prohibits a 10 AWG THWN;
  34.125A load requires an 8 AWG THWN
Answer: 8 AWG THWN circuit conductors

Calculation 2
Overcurrent protective device (OCPD)
424.22(A)
Table 310.16
  75°C copper column
  8 AWG THWN permits a 50A OCPD
Answer: 50A fuse or circuit breaker

Calculation 3
Equipment grounding conductor (EGC)
Table 250.122
  50A OCPD requires a 10 AWG EGC
Answer: 10 AWG equipment grounding conductor

DEFINITIONS AND TERMS

Appliance - Utilization equipment, generally other than industrial, that is normally built in standardized sizes or types and is installed or connected as a unit to perform one or more functions, such as clothes washing, air conditioning, food mixing, deep frying, and so forth. [**70**:100]

Branch Circuit - The circuit conductors between the final overcurrent device protecting the circuit and the outlet(s). [**70**:100]

Branch Circuit, Appliance - A branch circuit that supplies energy to one or more outlets to which appliances are to be connected and that has no permanently connected luminaires that are not a part of an appliance. [**70**:100]

Continuous Load - A load where the maximum current is expected to continue for 3 hours or more. [**70**:100]

Cooking Unit, Counter Mounted - A cooking appliance designed for mounting in or on a counter and consisting of one or more heating elements, internal wiring, and built-in or mountable controls. [**70**:100]

Demand Factor - The ratio of the maximum demand of a system, or part of a system, to the total connected load of a system or the part of the system under consideration. [**70**:100]

Dwelling Unit - A single unit, providing complete and independent living facilities for one or more persons, including permanent provisions for living, sleeping, cooking, and sanitation. [**70**:100]

Feeder - All circuit conductors between the service equipment, the source of a separately derived system, or other power supply source and the final branch-circuit overcurrent device. [**70**:100]

Reproduced with permission of NFPA from NFPA 70®, *National Electrical Code®* (NEC®), 2020 edition. Copyright© 2019, National Fire Protection Association. For a full copy of the NEC®, please go to www.nfpa.org.

SUMMARY

NEC **210.19(A)(3)** requires that branch-circuit conductors supplying household ranges, wall-mounted ovens, counter-mounted cooking units, and other household cooking appliances have an ampacity of not less than the rating of the branch circuit and not less than the maximum load to be served. For ranges rated $8^{3}/_{4}$ kW or more, the minimum branch-circuit rating must be at least 40 amperes. NEC **220.14(B)** permits the use of the demand factors from **220.55** to be used for the branch-circuit load. Generally, the demand factors and loads of **Table 220.55** apply to services and feeders for household electric ranges, wall-mounted ovens, counter-mounted cooking units, and other household cooking appliances over $1^{3}/_{4}$ kW but not over 27 kW. **Section 220.61** permits the neutral conductor of a single-phase, 3-wire circuit to be reduced to 70% of the phase conductor for household ranges and dryers.

As required by **220.54**, the minimum load to be used for calculations of electric clothes dryer circuits is the larger of either 5,000 volt-amperes or the nameplate rating of each dryer served. It also permits the use of the demand factors in **Table 220.54** to determine the final load for services and feeders.

Commercial electric cooking equipment, dishwasher booster heaters, water heaters, and other kitchen equipment loads are permitted to be calculated in accordance with the demand factors of **Table 220.56**.

Appliances are required to comply with **422.10** and **422.11** for minimum branch-circuit conductors and maximum overcurrent protective ratings. Some appliances, such as storage-type water heaters, require the conductors and overcurrent protective device to be sized at 125% in accordance with **422.13**. In the end, the electrical installer is required to comply with many sections of the *NEC* for a safe and *Code*-compliant installation for appliances.

REVIEW QUESTIONS

1. What is the minimum rating for a branch circuit supplying a household range that is rated 8 3/4 kW or more?
   a. 30 A
   b. 40 A
   c. 50 A
   d. 60 A

2. The minimum volt-amperes required to be used to determine the feeder or service load for electric household clothes dryers is __?__.
   a. 125% of the nameplate rating
   b. 5,000 VA
   c. the larger of 5,000 VA or the nameplate rating
   d. the nameplate rating

3. The feeder or service neutral for household electric ranges and dryers is permitted to have a __?__ demand factor applied to the line load to determine the neutral load.
   a. 70%
   b. 80%
   c. 100%
   d. 125%

4. The minimum kilowatt demand for one 12-kW range is __?__.
   a. 8 kW
   b. 9.6 kW
   c. 10 kW
   d. 12 kW

5. When multiple household electric ranges of more than a 12-kW rating (all equal ratings) are installed on a service or feeder, the demand in Column C shall be increased by __?__ for each kilowatt or major fraction of a kilowatt for which the rating exceeds 12 kW.
   a. 5%
   b. 10%
   c. the percentage determined by dividing the range rating by 12 kW
   d. No increase in percentage is required

6. When calculating the feeder or service load for household ranges supplied by a 3-phase, 4-wire, wye system, the demand from Column C that is determined on the basis of twice the maximum number of ranges connected to two phases is required to have which calculation performed to determine the final load?
   a. Divide by two, then multiply by three to determine the final load
   b. Divide by three, then multiply by two to determine the final load
   c. Multiply by three to determine the final load
   d. No calculations required; it is the final load

7. When using **Table 220.55** for ranges rated over 1 3/4 kW through 12 kW, Column C is always permitted to be used.
   a. True
   b. False

8. For determining the feeder and service load for electric household ranges and dryers, kilovolt-amperes is considered to be the same as kilowatts since the loads are primarily resistive.
   a. True
   b. False

9. The branch-circuit conductors for fixed electric space-heating equipment are required to be sized to 125% of the load.
   a. True
   b. False

10. A 120-gallon storage-type electric water heater is required to have only the branch-circuit conductors sized to 125% of the nameplate current rating and not the overcurrent protective device.
    a. True
    b. False

CHAPTER 9
LOAD CALCULATIONS

A one-family dwelling unit load calculation is one of the simplest of calculations presented. The loads in the dwelling are simply converted to volt-amperes (VA), with some loads permitted to be reduced by applicable demand factors. There are two different methods of performing these one-family dwelling unit calculations: the standard method or the optional method. The optional method is reserved for service sizes greater than 100 amperes.

Multifamily dwelling unit calculations, in some ways, are similar to one-family dwelling unit calculations. However, in addition to a calculation for each dwelling unit within the structure, there are feeders and their associated demand factors that may be permitted to be applied. In addition, the services to multifamily dwelling structures are generally larger than one-family dwelling structures. Continuous-duty loads do not generally apply to one-family and multifamily dwellings, unless fixed electric space-heating equipment is installed within the unit(s) or common area(s).

Commercial and industrial load calculations have different demand factors compared to dwelling occupancies. Different types of commercial and industrial occupancies utilize different demand factors for the branch circuits, feeders, and services. In addition, differentialing between continuous and noncontinuous loads is even more important in nondwelling occupancies as continuous loads are more prevalent than in dwelling occupancies and need to be addressed differently due to the additional heat factor from continuous use. The *Code* user needs to have a thorough understanding of all requirements to safely size commercial and industrial branch circuits, feeders, and services.

OBJECTIVES

- List all of the required branch circuits for a one-family dwelling unit for load calculation purposes.
- Calculate the feeder and service demand, conductor sizes, and service equipment for a one-family dwelling unit using the standard method.
- Calculate the feeder and service demand for a multifamily dwelling unit using both the standard method and optional method.
- Size the feeder and service-entrance conductors for the individual units and the main service equipment for a multifamily dwelling unit.
- Calculate branch-circuit loads for commercial occupancies accounting for continuous and noncontinuous loads.
- Calculate feeder and service demand, conductors, and service equipment for commercial occupancies.
- Determine the minimum size neutral conductor based upon load for commercial occupancies.

TABLE OF CONTENTS

9.1 GENERAL REQUIREMENTS FOR RESIDENTIAL LOADS 198

9.2 DWELLING UNIT—STANDARD CALCULATION METHOD 198
- .1 Dwelling Unit—General Lighting and General-Use Receptacle Load 198
- .2 Dwelling Unit—Number of Branch Circuits 199
- .3 Dwelling Unit—Required Branch Circuits 199
- .4 Summary Dwelling Unit—Smith House, Standard Calculation Method 202
- .5 Dwelling Unit—Smith House, Optional Calculation Method 205

9.3 MULTIFAMILY DWELLINGS 207
- .1 Introduction to Multifamily Dwellings 207
- .2 Homestead Apartments – Using the Standard Method 210
- .3 Homestead Apartments – Optional Calculations 213

9.4 COMMERCIAL BUILDINGS 215
- .1 Variety Store with Warehouse 215
- .2 Variety Store Calculation Summary 218

9.5 OFFICE BUILDINGS 221
- .1 Method of Feeder Demand Calculation 221
- .2 Office Building Calculation Summary 225

DEFINITIONS AND TERMS 225
SUMMARY 226
REVIEW QUESTIONS 227

9.1 GENERAL REQUIREMENTS FOR RESIDENTIAL LOADS

Load calculations can be done in simple or complex form. The complex calculations convert all loads into amperes and allot specific loads to the neutral conductor. The simple calculations convert all loads to volt-amperes (VA) and consider all neutral conductor loads to be evenly divided.

To begin, use the simplified (volt-ampere) method of calculation and round off all loads to a whole number.

For certain equipment, the *Code* permits the neutral conductor to be smaller than the line conductors, and this is reflected back into the feeder demand. To avoid overlooking the neutral conductor, neutral calculations can be made following the feeder demand calculations for the ungrounded conductors as each particular item is calculated.

The *Code* recognizes two methods of calculation. One is the standard method, usually called the *long method*, and the other is the optional method, usually referred to as the *short method*.

Although most of these calculations are directed at feeder demand loads, there are opportune times when certain branch-circuit calculations can be used.

9.2 DWELLING UNIT—STANDARD CALCULATION METHOD

Dwelling unit loads are more commonly called *residential loads*. They include one-family dwellings, two-family dwellings, townhouses, individual apartments, and multifamily apartment complexes. Dwelling unit loads can be applied for an entire building or an area of a building. Focus is directed mainly at "feeder" loads, which, for the dwelling unit, are most often the service-entrance conductors. Some calculations apply to branch-circuit loads.

The *Code* lists requirements for specific loads that might be installed in a dwelling unit. The following outline of these loads can be used as a checklist for calculating residential loads:

- General lighting and general-use receptacle load
- Small appliance load
- Laundry load
- Other fastened-in-place appliance loads
- Cooking appliance load
- Clothes dryer load
- Heating load
- Air-conditioning load
- 25% of largest motor installed
- Other loads

9.2.1 Dwelling Unit—General Lighting and General-Use Receptacle Load

In *NEC* **220.11**, the minimum lighting load is based upon the square footage (ft^2) area of a building using the outside measurements of the building. For dwelling units, the calculated floor area does not include open porches, garages, and unused or unfinished spaces not adaptable for future use. The assigned minimum unit load is three volt-amperes per square foot according to *NEC* **220.14(J)**. Included in the unit load are all 20-ampere or less general-use receptacles, including bathroom, garage, outdoor, and basement receptacles. Additionally, new for the 2020 *National Electrical Code*, any motor load less than $1/8$-horsepower and connected to a lighting circuit is included in the load.

Consider a home which a family, the Smiths, is planning to build. In the planning stages, the process is called *calculating loads*. Initially, all that is known is that the house is to be a single story and will measure 55 feet wide by 65 feet long, excluding open porches and garage areas, and that the service will be 120/240-volt, 3-wire. Other items will be added as the planning progresses. **See Problem 9-1**.

PROBLEM 9-1

Calculate the general lighting and general-use receptacle load for the Smith house.

Solution

Area = length × width
= 55 × 65
= 3,575 ft²

220.14(J)
Dwelling unit = 3 VA per ft²
Load = area × VA per ft²
= 3,575 × 3
= 10,725

Answer: 10,725 VA

9.2.2 Dwelling Unit—Number of Branch Circuits

A branch-circuit calculation is appropriate, since 210.11(A) requires that the total calculated lighting load (prior to the application of demand factors) be expressed in volt-amperes and used to calculate the minimum number of lighting branch-circuits needed. This lighting circuit will cover the general lighting and general-purpose receptacles. The two or more required small-appliance branch circuits and the required laundry circuit(s) are in addition to the lighting branch circuits. **See Problem 9-2**.

PROBLEM 9-2

Calculate the number of 120-volt, 15-ampere lighting and general-use receptacle branch circuits needed for the Smith house.

Solution

210.11(A)

$$\text{Amperes} = \frac{\text{Calculated VA}}{E}$$
$$= \frac{10,725}{120}$$
$$= 89.38 \text{ A}$$

$$\text{Number of circuits} = \frac{\text{Amperes}}{\text{Circuit size}}$$
$$= \frac{89.38}{15}$$
$$= 5.9 \text{ or 6 circuits}$$

Answer: 6 circuits

9.2.3 Dwelling Unit— Required Branch Circuits

When calculating the number of branch circuits, the calculated load is used before any demand factors are applied. When the number of calculated branch circuits is a fraction of a circuit, the next higher whole number must be used. For example, a calculated quantity of 4.1 actually requires five circuits. If 20-ampere circuits had been called for, the calculated ampere load would have been divided by 20. **See Figure 9-1**.

9.2.3.1 General Lighting, General-Use Receptacle, Small-Appliance, and Laundry Circuits

NEC **220.52(A)** and **220.52(B)** permit the required small-appliance and laundry loads to be included with the lighting and general-use receptacle load before the lighting load demand factors are applied. The permitted combined lighting and receptacle loads may seem strange at first, but it serves to greatly simplify dwelling unit calculations, while providing safe and ample feeders and services.

The required minimum of two small-appliance circuits for the Smith house will be installed and calculated at 1,500 volt-amperes each, according to **220.52(A)**. The required laundry circuit will be installed and calculated at 1,500 volt-amperes, according to **220.52(B)**.

All the lighting will not be utilized at the same time; therefore, the *Code* permits the calculated lighting load to be reduced by a percentage, called a demand factor, which is given in **Table 220.42**.

The Smith House			
Required number of branch circuits			
210.11(A) General Lighting and Receptacle	15-ampere branch circuits	6
210.11(C)(1) Small Appliance	20-ampere branch circuits	2
210.11(C)(2) Laundry	20-ampere branch circuits	1
210.11(C)(3) Bathroom	20-ampere branch circuits	1
210.11(C)(4) Garage	20-ampere branch circuits	1
Total branch circuits		11

Figure 9-1. NEC Required Branch Circuits. In addition to the branch circuits required by 210.11, when planning the construction of a home, other branch circuits may be required, such as for central heating equipment, microwaves, garbage disposals, and the like.

The lighting load demand factors for a dwelling unit are as follows:

- First 3,000 VA at 100%
- 3,001 to 120,000 VA at 35%
- Over 120,000 VA at 25%

See Problem 9-3.

PROBLEM 9-3

Calculate the lighting feeder demand for the Smith house.

Solution

Calculated lighting load = 10,725 VA

Lighting load total	10,725 VA
Small appliances: 2 circuits at 1,500	3,000 VA
Laundry: 1 circuit at 1,500	1,500 VA
Total	15,225 VA

Table 220.42

First 3,000 VA at 100%	3,000 VA
3,001 to 120,000 VA at 35%	
15,225 VA − 3,000 VA = 12,225	
= 12,225 × 0.35	
= 4,279 VA	4,279 VA
Lighting Feeder Demand	7,279 VA

Answer: 7,279 VA ungrounded conductor load
7,279 VA neutral conductor load

9.2.3.2 Feeder Demand: Clothes Dryer

Section 220.54 requires the minimum amount of feeder demand for a clothes dryer to be not less than 5,000 volt-amperes; or if the nameplate rating is larger than 5,000 volt-amperes, the nameplate rating is to be used. This means that a 4kW clothes dryer is calculated at 5,000 volt-amperes. A 6kW clothes dryer is calculated at 6,000 volt-amperes.

NEC **220.61(B)(1)** permits the neutral conductor load to be 70% of the calculated load on the ungrounded conductors for electric ranges, wall-mounted ovens, counter-mounted cooking units, and electric dryers. **See Problem 9-4.**

9.2.3.3 Feeder Demand: Appliance Loads

Many appliances installed in a dwelling unit are fastened in place. These fastened-in-place appliances are calculated at their nameplate rating. However, when four or more of these appliances, rated $1/4$-horsepower or greater, or 500 watts or greater, are installed in the same dwelling unit, a 75% demand factor is permitted by **Section 220.53**.

Fastened-in-place household electric cooking equipment, clothes dryers, space-heating equipment, and air-conditioning equipment are not permitted to have the 75% demand factor applied. These loads are to be calculated individually.

The following fastened-in-place appliances count toward the total of four and are then subject to the 75% demand factor.

- Water heater
- Microwave
- Dishwasher
- Disposer
- Trash compactor
- Ventilation hood (fan/light)
- Sump pump

See Problem 9-5.

9.2.3.4 Feeder Demand: Range Load

Calculations for range load and other cooking appliances have been covered previously. The neutral conductor for range loads is permitted to be reduced by 70%, according to **220.61(B)(1)**. **See Problem 9-6.**

PROBLEM 9-4

Calculate the feeder demand for a clothes dryer with a nameplate rating of 4.5 kW at 120/240 volts which is to be installed in the Smith house.

Solution

Calculation 1
Ungrounded conductors
Section 220.54
 Minimum for 1 dryer = 5,000 VA
Answer: 5,000 VA ungrounded conductor load

Calculation 2
Neutral conductor
220.61(B)(1)
 VA demand = VA × 70%
     = 5,000 × 0.70
     = 3,500 VA
Answer: 3,500 VA neutral conductor load

PROBLEM 9-5

Calculate the feeder demand for the following appliances to be installed in the Smith house:

120-volt, 6-ampere waste disposer

1.5kW dishwasher at 120 volts

5kW, 120-volt water heater

120-volt, 4.4-ampere ventilation hood (fan/light)

960-watt, 120-volt trash compactor

Solution

Convert all loads to VA

$VA = E \times I$ or $VA = kW \times 1,000$

Disposer:
$VA = E \times I$
$= 120 \times 6$
$= 720$ VA   720 VA

Dishwasher: 1.5 kW × 1,000   1,500 VA

Water heater: 5 kW × 1,000   5,000 VA

Ventilation hood:
$VA = E \times I$
$= 120 \times 4.4$
$= 528$ VA   528 VA

Compactor: 960 W   960 VA

Total appliance demand   8,708 VA

Section 220.53
Demand = VA × 75%
$= 8,708 \times 0.75$
$= 6,531$ VA

Answer: 6,531 VA ungrounded conductor load
6,531 VA neutral conductor load

9.2.3.5 Feeder Demand: Heating and Air Conditioning

Where fixed electric space-heating equipment is installed in a dwelling unit, the loads are calculated at 100% according to **220.51**. The same holds true for air-conditioning loads, which are also calculated at 100%. **Section 220.60** permits only the largest load of the two noncoincidental loads to be used for calculating feeder demand. *Noncoincidental loads* are loads that are unlikely to be used at the same time. While electric space-heating equipment and air-conditioning loads may be noncoincidental, a forced-air furnace may operate in conjunction with central air-conditioning equipment, and these are therefore not considered noncoincidental loads. **See Problem 9-7**.

PROBLEM 9-6

Calculate the feeder demand for a 12kW range to be installed in the Smith house.

Solution

Calculation 1
Table 220.55
  Column C
  One range 12 kW or less = 8,000 VA
Answer: 8,000 VA ungrounded conductor load

Calculation 2
220.61(B)(1)
  Neutral VA = VA × 70%
              = 8,000 VA × 0.70
              = 5,600 VA
Answer: 5,600 VA neutral grounded conductor load

PROBLEM 9-7

The Smith house will have four 500-watt strip heaters and two 750-watt bathroom heaters. Each heater is separately controlled and operated at 240 volts. In addition, there is a 7 1/2-horsepower, 240-volt air-conditioning unit. Calculate the heating and air-conditioning feeder demand and determine the noncoincidental load.

Solution

Calculation 1
Heating load
  4 strip heaters × 500 watts
  $= 4 \times 500$
  $= 2,000$ VA   2,000 VA
  2 heaters × 750 watts
  $= 2 \times 750$
  $= 1,500$ VA   1,500 VA
  Total heating load   3,500 VA

Answer: 3,500 VA heating load

Calculation 2
Air-conditioning load
Table 430.248
7 1/2 hp at 240 volts full-load current = 40 A
$VA = E \times I$
   $= 240 \times 40$
   $= 9,600$ VA
Answer: 9,600 VA air-conditioning load

Calculation 3
Noncoincidental load
Section 220.60
  Use larger load
  9,600 VA is larger than 3,500 VA
  Use air-conditioning load
Answer: 9,600 VA ungrounded conductor load
No neutral grounded conductor load

Fixed electric space-heating equipment comes in many different forms, such as customer-specified fixed electric space-heating cables in tile floors for dwelling unit bathrooms and kitchens. Courtesy of Raychem QuickNet, Tyco Thermal Controls.

9.2.3.6 Feeder Demand: Largest Motor
Section 220.50, by referencing sections in **Article 430** and specifically **Section 430.24**, requires 125% of the largest motor full-load current (FLC) to be part of the feeder load calculation. Typically, all motor loads are accounted for in the calculation at 100%. Therefore, when addressing the requirements of **430.24**, the calculation should not include 125%, but rather only the remaining 25%, which is added into the final calculation and used in the summary calculation as well. **See Problem 9-8**.

PROBLEM 9-8

What is 25% of the largest motor full-load current (FLC) planned for the Smith house?

Solution

The largest motor load is the air-conditioning motor
Section 430.24
  VA = Largest load × 25%
      = 9,600 × 0.25
      = 2,400 VA
Answer: 2,400 VA ungrounded conductor load

New for the 2020 *NEC*, clarification is provided for a motor that is part of a noncoincidental load. If it is the largest motor, it is used for the 25% largest motor calculation.

9.2.4 Summary Dwelling Unit—Smith House, Standard Calculation Method

The following is a summary for the Smith house:

- Area – 65 feet by 55 feet
- Service – 120/240-volts, single-phase, 3-wire
- Clothes dryer – 4.5 kW
- Disposer – 120-volt, 6 amperes
- Dishwasher – 1.5 kW
- Water heater – 5 kW
- Ventilation hood (fan/light) – 120-volts, 4.4 amperes
- Trash compactor – 960 watts
- Range – 10 kW
- Strip heaters – 4–500 watts, 240-volts each
- Heaters – 2–750 watts, 240-volts each
- Air-conditioning motor – 7-horsepower, 240-volts
- 25% of largest motor installed

9.2.4.1 Summary: Standard Calculation Method for One Dwelling Unit
According to **Article 220, Part III, Section 220.40**, the calculated load of a feeder or service shall not be less than the sum of the branch-circuit loads determined by **Part II**, after any applicable demand factors allowed by **Part III** have been applied. **See Problem 9-9**.

This summary step is arranged to provide two solutions using the standard calculation method: the total feeder demand in volt-amperes for ungrounded or line conductors and a separate total feeder demand in volt-amperes for the grounded conductor. Additional summary calculation examples are available for review using **Informative Annex D** of the *NEC*.

9.2.4.2 Service-Entrance Conductors: Ampacity
Now that everything is calculated in volt-amperes, the ampacity of the line and neutral conductors for the service-entrance conductors can be calculated for

CHAPTER 9 LOAD CALCULATIONS

PROBLEM 9-9

Summarize the total feeder demand for the Smith house using the standard calculations.

Solution

Area = length × width
 = 65 × 55
 = 3,575 ft^2

	Feeder Demand	VA Ungrounded Conductors	VA Neutral Conductor
Lighting			
Calculated lighting load = area × 3 VA per ft^2			
= 3,575 × 3			
= 10,725 VA	10,725 VA		
Small appliances: 2 circuits at 1,500	3,000 VA		
Laundry: 1 circuit at 1,500	1,500 VA		
Calculated total	15,225 VA		
First 3,000 at 100%	3,000 VA		
3,001 to 120,000 at 35%			
15,225 − 3,000 = 12,225			
= 12,225 × 0.35			
= 4,279	4,279 VA		
Lighting demand	7,279 VA	7,279	7,279
Clothes dryer:			
Minimum for 1 dryer = 5,000 VA		5,000	0
Neutral = 5,000 × 70%			
= 5,000 × 0.70			
= 3,500		0	3,500
Appliances			
Disposer: 120 V × 6 A	720 VA		
Dishwasher: 1.5 kW × 1,000	1,500 VA		
Water heater: 5 kW × 1,000	5,000 VA		
Ventilation hood: 120 V × 4.4 A	528 VA		
Compactor: 960 W	960 VA		
Total appliance demand	8,708 VA		
4 or more = 75%			
= 8,708 × 0.75			
= 6,531 VA		6,531	6,531
Range			
One range: 12 kW or less = 8,000 VA		8,000	0
Neutral = VA × 70%			
= 8,000 × 0.70			
= 5,600 VA		0	5,600
Heating			
4 strip heaters × 500 W			
= 2,000 VA	2,000 VA		
2 heaters × 750 W			
= 1,500 VA	1,500 VA		
Total heating load	3,500 VA	0	0
Air conditioning			
7 1/2 hp at 240 V FLC = 40 A			
VA = E × I			
= 240 × 40			
= 9,600 VA		9,600	0
Air-conditioning load is larger than heat load			
Air-conditioning motor is largest motor			
= 9,600 VA × 25%			
= 9,600 × 0.25		2,400	0
Total Demand		**38,810**	**22,910**

Answer: 38,810 VA ungrounded conductor load
 22,910 VA neutral grounded conductor load

the Smith house using Ohm's Law and the wire size selected. *NEC* **220.5(A)** specifies that the voltage to be used in this calculation is the nominal voltage of the system, which is 240 volts. **See Problem 9-10**.

PROBLEM 9-10

Calculate the ampacity of the service-entrance conductors for the Smith house.

Solution

Calculation 1
Ungrounded conductors
210.11(A)

$$I = \frac{VA}{E}$$
$$= \frac{38,810}{240}$$
$$= 161.71 \text{ A}$$

Answer: 161.71A ungrounded conductor

Calculation 2
Neutral conductor

$$I = \frac{VA}{E}$$
$$= \frac{22,910}{240}$$
$$= 95.46 \text{ A}$$

Answer: 95.46A neutral conductor

PROBLEM 9-11

What size THWN copper conductors are needed for the 120/240-volt, 3-wire service to the Smith house?

Solution

Calculation 1
Determine the ungrounded service conductor size, THWN, copper
Ungrounded conductor load = 161.71 A
Determine Service Rating: use next larger standard size, per 240.6(A)
  Next larger standard size Service Rating = 175 A
With no adjustment or correction factors, use Table 310.12
  For 175 A, use 1/0 copper THWN-2 copper conductor
Answer: 1/0 copper THWN-2 copper conductor

Calculation 2
Determine neutral service conductor size, THWN, copper
Ungrounded conductor load = 95.46 A
Using Table 310.16, for THWN, copper
  95.46 A requires a 3 AWG
Answer: 3 THWN copper neutral conductor
Comment: The 175-ampere service could use a 200-ampere switch with 175-ampere fuses or a 175-ampere circuit breaker. The standard sizes for fuses and circuit breakers are listed in 240.6(A).

9.2.4.3 Service-Entrance Conductors: Wire Size

The next step is to select the size of the dwelling unit service-entrance conductors. **Section 310.12** permits service conductors that supply the entire load for 120/240-volt single-phase dwelling services to have an ampacity not less than 83% of the service rating; if no adjustment or correction factors are required, **Table 310.12** is permitted. Service ratings are the same as standard size overcurrent protective devices from 100 through 400 amperes as found in **240.6(A)**. **Annex D** provides **Example D7** to assist the user with direct application of this percentage or the usage of the table.

The 120/240-volt, 3-wire service permits the usage of **Table 310.12** since there are no adjustment or correction factors and the service is not over 400 amperes. (Generally, not many one-family dwelling services are over 400 amperes.)

1. Unless the calculated amperage matches a service size, select the next larger standard size service rating from the calculated feeder load amperes and size the conductors from **Table 310.12**.
2. The service (or feeder) conductor supplying the entire load associated with the dwelling is permitted to have an ampacity of not less than 83% of the standard ampere rating between 100 and 400 amperes as found in the standard ampere rating of **240.6(A)** if adjustment and correction factors are required to be applied.
3. For the neutral conductor, use the amperes found using Ohm's Law and **Table 310.16** for conductor size.

See Problem 9-11.

Grounding rod electrodes are commonly installed at dwelling units. **Article 250, Part III** *provides requirements for the grounding electrode system and grounding electrode conductor size.*

9.2.4.5 Grounding Electrode Conductor: Wire Size

The size of the grounding electrode conductor is determined by its relationship to the size of the ungrounded conductor used for the service. **Section 250.66** is used to size the grounding electrode conductor. **See Problem 9-12**.

PROBLEM 9-12

What minimum size is needed for a copper grounding electrode conductor to a metal underground water pipe grounding electrode for the Smith house?

Solution

Largest ungrounded service-entrance conductor = 1/0 AWG
Table 250.66
1/0 AWG copper = 6 AWG copper
Answer: 6 AWG
Comment: For most residential services, the neutral conductor is not permitted to be smaller than as specified in Table 250.66. The minimum size grounded conductor for services is described in detail in 250.24(C)(1).

9.2.5 Dwelling Unit—Smith House, Optional Calculation Method

The optional feeder and service load calculations are found in **Article 220, Part IV**. The section only applies to a dwelling unit having a total connected load with an ampacity of 100 amperes or greater.

9.2.5.1 Summary: Optional Method for One Dwelling Unit

Using **Section 220.82**, the optional method of calculating feeder demand for a dwelling unit can be summed up in three statements:

1. Convert all loads to volt-amperes.
2. Calculate the first 10,000 volt-amperes at 100% and the balance at 40%.
3. Select the correct method of calculating the heating and air-conditioning feeder demand from **220.82(C)**.

See Problem 9-13.

PROBLEM 9-13

Calculate the feeder demand for the Smith house using the optional method.

Solution

Area = length × width
= 65 × 55
= 3,575 ft^2

Lighting
Calculated lighting load = area × 3 VA per ft^2
= 3,575 × 3
= 10,725 VA   10,725 VA
Small appliances: 2 circuits at 1,500   3,000 VA
Laundry: 1 circuit at 1,500   1,500 VA
Appliances
Clothes dryer: 4.5 kW × 1,000   4,500 VA
Disposer: 120 V × 6 A   720 VA
Dishwasher: 1.5 kW × 1,000   1,500 VA
Water heater: 5 kW × 1,000   5,000 VA
Ventilation hood: 120 V × 4.4 A   528 VA
Compactor: 960 watts   960 VA
Household cooking
Range: 12 kW (at nameplate)   10,000 VA
Total of nameplate ratings   38,433 VA

First 10,000 at 100%   10,000 VA
Balance at 40%
38,433 − 10,000 = 28,433
28,433 × 0.40
= 11,373   11,373 VA
Heating
220.82(C)(5)
40% demand factor
4 strip heaters × 500 watts
= 2,000 VA   2,000 VA
2 heaters × 750 watts
= 1,500 VA   1,500 VA
Subtotal   3,500 VA
6 units at 40%
3,500 VA × 0.40 = 1,400 VA
Heating load not used
Air conditioning
220.82(C)(1)
7 1/2 hp at 240 volts FLC = 40 A
VA = E × I
= 240 × 40
= 9,600 VA
Air-conditioning load is the largest load   9,600 VA
Total feeder demand optional method   30,973 VA

Answer: 30,973 VA total feeder demand

9.2.5.2 Using the Optional Method for Service-Entrance Conductor Ampacity, Line Size, Neutral Size, and Grounding Electrode Conductor Size

As long as a service fits the requirements of **310.12**, either **Table 310.12** or a factor of 0.83 (83%) is permitted to be used to reduce the size of the ungrounded service conductor for the optional method for determining the size of ungrounded service entrance conductors. The neutral is allowed to be sized in accordance with **220.61**. If the service does not fall within the parameters of **310.12**, the line conductors are required to be sized directly from **Table 310.16** without further reduction. However, **220.82(A)** still permits the neutral conductor to be calculated according to **220.61**, which is the same method by which the neutral was calculated using the previous standard calculation method. **See Problem 9-14**.

PROBLEM 9-14

Calculate the following for the Smith house using the optional calculation method:

1. Ampacity of service-entrance conductors
2. Minimum size service
3. Minimum size THWN copper service-entrance conductors
4. Minimum size neutral for service
5. Minimum size copper grounding electrode conductor using a metal water pipe grounding electrode

Solution

Calculation 1
Ampacity of service-entrance conductors
From **Problem 9-13**
Feeder Demand = 30,973 VA

$$I = \frac{VA}{E}$$
$$= \frac{30,973}{240}$$
$$= 129 \text{ A}$$

Answer: 129 A

Calculation 2
Determine minimum service size
Min. calculated service size = 129 A
240.6(A), next larger standard size OCPD
Minimum service size = 150 A

Calculation 3
Determine minimum conductor size
310.12 with no adjustment or correction factors permits Table 310.12
From Table 310.12 for 150 A = 1 AWG
Answer: 1 AWG THWN copper

Calculation 4
Neutral for service
220.61(A)
  Maximum unbalance

Lighting load
3,575 ft² × 3 VA per ft²		10,725 VA
Small appliances: 2 circuits at 1,500		3,000 VA
Laundry: 1 circuit at 1,500		1,500 VA
Subtotal		15,225 VA
3,000 VA at 100%		3,000 VA
Balance at 35%		
15,225 VA – 3,000 VA = 12,225		
12,225 × 0.35		
= 4,279 VA		4,279 VA

Appliances
Household range at 12 kW (8 kW at 70%)		5,600 VA
Clothes dryer at 4.5 kW (5 kVA at 70%)		3,500 VA
Disposer: 120 V × 6 A		720 VA
Dishwasher: 1.5 kW × 1,000		1,500 VA
Ventilation hood: 120 V × 4.4 A		528 VA
Compactor: 960 watts		960 VA
Total		20,087 VA

$$I = \frac{VA}{E}$$
$$= \frac{20,087}{240}$$
$$= 83.7 \text{ A}$$

Table 310.16
83.7 A = 4 AWG THWN copper
Answer: 4 AWG THWN neutral

Calculation 5
Grounding electrode conductor
Table 250.66
1 AWG copper = 6 AWG copper
Answer: 6 AWG copper

9.3 MULTIFAMILY DWELLINGS

Multifamily dwellings are permitted to be calculated according to the standard method of **Part III** or the optional method of **Part IV** within **Article 220**.

The standard methods will be used in **9.3.1 Introduction to Multifamily Dwellings** and in **9.3.2 Homestead Apartments**. Later in **9.3.3**, the optional calculations according to **Part IV** of **Article 220** are used.

9.3.1 Introduction to Multifamily Dwellings

The same standard calculation method used to calculate a one-family dwelling is used to calculate the feeder to each individual apartment of a multifamily dwelling. *NEC* **310.12(A)** through **(D)** applies to a 120/240-volt, 3-wire feeder installed to each apartment. If the feeder is a 3-wire feeder from a 208Y/120-volt, 3-phase, 4-wire system, **310.12(A)** through **(C)** is applicable.

The sequence of calculations for a multifamily dwelling are very similar to the calculations for a one-family dwelling. However, a few additional demand factors apply to a multifamily dwelling. The outline of these loads can be used as a checklist for calculating specific loads:

- Lighting load
- Small appliance loads
- Laundry load
- Other fastened-in-place appliance loads
- Cooking appliance load
- Clothes dryer load
- Heating load
- Air-conditioning load
- Other loads common to premises
- 25% of largest motor installed

Consider the planning of a multifamily dwelling, the Homestead Apartments. The basic plan calls for eighteen 1,400-square-foot units, each with a 120/240-volt, single-phase, 3-wire service. There is outdoor security lighting connected to the building panel (not supplied by any apartment unit), and there are no plans for general laundry facilities on the premises.

9.3.1.1 Lighting Load

The Homestead Apartments consists of 18 separate apartments. The apartment lighting load is based on the area of each apartment, which is 1,400 square feet. As a reminder, **220.14(J)** indicates that the general-use receptacles in one-family, two-family, and multifamily dwellings are included in the general lighting load calculation. In addition to lighting within each apartment, there is also outdoor security lighting connected to the structure load that is not associated with any apartment load. The security lighting load is a separate calculation. **See Problem 9-15**.

PROBLEM 9-15

Calculate the lighting load for the Homestead Apartments.

Solution

Area = ft^2 of each unit × number of units
= 1,400 × 18
= 25,200 ft^2

Table 220.12
Dwelling unit = 3 VA per ft^2
Lighting load = area × VA per ft^2
= 25,200 × 3
= 75,600 VA

Answer: 75,600 VA calculated lighting load

9.3.1.2 Feeder Demand: Lighting, Small-Appliance, and Laundry Circuits

Two small-appliance branch circuits are required for each unit. Since there are no general laundry facilities on the premises, the laundry branch-circuit load is required to be calculated for each unit according to **210.11(C)(2)**. Both of these loads are permitted to be added to the calculated lighting load for the complex, and the demand factors of **Table 220.42** are then applied. **See Problem 9-16**.

PROBLEM 9-16

Calculate the feeder demand for the lighting, small appliance, and laundry loads for the Homestead Apartments.

Solution

Calculated lighting load	75,600 VA
Small appliances load	
= 2 circuits × 18 units × 1,500 VA	
= 54,000 VA	54,000 VA
Laundry circuit load	
= 1 circuit × 18 units × 1,500	
= 27,000 VA	27,000 VA
Subtotal	156,600 VA
Table 220.42	
Apply demand factors	
First 3,000 VA at 100%	3,000 VA
3,001 to 120,000 VA at 35%	
120,000 − 3,001 = 117,000	
117,000 × 0.35	
= 40,950 VA	40,950 VA
Remaining at 25%	
156,600 − 3,000 − 117,000 = 36,600	
36,600 × 0.25	
= 9,150 VA	9,150 VA
Feeder demand for lighting	53,100 VA

Answer: 53,100 VA ungrounded and neutral conductor load

According to *LED Lighting Explained*, published by Philips Color Kinetics, LED light sources deliver high-quality white, colored, or color-changing light while consuming far less energy than conventional incandescent sources.

9.3.1.3 Feeder Demand: Appliance Loads

The fastened-in-place appliances installed in each apartment are additive for the multifamily complex and easily meet the four required appliances for the 75% reduction of **Section 220.53**. **See Problem 9-17**.

PROBLEM 9-17

Each unit of the Homestead Apartments will have one 2kW, 120-volt dishwasher, one 3kW, 120-volt water heater, and a 6.2-ampere, 120-volt waste disposer. Calculate the fastened-in-place appliance load for the Homestead Apartments.

Solution

VA = kW × 1,000

Dishwasher	
2 kW × 1,000 = 2,000 VA	
2,000 VA × 18 units = 36,000 VA	36,000 VA
Water heater	
3 kW × 1,000 = 3,000 VA	
3,000 VA × 18 units = 54,000 VA	54,000 VA
Disposer	
6.2 A × 120 V = 744 VA	
744 VA × 18 units = 13,392 VA	13,392 VA
Total	103,392 VA

Section 220.53
Over 4 appliances = 75% reduction
103,392 × 0.75 = 77,544 VA

Answer: 77,544 VA ungrounded and neutral conductor load

9.3.1.4 Feeder Demand: Dryer Loads

If a number of household dryers are installed, **Table 220.54** permits a demand factor according to the number of household dryers installed. **See Problem 9-18**.

In a multifamily complex, a number of appliances and dryers are often used.

PROBLEM 9-18

Plans are to install one 5kW, 120/240-volt dryer in each unit of the Homestead Apartments. Calculate the feeder demand for the dryer load.

Solution

Calculation 1
Line load
$$VA = \text{Dryer kW} \times 1{,}000$$
$$= 5 \times 1{,}000$$
$$= 5{,}000 \text{ VA}$$
Total number of dryers = 18
Table 220.54
12-23 dryers = 47% − 1% for each dryer exceeding 11
18 − 11 = 7
Demand factor = 47% − 7%
$$= 40\%$$
Load = number of dryers × VA × 40%
$$= 18 \times 5{,}000 \times 0.40$$
$$= 36{,}000 \text{ VA}$$
Answer: 36,000 VA ungrounded conductor load

Calculation 2
Neutral conductor load
220.61(B)
Neutral VA = VA × 70%
$$= 36{,}000 \times 0.70$$
$$= 25{,}200 \text{ VA}$$
Answer: 25,200 VA neutral conductor load

PROBLEM 9-19

Plans are to install one 9kW, 120/240-volt household electric range in each unit of the Homestead Apartments. Calculate the feeder demand for the ranges.

Solution

Calculation 1
Ungrounded conductor load
Table 220.55
  Column C
  18 ranges = 33 kW or 33,000 VA
Answer: 33,000 VA ungrounded conductor load

Calculation 2
Neutral conductor load
220.61(B)(1)
  Neutral VA = VA × 70%
$$= 33{,}000 \times 0.70$$
$$= 23{,}100 \text{ VA}$$
Answer: 23,100 VA neutral conductor load

9.3.1.5 Feeder Demand: Range Loads
Calculations for range load and other cooking appliances have been covered previously. The neutral conductor for range loads is permitted to be reduced by 70%, according to **220.61(B)(1)**. **See Problem 9-19**.

9.3.1.6 Feeder Demand: Heating and Air-Conditioning Loads
If air-conditioning loads are installed in a dwelling unit, the loads are calculated at 100%. **See Problem 9-20**.

PROBLEM 9-20

Plans call for one 3-horsepower, 240-volt, single-phase air conditioner in each unit of the Homestead Apartments. Calculate the feeder demand for the air-conditioning load.

Solution

Table 430.248
3 hp = 17 A
  $VA = E \times I \times$ number of units
$$= 240 \times 17 \times 18$$
$$= 73{,}440 \text{ VA}$$
Answer: 73,440 VA

9.3.1.7 Feeder Demand: 25% of Largest Motor
The calculation of the largest motor at 25% is also required for a multifamily dwelling. In this case, it is one of the 18 three-horsepower air conditioner motors. **See Problem 9-21**.

PROBLEM 9-21

What is 25% of the largest motor?

Solution

Largest motor
  Air conditioner motor
  240 V and 17 A
  $VA = E \times I$
$$= 240 \times 17$$
$$= 4{,}080 \text{ VA}$$
VA demand = 4,080 × 0.25
$$= 1{,}020 \text{ VA}$$
Answer: 1,020 VA ungrounded conductor load

9.3.1.8 Feeder Demand: Other Loads

Other loads that might be added are calculated at nameplate rating. **See Problem 9-22**.

PROBLEM 9-22

Plans are to have six 150-watt, 120-volt LED outdoor luminaires installed on the premises of the Homestead Apartments for security lighting. Calculate the feeder demand for the security lighting.

Solution

Load = 6 × 150 watts
= 900 VA

Answer: 900 VA ungrounded and neutral conductor load

*Other loads may include a self-contained hot tub or a hydro-massage bathtub as covered by **Article 680**.*

9.3.2 Homestead Apartments – Using the Standard Method

The following is a summary of the Homestead Apartments:

For the complex:

- Security lighting – six 150-watt LED outdoor luminaires
- Service to complex – 120/240-volt, single-phase, 3-wire
- Size – 18 units, each unit = 1,400 ft²

Within each unit:

- Dishwasher – 2 kW, 120 volts
- Water heater – 3 kW, 120 volts
- Disposer – 6.2 amperes, 120 volts
- Dryer – 5 kW, 120/240 volts
- Range – 9 kW, 120/240 volts
- Air Conditioner – 3 horsepower, 240 volts

9.3.2.1 Feeder Demand: Summary Using the Standard Calculation Method

According to **Article 220, Part II, Section 220.40**, the calculated load of a feeder or service shall not be less than the sum of the branch-circuit loads determined by **Part II**, after any applicable demand factors allowed by **Part III** have been applied. **See Problem 9-23**.

This summary step is arranged to provide two solutions using the standard calculation method: the total feeder demand in volt-amperes for ungrounded or line conductors, and a separate total feeder demand in volt-amperes for the grounded conductor. Additional summary calculations are available for review using **Informative Annex D** of the *NEC*.

Once the total feeder demands are calculated, several other items can be calculated. They include the ungrounded and grounded conductor ampacity, the corresponding conductor sizes, and the conduit size(s).

9.3.2.2 Service-Entrance Conductors: Ampacity

The ampacity calculation is performed by dividing the volt-amperes by the voltage. However, **220.61(B)(2)** permits an additional derating factor of 70% for the neutral conductor if the calculated neutral conductor current is over 200 amperes. If the supply is 120/240-volt, single-phase, there is no prohibited reduction for the neutral conductor according to **220.61(C)** as it only applies to 3-phase, 4-wire, wye systems. For multifamily

CHAPTER 9 LOAD CALCULATIONS

PROBLEM 9-23

Calculate the feeder load for the Homestead Apartments using the standard method.

Solution

Area = ft² × number of units
= 1,400 × 18
= 25,200 ft²
Lighting load = area × VA per ft²
= 25,200 × 3
= 75,600 VA

Feeder Demand		VA Ungrounded Conductors	VA Neutral Conductor
Lighting Demand			
Section 220.42			
Apply demand factor			
Calculated lighting load	75,600 VA		
2 small appliance branch circuits			
= 2 circuits × 18 units × 1,500			
= 54,000 VA	54,000 VA		
1 laundry branch circuit			
= 1 circuit × 18 units × 1,500			
= 27,000 VA	27,000 VA		
Subtotal	156,600 VA		
First 3,000 at 100%	3,000 VA		
Next 117,000 at 35%			
= 117,000 × 0.35			
= 40,950 VA	40,950 VA		
Remainder of 36,600 at 25%			
= 36,600 × 0.25			
= 9,150 VA	9,150 VA		
Lighting feeder demand	53,100 VA	53,100	53,100
Appliance loads			
Dishwasher: 2 kW × 18	36,000 VA		
Water heater: 3 kW × 18	54,000 VA		
Disposer: 6.2 A × 120 V × 18	13,392 VA		
Subtotal	103,392 VA		
Over 4 appliances at 75%			
= 103,392 × 0.75			
= 77,544 VA		77,544	77,544
Dryer Feeder Demand			
Table 220.54			
18 dryers = demand factor 40%			
= 18 × 5 kW × 0.40			
= 36,000 VA		36,000	0
Neutral = 36,000 × 70%			
= 25,200 VA		0	25,200
Household Cooking Feeder Demand			
Table 220.55			
18 ranges = 33 kW × 1,000		33,000	0
Neutral = 33,000 × 70%			
= 23,100 VA		0	23,100
Air-Conditioning Demand			
3 hp, 240 volt FLC = 17 A			
VA = 240 × 17 = 4,080 VA			
4,080 VA × 18 motors		73,440	0
25% of largest motor			
4,080 VA × 0.25			
= 1,020 VA		1,020	0
Other Loads			
Security lighting 6 × 150 W		900	900
Total Demand		275,004	179,844

Answer: 275,004 VA ungrounded conductor load
181,944 VA neutral grounded conductor load

dwellings supplied by 208Y/120-volt, 3-phase, 4-wire systems, the feeder neutrals for each individual unit are prohibited to be reduced in size; however, the service neutral would be permitted to have the additional 70% demand factor applied. If nonlinear loads are present, such as lighting loads other than incandescent, it is not permitted to apply the 70% demand factor to the nonlinear loads for the service neutral. **See Problem 9-24.**

PROBLEM 9-24

Calculate the minimum ampacity of the service-entrance conductors for the Homestead Apartments. The service equipment terminals are rated for 75°C aluminum conductors.

Solution

Calculation 1
Ungrounded service-entrance conductors
210.11(A)

$$I = \frac{VA}{E}$$
$$= \frac{275{,}004}{240}$$
$$= 1{,}145.85 \text{ A}$$

Answer: 1,146A ungrounded service-entrance conductors

Calculation 2
Neutral conductor

$$I = \frac{VA}{E}$$
$$= \frac{179{,}844}{240}$$
$$= 749.35 \text{ A}$$

220.61(B)(2)
Permitted reduction of neutral load

Total calculated neutral load	749 A
First 200 A at 100%	200 A
Remaining 549 A at 70%	
$= 549 \times 0.70$	384 A
Total neutral load = 200 + 384	584 A

Answer: 584A neutral service-entrance conductor
Comment: Since the service is 120/240-volt, single-phase, the nonlinear load of the LED security lighting is permitted to have the demand applied to the neutral load as it does not fit the requirements of 220.61(C)(2). Additionally, 220.5(B) permits calculations to be rounded to whole amperes.

9.3.2.3 Service-Entrance Conductors: Wire Size

The next step is to select the proper conductor size using parallel aluminum service-entrance conductors. The calculated load is divided by the number of conductors (per phase) connected in parallel. *NEC* **310.10(G)** restricts the minimum size parallel conductor permitted to 1/0 AWG (with few exceptions). **See Problem 9-25.**

PROBLEM 9-25

What size THHN aluminum conductors are needed when three conductors per phase are paralleled and installed in three runs of rigid metal conduit? The service equipment terminals are rated for 75°C aluminum conductors.

Solution

Calculation 1
Ungrounded service-entrance conductors
210.11(A)

$$\text{Single conductor amperes} = \frac{\text{Total amperes}}{3}$$
$$= \frac{1{,}146}{3}$$
$$= 382 \text{ A}$$

Table 310.16
75°C THHN aluminum column
385 A = 750 kcmil
Answer: Three 750 kcmil THHN aluminum conductors per phase

Calculation 2
Neutral service-entrance conductors
210.11(A)

$$\text{Single conductor amperes} = \frac{\text{Total amperes}}{3}$$
$$= \frac{584}{3}$$
$$= 195 \text{ A}$$

Table 310.16
75°C THHN aluminum column
205 A = 250 kcmil
Answer: Three 250 kcmil THHN aluminum conductors per phase
Comment: The line and neutral conductors are all over 1/0 AWG and are permitted to be paralleled by 310.10(G)(1). When the neutral calculations result in a conductor smaller than 1/0 AWG, the minimum 1/0 AWG size takes precedence.

CHAPTER 9 LOAD CALCULATIONS

Electrical continuity of service equipment and raceways is required to be ensured by proper bonding, such as with the use of a supply-side bonding jumper.

9.3.2.4 Service-Entrance Conductors: Conduit Size

Chapter 9, Tables 1, 4, 5, and **5A** are used to determine conduit size if a raceway contains mixed size aluminum conductors. **Table 5** or **5A** is used to calculate the total area of wire present in the conduit. Then, using the rigid metal conduit (RMC) portion of **Table 4**, the total calculated area (in²) of wire fill is applied to the 40% column such that the total fill does not exceed the total area of the selected conduit. **See Problem 9-26**.

PROBLEM 9-26

What is the minimum size rigid metal conduit (RMC) needed where compact aluminum conductors are installed in three parallel conduit sets?

Solution

Chapter 9 Table 5A
750 kcmil THHN aluminum = 0.9076 in.²
0.9076 in.² × 2 = 1.8152 in.²   1.8152 in.²
250 kcmil THHN aluminum = 0.3525 in.²
0.3525 in.² × 1 = 0.3525 in.²   0.3525 in.²
Total area of 3 conductors   2.1677 in.²

Chapter 9, Table 4; Article 344 (RMC)
Over two wires, 40% fill column
2.1677 in.² = 3 in. RMC
Answer: 3 in. RMC

9.3.3 Homestead Apartments – Optional Calculations

Optional calculations for multifamily dwellings are permitted to be used according to **Article 220, Part IV, Section 220.84**, instead of **Part III**. This section and associated table permit the use of additional demand factors based upon the number of dwelling units per service or feeder. Before using this option, verify that all of the qualifications are available.

9.3.3.1 Summary: Optional Calculation Method for Multifamily Dwellings

Specific qualifications are required to be met before a multifamily dwelling unit with three or more units is permitted to use the optional calculation:

1. Each dwelling unit must be supplied with one feeder.
2. Each dwelling unit must be equipped with electric cooking.
3. Each unit must have air conditioning, electric heat, or both.

The optional method of calculating the feeder demand for a multifamily dwelling unit is based upon **Section 220.84** and **Table 220.84**. All loads common to each unit are calculated at nameplate rating. The demand factor of **Table 220.84** is applied using the following steps:

1. Calculate the general lighting load and general-use receptacles at three volt-amperes per square foot.
2. Calculate the small appliance load at 1,500 volt-amperes per circuit.
3. Calculate the laundry circuit at 1,500 volt-amperes.
4. Use the nameplate rating of the following:

    a. All appliances fastened in place, permanently connected, or located to be on a specific circuit
    b. Ranges, wall-mounted ovens, and counter-mounted cooking units
    c. Clothes dryers not connected to the laundry circuit in item 3

5. Calculate the nameplate amperes or volt-ampere rating of permanently-connected motors not included in item 4.
6. Use the larger of the heating or air-conditioning load or fixed electric heating load.
7. Total the loads and apply the demand factor for the number of units as given in **Table 220.84**.

For additional information, visit qr.njatcdb.org Item #1038

8. Total the house loads according to **220.84(B)**. The term *house load* refers to all public electrical loads within a multifamily dwelling which are not directly associated with a particular dwelling unit within the property.

See Problem 9-27.

PROBLEM 9-27

Calculate the feeder demand for the Homestead Apartments using the optional method.

Solution

One Dwelling Unit

Lighting: 1,400 ft² × 3 VA per ft²	4,200 VA
Small appliances: 2 circuits at 1,500	3,000 VA
Laundry: 1 circuit at 1,500	1,500 VA
Dishwasher: 2 kW × 1,000	2,000 VA
Water heater: 3 kW × 1,000	3,000 VA
Disposer: 6.2 A × 120 V	744 VA
Dryer: 5 kW × 1,000	5,000 VA
Range: 9 kW × 1,000	9,000 VA

Heating and air conditioning
3 hp, 240 volts FLC = 71 A
VA = E × I × number of units
= 240 × 17 × 1
= 4,080 VA   4,080 VA

Subtotal   32,524 VA

Total = 18 units × 32,524 VA
= 585,432 VA

Table 220.84
18 units at 38%
= 585,432 × 0.38
= 222,464 VA   222,464 VA
Security lighting (house load)   900 VA
Total   223,364 VA

Answer: 223,364 VA demand using the optional method

9.3.3.2 Service-Entrance Conductors: Size and Ampacity

NEC **220.84(A)(3)** indicates the use of **220.61(B)** for calculating neutral conductors, which permits the application of a 70% demand factor on the neutral load. It also indicates that the optional method is used for ungrounded feeder and service-entrance conductors, while the standard method is used for neutral feeder and service-entrance conductors. See Problem 9-28.

PROBLEM 9-28

Calculate the ampacity of the feeder conductors for the Homestead Apartments when the optional method is used.

Solution

Calculation 1
Ungrounded service-entrance conductor (or feeder) ampacity

$$I = \frac{VA}{E}$$
$$= \frac{223{,}364}{240}$$
$$= 930.68 \text{ A}$$

Answer: 931 A ungrounded service-entrance conductors

Calculation 2
Grounded (neutral) service-entrance (or feeder conductor)
Same as standard method calculation

$$I = \frac{VA}{E}$$
$$= \frac{179{,}844}{240}$$
$$= 749.35 \text{ A}$$

220.61(B)(2)

Permitted reduction of neutral load
Total calculated neutral load = 749 A
First 200 A at 100%   200 A
Remaining 549 A at 70%
= 549 × 0.70   384 A
Total neutral load   584 A

Answer: 584 A neutral service-entrance conductor

Large quantities of service entrance (SE) cables are often visible in ceiling corridors outside the main electrical room of a large multifamily dwelling.

9.4 COMMERCIAL BUILDINGS

The calculations for commercial buildings are more restrictive as there are fewer demand factors that are applicable and there is not an optional calculation method except for schools and new restaurants. However, the basic system is very much like the residential calculations in that everything is converted to volt-amperes and all loads are considered to be balanced.

It is important to understand that commercial buildings often have continuous loads. *Continuous loads* are loads that continue for three hours or more. Continuous loads are required to be accounted for during load calculations specifically for the overcurrent protective devices and conductors.

9.4.1 Variety Store with Warehouse

The first commercial building to plan is a variety store. The store area has a 60-foot frontage and is 150 feet deep, with an additional 5,000 square feet of storage warehouse area in the basement. The service will be 208Y/120 volts, 3-phase, 4-wire. Plans call for the general lighting to be 120-volt LED throughout.

9.4.1.1 Feeder Demand: General Lighting
Table 220.12 lists the lighting volt-amperes per square foot for different types of locations by occupancy. More than one of these locations can be located in the same building. If they are, each area is calculated separately with the volt-amperes per square foot listed in **Table 220.12**. See Problem 9-29.

PROBLEM 9-29

Calculate the lighting load for the variety store. All of the lighting in the store, retail area, and storage area is considered to be continuous as it will be on for three hours or more.

Solution

Calculation 1
General store area (continuous load)
  Area = length × width
       = 150 × 60
       = 9,000 ft²
Table 220.12
  Retail lighting = 1.9 VA per ft²
  Lighting load = area × VA
                = 9,000 × 1.9
                = 17,100 VA
Answer: 17,100 VA of continuous load

Calculation 2
Storage area (continuous load) = 5,000 ft²
Table 220.12
  Warehouse (storage) lighting = 1.2 VA per ft²
  Lighting load = area × VA
                = 5,000 × 1.2
                = 6,000 VA
Answer: 6,000 VA of continuous load

Calculation 3
Neutral conductor load
Add retail and storage area together
  17,100 + 6,000 = 23,100 VA
Answer: 23,100 VA of continuous neutral load
Comment: A new Note in Table 220.12 of the 2020 *NEC* specifies that the values in Table 220.12 already include a 125% multiplier for continuous loads, requiring no further addition for such loads when calculating using the table.

9.4.1.2 Feeder Demand: Receptacle Loads
The number of general-purpose duplex receptacles in a store is not regulated. The receptacles are not factored in with the lighting load as they are for a dwelling unit. Each general-purpose duplex receptacle is required to be calculated at 180 volt-amperes, according to **220.14(I)**. If receptacles are installed in non-dwelling locations and calculated

A multifamily dwelling unit might utilize stackable apartment meter sockets and feeder disconnect circuit breakers, all supplied from one service disconnect.

at 180 volt-amperes per receptacle, the demand factor of **Table 220.44** is used. The demand factor is applied as follows:

1. The first 10,000 volt-amperes are calculated at 100%
2. The balance is calculated at 50%

See Problem 9-30.

PROBLEM 9-30

The variety store plans call for 36 receptacles to be installed. Calculate the receptacle load for the variety store.

Solution

Calculation 1
220.14(I)
VA load = number of receptacles × 180 VA
= 36 × 180
= 6,480 VA
Answer: 6,480 VA noncontinuous load

Calculation 2
Table 220.44
Receptacle load is less than 10,000 VA = 100% load
Answer: 6,480 VA neutral conductor load

9.4.1.3 Feeder Demand: Sign Circuit
Almost every store needs an electric sign. The *Code* anticipates this need, and **600.5(A)** requires a 20-ampere branch circuit to be installed inside or outside at the front of the store for signs. *NEC* **220.14(F)** requires the circuit to be calculated at 1,200 volt-amperes. This is in addition to other receptacle loads. **See Problem 9-31**.

Many commercial buildings include a neon tubing type sign.

PROBLEM 9-31

Calculate the feeder demand for the required 120-volt, 20-ampere sign circuit. The sign circuit is considered to be a continuous load according to 600.5(C).

Solution

600.5(A)
One 20A receptacle at 1,200 VA
Answer: 1,200 VA continuous and neutral conductor load

9.4.1.4 Feeder Demand:
Show Window Lighting
Stores often display their merchandise in well-lit show windows. *NEC* **220.43(A)** requires a special calculation of 200 volt-amperes per linear foot of show window. **See Problem 9-32**.

PROBLEM 9-32

Plans call for 120-volt lighting in two 20-foot show windows for the variety store. Calculate the load for the show window lighting. The show window lighting is considered to be a continuous load.

Solution

VA load = number of show windows × length × 200 VA
= 2 × 20 × 200
= 8,000 VA
Answer: 8,000 VA continuous and neutral conductor load

9.4.1.5 Feeder Demand:
Multioutlet Assembly
Multioutlet assemblies are very handy for use with 120-volt electrical appliances, lamps, etc., especially in retail stores. The *Code* allots a special load to multioutlet assemblies according to the likelihood that the load will be used simultaneously, per **220.14(H)**:

1. Light use: 180 volt-amperes per five feet of multioutlet assembly
2. Heavy use: 180 volt-amperes per foot of multioutlet assembly

See Problem 9-33.

PROBLEM 9-33

Plans call for 30 feet of multioutlet assembly to be installed in the variety store for lighting use. Calculate the feeder demand for the multioutlet assembly. This load is considered to be noncontinuous.

Solution

Ungrounded service-entrance conductor (or feeder) ampacity

$$\text{Units} = \frac{\text{Length}}{5 \text{ ft}}$$
$$= \frac{30}{5}$$
$$= 6 \text{ units}$$

VA load = units × 180 VA
= 6 × 180
= 1,080 VA

Answer: 1,080 VA noncontinuous and neutral conductor load

9.4.1.6 Feeder Demand: Other Loads—Commercial Store

There are numerous other loads that could be used in a store. Other loads are calculated at 100% of the nameplate rating. **See Problem 9-34**.

PROBLEM 9-34

A 10kW, 208-volt, 3-phase, 80-gallon storage-type water heater is to be installed in the variety store. Calculate the water heater load.

Solution

One water heater at nameplate rating
10 kW = 10,000 VA
Answer: 10,000 VA noncontinuous load
Neutral conductor load = 0

Comment: The line and neutral conductors are all over 1/0 AWG and are permitted to be paralleled by 310.10(G)(1). When the neutral calculations result in a conductor smaller than 1/0 AWG, the minimum 1/0 AWG size takes precedence.

9.4.1.7 Feeder Demand: Small Motor Loads

Single-phase motor loads are calculated using the full-load current tables given in **Article 430** when the horsepower is given. If the horsepower is not given but the full-load current is given, the full-load current is used. For continuous and noncontinuous loads, motor calculations should follow the structure, as well as the requirements of **Section 430.24**. **See Problem 9-35**.

PROBLEM 9-35

Three ⅓-horsepower, 120-volt, single-phase motors are to be installed for ventilation purposes in the variety store. Calculate the full-load current of the feeder demand for the single-phase motors.

Solution

Calculate at FLC rating
Table 430.248
⅓ hp at 120 volts FLC = 7.2 A
$VA = E \times I \times 3$
$= 120 \times 7.2 \times 3$
$= 2,592 \text{ VA}$

Answer: 2,592 VA noncontinuous and neutral conductor load

Comment: Problem 9-35 follows 430.24(2) since none of these motor loads will be considered the largest motor load.

9.4.1.8 Feeder Demand: Air Conditioning

If there is both electric heat and air conditioning, the noncoincidental load requirement is permitted. If no electric heat is indicated, air conditioning is calculated at 100%. **See Problem 9-36**.

PROBLEM 9-36

A 3-phase, 20-horsepower, 208-volt motor is used for air conditioning of the variety store. Calculate the feeder demand for the air conditioning.

Solution

Table 430.250
20 hp at 208 volts FLC = 59.4 A
$VA = E \times I \times 1.73$
$= 208 \times 59.4 \times 1.73$
$= 21,374 \text{ VA}$

Answer: 21,374 VA noncontinuous load
Neutral conductor load = 0

Comment: This calculation follows 430.24(2) so that it can be used with continuous and noncontinuous load calculations.

9.4.1.9 Feeder Demand: Largest Motor

Section 430.24 requires conductors that supply several motors or a motor and other loads to have an ampacity of not less than the sum of the following:

1. 125% of the FLC rating of the highest rated motor
2. The total FLC ratings of all other motors in the group
3. 100% of the noncontinuous non-motor load
4. 125% of the continuous non-motor load

For simplicity of calculations, it is easiest to add all motors together and have the largest motor multiplied by a factor of 25% and added as a separate line item. A sample calculation performed in this manner can be found in **Annex D, Example D3(A)**. See Problem 9-37.

PROBLEM 9-37

Determine the feeder demand of the largest motor at 25%. Use 430.24(1) which will enable the answer to be used with continuous and noncontinuous load calculations.

Solution

Air-conditioning motor is largest

Demand = VA × 25%
= 21,374 × 0.25
= 5,344 VA

Answer: Noncontinuous load = 5,344 VA
Neutral conductor load = 0

9.4.2 Variety Store Calculation Summary

Calculations for commercial buildings are viewed as more restrictive due to fewer applicable demand factors. Basic commercial calculations are very straightforward.

Since most commercial buildings have continuous loads, these loads must be accounted for during load calculations, specifically when overcurrent protective devices and conductor sizes are calculated and determined. This summary consists of three individual calculations: total noncontinuous, total continuous, and total neutral loads.

The feeder demand of the largest motor must be determined. Courtesy of Baldor Electric Company.

However, the basic summary is similar to a residential summary; all loads are converted to volt-amperes and are considered balanced loads. See Problem 9-38.

9.4.2.1 Variety Store Summary Feeder Demand

- Service – 120/208-volt, 3-phase, 4-wire
- Store area – 60 feet by 150 feet
- Basement storage area – 5,000 ft^2
- Discharge lighting will be used
- General-purpose duplex receptacles – Thirty-six 120-volt
- Sign circuit – One 20-ampere, 120-volt, required
- Show windows – Two 20-feet
- Multioutlet assembly, light use – 30-feet, 120-volt
- Water heater – One 10 kW at 208-volt, 3-phase
- Single-phase motors – Three $1/3$-horsepower, 120-volt
- Motor – One 20-horsepower, 208-volt, 3-phase
- 25% of largest motor

9.4.2.2 Service-Entrance Conductors: Ampacity and Overcurrent Protection

Once the total volt-ampere demand is calculated, the next step is to calculate the ampacity and size of the service-entrance conductors in accordance with **230.42(A)**. Consider this installation to be 3-phase, 4-wire with all four conductors in one conduit.

Determining the overcurrent protection will follow the same basic method except without considering **Table 310.15(C)(1)**.

Note that all of the lighting in the variety store is LED, and is a nonlinear load that can cause

PROBLEM 9-38

Calculate the total noncontinuous load, the continuous load, and the neutral load for this variety store.

Solution

Calculation 1

Noncontinuous loads	Noncontinuous load VA
Lighting storage area	
Load = area × VA per ft^2	
= 5,000 × 1.2	
= 6,000 VA	6,000 VA
Store area lighting	
Area = length × width	
= 150 × 60	
= 9,000 ft^2	
Load = area × VA per ft^2	
= 9,000 × 1.9	
= 17,100 VA	17,100 VA

Note: Although both the storage and store area lighting are considered continuous loads, they are added in the noncontinuous loads as the VA per ft^2 from Table 210.12 factors the multiplier of 1.25 into the load.

General-purpose receptacles	
Load = number × 180 VA	
= 36 × 180	
= 6,480 VA	6,480 VA
Multioutlet assembly	
180 VA per 5 ft, light use	
Units = $\frac{\text{Length}}{5 \text{ ft}}$	
= $\frac{30}{5}$	
= 6 units of 5 ft	
Load = units × 180 VA	
= 6 × 180 VA	
= 1,080 VA	1,080 VA
Water heater	
One at 10 kW, 208 volts, 3-phase	
VA = kW × 1,000	
= 10 × 1,000	
= 10,000 VA	10,000 VA
Single-phase motors	
Table 430.248	
⅓ hp at 120 volts	
FLC = 7.2 A	
Load = $E \times I \times 3$	
= 120 × 7.2 × 3	
= 2,592 VA	2,592 VA
Air conditioning	
Table 430.250	
20 hp, 208 volt, 3-phase	
FLC = 59.4 A	
Load = $E \times I \times 1.73$	
= 208 × 59.4 × 1.73	
= 21,374 VA	21,374 VA
Largest motor × 25%	
= 21,374 × 0.25	
= 5,344 VA	5,344 VA
Noncontinuous load subtotal	**69,970 VA**

Answer: 69,970 VA Noncontinuous load

Calculation 2

Continuous loads	Continuous load VA
Required sign receptacle	
1 circuit at 1,200 VA	1,200 VA
Show window lighting	
Load = windows × length × 200 VA per ft	
= 2 × 20 × 200	
= 8,000 VA	8,000 VA
Continuous load subtotal	**9,200 VA**

Answer: 9,200 VA Continuous load

Calculation 3

Neutral loads	Neutral load VA
Store area lighting	
Area = length × width	
= 150 × 60	
= 9,000 ft^2	
Load = area × VA per ft^2	
= 9,000 × 1.9	
= 17,100 VA	17,100 VA

Note: Store lighting is LED lighting

Storage area lighting	
Load = area × VA per ft^2	
= 5,000 × 1.2	
= 6,000 VA	6,000 VA
General-purpose receptacles	
Load = number × 180 VA	
= 36 × 180	
= 6,480 VA	6,480 VA
Required sign receptacle	
1 circuit at 1,200 VA	1,200 VA
Show window lighting	
Load = windows × length × 200 VA per ft	
= 2 × 20 × 200	
= 8,000 VA	8,000 VA
Multioutlet assembly	
180 VA per 5 ft, light use	
Units = $\frac{\text{Length}}{5 \text{ ft}}$	
= $\frac{30}{5}$	
= 6 units of 5 ft	
Load = units × 180 VA	
= 6 × 180	
= 1,080 VA	1,080 VA
Single-phase motors	
Table 430.248	
⅓ hp at 120 volt	
FLC = 7.2 A	
Load = $E \times I \times 3$	
= 120 × 7.2 × 3	
= 2,592 VA	2,592 VA
Neutral loads subtotal	**42,452 VA**

Answer: 42,452 VA Neutral loads

harmonic currents in the neutral conductor. Therefore, **310.15(E)(3)** requires the neutral to be counted as a conductor if the majority of the neutral load is nonlinear. With four conductors in the conduit, the adjustment factors of **310.15(C)(1)** will apply. No temperature is indicated, so it is assumed to be within the range of ordinary ambient, or 86°F. **See Problem 9-39**.

PROBLEM 9-39

Calculate the ampacity of the service conductors for the variety store and determine the minimum size of the overcurrent protection for this service.

Solution

Calculation 1

Service overcurrent protection
230.42(A)

Noncontinuous loads	69,970 VA
Continuous loads = 9,200 VA	
125% of the continuous loads	
9,200 × 1.25 = 11,500 VA	11,500 VA
Total load	81,470 VA

Ungrounded conductors

$$I = \frac{VA}{E \times 1.73}$$
$$= \frac{81,470}{208 \times 1.73}$$
$$= 226 \text{ A}$$

240.4(B)
 Next higher rating
240.6(A)
 250A overcurrent protective device

Answer: 250A overcurrent protective device

Calculation 2

Service conductor ampacity
Ampacity required before application of adjustment and correction factors

Noncontinuous loads	69,970 VA
Continuous loads = 9,200 VA	
125% of the continuous loads	
9,200 VA × 1.25 = 11,500 VA	11,500 VA
Total load	81,470 VA

Ungrounded conductors

$$I = \frac{VA}{E \times 1.73}$$
$$= \frac{81,470}{208 \times 1.73}$$
$$= 226 \text{ A}$$

230.42(A)(2)
 Ampacity of not less than the maximum load after the application of adjustment and correction factors

Maximum load = noncontinuous + continuous load
69,970 + 9,200 = 79,170 VA

$$I = \frac{VA}{E \times 1.73}$$
$$= \frac{79,170}{208 \times 1.73}$$
$$= 220 \text{ A}$$

310.15(E)(3)
 Neutral load is majority of LED lighting
 Neutral counts as a current-carrying conductor for Table 310.15(C)(1)
 Ampacity correction for 4 conductors = 80%

$$\text{Ampacity} = \frac{I}{80\%}$$
$$= \frac{220}{0.80}$$
$$= 275 \text{ A}$$

Answer: 275A ungrounded conductors from appropriate temperature column based on insulation rating of service conductors

Calculation 3

Neutral conductor load

$$I = \frac{VA}{E \times 1.73}$$
$$= \frac{42,452}{208 \times 1.73}$$
$$= 118 \text{ A}$$

310.15(E)(3)
 Neutral load is majority of LED lighting
 Neutral counts as a current-carrying conductor for conduit fill, use Table 310.15(C)(1)
 Ampacity correction for 4 conductors = 80%

$$\text{Ampacity} = \frac{I}{80\%}$$
$$= \frac{118}{0.80}$$
$$= 148 \text{ A}$$

Answer: 148A neutral conductor

Comment: The conductors are required to be a larger size than the overcurrent protective device because there are four current-carrying conductors in the conduit.

As smart grid technology grows, the common electric meter will see major changes. **Section 230.82** will help pave the way for future advancements in power management with renewable energy storage, microgrids, and energy arbitrage.

9.4.2.3 Service-Entrance Conductors and a Bare Neutral: Size

According to **Section 230.41**, service-entrance conductors are required to be insulated conductors. However, grounded service-entrance conductors are permitted to be bare according to the exception following this section. **See Problem 9-40**.

9.4.2.4 Service-Entrance Conductors: Conduit Size

Determining the minimum conduit size using bare conductors is different from previous conduit size calculations because bare conductor dimensions are smaller than insulated conductors. Bare conductor dimensions are found in **Chapter 9, Table 8**, whereas **Chapter 9, Table 5** is used for insulated conductor dimensions. **See Problem 9-41**.

9.5 OFFICE BUILDINGS

The general term *office building* is a broad classification of commercial property usually designated as a business occupancy and designed with spaces to be used for offices.

9.5.1 Method of Feeder Demand Calculation

There are multiple methods of calculating the lighting and receptacle loads for office buildings. Often, an office building is built before there are tenants and is constructed simply as a shell of a building, sometimes referred to as a speculative or "spec" type building. As there are no tenants, receptacles have not been planned. Other times, office buildings are built with tenants in mind.

PROBLEM 9-40

The variety store service is to consist of single THWN copper conductors for the line conductors and a bare neutral conductor installed in rigid metal conduit. *NEC* 230.41 Exception permits a bare neutral conductor. What is the minimum size service-entrance conductor required?

Solution

Calculation 1
230.42(A)(1) Ampacity adequate for noncontinuous and 125% of continuous load
  Noncontinuous and 125% of continuous load = 226 A
Table 310.16 with equipment over 100 A, equipment is 75°C
  250 kcmil THWN-2 allowable ampacity from 75°C column = 255 A
230.42(A)(2) Ampacity adequate for maximum load
  Maximum load = 220 A
Table 310.15(C)(1) Four current-carrying conductors requires 80%
Table 310.16 for 250 kcmil THWN-2, use 290 A for adjustments
  Ampacity = 0.8 × 290 = 232 A
250 kcmil meets both requirements of 230.42(A)(1) and (2)
Additionally, a 232A conductor is protected by a 250A overcurrent protective device in accordance with 230.90 and 240.4(B).

PROBLEM 9-41

What size of rigid metal conduit (RMC) is necessary for the service-entrance conductor calculated in Problem 9-40?

Solution

Line conductor area
Chapter 9, Table 5
  300 kcmil THWN-2 copper = 0.4608 in.²
  0.4608 × 3 = 1.3824 in.²   1.3824 in.²
Bare conductor area
Chapter 9, Table 8
  2/0 AWG bare = 0.137 in.²
  0.137 × 1 = 0.1370 in.²   0.1370 in.²
Total   1.5194 in.²
Chapter 9, Table 4, Rigid metal conduit (RMC)
  Over 2 wires = 40% fill
  1.5194 in.² = 2 1/2 in. trade size
Answer: 2 1/2 in. RMC

Section 220.14(K) accommodates either method of providing for receptacles. In practice, this section requires that the larger of either an actual count of receptacles or an allowance of an additional one volt-ampere per square foot be used.

Consider the Tower Office Building. A value of one volt-ampere per square foot for receptacle loads will be used in addition to the **Table 220.12** value of 1.3 volt-amperes per square foot for lighting loads.

Multiple calculations can be made for the Tower Office Building. The building will consist of five floors, with an outside dimension of 125 feet by 88 feet. The service is 277/480 volts, 3-phase, 4-wire, and the lighting is LED throughout.

9.5.1.1 Feeder Demand: Lighting without Including Receptacles

Determining the general lighting load in volt-amperes for an office building without considering receptacle loads is done by applying the volt-amperes per square foot of **Table 220.12** to the total building area. **See Problem 9-42**.

PROBLEM 9-42

Calculate the feeder demand for the lighting of the Tower Office Building when the number of receptacles is known.

Solution

$$\text{Area} = \text{length} \times \text{width} \times \text{number of floors}$$
$$= 125 \times 88 \times 5$$
$$= 55{,}000 \text{ ft}^2$$

Table 220.12
VA per ft² = 1.3 VA per ft²
Lighting load = area × VA per ft²
$$= 55{,}000 \times 1.3$$
$$= 71{,}500 \text{ VA}$$

Answer: 71,500 VA

9.5.1.2 Calculating the Required Number of Lighting Circuits

Office building lighting is considered a continuous load. For this reason, **210.20(A)** requires the branch-circuit overcurrent protective device, which is also the branch-circuit rating, to be 125% of the connected continuous load. **Section 215.3** requires the same for the feeder overcurrent protective device.

Most new lighting being installed in office buildings is LED.

New for the 2020 *NEC*, the **Note** in **Table 220.12** clarifies the 125% for continuous loads is already included with the volt-amperes per square foot calculation and is not needed to be added for purposes of *NEC* **210.19**, **210.20**, **215.2**, **215.3**, and **230.42**. When calculating the number of branch circuits needed, the load from **Table 220.12** is divided by the load rating of a circuit. See Problem 9-43.

PROBLEM 9-43

If the lighting circuits are 277-volt, single-phase, 20-ampere, what is the minimum number of lighting circuits needed?

Solution

Calculation 1
Basic Calculation
210.11(A)
Lighting Load = 71,500 VA
Circuit Rating = 20 × 277 = 5,540 VA

$$\text{Number of circuits} = \frac{\text{Lighting load}}{\text{Circuit rating}}$$
$$= \frac{71{,}500}{5{,}540}$$
$$= 12.9 \text{ or } 13 \text{ circuits}$$

Answer: 13 circuits are required

Comment: The 2020 *NEC* has made significant changes in lighting load calculations. It should be noted that the 2017 *NEC* would have required 3.5 volt-amperes per square foot and 125% multiplied by the table load, resulting in 44 circuits compared to the 13 circuits required by the 2020 *NEC*. As LED lighting has become more widespread, the values in Table 220.12 have been modified to reflect new technologies that have reduced lighting loads.

9.5.1.3 Feeder Demand: Including Receptacles with Lighting

Determining the general lighting load and the receptacle load in volt-amperes for an office building is done by following the requirements of both **Table 220.12** and **Section 220.14**. The total volt-amperes per square foot used in the calculation is the sum of the value of **Table 220.12** plus the value from **220.14(K)**. *NEC* **220.14(K)** requires using the larger value of either one volt-ampere per square foot or using 180 volt-amperes per receptacle if the number of receptacles is known. **See Problem 9-44**.

PROBLEM 9-44

Calculate the lighting and receptacle load for the Tower Office Building when the number of receptacles is not known.

Solution

Area = 55,000 ft^2
Table 220.12
VA per ft^2 = 1.3 VA per ft^2
220.14(K)
 Increase VA by 1 VA = 2.3 VA per ft^2
 Lighting load = area × VA per ft^2
  = 55,000 × 2.3
  = 126,500 VA
Answer: 126,500 VA

9.5.1.4 Feeder Demand: Number of Receptacles Known
According to **220.14(K)**, office building receptacle loads must be calculated according to the larger of either the 180 volt-amperes method used in **220.14(I)** or the one volt-ampere per square foot method used in **220.14(K)**. **See Problem 9-45**.

9.5.1.5 Sizing a Transformer for 120-Volt Receptacles
If the general distribution system is 480/277 volts, a transformer is needed to furnish the 120 volts for the general-purpose receptacle load. If the receptacle load is calculated in volt-amperes and transformers are rated in kilovolt-amperes (kVA), the calculated receptacle volt-ampere load can be divided by 1,000 to determine the minimum kilovolt-ampere transformer rating needed. **See Problem 9-46**.

9.5.1.6 Feeder Demand: Motor Loads
Much of the heating and cooling of commercial buildings is accomplished with 3-phase motors. Motor calculations are required to comply with

PROBLEM 9-45

Calculate the receptacle load for the Tower Office Building when plans call for fifty 120-volt duplex receptacles to be installed on each floor.

Solution

Calculation 1
180 VA method
Number of receptacles = 50 per floor × 5 floors
 = 250
220.14(I)
Receptacles calculated at 180 VA each
 Load = number of receptacles × 180 VA
  = 250 × 180
  = 45,000 VA
Table 220.44
Apply demand factors
Total calculated load = 45,000 VA

First 10,000 at 100%	10,000 VA
Remaining 35,000 VA at 50%	
= 35,000 × 0.50	
= 17,500 VA	17,500 VA
Total	27,500 VA

Answer: 27,500 VA

Calculation 2
One VA per ft^2 method
220.14(K)
 One VA per ft^2 = 55,000 VA
Table 220.44 does not apply
Answer: 55,000 VA

Calculation 3
220.14(K)
 Use larger load
 55,000 VA is larger than 27,500 VA
 Use One VA per ft^2 method
Answer: 55,000 VA

PROBLEM 9-46

The receptacle load will be supplied by a transformer with a 3-phase, 480-volt primary and a 120/208-volt, 3-phase, 4-wire secondary. Calculate the minimum kVA rating of the transformer.

Solution

Receptacle load = 55,000 VA

$$kVA = \frac{VA}{1,000}$$
$$= \frac{55,000}{1,000}$$
$$= 55 \text{ kVA}$$

Answer: 55 kVA

Comment: The answer of a 55 kVA transformer is not a standard size 3-phase transformer. Therefore, any size larger would be permitted.

PROBLEM 9-47

The following motors are to be installed in the Tower Office Building:

Two 5-horsepower, 460-volt, 3-phase   Two 50-horsepower, 460-volt, 3-phase

Two 10-horsepower, 460-volt, 3-phase

Calculate the VA feeder demand for the motor loads.

Solution

Table 430.250

5 hp, 460 volt FLC = 7.6 A

10 hp, 460 volt FLC = 14 A

50 hp, 460 volt FLC = 65 A

VA = E × I × 1.73 × number of motors

VA (5 hp) = 460 × 7.6 × 1.73 × 2 = 12,096	12,096
VA (10 hp) = 460 × 14 × 1.73 × 2 = 22,282	22,282
VA (50 hp) = 460 × 65 × 1.73 × 2 = 103,454	103,454
25% of largest	
VA hp = 460 × 65 × 1.73 × 0.25 = 12,932	12,932
Total motor VA	150,764

Answer: 150,764 VA

430.24 using the full-load currents from **Table 430.250**. The *NEC* **Informative Annex D, Example D3(a)** provides a sample calculation. **See Problem 9-47.**

Large motors are used for air-handling purposes in commercial buildings under construction.

PROBLEM 9-48

Calculate the total feeder demand based upon continuous and noncontinuous loads for the Tower Office Building when the number of receptacles is not known.

Summary of Tower Office Building:

- 5 floors, 125 ft by 88 ft
- Service: 480/277 volts, 3-phase, 4-wire
- LED lighting used throughout
- Motor loads: two 5 hp; two 10 hp, and two 50 hp; all of which are 460 volts, 3-phase

Solution

Building total area = length × width × floors
= 125 × 88 × 5
= 55,000 ft²

	Noncontinuous Load	Continuous Load
Lighting VA = total area × 1.3 VA per ft²		
= 55,000 × 1.3		
= 71,500 VA	71,500 VA	0
Receptacles VA = total area × 1 VA per ft²		
= 55,000 × 1		
= 55,000 VA	55,000 VA	0
Motor loads calculated in Problem 9-47		
Two 5 hp, 460 V 12,096 VA		
Two 10 hp, 460 V 22,282 VA		
Two 50 hp, 460 V 103,454 VA		
Total motor load 137,832 VA	137,832 VA	0
25% of largest (50 hp) motor calculated in Problem 9-47	12,932 VA	0
Totals	**277,264 VA**	**0**

Answer: 277,264 VA total feeder demand

Note: Although lighting typically is a continuous load and normally would be required to be adjusted by 125% for sizing conductors and overcurrent protective devices, the new note in Table 220.12 clarifies that 125% is already included in the lighting load from the Table.

9.5.2 Office Building Calculation Summary

This summary of the office building calculation follows the same procedures as previously outlined.

9.5.2.1 Total Feeder Demand for Office Building, Number of Receptacles Unknown

The general lighting load for the office building is calculated by using **Table 220.12**. The receptacles are calculated using **220.14(K)(2)**. The solution for Problem 9-48 could combine the office lighting load of 1.3 volt-amperes per square foot with the office receptacle's load of one volt-ampere per square foot, but because continuous and noncontinuous loads are being calculated, the calculations should remain separate. The motor load calculations follow **430.24(1)** and **430.24(2)**. See Problem 9-48.

9.5.2.2 Ampacity of Neutral Conductor

NEC **220.61(B)(2)** permits the size of the neutral conductor to be decreased to 70% after the first 200 amperes is calculated at 100%. However, the ampacity of the neutral is not permitted to be reduced for the portion of the load that supplies electric discharge lighting or other harmonic loads. See Problem 9-49.

PROBLEM 9-49

Calculate the ampacity of the neutral conductor for the following calculated office building loads when the service is 208/120 volts, 3-phase, 4-wire.

LED lighting load	210,000 VA
Receptacle load (after application of demand factors)	65,000 VA
Fixed electric space-heating load	85,000 VA
120-volt motor load	30,000 VA

Solution

LED lighting load

$$I = \frac{VA}{E \times 1.732}$$
$$= \frac{210,000}{208 \times 1.732}$$
$$= 583 \text{ A}$$

Other loads = receptacles, heat, and motor
= 65,000 + 85,000 + 30,000 = 180,000 VA

$$I = \frac{VA}{E \times 1.732}$$
$$= \frac{180,000}{208 \times 1.732}$$
$$= 500 \text{ A}$$

200 A at 100%	200 A
Remaining 300 A at 70% = 300 × 0.7 = 210 A	210 A
LED Lighting Load prohibited reduction (nonlinear load)	
583 A at 100%	583 A
Total	993 A

Answer: 993 A of neutral conductor load

DEFINITIONS AND TERMS

Appliance - Utilization equipment, generally other than industrial, that is normally built in standardized sizes or types and is installed or connected as a unit to perform one or more functions such as clothes washing, air conditioning, food mixing, deep frying, and so forth. [**70**:100]

Building - A structure that stands alone or that is separated from adjoining structures by fire walls. [**70**:100] All openings therein are protected by approved fire doors.

Demand Factor - The ratio of the maximum demand of a system, or part of a system, to the total connected load of a system or the part of the system under consideration. [**70**:100]

Dwelling, One-Family - A building that consists solely of one dwelling unit. [**70**:100]

Dwelling, Multifamily - A building that contains three or more dwelling units. [**70**:100]

Reproduced with permission of NFPA from NFPA 70®, *National Electrical Code*® (NEC®), 2020 edition. Copyright© 2019, National Fire Protection Association. For a full copy of the NEC®, please go to www.nfpa.org.

DEFINITIONS AND TERMS

Dwelling Unit - A single unit, providing complete and independent living facilities for one or more persons, including permanent provisions for living, sleeping, cooking, and sanitation. [**70**:100]

Feeder - All circuit conductors between the service equipment, the source of a separately derived system, or other power supply source and the final branch-circuit overcurrent device. [**70**:100]

Grounding Electrode Conductor - A conductor used to connect the system grounded conductor or the equipment to a grounding electrode or to a point on the grounding electrode system. [**70**:100]

Neutral Conductor - The conductor connected to the neutral point of a system that is intended to carry current under normal conditions. [**70**:100]

Neutral Point - The common point on a wye-connection in a polyphase system or midpoint on a single-phase, 3-wire system, or midpoint of a single-phase portion of a 3-phase delta system, or a midpoint of a 3-wire, direct-current system. [**70**:100]

Noncoincidental Loads - Two electrical loads are considered to be noncoincidental loads if the two electrical loads are unlikely to operate at the same time (see **220.60**).

Service - The conductors and equipment connecting the serving utility to the wiring system of the premises served. [**70**:100]

Service Conductors - The conductors from the service point to the service disconnecting means. [**70**:100]

Reproduced with permission of NFPA from NFPA 70®, *National Electrical Code*® (NEC®), 2020 edition. Copyright© 2019, National Fire Protection Association. For a full copy of the NEC®, please go to www.nfpa.org.

SUMMARY

Article 220, Part III provides the basic method for performing feeder and service load calculations for all occupancies. The feeder and service load is the sum of all the branch circuit loads as determined by **Part II** of **Article 220** with any applicable demand factors applied. It is also important to differentiate loads based on line and neutral loads, as well as continuous and noncontinuous loads for proper determination of overcurrent protective devices and conductor sizing. A properly performed load calculation will provide the correct service and feeder sizes that are neither dangerously undersized nor inefficiently oversized.

Annex D provides a variety of example load calculations and is an important reference source.

REVIEW QUESTIONS

1. For the total square footage of a dwelling unit required to be included for the general lighting load calculation, which area would not be included?
   a. A finished basement
   b. A garage
   c. A living room
   d. An unfinished basement

2. What is the minimum required load for either one of the 20-ampere small appliance branch circuits or the 20-ampere laundry circuit?
   a. 1,500 VA
   b. 1,800 VA
   c. 2,000 VA
   d. 2,400 VA

3. When using **Table 220.42** and applying demand to the lighting load for dwelling units, the 35% demand factor is applied to what maximum amount of load?
   a. 3,000 VA
   b. 117,000 VA
   c. 120,000 VA
   d. None – it is not permitted to be applied

4. What is the demand factor percentage permitted to be applied to four or more appliances fastened in place in a dwelling unit?
   a. 70%
   b. 75%
   c. 80%
   d. 100%

5. For fixed electric space-heating equipment installed on a feeder or service, the load is calculated by having which percentage applied?
   a. 75%
   b. 80%
   c. 100%
   d. 125%

6. For a 3-phase, 4-wire, wye service, the 70% demand factor permitted to be applied to the neutral load is not allowed to be applied to __?__.
   a. nonlinear loads
   b. the load in excess of 200 A
   c. the neutral of a single-phase, 120/240V feeder
   d. the neutral supplying household electric ranges and dryers

7. If multiple motors are supplied by a service or feeder and all motors and other loads have been added in the load calculation, which is required?
   a. Adding an additional 25% of any motor
   b. Adding an additional 25% of the largest motor
   c. Adding an additional 125% of the largest motor
   d. No further additions are required

8. Which is used when determining the receptacle load for a commercial office building?
   a. 1 VA per ft² of the office building
   b. 3 ½ VA per ft² of the office building
   c. 180 VA per receptacle
   d. The larger of 1 VA per ft² or 180 VA per receptacle

9. What is the feeder demand for a retail store that has 20 feet of multioutlet assembly where appliances are likely to be used simultaneously?
   a. 720 VA
   b. 900 VA
   c. 2,400 VA
   d. 3,600 VA

10. Which part of **Article 220** provides for optional feeder and service load calculations?
    a. Part I
    b. Part II
    c. Part III
    d. Part IV

CHAPTER 10
TRANSFORMER OVERCURRENT PROTECTION

Protection techniques of power transformers, their supply conductors, and their load conductors consist of basic overcurrent and overload protection. Calculations to determine and properly size this protection are broken down into four basic general categories.

The first category is general overcurrent protection afforded to the windings of a transformer. Calculations based upon **Table 450.3(B)** are used to demonstrate how to properly apply and select the maximum size overcurrent protection as "primary only" and "primary plus secondary" protection for a given transformer. Each of the three individual primary categories and each secondary category will be explored and calculated, as permitted.

The second category is the maximum overcurrent protective device along with the correct conductor size. Calculations and selection are based upon the load(s) served by the secondary and the primary circuit of a transformer with the use of **Table 450.3(B)**, along with more complex sections of overcurrent protection within **240.21(B), Feeder Taps**, and **240.21(C), Transformer Secondary Conductors**. The seven specific tap rules will be studied in depth.

The third category is the overcurrent protective device and the proper size conductor for transformers equipped with coordinated thermal overload protection by the manufacturer.

The fourth category is dedicated transformers used in fire pump circuits. Special calculations based upon **Article 695** are used to correctly size a transformer and apply short-circuit protection to a fire pump circuit.

This study of transformers is limited to 1,000 volts, nominal, or less.

OBJECTIVES

- Calculate the overcurrent protection for primary and secondary windings of a transformer.
- Select the standard size overcurrent protective devices.
- Calculate and select the primary and secondary transformer conductor sizes.
- Calculate and select the primary overcurrent devices for single-phase transformers with a 2-wire secondary.
- Apply the 10-foot and 25-foot tap rule to transformer secondary conductors.
- Apply the feeder tap rule, which supplies a transformer (primary plus secondary not over 25 feet long).

TABLE OF CONTENTS

10.1 PROTECTING TRANSFORMER WINDINGS (1,000 VOLTS, NOMINAL, OR LESS) — 230

- .1 General — 230
- .2 Primary Overcurrent Protection Only — 231
- .3 Secondary Overcurrent Protection — 235
- .4 Primary Protection at 250% and Secondary Protection at 125% — 236
- .5 Secondary Protection Using Multiple Overcurrent Devices — 236
- .6 Transformer Thermal Overload Protection — 237
- .7 Summary — 238

10.2 240.21(B) FEEDER TAPS AND 240.21(C) TRANSFORMER SECONDARY CONDUCTORS — 239

- .1 240.21(C)(1) Primary Protection, Including Secondary Protection — 240
- .2 Ten-Foot Feeder Tap Rule — Transformer Primary Conductors 240.21(B)(1) — 240
- .3 Ten-Foot Transformer Tap Rule — Transformer Secondary Conductors — 242
- .4 Ten-Foot Transformer Tap Rule — Supplying a Panelboard — 245
- .5 Twenty-Five-Foot Feeder Tap Rule — Transformer Primary 240.21(B)(2) — 245
- .6 Twenty-Five-Foot Transformer Tap Rule — Transformer Secondary Conductors 240.21(C)(6) — 246
- .7 Outside — Secondary Conductors 240.21(C)(4) — 247

10.3 DEDICATED TRANSFORMERS USED IN FIRE PUMP CIRCUITS — 248

DEFINITIONS AND TERMS — 249

SUMMARY — 250

REVIEW QUESTIONS — 250

10.1 PROTECTING TRANSFORMER WINDINGS (1,000 VOLTS, NOMINAL, OR LESS)

Section 450.3 provides the requirements for transformer protection. **Informational Note No. 1** is also provided to remind the *Code* user to see **240.4** and **240.21** for requirements for the protection of primary and secondary conductors.

10.1.1 General

The study of overcurrent protection of transformers begins with a look at the transformers used for power and lighting with an operating voltage of 1,000 volts, nominal, or less. Such transformers are used as premises distribution transformers, often in conjunction with lighting distribution panels.

The following primary sections of the *Code* will be used:

- **Table 450.3(B)** - This table is directed at the overcurrent protection of transformer windings for transformers operating at 1,000 volts, nominal, or less.
- **Table 450.3(B)**, **Note 1** - This note permits overcurrent protection, where limited to 125% of the transformer full-load current, to be increased to a higher rating that does not exceed the next higher standard size overcurrent protective device.
- **240.6(A)** - This section includes standard ampere ratings of fuses and circuit breakers used for selecting the proper final transformer size and conductor overcurrent protective device.
- **Table 450.3(B)**, **Note 2** - This note permits overcurrent protection on the secondary of a transformer to be not more than six circuit breakers or sets of fuses grouped at one location.

Primary overcurrent protection can be responsive to secondary short circuits but is not always responsive to secondary overcurrent caused by an unbalanced condition of a single-phase, 3-wire system or a 3-phase, 4-wire system. The *Code* calls attention to this in **240.21(C)(1)**, which states in part:

> **Protection by Primary Overcurrent Device.** Conductors supplied by the secondary side of a single-phase transformer having a 2-wire (single-voltage) secondary, or a three-phase, delta-delta connected transformer having a 3-wire (single-voltage) secondary, shall be permitted to be protected by overcurrent protection provided on the primary (supply) side of the transformer, provided…

The *Code* does not give a specific method for sizing the primary or secondary conductors of transformers 1,000 volts, nominal, or less, other than as required by the following general requirements for electrical conductors:

- **Section 215.2** requires feeder conductors to have sufficient ampacity to supply the load served.
- **Section 240.4** requires conductors to be protected against overcurrent according to their ampacities.

Table 450.3(B) requires transformer primary and secondary windings to be protected against overcurrents according to the ampacity rating of the transformer windings. The ampacity rating of the transformer windings is based upon the current rating of the transformer.

The sizing of primary or secondary conductors and the primary or secondary overcurrent protection need to be considered together. The reason is that the overcurrent device can be used to protect the transformer windings and the primary and secondary circuit conductors.

NEC **240.6(A)** is divided into the following three separate parts:

1. Standard ampere ratings for fuses and inverse-time circuit breakers

2. Additional standard ratings for fuses of only 1, 3, 6, 10, and 601 amperes
3. The use of nonstandard fixed ampere rated fuses and circuit breakers which could have any ampacity rating

The type of overcurrent protective device required for transformers is not specified. The overcurrent protective device can be time-delay or non–time-delay fuses, or adjustable or nonadjustable circuit breakers. Thermal overload protective devices are also permitted for use as transformer winding overcurrent protection.

When a transformer is energized, there is an inrush of current. The inrush of current is similar to the starting current of a motor. It will last until a counter-EMF is built up in the primary of the transformer, which takes only a short period of time. This initial current surge is called *inrush current*, *charging current*, or *excitation current*. The inrush current can be as much as eight to ten times the rated primary current. A time-delay type overcurrent protective device can be used to compensate for the inrush current.

> **SYMBOL IDENTIFICATION**
>
> Where transformer overcurrent protection examples are presented, the following standard references and symbols will be used:
>
> - OCPD – Overcurrent protective device
> - $OCPD_{pri}$ – Overcurrent protective device, primary side of the transformer
> - $OCPD_{sec}$ – Overcurrent protective device, secondary side of the transformer
> - I_{pri} – Primary current
> - E_{pri} – Primary voltage
> - I_{sec} – Secondary current
> - E_{sec} – Secondary voltage
> - kVA – Kilovolt-amperes
> - LRC – Locked-rotor current
> - CB – Circuit breaker

Table 310.16 is used for selecting the ampacity of conductors. Additionally, all equipment will be listed for use at 75°C temperature ratings. All conductors can be assumed to be copper, unless noted otherwise.

> **EQUATIONS**
>
> Transformer primary and secondary current ratings can be taken from tables or can be calculated using transformer power equations:
>
> Single-phase:
> $$I = \frac{kVA \times 1,000}{E}$$
>
> 3-phase:
> $$I = \frac{kVA \times 1,000}{E \times 1.73}$$

10.1.2 Primary Overcurrent Protection Only

Table 450.3(B) includes multiple transformer overcurrent protection schemes based upon the percentage of a transformer's rated current.

Notice that the table focuses only on the protection of the transformer windings and excludes the primary or secondary feeder conductor protection. Consider the overcurrent protection to be individually located at the transformer.

10.1.2.1 Primary Protection, Nine Amperes or More

Table 450.3(B) requires each 1,000-volt, nominal, or less transformer primary with a primary current of nine amperes or more to be protected by an individual overcurrent device on the primary side of the transformer. If the protection method is primary-only protection, the overcurrent protective device is required to be rated or set at not more than 125% of the rated primary current (I_{pri}). The equation is stated as follows:

$$OCPD_{pri} = I_{pri} \times 125\%$$

The title of **Table 450.3(B)** states, "Maximum Rating or Setting of Overcurrent Protection for Transformers," and therefore, the calculated value of multiplying the transformer rated current by the appropriate percentage in the table yields the maximum OCPD. For transformers with currents of nine amperes or more and primary or secondary protection at 125%, **Note 1** of **Table 450.3(B)** permits a higher rating that does not exceed the next higher standard size overcurrent protective device to be used. To determine the maximum primary overcurrent protective device if providing only primary protection for transformers rated nine amperes or more, always use **Note 1** of the table to increase to the next standard size.

The second protection method is primary and secondary protection. For this method, the overcurrent protective device is allowed to be rated or set at not more than 250% of the rated primary current (I_{pri}).

Maximum $OCPD_{pri} = I_{pri} \times 250\%$

Note 1 of the table is not applicable, and therefore, the result calculated at 250% is a maximum value. In order to select a standard size overcurrent protective device, the selection of the next lower standard size from the calculated 250% value is required.

10.1.2.2 Primary Protection, Less Than Nine Amperes

Table 450.3(B) requires each 1,000-volt, nominal, or less transformer primary with a primary current of less than nine amperes to be protected by an individual overcurrent protective device on the primary side of the transformer rated or set at not more than 167% of the rated primary current (I_{pri}). **Note 1** is not applicable. **See Problem 10-1**.

The front cover of the transformer is removed to expose the wiring terminal for view and connection. Notice that the low-voltage secondary wiring uses parallel conductors.

PROBLEM 10-1

Calculate the maximum size overcurrent protective device permitted on the primary of a 15kVA, 3-phase, 480-volt transformer for both protection methods of Table 450.3(B).

Solution

Calculation 1
Primary only protection
3-phase

$$I = \frac{kVA \times 1,000}{E_{pri} \times 1.73}$$

$$= \frac{15 \times 1,000}{480 \times 1.73}$$

$$= 18.06 \text{ A}$$

Table 450.3(B)
 Currents of 9 amperes or more column
 Primary only protection = 125%
 Max. $OCPD_{pri} = I_{pri} \times 125\%$
  $= 18.06 \times 1.25$
  $= 22.58$ A
Table 450.3(B) Note 1
 Next larger std. size permitted
240.6(A)
 Next larger = 25 A
Answer: 25 A Max. $OCPD_{pri}$

Calculation 2
Primary and secondary protection
$I_{pri} = 18.06$ A
Table 450.3(B)
 Currents of 9 amperes or more column
 Primary and secondary protection = 250%
 Max. $OCPD_{pri} = I_{pri} \times 250\%$
  $= 18.06 \times 2.50$
  $= 45.15$ A
Table 450.3(B) Note 1
 Does not apply, use next smaller
240.6(A)
 Next smaller = 45 A
Answer: 45 A max. $OCPD_{pri}$

Comment: The dual solution calculations from Problem 10-1 demonstrate a stark difference in the maximum overcurrent protection permitted for a 15kVA transformer. Using **Calculation 1**, the transformer primary OCPD maximum is limited to 25 amperes, whereas using **Calculation 2**, the transformer primary OCPD max is limited to 45 amperes. For a 150kVA transformer, the differences could be as large as 250 amperes versus 500 amperes. The primary only protection demonstrated by **Calculation 1** is often recommended for transformers with stable loads and other loads without high inrush currents. The primary protection demonstrated by **Calculation 2** is often recommended for transformers with varying loads or loads with high inrush currents.

The reason for the increase in the permitted sizing of the protective device is that the transformer "charging current" for the smaller transformers is proportionally larger for the ampere rating of the transformer.

For additional information, visit qr.njatcdb.org Item #1039

Some transformers are designed for specific applications and have single winding primaries or single winding secondaries. Most transformers, however, have dual windings on both the primary and the secondary. **See Problem 10-2.**

PROBLEM 10-2

Calculate the maximum primary overcurrent protection permitted for the primary of a 2.5kVA single-phase, 480-volt transformer where fuses are used and secondary overcurrent protection for the transformer is not desired.

Solution

Primary overcurrent protection

$$I_{pri} = \frac{kVA \times 1{,}000}{E_{pri}}$$
$$= \frac{2.5 \times 1{,}000}{480}$$
$$= 5.2 \text{ A}$$

Table 450.3(B)
  Currents less than 9 amperes column
  Primary only protection = 167%
  Max. OCPD$_{pri}$ = I_{pri} × 1.67
    = 5.2 × 1.67
    = 8.68 A
Table 450.3(B) Note 1
  Does not apply, any less permitted
240.6(A)
  Next smaller = 6 A
Answer: Fuse size of 8.68 A or less

10.1.2.3 Primary Protection, Less Than Two Amperes

Table 450.3(B) requires each 1,000-volt, nominal, or less transformer primary with a primary current of less than two amperes to be protected by an individual overcurrent protective device on the primary side of the transformer rated or set at not more than 300% of the rated primary current (I_{pri}). **Note 1** is not applicable. **See Problem 10-3.**

PROBLEM 10-3

Calculate the maximum overcurrent protection using the primary-only method of protection for a 200VA, single-phase, 120-volt primary transformer when fuses are used.

Solution

Primary overcurrent protection

$$I_{pri} = \frac{VA}{E_{pri}}$$
$$= \frac{200}{120}$$
$$= 1.67 \text{ A}$$

Table 450.3(B)
  Currents less than 2 amperes column
  Primary only protection = 300%
  Max. OCPD$_{pri}$ = I_{pri} × 300%
    = 1.67 × 3.00
    = 5.01 A
Table 450.3(B) Note 1
  Does not apply, any less permitted
240.6(A)
  Next smaller = 3 A
Answer: Fuse size of 5.01 A or less

The primary winding is connected to the AC input, and the secondary is connected to the load.

10.1.2.4 Overcurrent Protection Primary Windings and Primary Feeder Conductors

Provided the overcurrent device protects the primary transformer windings according to **Table 450.3(B)**, the overcurrent protective device protecting the primary of a transformer may be located other than at the transformer.

Therefore, the overcurrent protective device used to protect the primary windings of the transformer is commonly used to also protect the circuit conductors supplying the primary side of the transformer. Remember:

1. The overcurrent protective device is required to protect the primary of the transformer, according to **Table 450.3(B)**.
2. It is also required to protect the conductors according to **Section 240.4**.

The overcurrent protective device is responsible for the protection of the transformer windings

PROBLEM 10-4

The primary of a 45kVA, 440-volt, 3-phase transformer is supplied with THWN copper conductors. Calculate the maximum primary overcurrent protective device and the minimum primary conductors for the transformer. The method of protection is selected to be primary only.

Primary Overcurrent Protective Device
80 A
4 AWG THWN Copper
440 V 3-Phase
59.1 A
Primary
Secondary
45 kVA

Solution

Calculation 1
Primary only protection
3-phase

$$I = \frac{kVA \times 1,000}{E_{pri} \times 1.73}$$

$$= \frac{45 \times 1,000}{440 \times 1.73}$$

$$= 59.1 \text{ A}$$

Table 450.3(B)
Currents of 9 amperes or more column
Primary only protection = 125%
Max. OCPD$_{pri}$ = I_{pri} × 125%
$= 59.1 \times 1.25$
$= 73.87$ A
Table 450.3(B) Note 1
Next larger std. size permitted
240.6(A)
Next larger = 80 A
Max. OCPD$_{pri}$ = 80A OCPD
Table 310.16
THWN copper column
80 A = 4 AWG THWN
4 AWG THWN = 85 A
Answer: 80A OCPD$_{pri}$ with 4 AWG THWN copper

Calculation 2
Primary overcurrent protection
I_{pri} = 59.1 A
Table 310.16
THWN copper column
59.1 A = 6 AWG THWN
6 AWG THWN copper = 65 A
240.4(A)
Next larger std. size permitted
240.6(A)
Next larger = 70 A
Table 450.3(B)
Currents of 9 amperes or more column
Primary only protection = 125%
Max. OCPD$_{pri}$ = I_{pri} × 125%
$= 59.1 \times 1.25$
$= 73.87$ A
Table 450.3(B) Note 1
Next larger std. size permitted
240.6(A)
Next larger = 80 A
Select 6 AWG THWN Copper with 70A OCPD
Reason: Neither method exceeds 125% of I_{pri}
Answer: 70A OCPD$_{pri}$ with 6 AWG THWN copper

Selection of Answers:
4 AWG THWN copper with 80A OCPD$_{pri}$
6 AWG THWN copper with 70A OCPD$_{pri}$

Comment: Notice that when a 6 AWG conductor is used with a 70-ampere overcurrent protective device, both the conductor and the transformer are protected. No transformer capacity is being lost by using a conductor one size smaller and keeping the conductor and the primary windings protected. When the smaller overcurrent protective device is used, less transformer overload current will be permitted before the primary overcurrent protective device operates.

and the circuit conductors, and both are required to be considered. Additionally, there is more risk of nuisance tripping where a transformer is fully loaded since the OCPD is less than 125% of the primary full-load current.

10.1.3 Secondary Overcurrent Protection

Table 450.3(B) does not require secondary overcurrent protection for the transformer when primary-only overcurrent protection is provided. When providing primary and secondary protection for the transformer, the secondary device is only able to provide overload protection to the transformer, and the primary device is still required to provide short-circuit and ground-fault protection. **See Problem 10-4**.

10.1.3.1 Secondary Protection, Nine Amperes or More

Table 450.3(B) requires each 1,000-volt, nominal, or less transformer secondary with a secondary current of nine amperes or more to be protected by an individual overcurrent protective device on the secondary side of the transformer rated or set at not more than 125% of the rated secondary current (I_{sec}). **Note 1** of the table permits a higher rating that does not exceed the next higher standard size overcurrent protective device to be used for the transformer overcurrent protection. According to **Note 1**, using the next higher standard size OCPD is permitted. **See Problem 10-5**.

10.1.3.2 Secondary Protection, Less Than Nine Amperes

Table 450.3(B) requires each 1,000-volt or less transformer with a secondary current of less than nine amperes to be protected by an individual overcurrent protective device on the secondary side of the transformer rated or set at not more than 167% of the rated secondary current (I_{sec}). **Note 1** is not applicable. **See Problem 10-6**.

Small transformers are often more vital to the successful operation of a building than may be realized. Small transformers are responsible for building automation systems, mass notification and fire alarm systems, elevator control, and a myriad of other very important electrical systems.

PROBLEM 10-5

Calculate the maximum secondary overcurrent protection for a 40kVA, 3-phase transformer with a secondary voltage of 240 volts.

Primary 40 kVA
Secondary 240 V 3-Phase
96.3 A
Secondary Overcurrent Protective Device → 125 A

Solution

Transformer secondary current 3-phase

$$I_{sec} = \frac{kVA \times 1,000}{E_{sec} \times 1.73}$$
$$= \frac{40 \times 1,000}{240 \times 1.73}$$
$$= 96.3 \text{ A}$$

Secondary overcurrent protection
Table 450.3(B)
Currents of 9 amperes or more column
Primary and secondary protection = 125%
Max. OCPD$_{sec}$ = I_{sec} × 125%
  = 96.3 × 1.25
  = 120.37 A
Table 450.3(B) Note 1
Next larger std. size permitted
240.6(A)
Next larger = 125 A
Answer: 125A max. OCPD$_{sec}$

PROBLEM 10-6

Calculate the maximum secondary overcurrent fuse protection for a single-phase, 2kVA transformer with a secondary voltage of 240 volts.

Primary 2 kVA
Secondary 240 V 1-Phase
Secondary Overcurrent Protective Device →

Solution

Transformer secondary current 3-phase

$$I_{sec} = \frac{kVA \times 1,000}{E_{sec}}$$
$$= \frac{2 \times 1,000}{240}$$
$$= 8.3 \text{ A}$$

Secondary overcurrent protection
Table 450.3(B)
Currents less than 9 amperes column
Secondary protection = 167%
Max. OCPD$_{sec}$ = I_{sec} × 167%
  = 8.3 × 1.67
  = 13.9 A
Table 450.3(B) Note 1
Does not apply, any less permitted
240.6(A)
Next smaller = 10 A
Answer: Fuse size of 13.9 A or less

PROBLEM 10-7

Calculate the maximum primary and secondary overcurrent protection and size of the primary THWN copper conductors.

- Primary Overcurrent Protective Device
- 3 AWG THWN Copper
- 480 V 3-Phase, 48.2 A
- Primary / Secondary
- 40 kVA
- 240 V 3-Phase, 96.3 A
- Secondary Overcurrent Protective Device

Solution

Calculation 1

Secondary overcurrent protection
I_{sec} = 96.3 A
Table 450.3(B)
  Currents of 9 amperes or more column
  Secondary protection = 125%
  Max. OCPD$_{sec}$ = I_{sec} × 125%
      = 96.3 × 1.25
      = 120.37 A
Table 450.3(B) Note 1
  Next larger std. size permitted
240.6(A)
  Next larger = 125 A
Answer: 125A Max. OCPD$_{sec}$

Calculation 2

Primary overcurrent protection
I_{pri} = 48.2 A
Table 450.3(B)
  Currents of 9 amperes or more column
  Primary and secondary protection = 250%
  OCPD$_{pri}$ = I_{pri} × 250%
      = 48.2 × 2.50
      = 120.5 A
Table 450.3(B) Note 1
  Does not apply, any less permitted
240.6(A)
  Next smaller = 110 A
Answer: 110A max. OCPD$_{pri}$

Calculation 3

Primary conductor size
  OCPD$_{pri}$ = 110 A
  Match conductor to OCPD
Table 310.16
  THWN copper column
  110 A = 2 AWG THWN
  2 AWG THWN = 115 A
  Therefore, it is protected at 110 A
Answer: 2 AWG THWN copper

10.1.4 Primary Protection at 250% and Secondary Protection at 125%

Two parts of **Table 450.3(B)** are considered in this situation. One part applies to overcurrent protection on the secondary side of the transformer. The second part applies to the overcurrent protection on the primary side of the transformer.

1. The secondary overcurrent protection is sized according to the 125% rule.
2. The primary overcurrent protective device is permitted to be set at not over 250% of the primary current.

Although the primary overcurrent protective device is permitted to be set up to 250% of the primary current, the transformer is still protected at 125% by the secondary overcurrent protective device. So in either scenario of primary-only protection or primary and secondary protection, the transformer is protected at 125%. With the primary overcurrent protection set at 250%, larger equipment and larger conductor sizes are required, which is not always desirable. A typical design practice is to set both primary and secondary protective devices at 125%, although the *NEC* does not specifically require this. **See Problem 10-7.**

10.1.5 Secondary Protection Using Multiple Overcurrent Devices

As pointed out in **Note 2** of **Table 450.3(B)**, multiple overcurrent protective devices, including fuses and circuit breakers, are allowed to be substituted for a single individual overcurrent protective device where the individual device is required for secondary protection according to **450.3(B)**.

Table 450.3(B) Note 2 permits overcurrent protection for the secondary of a transformer to consist of the following:

- Up to six overcurrent protective devices
- Grouped in one location
- Total device ratings not exceeding the allowed rating of a single overcurrent protective device

For example, if the calculated size of a circuit breaker or fuse used for the transformer secondary overcurrent protection is 200 amperes, it would also be permissible to use two 100-ampere or four 50-ampere overcurrent protective devices. **See Problem 10-8**.

The required disconnect for this transformer is not located within sight of the transformer location. Where a transformer disconnect is remotely located and not within sight, the transformer is required to be field marked with the location of the disconnecting means. Additionally, the remote disconnecting means is required to be lockable per **Section 110.25**.

10.1.6 Transformer Thermal Overload Protection

Thermal overload protection is sometimes built into the transformer by the manufacturer. This is also called self-contained protection (SCP). The thermal overload unit is sensitive to the heat generated within the transformer, which could damage the windings of the transformer. In case of dangerous overheating within the transformer, the thermal overload operates very much like the overload heaters in a magnetic switch and opens the control circuit to the overcurrent protective device protecting the circuit to the primary windings of the transformer. The primary feeder overcurrent protection is sized according to the impedance (Z) of the transformer. The impedance of a transformer is marked on the nameplate of the transformer.

PROBLEM 10-8

Transformer Secondary

300 Amp Calculated Maximum Overcurrent Protection Device

Two 150 Amp Permitted

Six 50 Amp Permitted

What is the maximum number of 50-ampere circuit breakers permitted to be used as overcurrent protection on the secondary of a 480//208-volt, 3-phase, 75kVA transformer? The transformer primary is protected by an overcurrent protective device set at not more than 250% of the rated transformer current.

Solution

Secondary overcurrent protection
3-phase

$$I_{sec} = \frac{kVA \times 1{,}000}{E_{sec} \times 1.73}$$

$$= \frac{75 \times 1{,}000}{208 \times 1.73}$$

$$= 208.4 \text{ A}$$

Table 450.3(B)
 Currents of 9 amperes or more column
 Primary and secondary protection = 125%
 Max. OCPD$_{sec}$ = $I_{sec} \times 125\%$
  = 208.4 × 1.25
  = 260.5 A

Table 450.3(B) Note 1
 Next larger std. size permitted
240.6(A)
 Next larger = 300 A

$$\text{Number of 50A circuit breakers} = \frac{OCPD_{sec}}{50}$$

$$= \frac{300}{50}$$

$$= \text{Six 50A circuit breakers}$$

Answer: Six 50A circuit breakers

The following values are listed in **Note 3** of **Table 450.3(B)**:

Where Z is 6% or less

$$\text{Max. OCPD}_{pri} = I_{pri} \times 6$$

Where Z is over 6%, but less than 10%

$$\text{Max. OCPD}_{pri} = I_{pri} \times 4$$

See Problems 10-9 and 10-10.

PROBLEM 10-9

Calculate the maximum standard-size overcurrent protection permitted for the transformer feeder with built-in thermal overload protection in the primary of the transformer. The transformer impedance is 3%.

Solution

Primary overcurrent protection
I_{pri} = 54.2 A
Table 450.3(B) Note 3
  Transformer Z is 6% or less
  Max. OCPD$_{pri}$ = $I_{pri} \times 6$
    = 54.2 × 6
    = 325.2 A
Table 450.3(B) Note 1
  Does not apply, any less permitted
240.6(A)
  Next smaller = 300 A
Answer: 300A max. OCPD$_{pri}$ or less

PROBLEM 10-10

Calculate the feeder overcurrent protection permitted for the transformer with built-in thermal overload protection for the primary with an 8% impedance rating.

Solution

Primary overcurrent protection
I_{pri} = 54 A
Table 450.3(B) Note 3
  Transformer Z is over 6%, but less than 10%
  Max. OCPD$_{pri}$ = $I_{pri} \times 4$
    = 54.2 × 4
    = 216.8 A
Table 450.3(B) Note 1
  Does not apply, any less permitted
240.6(A)
  Next smaller = 200 A
Answer: 200A max. OCPD$_{pri}$ or less

10.1.7 Summary

For installation of a transformer rated 1,000 volts, nominal, or less, the first consideration is for overcurrent protection of the transformer primary and secondary windings. Often the overcurrent protection is located remotely from the transformer and serves a dual function of protecting both the transformer windings and the supply conductors to the transformer.

The following is a summary of **Table 450.3(B)**:

1. If the primary current rating is nine amperes or more, overcurrent protection is permitted to be 125% of the rated primary current.
   OCPD selection – See **Note 1**. Use the next higher standard size.
2. If the primary current rating is less than nine amperes, overcurrent protection is permitted to be 167% of the primary current.
   OCPD selection - Use the 167% value or any lower size.

3. If the primary current rating is less than two amperes, overcurrent protection is permitted to be 300% of the primary current.
   OCPD selection - Use the 300% value or any lower size.
4. If the overcurrent protection for the primary windings is located remotely from the transformer, the overcurrent protective device is required to protect both the transformer primary winding and the conductors supplying that transformer primary.
5. If the secondary current rating is nine amperes or more, overcurrent protection is permitted to be 125% of the rated secondary current.
   OCPD selection – See **Note 1**. Use the next higher standard size.
6. If the secondary current is less than nine amperes, overcurrent protection is permitted to be up to 167% of the rated secondary current.
   OCPD selection - Use the 167% value or any lower size.
7. If the secondary windings are protected at 125%, then the overcurrent protection on the primary is permitted to be 250% of the rated primary current, and it will protect both the primary windings and the transformer primary conductors.
   OCPD selection, secondary – See **Note 1**. Use the next higher standard size.
   OCPD selection, primary – Use the 250% value or any lower size.
8. A maximum of six overcurrent devices is permitted for the protection of the secondary, provided the total rating of the six overcurrent devices does not exceed the value required of a single device.
9. Feeder protection with thermal overload and 6% or less impedance requires not more than six times the primary current.
   OCPD selection, primary feeder - Use the 600% value or any lower size.
10. Feeder protection with thermal overload and more than 6%, but less than 10% impedance, requires not more than four times the primary current.
    OCPD selection, primary feeder - Use the 400% value or any lower size.

10.2 240.21(B) FEEDER TAPS AND 240.21(C) TRANSFORMER SECONDARY CONDUCTORS

The location of the overcurrent protection for conductors, as required by **Section 240.21**, may be applied in conjunction with transformer overcurrent protection.

The basic rule of **Section 240.21** is that an overcurrent protective device is required to be located at the point where a conductor receives its supply.

The primary of a transformer typically receives its supply from a feeder overcurrent protective device located remotely from the transformer and supplies feeder conductors connected to the primary of the transformer. Although not as common, a transformer may also be supplied by a primary feeder tap.

The secondary of a transformer is the source of supply for the secondary conductors. Generally, the overcurrent protection for the secondary conductors is required to be located at the transformer; however, this is typically not practicable. The permissive rules in **240.21(C)** permit the overcurrent protection for the secondary conductors to be located at a point other than the supply.

For transformer secondary conductors, there are six permissive rules. Each permissive rule has a number of specific requirements that are required to be met before the conductors can be installed without overcurrent protection at the point at which the conductor receives its supply. Each of the permissive rules should be looked at individually as they apply to the primary or secondary of the transformer.

10.2.1 240.21(C)(1) Primary Protection, Including Secondary Protection

NEC **240.21(C)(1)** applies to the secondary conductors of a transformer. The first statement in the requirement stipulates that the transformer secondary is not permitted to be protected by the primary overcurrent protective device unless it is one of the following transformer connections:

- Single-phase, 2-wire, single-voltage secondary
- Delta-delta, 3-phase, 3-wire, single-voltage secondary

Secondary conductors, as such, are not limited in length. However, if the primary overcurrent protective device is used to also protect the secondary, the following are required:

1. The primary overcurrent is required to be in accordance with **Section 450.3**.
2. The primary overcurrent protection is required not to exceed the value determined by multiplying the ampacity of the secondary conductors by the secondary-to-primary voltage ratio.

Examples of application:

1. Single-phase, 2-wire, 480-volt primary with a single-phase, 2-wire, 120-volt ungrounded secondary
2. Single-phase, 2-wire, 480-volt primary with a single-phase, 2-wire, 120-volt secondary with one conductor grounded
3. Single-phase, 2-wire, 120-volt primary with a single-phase, 2-wire, 120-volt ungrounded secondary used as an isolation transformer
4. Delta, 3-phase, 480-volt primary with a 240-volt, 3-phase, 3-wire delta secondary

See Problem 10-11.

NEC **240.21(C)(1)** cannot be applied to a transformer with a single-phase, 2-wire, 480-volt or 277-volt primary and a 120/240-volt, 3-wire secondary, as is commonly used for 120-volt receptacles with a 277/480-volt system. Nor can the rule be applied to a 480-volt delta primary and a 120/208-volt, 4-wire wye secondary. Summarizing the calculation requirements of **240.21(C)(1)**, the following two rules apply:

1. The rating of the primary OCPD cannot exceed the requirements of **Table 450.3(B)**.
2. The rating of the primary OCPD cannot exceed the value of the secondary conductor ampacity multiplied by the voltage ratio of the secondary voltage divided by the primary voltage.

10.2.2 Ten-Foot Feeder Tap Rule — Transformer Primary Conductors 240.21(B)(1)

The basic rule for overcurrent protection of conductors requires the overcurrent protective device to be located at the point the conductor receives its supply. **Section 240.21** lists several permissive rules for the installation of tap conductors without overcurrent protection. *NEC* **240.21(B)(1), Feeder Taps**, permits a 10-foot tap from a feeder without overcurrent protection on the primary side of the transformer, provided all of the following conditions are met:

1. The tap conductors are not over 10 feet in length
2. The ampacity of the tap conductors is not less than:
   a. The combined calculated loads on the circuit supplied by the tap
   b. The current rating of the equipment containing an overcurrent protective device supplied
3. The tap conductors do not extend beyond the transformer, switchgear, panelboard, or disconnecting means they supply
4. Except at the point of connection, the conductors are protected and enclosed in a raceway
5. For field installations, if the tap conductors leave the enclosure where the tap is made, the ampacity of the tap conductors cannot be less than one-tenth of the rating of the overcurrent protective device protecting the feeder conductors

PROBLEM 10-11

A single-phase 10kVA transformer has a 480-volt, 20.8-ampere, 2-wire primary and a 120-volt, 83.3-ampere, 2-wire secondary. Calculate the primary overcurrent protection, which also serves as the secondary overcurrent protection for this single-phase, 2-wire transformer.

Primary 480 V 20.8 A
10 kVA
Secondary 120 V 83.3 A

Solution

Calculation 1
Primary overcurrent protection
Table 450.3(B)
  Currents of 9 amperes or more column
  Primary protection only = 125%
  Max. OCPD$_{pri}$ = I_{pri} × 125%
           = 20.8 × 1.25
           = 26 A
Table 450.3(B) Note 1
  Next larger std. size permitted
240.6(A)
  Next larger = 30 A
Answer: 30A OCPD$_{pri}$
Note: The use of a 25A OCPD$_{pri}$ is not prohibited as an alternate (less than maximum) solution.

Calculation 2
Secondary conductor ampacity
I_{sec} = 83.3 A
Table 310.16
  THWN copper column
  83.3 A = 4 AWG THWN
  4 AWG THWN = 85A ampacity
Answer: Ampacity of 85 A

Calculation 3
Secondary-to-primary voltage ratio

$V_{ratio} = \dfrac{E_{sec}}{E_{pri}}$
$= \dfrac{120}{480}$
$= 0.25$

Answer: 0.25 voltage ratio

Calculation 4
Verification No. 1
  Confirm acceptable secondary conductor size
  4 AWG THWN = 85 A
  OCPD$_{pri}$ = I_{sec} × V_{ratio}
       = 85 × 0.25
       = 21.25 A
  OCPD$_{pri}$ (30 A or 25 A) rating exceeds 21.25 A
  Verification No. 1 fails
Verification No. 2
  Increase size secondary conductors
Table 310.16
  THWN copper column
  3 AWG THWN = 100 A
  OCPD$_{pri}$ = I_{sec} × V_{ratio}
       = 100 × 0.25
       = 25 A
  OCPD$_{pri}$ (25 A) rating does not exceed 25 A
  Verification No. 2 is acceptable installation
  OCPD$_{pri}$ 25 A, 10 AWG on primary and 3 AWG on secondary
Verification No. 3
  Increase secondary conductors to 1 AWG
Table 310.16
  THWN copper column
  1 AWG THWN = 130 A
  OCPD$_{pri}$ = I_{sec} × V_{ratio}
       = 130 × 0.25
       = 33 A
  Use 30 A OCPD$_{pri}$
  30A OCPD$_{pri}$, 10 AWG THWN copper primary conductors, and
    1 AWG THWN copper secondary conductors
  Verification No. 3 is an acceptable installation
Answer: OCPD$_{pri}$ 25 A, 10 AWG on primary and 3 AWG THWN copper on secondary
Answer: OCPD$_{pri}$ 30 A, 10 AWG on primary and 1 AWG THWN copper on secondary

PROBLEM 10-12

Calculate the minimum size tap conductor using THWN copper, and the maximum setting of the overcurrent protective device on the primary feeder for a 10kVA, 480-volt, 3-phase transformer with a full-load primary current of 12 amperes.

Diagram: Feeder with 10 ft Tap to Primary Overcurrent Protection Device, 480 V 3 Phase, 12 A, 10 kVA transformer.

Solution

Calculation 1
Primary overcurrent protection
Table 450.3(B)
  Currents of 9 amperes or more column
  Primary protection = 125%
  Max. OCPD$_{pri}$ = I_{pri} × 125%
           = 12 × 1.25
           = 15 A
  15 A is a standard size
Answer: 15A Max. OCPD$_{pri}$

Calculation 2
Primary conductor size
  Tap conductor (TC) amps = I_{pri}
                = 12 A
Table 310.16
  THWN copper column
  12 A = 14 AWG THWN copper
  240.21(B) indicates that 240.4(D) does not apply
  240.4(E) applies
  14 AWG THWN = 20 A
Answer: 14 AWG THWN copper

Calculation 3
Feeder CB ratio compliance
240.21(B)(1)(4)
  Feeder CB cannot exceed ten times the tap conductor ampacity
  Tap conductor ampacity
  14 AWG THWN = 20 A
  Feeder OCPD max = 20 A × 10
             = 200 A
  Feeder CB cannot exceed 200 A
Answer: Feeder OCPD cannot exceed 200 A
Comment: Without the limitation of the "one-tenth" rule, in 240.21(B)(1)(4), a small conductor could be severely damaged by high let-through current of a larger overcurrent protective device. For example, if an insulated 14 AWG conductor were on the load side of a 400-ampere circuit breaker, the insulated 14 AWG conductor could "see" a maximum of 400 amperes for a long period of time without ever tripping. Four hundred amperes on an insulated 14 AWG conductor will far exceed the damage curve of that conductor and may cause a fire. So, for the case of a 400-ampere feeder overcurrent protective device, instead of an insulated 14 AWG conductor, at least an insulated 8 AWG (40-ampere) conductor would be necessary.

According to **240.21(B)**, the provisions of **240.4(B)** do not apply to feeder tap conductors. Also, the small conductor requirements of **240.4(D)** do not apply since they are specifically mentioned in **240.4(E)(3)**. **See Problem 10-12.**

10.2.3 Ten-Foot Transformer Tap Rule — Transformer Secondary Conductors

NEC **240.21(C)(2)** covers transformer secondary conductors not over 10 feet long and permits them to be without overcurrent protection on the secondary side of the transformer provided all of the following conditions are met:

1. The length of secondary conductors is limited to 10 feet.
2. The ampacity of the secondary conductors is not less than:
   a. The combined calculated load served
   b. The rating of the equipment containing an overcurrent protective device or the overcurrent protective device at its termination
3. The tap conductors do not extend beyond the panel or equipment supplied.
4. The conductors are protected and enclosed in a raceway.
5. For field installations, if the secondary conductors leave the enclosure where the connections are made, the rating of the overcurrent protective device protecting the primary of the transformer, multiplied by the primary-to-secondary transformer voltage ratio, cannot exceed 10 times the ampacity of the secondary conductor.

Note that the secondary conductors of a transformer are not considered tap conductors. The secondary conductors should be considered feeders that originate at the secondary of the transformer.

The 10-foot secondary conductor rule requires secondary conductors to terminate on a set of fuses or a circuit breaker. The 10-foot tap rule no longer allows conductors to land directly onto the main-lug-only type switchboards or panelboards. Now, all other secondary tap rules require conductors to terminate on a single set of fuses or a single circuit breaker. **See Problem 10-13.**

CHAPTER 10 TRANSFORMER OVERCURRENT PROTECTION 243

PROBLEM 10-13

The following calculation illustrates an alternate or different use of the 10-foot secondary conductor rule of 240.21(C)(2). The drawing shows two separate sets of 10-foot secondary conductors used on the secondary side of a 120/208-volt, 3-phase, 4-wire, 112.5kVA transformer. One set of secondary conductors supplies a panelboard protected by a 300-ampere main circuit breaker. Another set of secondary conductors supplies a 60-ampere fusible disconnect switch. Both transformer primary and secondary overcurrent protection are to be used according to Table 450.3(B).

Solution

Calculation 1
Primary overcurrent protection
I_{pri} = 135 A
Table 450.3(B)
  Currents of 9 amperes or more column
  Primary and secondary protection = 250%
  Max. OCPD$_{pri}$ = I_{pri} × 250%
    = 135 × 2.5
    = 337.5 A
Table 450.3(B) Note 1
  Does not apply, use next smaller
240.6(A)
  Next smaller = 300A fuse or circuit breaker
  Answer: 300A max. OCPD$_{pri}$

Calculation 2
Primary conductor size
  Match conductors to 300A OCPD$_{pri}$
Table 310.16
  THWN copper column
  350 kcmil THWN copper = 310 A
  Answer: 350 kcmil THWN copper per phase

Calculation 3
Secondary conductors (300A circuit)
240.21(C)(2)
  300A OCPD$_{sec}$
240.4(B) not permitted
  300A minimum ampacity
Table 310.16
  THWN copper column
  350 kcmil THWN copper = 310 A
  Answer: 350 kcmil THWN copper per phase and neutral

Calculation 4
Secondary overcurrent protection
  60A fused circuit
215.3
  Maximum calculated load is 60 A
  Maximum OCPD is 60 A
  Answer: 60A max. OCPD$_{sec}$

Calculation 5
Secondary conductors
  60A circuit
240.21(C)(2)(4)
  Max. ratio for field installation
  Max. ratio = $^1/_{10}$ × OCPD$_{pri}$
    = 0.10 × 300
    = 30 A
Calculate primary-to-secondary voltage ratio
$$V_{ratio} = \frac{E_{pri}}{E_{sec}}$$
$$= \frac{480}{208}$$
$$= 2.31$$

OCPD$_{pri}$ × V_{ratio}
30 A × 2.31 = 69 A
Table 310.16
  4 AWG THWN copper rated 85 A
  Answer: 4 AWG THWN copper (60A circuit)

Calculation 6
Table 450.3(B) Note 2
  Verify maximum secondary overcurrent protection is not exceeded
Step 1
  Calculate max. value of a single OCPD$_{sec}$
  I_{sec} = 312 A
Table 450.3(B)
  Currents of 9 amperes or more column
  Secondary protection = 125%
  OCPD$_{sec}$ = I_{sec} × 125%
    = 312 × 1.25
    = 390 A
Table 450.3(B) Note 1
  Next larger std. size permitted
240.6(A)
  Next larger = 400 A
  Answer: 400 A
Step 2
  Verify total max. OCPD$_{sec}$ does not exceed 400 A by adding both OCPD$_{sec}$
  300A OCPD$_{sec}$ + 60A OCPD$_{sec}$ = 360 A
  Answer: Total max. OCPD$_{sec}$ not exceeded

Comment: For a configuration such as this example, a load calculation for these two combined secondary circuits must be done according to Article 220. In addition, all loads must be calculated at 100% of the noncontinuous load and 125% of the continuous load according to 215.2(A)(1) for conductors and 215.3 for overcurrent protection. Finally, the total calculated load cannot exceed the maximum permitted load on the selected transformer.

PROBLEM 10-14

Calculate the overcurrent protection and conductor sizes permitted for the 75kVA transformer using the 10-foot secondary conductor rule to supply a panelboard.

Diagram: 3-Phase 480 V, 90 A primary feeding a 75 kVA transformer; Secondary 3-Phase 4-Wire 120/208 V, 208 A; 10 ft Tap to a Panelboard with 200 A Main Circuit Breaker.

Solution

Calculation 1
Primary overcurrent protection
$I_{pri} = 90$ A
Table 450.3(B)
  Currents of 9 amperes or more column
  Primary protection = 125%
  Max. $OCPD_{pri} = I_{pri} \times 125\%$
       $= 90 \times 1.25$
       $= 113$ A
Table 450.3(B) Note 1
  Next larger std. size permitted
240.6(A)
  Next larger = 125 A
Answer: 125A max. $OCPD_{pri}$

Calculation 2
Primary conductors
Table 310.16
  THWN copper column
  113 A = 2 AWG THWN copper
  2 AWG THWN = 115 A
240.4(B)
  Next larger higher rating permitted
  OCPD for conductor = 125 A
Table 310.16
  THWN copper column
  115 A = 2 AWG THWN copper
Answer: 2 AWG THWN copper

The 125 ampere overcurrent protection will protect the conductors supplying the transformer and the primary windings of the transformer.

Calculation 3
Secondary overcurrent protection
$I_{sec} = 208$ A
Table 450.3(B) and 408.36
  Currents of 9 amperes or more column
  Secondary protection = 125%
  $OCPD_{sec} = I_{sec} \times 125\%$
       $= 208 \times 1.25$
       $= 260$ A
Table 450.3(B) Note 1
  Next larger std. size permitted
240.6(A)
  Next larger = 300 A
  Max. $OCPD_{sec} = 300$ A
  But 200A panel is less than secondary full-load current
  200A $OCPD_{sec}$ is the max. permitted
Answer: 200A max. $OCPD_{sec}$

Calculation 4
Secondary conductors
  $OCPD_{sec} = 200$ A
Table 310.16
  THWN copper column
  200 A = 3/0 AWG THWN copper
Answer: 3/0 AWG THWN copper

Comment: In this particular case, the 200-ampere main overcurrent protection in the panelboard has three responsibilities:
1. Protect the transformer secondary windings
2. Limit the current on the 3/0 AWG 10-foot secondary conductors to 200 amperes
3. Protect the 200-ampere panelboard

CHAPTER 10   TRANSFORMER OVERCURRENT PROTECTION   245

A separately derived system supplying a main circuit breaker panelboard using the 10-foot transformer tap rule must comply with **408.36**.

10.2.4 Ten-Foot Transformer Tap Rule — Supplying a Panelboard

If the 10-foot tap rule is used to supply a panelboard, **Section 408.36** requires an overcurrent protective device to protect the panelboard. It permits the required overcurrent protective device to be located on any point in the feeder circuit or within the panelboard itself.

10.2.5 Twenty-Five-Foot Feeder Tap Rule — Transformer Primary 240.21(B)(2)

NEC **240.21(B)(2), Feeder Taps,** is a permissive rule permitting a maximum conductor tap length of 25 feet without overcurrent protection at the point where the conductor receives its supply. This permissive rule is applicable to the primary of a transformer when all of the following conditions are met:

1. The tap is not over 25 feet in length.
2. The ampacity of the tap conductors is at least one-third the rating of the overcurrent protective device protecting the conductors.
3. The tap conductors terminate in a single set of fuses or a circuit breaker, which will limit the current on the tap conductors.
4. The tap conductors are protected from physical damage.

There is more than one solution for these calculations. The final solution should always be verified for compliance with all *Code* text. See Problems 10-14 and 10-15.

PROBLEM 10-15

A 300-ampere feeder is tapped to supply a 75kVA transformer. The total length of the tap leading to the primary circuit breaker does not exceed 25 feet. Calculate the minimum THWN copper conductor size of the tap conductor leading to the 75kVA transformer. Also, calculate the size of the primary circuit breaker protecting the transformer using the primary-only protection rule of Table 450.3(B).

Solution

Calculation 1
Primary overcurrent protection at transformer
Table 450.3(B)
  Currents of 9 amperes or more column
  Primary protection = 125%
  $OCPD_{pri} = I_{pri} \times 125\%$
          $= 90 \times 1.25$
          $= 113$ A
Table 450.3(B) Note 1
  Next larger std. size permitted
240.6(A)
  Next larger = 125 A
  $OCPD_{pri} = 125$A circuit breaker
Answer: 125A circuit breaker

Calculation 2
Primary tap conductor size
  125A circuit breaker
Table 310.16
  2 AWG THWN copper or 1 AWG THW copper
Answer: 2 AWG THWN copper wire rated 115 A

Calculation 3
Verify primary tap conductor size
240.21(B)(2)(1)
  Not less than ⅓ rating of feeder CB
  300 ÷ 3 = 100 A
  Primary tap conductor must be 100 A or greater
  Primary tap conductor = 2 AWG THWN copper
Answer: 2 AWG THWN copper is sufficient

Grounded, Solidly

Solidly Grounded

Grounded Through Inductor

Grounded Through Resistor

While **Section 250.36** permits high-impedance grounded systems with a number of conditions and typically with the use of a resistor or impedance device, most transformers are solidly grounded as required in **250.20**. See also **250.30** for grounding of separately derived systems.

10.2.6 Twenty-Five-Foot Transformer Tap Rule — Transformer Secondary Conductors 240.21(C)(6)

NEC **240.21(C)(6)** is what is commonly referred to as the 25-foot rule for secondary conductors of a transformer. Like the others, this rule is comprised of several requirements:

1. Secondary conductors are not over 25 feet long.
2. The secondary conductor ampacity is not less than the primary-to-secondary voltage ratio multiplied by one-third the rating of the primary OCPD.
3. Secondary conductors terminate in a single circuit breaker or set of fuses, which limits the current to the ampacity of the secondary conductor.

PROBLEM 10-16

A 3-phase 80kVA transformer with a full-load secondary current of 193 amperes supplies a 240-volt, 3-phase, 3-wire panelboard equipped with a 250-ampere main circuit breaker. The transformer secondary conductors supplying the panelboard do not exceed 25 feet in length. Determine if the 250-ampere circuit breaker complies with Table 450.3(B) secondary protection and calculate the size of the copper THWN secondary conductors supplying the transformer.

Solution

Calculation 1

Secondary overcurrent protection

$$I_{sec} = \frac{kVA \times 1{,}000}{E_{sec} \times 1.73}$$

$$= \frac{80 \times 1{,}000}{240 \times 1.73}$$

$$= 193 \text{ A}$$

Table 450.3(B)
 Currents of 9 amperes or more column
 Secondary protection = 125%
  Max. OCPD$_{sec}$ = I_{sec} × 125%
   = 193 × 1.25
   = 241.25 A
Table 450.3(B) Note 1
 Next larger std. size permitted
 240.6(A)
  Next larger = 250 A
Answer: 250A max. OCPD$_{sec}$

Calculation 2

Secondary conductors
Table 310.16
 THWN copper column
 250 kcmil THWN = 255 A
 250 kcmil will carry 193A secondary
Answer: 250 kcmil THWN copper

CHAPTER 10 TRANSFORMER OVERCURRENT PROTECTION

4. Secondary conductors are protected from physical damage, for example by being enclosed in an approved raceway.

See Problem 10-16.

10.2.7 Outside — Secondary Conductors 240.21(C)(4)

NEC **240.21(C)(4)** is a permissive rule for outside secondary conductors and applies to the secondary conductors of a transformer installed with the following limitations:

1. Conductors must be installed outdoors except at the point of load termination.
2. Conductors must be protected from physical damage.
3. Conductors are required to be terminated on a single overcurrent protective device, which will limit the load to the ampacity of the conductors.
4. The overcurrent protective device must be an integral part of a disconnecting means or be adjacent to the disconnecting means.
5. The disconnecting means must be readily accessible outside of the building or inside the nearest point of entrance of the conductors, or it must be installed in accordance with **Section 230.6** at the nearest point of entrance of the conductors.

An example of use would be a 480-volt feeder to a second building on the premises where a transformer is set outside the second building. The transformer secondary conductors terminate in a circuit breaker either outside the building or inside the building. Note: **240.21(C)(4)** does not limit the length of outside secondary conductors.

Power supply to a sign panelboard via a transformer would use **240.21(C)(6)**.

A delta connection has the wires from the ends of each coil connected end-to-end to form a closed loop.

PROBLEM 10-17

What size THWN copper secondary conductors are needed for a 45kVA, 3-phase, 480-volt primary and a 208/120-volt secondary pad-mounted transformer set outside of a second building? The secondary feeder conductors terminate immediately inside the building, in a single circuit breaker, for secondary overcurrent protection.

Solution

Secondary conductor size

$$I_{sec} = \frac{kVA \times 1{,}000}{E_{sec} \times 1.73}$$

$$= \frac{45 \times 1{,}000}{208 \times 1.73}$$

$$= 125 \text{ A}$$

Table 450.3(B)(2)
  Currents of 9 amperes or more column
  Secondary protection = 125%
  $OCPD_{sec} = I_{sec} \times 125\%$
  $= 125 \times 1.25$
  $= 156.25$ A
Table 450.3(B) Note 1
  Next larger std. size permitted
240.6(A)
  Next larger = 175 A
Table 310.16
  THWN copper column
  175 A = 2/0 AWG THWN
Answer: 2/0 AWG THWN copper

10.3 DEDICATED TRANSFORMERS USED IN FIRE PUMP CIRCUITS

NEC **695.5(A)** and **695.5(B)** give special attention to fire pump installations with a transformer dedicated to supplying only the power to a fire pump and its related equipment. No overcurrent protection is permitted on the secondary side of the transformer. The primary overcurrent protection rating or setting must be large enough to carry all of the following loads:

1. The locked-rotor current (LRC) of the fire pump motor(s)
2. The locked-rotor current of the pressure maintenance or jockey pump motor(s) when connected to this power supply
3. 100% of the current(s) of any associated fire pump accessory equipment when connected to this power supply

See Problems 10-17 and 10-18.

CHAPTER 10 TRANSFORMER OVERCURRENT PROTECTION

PROBLEM 10-18

Calculate the minimum primary overcurrent protection for a 480/240-volt dedicated fire pump transformer where it supplies a 240-volt, 3-phase, 25-horsepower fire pump; a 240-volt, 3-phase, 5-horsepower pressure maintenance pump; and 3-phase accessory equipment with a full-load rating of 60 amperes.

Solution

Primary overcurrent protection
 Using locked-rotor current (LRC)
 LRC for 3-phase motors
 Table 430.251(B)
  230 V column
  LRC of a 25 hp = 365 A
  LRC of a 5 hp = 92 A
 Min. I_{sec} = LRC motor 1 + LRC motor 2 + I (accessories)
  = 365 + 92 + 60
  = 517 A
Transfer I_{sec} (secondary current) to I_{pri} (primary current)
By using secondary-to-primary voltage ratio

$$V_{ratio} = \frac{E_{sec}}{E_{pri}}$$
$$= \frac{240}{480}$$
$$= 0.5$$

Min. I_{pri} = Min. $I_{sec} \times V_{ratio}$
 = 517 × 0.5
 = 258.5 A
Min. $OCPD_{pri}$ = I_{pri}
 = 258.5 A
240.4(B)
Next larger rating permitted
Min. $OCPD_{pri}$ = 300 A
Answer: 300A min. $OCPD_{pri}$

DEFINITIONS AND TERMS

Overcurrent - Any current in excess of the rated current of equipment or the ampacity of a conductor. It may result from overload, short circuit, or ground fault. [**70**:100]

Overload - Operation of equipment in excess of normal, full-load rating, or of a conductor in excess of rated ampacity that, when it persists for a sufficient length of time, would cause damage or dangerous overheating. A fault, such as a short circuit or ground fault, is not an overload. [**70**:100]

Tap Conductor - A conductor, other than a service conductor, that has overcurrent protection ahead of its point of supply that exceeds the value permitted for similar conductors that are protected as described elsewhere in **240.4**. [**70**:240.2] The application of tap conductor is limited to **Article 240**, and does not apply to other areas of the *Code*.

Transformer - An individual transformer, single- or polyphase, identified by a single nameplate, unless otherwise indicated in [**Article 450**]. [**70**:450.2]

SUMMARY

For transformers rated 1,000 volts, nominal, or less, protection is required in accordance with **Table 450.3(B)**. As provided in the table, the rated transformer currents are multiplied by the appropriate percentage in the table to give a maximum rating or setting of the overcurrent protective device. Generally, the calculated value is the maximum; however, **Note 1** of the table permits the 125% calculation and an increase to the next standard size. Two methods of protection for a transformer are permitted as primary-only protection and primary and secondary protection, and it is left to the *Code* user to decide which method to use.

Once overcurrent protective devices are selected, the primary conductors are selected based upon the overcurrent protective device and the use of **240.4** for the protection of conductors. For the secondary conductors, two general rules are commonly used: a 10-foot and 25-foot rule, as provided in **240.21(C)**. While the primary transformer conductors are permitted to use the rule of **240.4(B)**, transformer secondary conductors are not allowed to use the permissive rule of **240.4(B)** but are required to have an ampacity of not less than the rating of the overcurrent protective device they supply. Transformer installations supplying fire pump motors are sized to allow the fire pump motor to run until a locked-rotor condition.

REVIEW QUESTIONS

1. A transformer rated 1,000 volts, nominal, or less, with a primary current of more than nine amperes, is to be provided with primary-only protection. To select the maximum size, which one of the following is permitted by **Table 450.3(B)**?
   a. Primary current multiplied by 125%
   b. Primary current multiplied by 125% and, based on the result, increased to the next higher standard size
   c. Primary current multiplied by 250%
   d. Primary current multiplied by 250% and, based on the result, decreased to the next lower standard size

2. A primary overcurrent protective device will protect which two items?
   a. The feeder supplying the primary overcurrent protective device and the secondary conductors
   b. The primary and secondary conductors
   c. The transformer windings and the primary conductors supplying the transformer
   d. The transformer windings and the secondary conductors from the transformer

3. A transformer rated 1,000 volts, nominal, or less, with a primary current of more than nine amperes, is to be provided with primary and secondary protection. In order to select the maximum standard size primary overcurrent protective device, which is permitted by **Table 450.3(B)**?
   a. Primary current multiplied by 125%
   b. Primary current multiplied by 125% and, based on the result, increased to the next higher standard size
   c. Primary current multiplied by 250%
   d. Primary current multiplied by 250% and, based on the result, decreased to the next lower standard size

4. A transformer rated 1,000 volts, nominal, or less, with a secondary current of more than nine amperes, is to be provided with primary and secondary protection. In order to select the maximum size secondary overcurrent protective device, which is permitted by **Table 450.3(B)**?
   a. Secondary current multiplied by 125%
   b. Secondary current multiplied by 125% and, based on the result, increased to the next higher standard size
   c. Secondary current multiplied by 167%
   d. Secondary current multiplied by 167% and, based on the result, decreased to the next lower standard size

5. Which one of the following transformers would permit the use of the primary overcurrent protective device to protect the secondary conductors?
   a. A single-phase, 480/120 V transformer
   b. A single-phase, 480//120/240 V transformer
   c. A 3-phase, 480//120/240 V transformer
   d. A 3-phase, 480//208Y/120 V transformer

6. A single-phase transformer with a primary current of 3.5 amperes is permitted to be protected by which maximum size fuse when providing primary-only protection?
   a. 4.4A fuse
   b. 5.8A fuse
   c. 6A fuse
   d. 10A fuse

7. A transformer is installed with the secondary conductors run inside a building to supply a panelboard. What is the maximum permitted length of the transformer secondary conductors?
   a. 10'
   b. 25'
   c. No restriction provided the raceway from the transformer to the panelboard is a maximum of 25' in length
   d. There is no restriction in length

8. Transformer secondary conductors that are 25 feet in length are required to land in __?__.
   a. a main-lug-only panelboard
   b. a single circuit breaker
   c. a single set of fuses
   d. either b. or c.

9. A dry-type transformer supplies a main circuit breaker panelboard. The rating of the main breaker is 150 amperes. If the transformer secondary conductors are no more than ten feet in length, what minimum size copper THWN secondary conductors are required to supply the panelboard?
   a. 1 AWG THWN
   b. 1/0 AWG THWN
   c. 2/0 AWG THWN
   d. 3/0 AWG THWN

10. The primary overcurrent protective device installed for protection of a transformer supplying a fire pump installation shall be sized by __?__.
    a. 125% of the transformer primary current
    b. 600% of the transformer primary current
    c. the sum of the fire pump motor(s) locked-rotor current, pressure maintenance pump motor(s), and associated fire pump accessory equipment
    d. the sum of the fire pump motor(s), pressure maintenance pump motor(s), and associated fire pump accessory equipment

CHAPTER 11
CABLE TRAY

Cable tray calculations and new cable tray fill tables are used to determine the proper cable tray fill using single- or multiconductor cables in different types of cable trays for conductors rated 2,000 volts or less. The standard cable tray sizes (based upon inside width) are listed in the first column of **Table 392.22(A)**. According to this table, cable tray sizes are related to both the "sum of diameters of cables placed within the tray" as well as "the cross-sectional area of fill in the cable tray." To determine single-conductor cable diameters and cross-sectional areas, use **Table 5** of **Chapter 9** for concentric conductors and **Table 5A** for compact conductors.

The types of cable tray include ladder, ventilated and solid-bottom trough, ventilated and solid-bottom channel, and wire mesh tray.

Fill calculations are somewhat similar to conduit and wireway fill calculations, in that tray fill calculations follow the tables found in **Section 392.22** and the new cable tray fill tables provided in **Annex C**. When calculating the maximum conductor fill for a circular raceway, the most commonly-used column for those calculations is the 40% fill column of **Chapter 9, Table 4**. Therefore, Column 1 of **Table 392.22(A)** can be compared to the 40% column of **Chapter 9, Table 4**.

Ampacity calculations of single- and multiconductor cables are generally more liberal than the calculations for wiring methods in the *National Electrical Code* (*NEC*) **Chapter 3**. The ampacity of the conductors installed in cable trays is based upon the installation of the conductors being made according to **392.80(A)(1)** for multiconductor cables and **392.80(B)(1)** for single-conductor cables with few variations. Final ampacity calculations also include **110.14(C)(1)** regarding terminal temperature limitations. The final ampacities for cables in cable trays may require stepping down to the ampacities of

OBJECTIVES

- Calculate cable tray fills for single-conductor and multiconductor cables in various types of cable trays.

- Determine the ampacity of single-conductor and multiconductor cables for given cables, conductors, and cable tray installation arrangements.

- Demonstrate how to calculate cable tray fills for multiconductor control cables, signal cables, and any mixture of cables.

- For an existing cable tray, determine the presence of additional space within the cable tray and show the necessary steps to place additional cables into the cable tray.

TABLE OF CONTENTS

11.1 CABLE TRAY FILL CALCULATIONS FOR MULTICONDUCTOR INSTALLATIONS — 254

- .1 Multiconductor, Single-Layer, Ventilated Tray — 256
- .2 Multiconductor, More Than One Layer, Ventilated Tray — 257
- .3 Mixing Multiconductor Single-Layer and Multilayer Ventilated Tray — 258
- .4 Multiconductor, Signal and Control-Only Ventilated Tray — 259
- .5 Multiconductor, Single-Layer, Solid-Bottom Tray — 260
- .6 Multiconductor, More Than One Layer, Solid-Bottom — 261
- .7 Mixing Multiconductor Single-Layer and Multilayer Solid-Bottom Tray — 262
- .8 Multiconductor Signal and Control-Only Solid-Bottom Tray — 263
- .9 Multiconductor Ventilated Channel Tray — 264

11.2 CABLE TRAY FILL CALCULATIONS FOR SINGLE-CONDUCTOR INSTALLATIONS — 264

- .1 Single-Conductor, 1,000 kcmil and Over Ventilated Tray — 265
- .2 Single-Conductor, From 250 kcmil through 900 kcmil, More Than One Layer Ventilated Tray — 265
- .3 Single-Conductor, One Layer and Multilayer, Same Ventilated Tray — 267
- .4 Single-Conductor, 1/0 through 4/0 AWG, One Layer Ventilated Tray — 267
- .5 Single-Conductor in Ventilated Channel Tray — 268

11.3 AMPACITY OF MULTICONDUCTOR INSTALLATIONS — 268

- .1 Multiconductor, Single-Layer and Multilayer, Same Uncovered Tray — 268
- .2 Multiconductor, Single-Layer and Multilayer, Same Solid Covered Tray — 269

11.4 AMPACITY OF SINGLE-CONDUCTOR INSTALLATIONS — 269

- .1 General — 270
- .2 Single-Conductor, 600 kcmil and Larger, Uncovered Tray and Covered Tray — 270
- .3 Single-Conductor, 1/0 AWG through 500 kcmil, Uncovered and Covered Tray — 271
- .4 Single-Conductor Uncovered Tray, One-Diameter Spacing — 271

DEFINITIONS AND TERMS — 272
SUMMARY — 272
REVIEW QUESTIONS — 273

11.1 CABLE TRAY FILL CALCULATIONS FOR MULTI-CONDUCTOR INSTALLATIONS

Cable trays are not considered a wiring method, but are a support system for wiring methods. Type TC cable, or tray cable, is just one of the recognized wiring methods that may be supported by cable trays. Many other wiring methods are permitted to be installed in cable trays.

The types of cable tray installations include:

- Ladder
- Ventilated trough
- Solid-bottom trough
- Cable tray with a solid fixed barrier
- Any of the above with a cover
- Ventilated and solid-bottom channel
- Wire mesh

Each of these trays provides strength for conductor support, physical protection from damage, and ventilation functions to a greater or lesser degree. All ventilated types of cable tray are designed to allow significant airflow around cables to allow dissipation of heat from conductors. See Figure 11-1.

Ladder, ventilated trough, and wire mesh cable trays allow better circulation of air for better heat dissipation. Therefore, it is understandable that the cable tray fill for a solid-bottom tray will be less than that for a ventilated tray.

Whether the cable tray is or is not covered is not taken into consideration when deciding cable tray fill, but it is factored in when calculating the ampacity of the conductors in cable trays.

For all practical purposes, when a solid fixed barrier is installed in a cable tray, the tray can be considered to be two cable trays. Ventilated and solid-bottom channel trays are used for cable dropouts, and have a smaller width measurement.

According to **392.10, Uses Permitted**, cable tray installations may be used as a support system for:

- Service conductors
- Feeders
- Branch circuits
- Communication cables and raceways
- Control circuits
- Signaling circuits

A cable tray can be dedicated to any one type of circuit or any combination within the range of 2,000 volts or less; some combinations require cable tray barriers. Cable tray installations are not restricted to industrial installations, and are used in a wide variety of installations in many commercial establishments.

The following is a partial list of the many wiring methods found in **Table 392.10(A)** that are permitted to be supported by cable trays:

- Armored cable (AC)
- Communication cables and raceways
- Class 2 and Class 3 cables
- Electrical metallic tubing (EMT)
- Fire alarm cables
- Flexible metal conduit (FMC)
- Instrument tray cable (ITC)
- Intermediate metal conduit (IMC)
- Liquidtight flexible metal conduit (LFMC)
- Liquidtight flexible nonmetallic conduit (LFNC)
- Metal-clad cable (MC)
- Mineral-insulated, metal-sheathed cable (MI)
- Network-powered broadband communications cables

Type of Tray	Ventilation	Heat Dissipation
Ladder	Yes	Yes
Wire Mesh	Yes	Yes
Trough	Yes	Less than ladder type
Solid-Bottom	No	Less than trough type
Covered (all types)	Limited	Reduced

Figure 11-1. Types of Cable Tray. Ladder and wire mesh trays are inherently better at dissipating heat due to the exposure of the cables and conductors to free air as compared to the trough and solid bottom, which restrict air movement.

- Optical fiber cables and optical fiber raceways
- Power and control tray cable (TC)
- Power-limited tray cable (PLTC)
- Other factory-assembled multiconductor control, signal, or power cables that are specifically approved for installation in cable tray
- Rigid metal conduit (RMC)
- Rigid polyvinyl chloride conduit (PVC)
- Reinforced thermosetting resin conduit (RTRC)

Cable and conductor installation requirements of **392.20(A)** and **(B)** are:

(A) Multiconductor Cables Operating at 1000 Volts or Less. Multiconductor cables operating at 1000 volts or less shall be permitted to be installed in the same tray.

(B) Cables Operating at Over 1000 Volts. Cables operating at over 1000 volts and those operating at 1000 volts or less installed in the same cable tray shall comply with either of the following:

(1) The cables operating at over 1000 volts are Type MC.

(2) The cables operating at over 1000 volts are separated from cables operating at 1000 volts or less by a solid fixed barrier of a material compatible with the cable tray.

Examples of performing fill calculations are based upon cable ratings of 2,000 volts or less, in accordance with **392.22(A)** and **392.22(B)**.

New for the 2020 *NEC* are seven cable tray fill tables in **Annex C**. It should be noted that the new tables are in an informative annex, and are therefore not part of the requirements of the *Code* but are included for informational purposes only. While the use of these tables may be easier and more efficient for installations using the same size and types of conductors, **392.22** provides the minimum *Code* requirements. It is also to be used for cable tray calculations when cables of different sizes are present.

Table 392.22(A) and **Table 392.22(B)(1)** are both used for cable tray fill. The tables look somewhat different and contain different symbols.

Ventilated Tray Size	Cross-Sectional Area	Percent Fill	Total Fill	Table 392.22(A) Columns 1 and 2
6 in. × 3 in. =	18 in.² ×	40% =	7.2 in.²	7 in.²
12 in. × 3 in. =	36 in.² ×	40% =	14.4 in.²	14 in.²
18 in. × 3 in. =	54 in.² ×	40% =	21.6 in.²	21 in.²

*Figure 11-2. Cable Tray Allowable Area Calculation. The calculation is only an approximation. For actual allowable fill areas, refer to **Table 392.22(A)** and **Table 392.22(B)(1)**.*

When calculating the maximum raceway fill for conductors in a raceway, **Chapter 9, Table 4** is used. The most commonly used column is for 40% fill. Column 1 of **Table 392.22(A)** can be compared to the 40% column of **Chapter 9, Table 4**. The same square inch area used in Column 1 is also used in Column 2 of **Table 392.22(A)**.

Using a 40% fill for a cable tray measuring three inches in cross-sectional depth, an approximation for allowable fill for a tray can be made that is similar to Column 1 of **Table 392.22(A)**. After multiplying the width by three inches and by 0.4, the area in Column 1 of **Table 392.22(A)** is rounded down to the next full square inch (in.²). **See Figure 11-2**.

Columns 1 and 2 of **Table 392.22(A)** are used for ladder or ventilated trough cable trays. Columns 3 and 4 are used for solid-bottom cable trays. Solid-bottom trays will not have as much ventilation; therefore, their fill can be expected to be less. Setting up a comparison table for solid-bottom trays using a three-inch high tray and a 30% fill and comparing to Columns 3 and 4 of **Table 392.22(A)**, the calculated values are rounded up to the next one-half square inch (0.5 in.²). **See Figure 11-3**.

Solid-Bottom Tray Size	Cross-Sectional Area	Percent Fill	Total Fill	Table 392.22(A) Columns 3 and 4
6 in. × 3 in. =	18 in.² ×	30% =	5.4 in.²	5.5 in.²
12 in. × 3 in. =	36 in.² ×	30% =	10.8 in.²	11.0 in.²
18 in. × 3 in. =	54 in.² ×	30% =	16.2 in.²	16.5 in.²

*Figure 11-3. Cable Tray Allowable Area Calculation. The calculation is only an approximation. For actual allowable fill areas, refer to **Table 392.22(A)** and **Table 392.22(B)(1)**.*

Code excerpts reproduced with permission of NFPA from NFPA 70®, *National Electrical Code®* (NEC®), 2020 edition. Copyright© 2019, National Fire Protection Association. For a full copy of the NEC®, please go to www.nfpa.org.

NEC **392.22(A)** and the accompanying **Table 392.22(A)** are used to determine the maximum number of multiconductor cables rated 2,000 volts or less which may be placed within a cable tray. This is commonly referred to as allowable cable fill.

EXAMPLE

In the following case studies, Case 1 is based upon a single layer of multiconductor cables. From a cross-sectional viewpoint, the arranged cables are added as a "sum of the cable diameters" to determine the inside width of the cable tray. Case 2 is based upon 40% of the cross-sectional cable tray fill area according to Column 1 of **Table 392.22(A)**.

Case 1: Using **392.22(A)(1)(a)** for multiconductor cables in ladder, ventilated trough, and wire mesh tray with conductor sizes 4/0 AWG or larger, the predetermined fill is based upon the "sum of diameters" for all cable placed in a single layer. For example, six 2.5-inch diameter multiconductor cables would require a 15-inch (2.5 in. × 6 cables = 15 in.) absolute minimum width cable tray. Using **Table 392.22(A)**, standard tray width results in the minimum selection of a 16-inch wide tray for practical reasons.

Case 2: Using **392.22(A)(1)(b)** and the accompanying **Table 392.22(A)** Column 1 for multiconductor cables in ladder, ventilated trough, and wire-mesh tray with all conductor sizes smaller than 4/0 AWG, the predetermined fill is based upon the Column 1 maximum allowable cable fill expressed in square inches (in.²). For example, 10 multiconductor cables with an individual cross-sectional area of 1.329 square inches would require a 13.29-square inch (1.329 in.² × 10 cables = 13.29 in.²) absolute minimum cross-sectional area cable tray. Again, according to **Table 392.22(A)**, the next standard tray width with an allowable fill area larger than 13.29 square inches is a 12-inch tray with an allowable fill area of 14.0 square inches.

Read *NEC* **392.22(A)(1)(a)** through **(c)** and carefully review **Table 392.22(A)** which includes pertinent points such as:

1. When 4/0 AWG and larger multiconductor cables are installed in a cable tray, they must be installed in a single layer.
2. The term "Sd" is used in **Table 392.22(A)** to denote the sum of the diameters of 4/0 AWG and larger multiconductor cables installed in the single layer area of the cable tray, which also includes multiconductor cables smaller than 4/0 AWG according to **392.22(A)(1)**.
3. The calculation of "1.2 Sd" means 1.2 multiplied by the sum of the cable diameters.
4. The factor of 1.2 results in adding one inch for every five inches of total cable diameter. This factor provides 20% additional linear space to ensure these large multiconductor cables are not too crowded. In addition, it will allow a limited amount of natural cooling to occur.

Cable trays containing only multiconductor cables with a rating of 2,000 volts or less are used in the first set of problems to determine cable tray fills. The cable tray widths listed in **Table 392.22(A)** are used for standard cable tray widths.

There are a number of symbols and abbreviations that are used for cables and cable tray calculations. **See Figure 11-4**.

11.1.1 Multiconductor, Single-Layer, Ventilated Tray

NEC **392.22(A)(1)** applies to ladder, ventilated trough, and wire mesh cable tray fill where only multiconductor cables 2,000 volts or less are installed. The section divides the installation into four groups:

1. All cables containing conductors 4/0 AWG or larger
2. All cables containing conductors smaller than 4/0 AWG
3. Mixing of cables containing conductors of all sizes
4. All cables that are signal or control cables

NEC **392.22(A)(1)(a)** applies to the following:
- Multiconductor cables
- 2,000 volts or less

Symbol Identification

/C	Number of conductors in a cable (for example, 3/C means three conductors in a multiconductor cable)
P	Power cable
L	Lightning cable
S	Signal cable
OD	Outside diameter (of a cable)
r	Radius (of a cable); equal to OD ÷ 2
A	Cross-sectional area (of a cable); equal to $r \times r \times 3.1416$
Sd	Sum of the OD of all cables (often laid adjacent in a single layer)

Figure 11-4. Cable and Tray Symbol Identification. If the outside diameter is given for the cable, it is required to calculate the cable area based on the radius with the formulas given in the table.

CHAPTER 11 CABLE TRAY

- 4/0 AWG or larger
- Installation in a single layer
- Installation in a ladder, ventilated trough, or wire mesh cable tray

NEC **392.22(A)(1)(a)** requires the cables to be installed in a single layer and that the sum of all cable diameters not exceed the inside cable tray width. Where this is done, then the ampacity of these cables can be determined by using **392.80(A)(1)**. See Problem 11-1.

PROBLEM 11-1

What is the minimum width of ladder-type cable tray for two 3-conductor, 4/0 AWG, 480-volt power cables and one 3-conductor, 250 kcmil, 480-volt power cable?

(OD 4/0 AWG = 1.875 inch; OD 250 kcmil = 2.25 inches)

Solution

392.22(A)(1)(a)
Single layer of conductors
Sd = Sum of all cable diameters
= (2 × OD of 4/0 AWG) + OD of 250 kcmil
= (2 × 1.875) + 2.25
= 6 in.
Answer: 6 in. minimum inside width

11.1.2 Multiconductor, More Than One Layer, Ventilated Tray

NEC **392.22(A)(1)(b)** applies to the following:

- Multiconductor cables
- 2,000 volts or less
- All cables smaller than 4/0 AWG
- Installation in a ladder, ventilated trough, or wire mesh cable tray
- Cables permitted to be stacked

NEC **392.22(A)(1)(b)** requires the cross-sectional area fill not to exceed Column 1 of **Table 392.22(A)** for appropriate cable tray width. See Problems 11-2 and 11-3.

PROBLEM 11-2

What is the minimum size ladder-type cable tray needed for the installation of four 3-conductor, 1 AWG cables for power; three 3-conductor, 8 AWG cables for lighting; and one 7-conductor cable for signaling?

(OD 1 AWG = 1.5 inches; OD 8 AWG = 0.875 inch; OD 7/C = 1 inch)

Solution

All conductors are smaller than 4/0 AWG
Fill is based on cross-sectional area occupied by all cables

Step 1
Area of four 3-conductor 1 AWG cables
3/C 1 AWG OD = 1.5 in.

$r = \dfrac{OD}{2} = \dfrac{1.5}{2} = 0.75$ in.

$A = r \times r \times 3.1416$
$= 0.75 \times 0.75 \times 3.1416$
$= 1.7672$ in.^{2}

Total area for four cables = 1.7672×4
= 7.0688 in.^{2}

Answer: 7.0688 in.^{2}

Step 2
Area of three 3-conductor 8 AWG cables
3/C 8 AWG OD = 0.875 in.

$r = \dfrac{OD}{2} = \dfrac{0.875}{2} = 0.4375$ in.

$A = r \times r \times 3.1416$
$= 0.4375 \times 0.4375 \times 3.1416$
$= 0.6013$ in.^{2}

Total area for three cables = 0.6013×3
= 1.8039 in.^{2}

Answer: 1.8039 in.^{2}

Step 3
Area of one 7-conductor signal cable
7/C OD = 1 in.

$r = \dfrac{OD}{2} = \dfrac{1}{2} = 0.5$ in.

$A = r \times r \times 3.1416$
$= 0.5 \times 0.5 \times 3.1416$
$= 0.7854$ in.^{2}

Total area for one cable = 0.7854 in.^{2}

Answer: 0.7854 in.^{2}

Calculation
Total area from all three types of cable
Area total = 7.0688 + 1.8039 + 0.7854
= 9.6581 in.^{2}
Table 392.22(A)
Column 1
9 in. tray max. fill = 10.5 in.^{2}
Answer: 9 in. cable tray

PROBLEM 11-3

When using Informative Annex C, what is the maximum number of 8 AWG 4-conductor non-jacketed assembly Type MC cables permitted to be installed in a 24-inch ventilated cable tray?

Solution

From Annex C, Table C.15
   For 8 AWG and 24-inch tray, the table gives 67 cables
Answer: 67 cables

11.1.3 Mixing Multiconductor Single-Layer and Multilayer Ventilated Tray

NEC **392.22(A)(1)(c)** applies to the following:

- Multiconductor cables
- 2,000 volts or less
- Cables 4/0 AWG and larger installed with cables smaller than 4/0 AWG
- Using ladder, ventilated trough, or wire mesh cable tray

For additional information, visit qr.njatcdb.org Item #1042

All are installed in a ladder, ventilated trough, or wire mesh cable tray and require the use of **Table 392.22(A)** Column 2, where the outside diameter of cables 4/0 AWG and larger are added and then multiplied by 1.2. **See Problem 11-4.**

Multiconductor cables may be installed in a ladder cable tray.

Reproduced with permission of NFPA from NFPA 70®, *National Electrical Code*® (NEC®), 2020 edition. Copyright© 2019, National Fire Protection Association. For a full copy of the NEC®, please go to www.nfpa.org.

Table C.14 Number of Type MC Cables Permitted in Cable Tray (3C Multiconductor MC Cable Non-Jacketed Assembly) (Based on fill in accordance with 392.9, Table 392.9, column 1, ampacity in accordance with 392.11)

Conductor Insulation Type	Conductor Size (AWG/kcmil)	50 (2)	100 (4)	150 (6)	200 (8)	300 (12)	400 (16)	450 (18)	500 (20)	600 (24)	750 (30)	900 (36)	Cable Diameter
THHN													
	14	13	27	41	55	82	110	124	138	165	206	248	0.46
	12	10	20	31	41	62	83	93	104	124	160	192	0.53
	10	7	15	23	31	47	62	70	78	94	119	149	0.61
	8	6	12	18	25	37	50	56	63	75	96	116	0.68
	6	4	8	13	17	26	34	39	43	52	66	79	0.82
	4	2	5	8	11	17	23	26	29	35	45	55	0.99
	3	2	5	7	10	15	21	23	26	31	40	48	1.05
	2	2	4	6	9	13	18	20	22	27	34	41	1.13
	1	2	4	6	8	12	16	18	20	24	30	36	1.2
	1/0	1	3	5	7	11	14	16	18	22	28	34	1.25
	2/0	1	3	4	6	9	13	14	16	19	24	29	1.34
	3/0	1	2	3	5	7	10	11	13	15	20	24	1.49
	4/0	1	2	3	5	7	10	11	12	15	19	22	1.57
	250	1	2	3	4	6	9	10	11	13	17	20	1.74
	300	1	2	3	4	6	8	9	10	12	16	19	1.86
	350	1	2	3	4	6	8	9	10	12	15	18	1.96
	400	0	1	2	3	5	7	8	9	11	14	17	2.11
	500	0	1	2	3	5	7	7	8	10	13	16	2.24
	600	0	1	2	3	4	6	7	8	9	12	15	2.38
	700	0	1	2	3	4	6	7	7	9	11	14	2.52
	750	0	1	2	2	4	5	6	7	8	11	13	2.67
	800	0	1	2	2	4	5	6	6	8	10	12	2.85
	900	0	1	1	2	3	5	5	6	7	10	12	2.99
	1000	0	1	1	2	3	4	5	6	7	9	11	3.25

Note: Single conductor diameters were obtained from Chapter 9, Table 5.

New for the 2020 NEC are seven new cable tray fill tables to be used when all of the conductors in a cable tray are the same size.

CHAPTER 11 CABLE TRAY

PROBLEM 11-4

A 12-inch wide cable tray contains one 3-conductor, 4/0 AWG cable and one 3-conductor, 250 kcmil cable. What is the remaining cross-sectional area that may be used by multiconductor cables less than 4/0 AWG?

(OD 4/0 AWG = 2.32 inches; OD 250 kcmil = 2.96 inches)

Solution

Step 1
Determine the capacity of a 12-in. cable tray
Table 392.22(A)
 Column 2
 12 in. cable tray = 14 in.²
Answer: 14 in.²

Step 2
Calculate the area used by the larger multiconductor cables
 A = 4/0 and larger (Sd × 1.2) or
   = (OD1 + OD2) × 1.2
   = (OD 4/0 AWG + OD 250 kcmil) × 1.2
   = (2.32 + 2.96) × 1.2
   = 6.336 in.²
Answer: 6.336 in.²

Calculation
Calculate the remaining area within the tray to be used for cables smaller than 4/0 AWG
Table 392.22(A)
 Column 2
 Remaining area = tray capacity − occupied area
        = 14 in.² − 6.336 in.²
        = 7.664 in.²
Answer: 7.664 in.² is the remaining area for additional cables smaller than 4/0 AWG

11.1.4 Multiconductor, Signal and Control-Only Ventilated Tray

NEC **392.22(A)(2)** applies to the following:

- Multiconductor cables
- 2,000 volts or less
- Signal and control cable only
- Installation in a ladder or ventilated trough cable tray

NEC **392.22(A)(2)** requires limited use of 50% of inside cross-sectional area. Cable tray with over six inches of usable depth will have calculations based upon six inches of depth only for calculating cross-sectional area. See Problem 11-5.

Multiconductor Type MC cables can be installed in a wire mesh cable tray.

PROBLEM 11-5

Ventilated

A ladder-type cable tray has an internal width of 12 inches and a depth of eight inches, and contains five 9-conductor signal cables with an outside diameter of 1.27 inches each. How many 7-conductor control cables with an individual outside diameter of 0.976 inches can be added without exceeding the cable tray fill limitation for a cable tray dedicated to control and signal cables?

Solution

Step 1
Calculate usable cross-sectional area of the cable tray
392.22(A)(2)
 Only 6 in. of the 8-in. depth may be used
 Cable tray area:
  A = depth × width
   = 6 × 12
   = 72 in.^{2}
 Permitted use is limited to 50% of cross-sectional area
 Usable area = 72 in.^{2} × 0.5
       = 36 in.^{2}
Answer: 36 in.^{2}

Step 2
Calculate the occupied area of the cable tray
 9/C cable OD = 1.27 in.
 $r = \dfrac{OD}{2}$
  $= \dfrac{1.27}{2}$
  $= 0.635$ in.
 $A = r \times r \times 3.1416$
  $= 0.635 \times 0.635 \times 3.1416$
  $= 1.2668$ in.^{2}
 Total occupied area = 1.2668 × 5 cables
           = 6.334 in.^{2}
Answer: 6.334 in.^{2}

Step 3
Calculate the available area of the cable tray
 Available area = usable area − occupied area
         = 36 − 6.334
         = 29.66 in.^{2}
Answer: 29.66 in.^{2}

Step 4
Calculate the area needed for each 7-conductor cable
 7/C cable OD = 0.976 in.
 $r = \dfrac{OD}{2}$
  $= \dfrac{0.976}{2}$
  $= 0.488$ in.
 $A = r \times r \times 3.1416$
  $= 0.488 \times 0.488 \times 3.1416$
  $= 0.7482$ in.^{2}

Calculation
Calculate the maximum number of cables permitted in the available area of the cable tray

Number of conductors = $\dfrac{\text{available area}}{\text{7/C cable area}}$
  $= \dfrac{29.66}{0.7482}$
  = 39.6 or 39 more 7/C cables

Answer: 39 additional 7/C cables can be added before 50% fill is reached

11.1.5 Multiconductor, Single-Layer, Solid-Bottom Tray

Although solid-bottom cable tray installations may provide additional physical damage protection to the contained cables, a solid-bottom tray also presents challenges of elevated cable temperatures due to the lack of natural cooling. Because a solid-bottom tray provides less ventilation, the *Code* does not permit solid-bottom trays to be filled to the same capacity as ventilated trays. Due to the reduced ventilation, the ampacity of conductors within solid-bottom cable trays is also reduced. **See Figure 11-5**.

NEC **392.22(A)(3)(a)** applies to solid-bottom cable tray using only multiconductor cables rated 2,000 volts or less and in sizes of 4/0 AWG or

For additional information, visit qr.njatcdb.org
Item #1043

CHAPTER 11 CABLE TRAY

larger. *NEC* **392.22(A)(3)(a)** requires the cables to be installed in a single layer. Also, the sum of the diameters of all multiconductor cables must not exceed 90% of the width of the cable tray. **See Problem 11-6**.

PROBLEM 11-6

Cable Tray Width	Limitation	Usable Width
6 in.	90%	5.4 in.
12 in.	90%	10.8 in.
18 in.	90%	16.2 in.

Figure 11-5. Solid-Bottom Tray Limitations. Cable tray widths are reduced accordingly.

Determine the minimum standard size solid-bottom cable tray to accommodate two 3-conductor, 4/0 AWG power cables and one 3-conductor, 250 kcmil power cable. (OD 4/0 AWG = 1.875 inches; OD 250 kcmil = 2.25 inches)

Solution

Solid Bottom Tray
  All conductors are 4/0 AWG and larger
  Sd = (4/0 AWG OD × 2) + 250 kcmil OD
  = (1.875 × 2) + 2.25
  = 3.75 + 2.25
  = 6 in.
392.22(A)(3)(a)

$$\text{Cable tray width (min.)} = \frac{Sd}{90\%}$$
$$= \frac{6}{0.90}$$
$$= 6.667 \text{ in.}$$

Table 392.22(A), Column 1
  Next larger standard size = 8 in.
  Answer: 8-in. cable tray

11.1.6 Multiconductor, More Than One Layer, Solid-Bottom

NEC **392.22(A)(3)(b)** applies to solid-bottom trays using only multiconductor cables rated 2,000 volts or less and smaller than 4/0 AWG. This section permits the multiconductor cables to be stacked and requires the sum of the cross-sectional area not to exceed the cable tray fill of Column 3 in **Table 392.22(A)**. **See Problem 11-7**.

PROBLEM 11-7

What is the minimum standard size solid-bottom cable tray needed for two 3-conductor, 1/0 AWG cables; three 3-conductor, 2 AWG cables; and six 9-conductor, 3 AWG control cables? (OD 1/0 AWG = 1.52 inches; OD 2 AWG = 1.14 inch; OD 9/C = 1.625 inch)

Solution

All conductors are smaller than 4/0 AWG
Fill is based upon cross-sectional area occupied
Determine the cross-sectional area for each size cable

Step 1
3/C 1/0 AWG OD = 1.52 in.
$$r = \frac{OD}{2}$$
$$= \frac{1.52}{2}$$
$$= 0.76 \text{ in.}$$
$A = r \times r \times 3.1416$
$ = 0.76 \times 0.76 \times 3.1416$
$ = 1.8146 \text{ in.}^2$
Total 1/0 AWG area = 1.8146 in.² × 2
$\phantom{\text{Total 1/0 AWG area}} = 3.6292 \text{ in.}^2$
Answer: 3.6292 in.²

Step 2
3/C 2 AWG OD = 1.14 in.
$$r = \frac{OD}{2}$$
$$= \frac{1.14}{2}$$
$$= 0.57 \text{ in.}$$
$A = r \times r \times 3.1416$
$ = 0.57 \times 0.57 \times 3.1416$
$ = 1.0207 \text{ in.}^2$
Total 3/C 2 AWG area = 1.0207 in.² × 3
$\phantom{\text{Total 3/C 2 AWG area}} = 3.0621 \text{ in.}^2$
Answer: = 3.0621 in.²

Step 3
9/C 3 AWG control cable OD = 1.625 in.
$$r = \frac{OD}{2}$$
$$= \frac{1.625}{2}$$
$$= 0.8125 \text{ in.}$$
$A = r \times r \times 3.1416$
$ = 0.8125 \times 0.8125 \times 3.1416$
$ = 2.0739 \text{ in.}^2$
Total 9/C area = 2.0739 in.² × 6
$\phantom{\text{Total 9/C area}} = 12.4434 \text{ in.}^2$
Answer: 12.4434 in.²

Calculation
Determine the total cross-sectional area of all cables
  Total Area = 3.6292 + 3.0621 + 12.4434
  = 19.1347 in.²
Table 392.22(A), Column 3
  Select next larger standard volume cable tray = 22 in.²
  Maximum fill of 22 in.² = 24 in. tray
  Answer: 24-in. solid-bottom cable tray required

261

PROBLEM 11-8

How many 3-conductor, 4 AWG cables can be installed in the same 12-inch solid-bottom cable tray with two 4-conductor, 500 kcmil cables?

(OD 4/C 500 kcmil = 3.12 inches; OD 3/C 4 AWG = 1.07 inch)

Solution

Step 1
Determine the maximum capacity of a 12-inch solid bottom cable tray
Table 392.22(A), Column 4
  12 in. cable tray capacity = 11 in.^{2}
Answer: 11 in.^{2}

Step 2
Determine the occupied width (using a single layer fill)
  Sd = OD 4/C 500 kcmil × 2
   = 3.12 × 2
   = 6.24 in.
  (for in.^{2} units, 6.24 in. is multiplied by 1.0 in.)*
  Used area = 6.24 in.^{2}
Answer: 6.24 in.^{2}

Step 3
Determine available area using stacked fill
Table 392.22(A), Column 4
  12 in. tray = 11.0 − Sd
   = 11 − 6.24
   = 4.76 in.^{2}
Answer: 4.76 in.^{2}

Step 4
Calculate the area needed for each 3/C cable
$$r = \frac{OD}{2}$$
$$= \frac{1.07}{2}$$
$$= 0.535 \text{ in.}$$
  A = r × r × 3.1416
   = 0.535 × 0.535 × 3.1416
   = 0.8992 in.^{2}
Answer: 0.8992 in.^{2}

Calculation
Determine the quantity of 3-conductor cables using stacked fill

$$\text{Number of conductors} = \frac{\text{available area}}{\text{3/C cable area}}$$
$$= \frac{4.76}{0.8992}$$
$$= 5.29 \text{ or five 3/C cables}$$

Answer: Five 3-conductor 4 AWG cables

Comment: Regarding units of measure, fill calculations from Column 2 and 4 of Table 392.22(A) are based upon square inch (in.^{2}) fill. The sum of diameters (Sd) is actually a linear measure of inches (in.) However, multiplying Sd by 1.2 inches from Column 2 or multiplying Sd by 1.0 inch from Column 4 allows the Sd units of measure to match the table units of square inches (in.^{2})

11.1.7 Mixing Multiconductor Single-Layer and Multilayer Solid-Bottom Tray

NEC **392.22(A)(3)(c)** applies to solid-bottom cable tray using multiconductor cables of mixed sizes, all rated 2,000 volts or less. This section requires all 4/0 AWG or larger cables to be installed in a single layer with no other cables on top of cables 4/0 AWG or larger. Column 4 of **Table 392.22(A)** with "Sd" factor for maximum fill applies. **See Problem 11-8**.

Note: The Sd factor for solid-bottom cable tray is not increased. See **Table 392.22(A) Column 4**.

11.1.8 Multiconductor Signal and Control-Only Solid-Bottom Tray

NEC **392.22(A)(4)** applies to the following:

- Multiconductor cables
- 2,000 volts or less
- Signal and control cable only
- Installation in a solid-bottom cable tray

NEC **392.22(A)(4)** requires limited use of 40% of inside cross-sectional area. Where the usable cable tray depth is six inches or less, the actual depth may be used in the calculation. Cable tray with over six inches of usable depth will have calculations based on a maximum depth of six inches only for calculating the cross-sectional area of a given tray. **See Problem 11-9**.

PROBLEM 11-9

A cable tray with internal measurements of six inches wide × four inches deep dedicated to signal and control cables contains five 4-conductor control cables. How many 7-conductor control cables can be added to the solid-bottom tray without exceeding the *Code* limitations?

(OD 4/C = 0.537 inch; OD 7/C = 0.975 inch)

Solution

Step 1
Calculate the usable area of the cable tray

Cable tray area = width × depth
= 6 × 4
= 24 in.²

392.22(A)(4)
Usable area = total × 40%
= 24 × 0.40
= 9.6 in.²

Answer: 9.6 in.²

Step 2
Calculate the occupied 4-conductor cable area fill

$r = \dfrac{OD}{2}$
$= \dfrac{0.537}{2}$
= 0.2685 in.

A = r × r × 3.1416
= 0.2685 × 0.2685 × 3.1416
= 0.2265 in.²

Total occupied area = 0.2265 × 5
= 1.1325 in.²

Answer: 1.1325 in.²

Step 3
Calculate the available area

Available area = usable area − occupied area
= 9.6 − 1.1325
= 8.4675 in.²

Answer: 8.4675 in.²

Step 4
Calculate the area needed for each 7-conductor cable

$r = \dfrac{OD}{2}$
$= \dfrac{0.975}{2}$
= 0.4875 in.

A = r × r × 3.1416
= 0.4875 × 0.4875 × 3.1416
= 0.7466 in.²

Answer: 0.7466 in.²

Calculation
Calculate the maximum number of 7-conductor cables permitted

Number of conductors = $\dfrac{\text{available area}}{\text{7/C cable area}}$
$= \dfrac{8.4675}{0.7466}$
= 11.34 or 11

Answer: Eleven 7-conductor cables

11.1.9 Multiconductor Ventilated Channel Tray

Ventilated channel cable tray has a smaller internal width than a regular cable tray and is often used for cable tray dropouts. *NEC* **392.22(A)(5)** and **Table 392.22(A)(5)** apply to the following:

- Multiconductor cable(s)
- 2,000 volts or less
- Installation in ventilated channel cable tray
- When one or more cable is installed

See Problems 11-10 and 11-11.

NEC **392.22(A)(5)** and **Table 392.22(A)(5)** of the *Code* have limitations for ventilated channel tray for a single cable and multiple cables. **See Figure 11-6**.

Table 392.22(A)(5), Column 2, More than One Cable	
Cable Tray Width	Maximum Fill
3 in.	1.3 in.²
4 in.	2.5 in.²
6 in.	3.8 in.²

Table 392.22(A)(5), Column 1, One Cable	
Cable Tray Width	Maximum Fill
3 in.	2.3 in.²
4 in.	4.5 in.²
6 in.	7.0 in.²

Figure 11-6. Ventilated Channel Tray. Ventilated channel tray is often used for indoor, lightweight applications.

PROBLEM 11-10

What width of ventilated channel cable tray would be needed for one 3-conductor, 3/0 AWG cable?

(OD 3-conductor 3/0 AWG = 1.7 inches)

Solution

Calculate area needed for 3-conductor, 3/0 AWG cable

$$r = \frac{OD}{2}$$
$$= \frac{1.7}{2}$$
$$= 0.85 \text{ in.}$$

$$A = r \times r \times 3.1416$$
$$= 0.85 \times 0.85 \times 3.1416$$
$$= 2.27 \text{ in.}^2$$

Table 392.22(A)(5), Column 1

2.3 in.² for one multiconductor cable = 3-inch cable tray

Answer: 3-in. ventilated channel cable tray

PROBLEM 11-11

Is it permissible to install one 4-conductor, 500-kcmil power cable with an outside diameter of 2.5 inches in a 4-inch wide ventilated channel cable tray?

Solution

$$r = \frac{OD}{2}$$
$$= \frac{2.5}{2}$$
$$= 1.25 \text{ in.}$$

$$A = r \times r \times 3.1416$$
$$= 1.25 \times 1.25 \times 3.1416$$
$$= 4.9088 \text{ in.}^2$$

Table 392.22(A)(5), Column 1

Maximum fill one cable

4-in. cable tray, with a fill of 4.5 in.² is too small

Use 6-in. cable tray with a fill of 7 in.²

Answer: No. A 6-inch ventilated channel cable tray is the minimum size required

11.2 CABLE TRAY FILL CALCULATIONS FOR SINGLE-CONDUCTOR INSTALLATIONS

The next group of cable tray illustrations is directed at the installation of single-conductor cables used in cable trays. Unless the dimensions of the insulated conductors are given, the dimensions of the diameter and cross-sectional area as given in **Chapter 9, Table 5** for copper and aluminum and **Chapter 9, Table 5A** for compact copper and aluminum are used.

NEC **392.10(B)(1)(a)** limits the smallest single-conductor cable installed in a cable tray to 1/0 AWG, and **392.10(B)(1)(c)** permits an equipment grounding conductor as small as 4 AWG.

NEC **392.22(B)** applies to the following:

- Cables 2,000 volts or less
- Where only single-conductor cable is installed or where single-conductor cable assemblies (such as triplex) are installed
- When in ladder, ventilated trough, and wire mesh cable tray
- Where cable is evenly distributed across the cable tray

The installations of single-conductor cables rated 2,000 volts or less are divided into five groups:

1. Where all cables are 1,000 kcmil or larger
2. Where all cables are from 250 kcmil through 900 kcmil
3. Where 1,000 kcmil cables or larger are mixed within the same tray as cables smaller than 1,000 kcmil
4. Where any 1/0 AWG through 4/0 AWG cables only are in the cable tray
5. Where single-conductor cables are installed in ventilated channel cable trays

11.2.1 Single-Conductor, 1,000 kcmil and Over Ventilated Tray

NEC **392.22(B)(1)(a)** applies to the following:

- Single-conductor cables
- 2,000 volts or less
- Installation in a ladder, ventilated trough, or wire mesh cable tray
- Conductor sizes 1,000 kcmil and over
- Single layer of cables evenly distributed

NEC **392.22(B)(1)(a)** requires the sum of all cable diameters not to exceed the inside width of the cable tray. **See Problem 11-12.**

PROBLEM 11-12

What is the minimum inside width of ladder-type cable tray required for the installation of nine 480-volt, 1,000 kcmil THWN single copper conductors?

Solution

Calculation 1

All conductors are 1,000 kcmil or larger
392.22(B)(1)(a) applies
Diameters of cables not to exceed inside width of cable tray
Chapter 9, Table 5
1,000 kcmil THWN copper OD = 1.31 in.
Min. width = No. conductors × OD of 1/C
= 9 × 1.31 in.
= 11.79 in.
Table 392.22(A)
Select next standard width greater than 11.79 inch
Standard cable tray width = 12 inches

Calculation 2

From Annex C, Table C.18
For 1,000 kcmil THHN and 9 conductors: 12-inch tray
Answer: 12-in. cable tray
Comment: While the use of 392.22 calculates the correct answer, Table C.18 also gives the correct answer, but only when the cables are the same size. It should be noted that Table C.18 only lists THHN insulation, but a quick comparison to Chapter 9, Table 5 provides the same outside diameter for a 1,000 kcmil THHN conductor as a THWN insulated conductor, allowing the use of the Annex table.

11.2.2 Single-Conductor, From 250 kcmil through 900 kcmil, More Than One Layer Ventilated Tray

NEC **392.22(B)(1)(b)** applies to the following:

- Single-conductor cables
- 2,000 volts or less
- Installation in a ladder, ventilated trough, or wire mesh cable tray
- Conductor sizes from 250 kcmil through 900 kcmil
- Conductors permitted to be stacked

PROBLEM 11-13

What is the minimum width of a ventilated trough cable tray needed for three 250 kcmil, THWN, copper single conductors; six 500 kcmil, THWN, copper single conductors; and three 750 kcmil, XHHW, compact aluminum single conductors? All conductors have 600-volt insulation.

Ventilated

Solution

392.22(B)(1)(b)
Chapter 9, Table 5 and Table 5A
Approximate area (using in.^{2})

Table 5:	500 kcmil THWN copper	= 0.7073 in.^{2}
Table 5:	250 kcmil THWN copper	= 0.3970 in.^{2}
Table 5A:	750 kcmil XHHW compact alum.	= 0.9331 in.^{2}

500 kcmil A =	6 × 0.7073 =	4.2438 in.^{2}
250 kcmil A =	3 × 0.3970 =	1.1910 in.^{2}
750 kcmil A =	3 × 0.9331 =	2.7993 in.^{2}
Total		8.2341 in.^{2}

Table 392.22(B)(1), Column 1
8 in. wide cable tray fill permitted to be 8.5 in.^{2}
Answer: 8-in. cable tray

PROBLEM 11-14

How many single-conductor 500 kcmil XHHW copper conductors can be installed with three 1,250 kcmil XHHW copper conductors and three 1,000 kcmil XHHW copper conductors in a 12-inch wide ventilated cable tray?

Solution

392.22(B)(1)(c) and Table 392.22(B)(1) Column 2 applies

Step 1
Occupied space
Find Sd for all 1,000 kcmil and over
Chapter 9, Table 5 OD of cables
Three 1/C 1,250 kcmil XHHW = 1.479 in. × 3
= 4.437 in.
Three 1/C 1,000 kcmil XHHW = 1.312 in. × 3
= 3.936 in.
Sd = 4.437 + 3.936
= 8.373 in.
Answer: 8.373 in.

Step 2
Remaining space (area for 500 kcmil only)
Table 392.22(B)(1), Column 2
Remaining area = usable area − (Sd factor × occupied area)
= 13 in.^{2} − (1.1 in. × 8.373 in.)
= 3.7897 in.^{2}
Answer: 3.7897 in.^{2}

Step 3
Quantity of 500 kcmil conductors

$$\text{Number of conductors} = \frac{\text{remaining space}}{\text{area of 500 kcmil XHHW}}$$

Chapter 9, Table 5
500 kcmil XHHW = 0.6984 in.^{2}

$$\text{Number of conductors} = \frac{3.7897 \text{ in.}^2}{0.6984 \text{ in.}^2}$$

= 5.426 or 5 conductors

Answer: Five 500 kcmil XHHW conductors

NEC **392.22(B)(1)(b)** requires cross-sectional area fill in square inches not to exceed the cable tray fill of Column 1 of **Table 392.22(B)(1)**. **See Problem 11-13**.

The *Code* permits single conductors from 250 kcmil through 900 kcmil to be stacked in a cable tray because the larger cables are less flexible and are not damaged or crushed as easily when other cables are placed on top of them. Smaller size cables, 1/0 AWG through 4/0 AWG, are easily damaged or crushed when significant weight is placed on them.

11.2.3 Single-Conductor, One Layer and Multilayer, Same Ventilated Tray

NEC **392.22(B)(1)(c)** applies to the following:

- Single-conductor cables
- 2,000 volts or less
- Installation in a ladder or ventilated trough cable tray

- Some 1,000 kcmil or over
- Some from 250 kcmil through 900 kcmil

NEC **392.22(B)(1)(c)** requires the use of the Sd factor of **Table 392.22(B)(1)** Column 2 for maximum fill. **See Problem 11-14**.

11.2.4 Single-Conductor, 1/0 through 4/0 AWG, One Layer Ventilated Tray

NEC **392.22(B)(1)(d)** applies to the following:

- Single-conductor cables
- 2,000 volts or less
- Sizes 1/0 AWG through 4/0 AWG
- Installation in a ladder, ventilated trough, or wire mesh cable tray

NEC **392.22(B)(1)(d)** requires the cable to be installed in a single layer, with the total diameter of all conductors not exceeding the cable tray width. **See Problem 11-15**.

PROBLEM 11-15

What is the minimum standard width of ventilated cable tray needed for four 1/0 AWG, three 2/0 AWG, and three 4/0 AWG conductors, if all are THWN-2 copper single conductors?

Solution

392.22(B)(1)(d)
  Cable tray width not to exceed Sd of single-conductor cables
Chapter 9, Table 5
  OD of cables
    1/0 AWG THWN-2 =   0.486 × 4 =   1.944 in.
    2/0 AWG THWN-2 =   0.532 × 3 =   1.596 in.
    4/0 AWG THWN-2 =   0.642 × 3 =   1.926 in.
    Total   5.466 in.

  Does not exceed the width of the 6 in. tray
  Answer: 6-in. cable tray

11.2.5 Single-Conductor in Ventilated Channel Tray

NEC **392.22(B)(2)** applies to the following:

- Single-conductor cables
- 2,000 volts or less
- Installed in 2-inch, 3-inch, 4-inch, or 6-inch ventilated channel-type cable trays

NEC **392.22(B)(2)** requires the sum of the diameter of all conductors not to exceed the inside width of the cable tray. **See Problem 11-16**.

11.3 AMPACITY OF MULTICONDUCTOR INSTALLATIONS

The ampacity of the conductors installed in cable trays is based upon the installation of the conductors being made according to **392.80(A)(1)** for multiconductor cables and **392.80(A)(2)** for single-conductor cables, with few variations.

The adjustment factors of **310.15(B)(1)** for the ampacity tables of **Article 310** are applicable to multiconductor cables installed in a cable tray. The individual adjustment factors will be based upon the number of current-carrying conductors in the cable and not the whole of the cable tray. Each cable must be looked at individually.

For multiconductor cables, **Table 310.16** and **Table 310.18** are used. These are the tables listing the ampacity of conductors when there are not more than three conductors in a raceway or cable.

For single-conductor cables, triplex, or smaller cables, **Table 310.17** and **Table 310.19** are used. These are the tables listing the ampacities of single conductors installed in open air. **Table 310.17** is based upon a 30°C ambient temperature and **Table 310.19** is based upon a 40°C temperature. However, final ampacities for single-conductor cables may be less than the given values in **Table 310.17** and **Table 310.19** if the cable terminations in equipment are marked to accept only such ampacities in accordance with **110.14(C)(1)** and those found in **Table 310.16**.

In the following problems, all conductors will be considered to be operating in an ambient area where the temperature will not exceed the temperatures listed in **Table 310.16** and **Table 310.17**. Should the installation be in an area with an ambient temperature other than the temperature listed in these ampacity tables, the calculated ampacities may be different.

The ampacities for conductors in different types of cable trays are the same, provided the cable tray is installed without covers. When covers over six feet in length are used on any type of cable tray, the ampacity of the conductors will be less than that of uncovered cable tray installations.

11.3.1 Multiconductor, Single-Layer and Multilayer, Same Uncovered Tray

Provided the installation is in accordance with **392.22(A)**, **392.80(A)(1)** is used to determine the ampacity of multiconductor cables rated 2,000 volts or less installed in cable trays. The calculation begins by applying the ampacities of **Table 310.16** appropriately to each multiconductor cable. The

PROBLEM 11-16

What is the minimum size ventilated channel cable tray needed for four 600 kcmil, THWN, single copper conductors?

Solution

392.22(B)(2)
  Cable tray width not to exceed Sd of single-conductor cables
Chapter 9, Table 5
  OD of cables
  600 kcmil THWN = 1.051 in.
  Total width = conductors × OD
              = 4 × 1.051
              = 4.204 in.
  Exceeds 4 in. width
Table 392.22(B)(1)
  Next larger standard size = 6 in. width
Answer: 6-in. ventilated channel cable tray

application of adjustment factors according to **310.15(B)(1)** is only necessary if the number of current-carrying conductors within each multi-conductor cable exceeds three current-carrying conductors. Each multiconductor cable is reviewed individually. The total sum of current-carrying conductors within all of the cables contained in a cable tray is not reviewed. **See Problem 11-17**.

11.3.2 Multiconductor, Single-Layer and Multilayer, Same Solid Covered Tray

The ampacity of multiconductor cables installed in cable trays is based upon the requirements of **392.80(A)(1)**. Where a cable tray is continuously covered for more than six feet, **392.80(A)(1)(b)** indicates the ampacity of the conductors is required to be reduced to 95% of the ampacities of **Table 310.16** or **Table 310.18**. **See Problem 11-18**.

PROBLEM 11-18

What is the ampacity of the conductors in Problem 11-17 when a solid cover is installed over the entire cable tray?

Solution

Calculation 1
Ampacity of 4-conductor 500 kcmil
Table 310.16 Ampacity
  4/C 500 kcmil at 75°C = 380 A
392.80(A)(1)(a)
  More than 3 current-carrying conductors
310.15(B)(1)
Table 310.15(B)(1)
  Adjustment factor for four conductors = 80%
392.80(A)(1)(b)
  Covered tray adjustment factor = 95%
  500 kcmil = 380 A × 0.80 × 0.95
         = 288.8 A
Answer: 288.8 A

Calculation 2
Ampacity of 3/C 4 AWG
Table 310.16 Ampacity
  3/C 4 AWG at 75°C = 85 A
392.80(A)(1)(b)
  Covered tray adjustment factor = 95%
  4 AWG = 85 × 0.95
        = 80.75 A
Answer: 80.75 A

PROBLEM 11-17

What is the ampacity of each conductor of the multiconductor cables installed in an uncovered cable tray, as shown in the given illustration? All conductors are 75°C insulated, current-carrying copper conductors.

Note: This problem is a logical extension of Problem 11-8 using the matching cables and cable tray. The fill requirement according to 392.22(A) and associated Table 392.22(A) are satisfied.

Solution

Calculation 1
Ampacity of 4-conductor 500 kcmil
Table 310.16 Ampacity
  4/C 500 kcmil at 75°C = 380 A
392.80(A)(1)(a)
  More than 3 current-carrying conductors
310.15(B)(1)
Table 310.15(B)(1)
  Adjustment factor for four conductors = 80%
  500 kcmil = 380 × 0.80
         = 304 A
Answer: 304 A

Calculation 2
Ampacity of 3-conductor 4 AWG
Table 310.16 Ampacity
  3/C 4 AWG at 75°C = 85 A
  No adjustment factor necessary
  4 AWG = 85 A
Answer: 85 A

11.4 AMPACITY OF SINGLE-CONDUCTOR INSTALLATIONS

The ampacity of the single-conductor cables installed in cable trays is based upon the installation of the conductors being made according to **392.80(A)(2)**, with one variation used where cable separation is significant.

The adjustment factors of **310.15(C)(1)** do not apply to single-conductor cables in cable tray. The ampacity tables of **Article 310** are applicable to multiconductor cables installed in cable tray.

As a reminder, whenever ampacity calculations are made using tables other than **Table 310.16**, the final ampacity calculation for terminations may need to be adjusted according to the termination marking requirements and **110.14(C)(1)**.

11.4.1 General

The ampacities of single-conductor cables are regulated by **392.80(A)(2)**. This section is further divided into four subdivisions, three of which are:

a. Provided the conductors are installed in accordance with **392.22(B)**, 600 kcmil and larger, ampacities must not exceed 75% of the value given in either **Table 310.17** or **Table 310.19**. For covered tray installations, the factor of 75% is reduced to 70%.
b. Provided the conductors are installed in accordance with **392.22(B)**, for 1/0 AWG through 500 kcmil and larger, ampacities must not exceed 65% of the value given in either **Table 310.17** or **Table 310.19**. For covered tray installations, the factor of 65% is reduced to 60%.
c. Where single conductors are installed with maintained spacing not less than one cable diameter between individual conductors, the ampacity of 1/0 AWG and larger must not exceed the value given in either **Table 310.17** or **Table 310.19**.

*Cable trays containing conductors rated over 600 volts are required to be marked according to NEC **392.18(H)** and **110.21(B)**.*

11.4.2 Single-Conductor, 600 kcmil and Larger, Uncovered Tray and Covered Tray

NEC **392.80(A)(2)(a)** applies to single-conductor cables rated 2,000 volts or less and the following:

- Conductors 600 kcmil and larger
- In ventilated or solid-bottom cable trays
- Requires the use of ampacity **Table 310.17** or **Table 310.19**
- Cable tray fill complies with **392.22(B)**

For these types of installations, conductors in an uncovered tray are restricted to 75% of the table ampacity. Conductors in a covered tray are restricted to 70% of table ampacity. **See Problem 11-19**.

PROBLEM 11-19

Ventilated

What is the ampacity of each conductor when four 600 kcmil aluminum single conductors with 75°C insulation are installed in the following:

1. An uncovered cable tray?
2. Cable tray with a full-length covering?

Solution

Calculation 1
Uncovered tray
392.80(B)(2)(a)
Table 310.17 Ampacity
  600 kcmil 75°C insulation = 545 A
  Ampacity = table value × 75%
           = 545 × 0.75
           = 408.75 A
Answer: 408.75 A

Calculation 2
Covered tray
392.80(B)(2)(a)
Table 310.17 Ampacity
  600 kcmil 75°C insulation = 545 A
  Ampacity = table value × 70%
           = 545 × 0.70
           = 381.5 A
Answer: 381.5 A

11.4.3 Single-Conductor, 1/0 AWG through 500 kcmil, Uncovered and Covered Tray

NEC **392.80(A)(2)(b)** applies to single-conductor cables rated 2,000 volts or less and the following:

- Sizes 1/0 AWG through 500 kcmil
- Within ventilated or solid-bottom cable trays
- Requires the use of ampacity **Table 310.17** or **Table 310.19**
- Ampacity for uncovered tray = 65% of table ampacity
- Ampacity for covered tray = 60% of table ampacity
- Cable tray fill complies with **392.22(B)**

See Problem 11-20.

11.4.4 Single-Conductor Uncovered Tray, One-Diameter Spacing

NEC **392.80(A)(2)(c)** applies to single-conductor cables rated 2,000 volts or less and the following:

- Sizes 1/0 AWG and larger
- Single layer
- Requires conductor being spaced apart one cable diameter in an uncovered tray
- Ampacity read directly from **Table 310.17** or **Table 310.19**

NEC **392.80(A)(2)(c)** provides an economical solution for cable tray circuits. For example, a 600 kcmil copper conductor using **Table 310.16** has a 75°C ampacity of 420 amperes, whereas the same 600 kcmil conductor using **Table 310.17** has a 75°C ampacity of 690 amperes. The permission to use **Table 310.17** allows a 64% increase in ampacity using the same conductors. **See Problem 11-21**.

PROBLEM 11-20

What is the ampacity of each conductor when four 350 kcmil, 75°C copper conductors are installed in both an uncovered and a covered cable tray?

Solution

Calculation 1
Uncovered tray
392.80(B)(2)(b)
Table 310.17 Ampacity
  350 kcmil 75°C = 505 A
  Ampacity = table value × 65%
          = 505 × 0.65
          = 328.25 A
Answer: 328.25 A

Calculation 2
Covered tray
392.80(B)(2)(b)
Table 310.17 Ampacity
  350 kcmil 75°C = 505 A
  Ampacity = table value × 60%
          = 505 × 0.60
          = 303 A
Answer: 303 A

PROBLEM 11-21

What is the ampacity of a single 500 kcmil THHN copper conductor installed in an uncovered ventilated cable tray when each conductor is separated by at least a cable diameter?

Solution

392.80(A)(2)(c)
Table 310.17 Ampacity
  500 kcmil THHN copper = 700 A
Answer: 700 A

DEFINITIONS AND TERMS

Cable Tray System - A unit or assembly of units or sections and associated fittings forming a structural system used to securely fasten or support cables and raceways.

Channel Cable Tray* - A fabricated structure consisting of a one-piece ventilated-bottom or solid-bottom channel section.

Ladder Cable Tray* - A fabricated structure consisting of two longitudinal side rails connected by individual transverse members (rungs).

Single-Rail Cable Tray* - A fabricated structure consisting of a longitudinal rail with transversely connected members (rungs) that project from one side (side-supported) or both sides (center-supported), which may be single- or multi-tier.

Solid Bottom or Nonventilated Cable Tray* - A fabricated structure consisting of a bottom without ventilation openings within integral or separate longitudinal side rails.

Trough or Ventilated Cable Tray* - A fabricated structure consisting of integral or separate longitudinal rails, and a bottom having openings sufficient for the passage of air and utilizing 75% or less of the plan area of the surface to support cables where the maximum open spacings between cable support surfaces of transverse elements do not exceed 100 millimeters (4 in.) in the direction parallel to the tray side rails.

Wire Mesh Cable Tray* - A manufactured wire mesh tray consisting of steel wires welded at all intersections. Longitudinal wires located on the exterior of the tray are spaced at a maximum of 50 millimeters (2 in.) and transverse wires are spaced at a maximum of 100 millimeters (4 in.).

***NEMA VE 1-2009, Metal Cable Tray Systems**

SUMMARY

Cable tray is an economical support system for multiconductor cable-type wiring methods and is available in ladder, ventilated trough, wire mesh, and solid-bottom systems. Cable tray may be installed with or without covers, and the covers are permitted to be solid or ventilated. **Section 392.22** provides fill requirements that are specific to tray type and cable type, and by following the requirements accurately, the installer will not dangerously overfill the tray. **Section 392.80** provides ampacity requirements to additionally ensure the cables are not overloaded and will operate safely. Cable trays, whether installed in commercial or industrial locations, provide for a safe, economical, and flexible electrical installation.

REVIEW QUESTIONS

1. Cable trays are considered to be a __?__ .
   a. conduit
   b. raceway
   c. support system
   d. wiring method

2. Which of the following is not a type of cable tray?
   a. Ladder
   b. Solid-bottom
   c. Ventilated channel
   d. Wooden rail

3. When installing 4/0 AWG and larger multiconductor cables in a ladder cable tray, the maximum number of cables permitted in the tray is based upon the __?__ .
   a. allowable fill area of the tray not exceeded by the sum of the cross-sectional areas of all the cables
   b. width of the tray not exceeded by the sum of the outside diameters of the cables
   c. width times the height of the tray multiplied by 50% and not exceeded by the sum of the cross-sectional areas of all the cables
   d. width times the height of the tray not exceeded by the sum of the cross-sectional areas of all the cables

4. When determining the maximum number of smaller than 4/0 AWG multiconductor cables in a ladder cable tray, the __?__ of the cable must be known.
   a. circumference
   b. cross-sectional area
   c. internal diameter
   d. number of conductors

5. Given a 24-inch ladder cable tray with an allowable fill area of 28 square inches from **Table 392.22(A)**, what is the maximum number of 4-conductor, 50 kcmil multiconductor cables permitted to be installed if the cables each have an outside diameter of three inches?
   a. 3
   b. 4
   c. 8
   d. 9

6. For determining the maximum number of multiconductor control and signal cables in a solid-bottom cable tray, what is the maximum height permitted to be used for determining the allowable fill area?
   a. 3"
   b. 6"
   c. 8"
   d. The height of the tray

7. As used in **Table 392.22(A)** and **Table 392.22(B)(1)**, the term *Sd* means __?__ .
   a. single depth
   b. smaller density
   c. square dimensions
   d. sum of diameters

8. For determining the maximum number of multiconductor control and signal cables in a ladder cable tray, what is the maximum percentage of the tray's cross-sectional area that is permitted to be filled by the cables?
   a. 40%
   b. 50%
   c. 60%
   d. 100%

9. Under which requirement are the adjustment factors of **310.15(B)(1)** required to be applied to multiconductor cables installed in an uncovered cable tray?
   a. If there are more than three current-carrying cables in the tray
   b. If there are more than three current-carrying conductors in a cable
   c. If there are more than three current-carrying cables without one cable diameter of spacing between the cables
   d. If the cable tray is solid-bottom

10. A 500 kcmil single-conductor cable with 90°C insulation is installed in a ladder cable tray. Which table would be used to determine the ampacity of the conductor?
    a. Table 310.16
    b. Table 310.17
    c. Table 310.18
    d. Table 310.19

CHAPTER 12
ELECTRIC WELDERS

Branch circuits and feeders supplying welders require ampacity calculations based upon those found in **Article 630, Electric Welders**. The two basic types of electric welders covered within **Article 630** are arc welders and resistance welders.

Welder loads are often substantially less than the supply current marked on the product nameplate, or as the *National Electrical Code* (*NEC*) calls it, the rating plate. Most welders operate on a duty cycle and a multiplication factor of less than 100%. Where more than one welder is placed on a branch circuit or feeder, additional demand factors may be applied, which further reduces the overall calculated load.

Overcurrent protection of arc welder circuits is required to be set at not more than 200% of its rated supply current at maximum rated output (I_{1max}). The conductors that supply welders are permitted to be protected by an overcurrent protective device also set at 200%. The branch-circuit overcurrent protective device may serve as the welder overcurrent protective device as well if it is sized at not over 200%. The 200% rating also serves as the rating of the identified disconnecting means.

OBJECTIVES

- Name the two types of electric welders and their identifying characteristics.
- Calculate the ampacity of supply conductors for individual welders of various types.
- Identify the additional calculations necessary when determining the ampacity of supply conductors for various types of electric welders when operated in groups.
- Calculate the duty cycle of various types of welders.

TABLE OF CONTENTS

12.1 ARTICLE 630, ELECTRIC WELDERS 276
- .1 Types of Welders 276
- .2 Duty Cycle 276
- .3 Ampacity Multiplier 276
- .4 Number of Welders 277

12.2 ARC WELDERS 277
- .1 AC Transformer and DC Rectifier Type Welders 277
- .2 Motor Generator Type 283

12.3 RESISTANCE WELDERS 285
- .1 Load Calculation for Individual Welders 285
- .2 Load Calculation for Multiple Welders 286
- .3 Calculating Duty Cycle 286

DEFINITIONS AND TERMS 288
SUMMARY 288
REVIEW QUESTIONS 289

12.1 ARTICLE 630, ELECTRIC WELDERS

Article 630, Electric Welders, was introduced into the *NEC* just after 1942. At that time, productivity for the war effort, especially welding, was very important.

Welding machines are covered in **Article 630** of **Chapter 6, Special Equipment**. It is important to remember that according to **Section 90.3**, **Chapters 1, 2, 3, and 4** apply generally and **Chapters 5, 6**, and **7** apply to special occupancies, special equipment, or other special conditions. These latter chapters supplement or modify the general rules. **Chapters 1** through **4** apply except as amended by **Chapters 5, 6**, and **7** for the particular conditions. Therefore, **Article 630** may amend the requirements of any other chapter in the *Code*.

Fundamental electric welding is accomplished by the use of a low voltage and an exceptionally high current.

12.1.1 Types of Welders

The *Code* contains specific requirements for the different types of welders. **Article 630** covers two basic types of welders:

1. Arc Welders

   Nonmotor Generator Type - This type of welder looks like a box and has no moving parts. It contains a transformer to step down the voltage and a bank of rectifiers to change the voltage from AC to DC, which is used for the welding process. Modern welding equipment no longer uses DC secondary circuits exclusively. This welder is used to join two pieces of metal with the use of a welding rod by properly flowing the liquid metal to bond the two pieces of metal. The AC transformer and DC rectifier welder is a nonmotor generator type welder.

   Motor Generator Type - This type of welder is often referred to as a rotary welder because it has moving parts that rotate. As the name indicates, it is a motor generator. It has an AC motor that drives a DC generator used for the actual welding. It is used in the same manner as the AC transformer and DC rectifier type.

2. Resistance Welders

   Resistance Welders - Resistance welders furnish a high current to two electrodes. When pieces of metal are placed between the electrodes, current flows and the resistance of the metal causes the metal to heat and fuse together. Resistance welding is often referred to as "spot welding" or "seam welding" when used in the manufacturing process.

Electric welders include portable and fixed AC arc welding machines, DC arc welding machines, TIG welding machines, MIG/MAG welding machines, plasma arc cutting machines, plasma arc welding equipment, and resistance ("spot") welding machines. **See Figure 12-1**.

12.1.2 Duty Cycle

The term *duty cycle* used in conjunction with welders refers to the length of time there will be a demand for current flow in the circuit and the length of the time the circuit will be at rest. The duty cycle is expressed as a percentage. A duty cycle of 40% indicates that the welding circuit operates 40% of the time and is at rest 60% of the time. Another way to look at it is that the current flow is heating the conductors 40% of the time, and the lack of current flow allows the conductors to cool 60% of the time. The welding current flow varies from full-load to partial load during the duty cycle. Since the circuit conductors are not required to carry their full ampacity at all times, the ampacity of the circuit conductors is permitted to be reduced according to the duty cycle of the welder.

12.1.3 Ampacity Multiplier

The multiplier is a number used to determine the ampacity of the circuit conductors for welding machines. The smaller the duty cycle, the less time the current will flow and the less ampacity the conductor is required to have. When a welder is used 100% of the time, it has a duty cycle of one and the circuit conductors are calculated at 100% of the rated primary current.

The multiplier is given as a decimal, which is a percentage. The multiplier given means that the ampacity of the primary conductors can have an ampacity rating less than the ampacity rating on the nameplate of the welder. Each type of welder has its own characteristics, resulting in separate multipliers for arc welders and resistance welders based upon the duty cycle.

12.1.4 Number of Welders

The duty cycle multiplier tables in **Article 630** are for the installation of a single welder. When more than one welder or a group of welders is installed on the same circuit, different calculations are used. These calculations are explained in **630.11(B)** and **630.31(B)** and are used to determine the ampacity of the feeder circuit conductors supplying a group of welding machines. These calculations are somewhat similar to the application of feeder demand factors of **Article 220**.

As previously noted, welders do not draw current 100% of the time, even when a group of welders is installed on the same circuit. Therefore, it is not anticipated that all the welders will be operating at full-load current 100% of the time.

12.2 ARC WELDERS

Arc welders are covered by **Part II** of **Article 630**.

According to **Section 630.14**, the rating plate of arc welders is required to be marked with either the I_{1max} and the I_{1eff} or the rated primary current (RPC).

I_{1eff} – This symbol is used on the rating plate of arc welders to indicate the effective input current required by the welder. This rating more accurately reflects the heating effect of the supply conductors because it considers both

Type of Welder	Identification	Identification
AC Transformer and DC Rectifier	Box	Nonmotor Generator
Motor Generator Arc Welder	Rotary	Motor Generator
Resistance Spot Welder	Resistance	

Figure 12-1. Arc Welder Types. *The welder and process selected are dependent upon the type of material to be welded and its thickness.*

the current at idle as well as the current while welding. When calculating the conductor size, the I_{1eff} given on the rating plate is used. When the I_{1eff} is not given, the RPC rating is used to calculate the conductor size for arc welders.

I_{1max} – This symbol is used on the rating plate of arc welders to indicate the current value to be used when calculating the overcurrent protective device for the welder circuit. When the I_{1max} is not given, the RPC rating is used to calculate the overcurrent protection for arc welders.

12.2.1 AC Transformer and DC Rectifier Type Welders

AC transformer and DC rectifier welders are just one type of welder under the category of arc welder or nonmotor generator welder. Other nonmotor generator welders include AC arc welding machines, DC arc welding machines, TIG welding machines, MIG/MAG welding machines, plasma arc cutting machines, and plasma arc welding equipment.

AC transformer and DC rectifier welders operate more efficiently than motor generator welders because they have no rotational losses.

12.2.1.1 Load Calculation for Individual Welders

Load calculations for individual welders are the simplest of welder calculations and follow **630.11(A)** for individual welders. The demand factor of the welder is obtained from the rating plate and the multiplier is determined using **Table 630.11(A)**, Columns 1 and 2 only. Simply match the machine duty cycle in Column 1 to the multiplier in Column 2 in the same row.

Where RPC equals the rating plate current, the following formula is used to determine the ampacity (*I*) of the welder branch circuit:

$$I = RPC \times \text{multiplier}$$

Where the rating plate contains the value for $I_{1\text{eff}}$, no calculations are necessary since the demand factor and the multiplier have already been accounted for.

$$I = I_{1\text{eff}}$$

Overcurrent protection must also be provided for the welding machine, as well as for the conductors that supply it. For arc welders, **Section 630.12** sets forth the maximum limit of 200% for the overcurrent protective device selection in order to provide protection against short circuits. Proper operation of the welder, together with overload circuit controls within the apparatus, will protect against overloads. However, most manufacturer installation instructions recommend an overcurrent protective device sized less than 200%. Where a welding machine is a listed or labeled product, the manufacturer instructions become part of the listing requirements and must be followed as if they were part of the *Code*.

NEC **110.3(B)** indicates that listed or labeled equipment shall be installed and used in accordance with any instructions included in the listing or labeling. **See Problems 12-1 and 12-2.**

For additional information, visit qr.njatcdb.org Item #1044

12.2.1.2 Load Calculation for Multiple Welders

NEC **630.11(B)** addresses the installation of a group of welders on the same circuit. The following conditions apply:

1. Calculate each welder using the multiplier listed in **Table 630.11(A)**.
2. Each welder is considered for its particular duty.
3. The total load is not the sum of the calculated individual currents.
4. All welders are not considered to be operating at the same time.
5. The ampacity of the circuit conductors is permitted to be a percentage of the total calculated duty load.
6. The percentage of calculated current varies for each welder in the group. **See Figure 12-2.**

See Problems 12-3, 12-4, 12-5, and 12-6.

Number of Welders	% of Calculated Current
Largest	100%
2nd Largest	100%
3rd Largest	85%
4th Largest	70%
5th Largest and More	60%

Figure 12-2. NEC 630.11(B) Summary. *On construction sites and in fabrication shops, it is common to encounter 4-pack and 6-pack multioperator welders.*

PROBLEM 12-1

An AC transformer and a DC rectifier welder has a rated primary current (RPC) of 40 amperes with a duty cycle of 70%.

Calculate the ampacity of the circuit conductors.

Solution

Table 630.11(A)
Nonmotor generator column; duty cycle 70%
Multiplier = 0.84
I = RPC × multiplier
   = 40 × 0.84
   = 33.6 A
Answer: 33.6 A

On a typical nameplate of a nonmotor generator arc welder, the primary current is listed along with the duty cycle rating under the secondary side as needed to size the conductors and overcurrent protection.

CHAPTER 12 ELECTRIC WELDERS

PROBLEM 12-2

An AC transformer and DC rectifier arc welder have a duty cycle of 50% and a rated primary current of 38 amperes. Calculate the following:

1. Ampacity
2. Size of copper conductors with THWN 75°C rated insulation
3. Maximum overcurrent protective device (OCPD)

Solution

Calculation 1
Ampacity
Table 630.11(A)
  Nonmotor generator column; duty cycle of 50%
  Multiplier = 0.71
  I = RPC × multiplier
     = 38 × 0.71
     = 26.98 A
Answer: 26.98 A

Calculation 2
Circuit conductors
Table 310.15(B)(16)
  75°C copper column
  26.98 A = 10 AWG THWN
  Double asterisk note does not apply
Answer: 10 AWG THWN

Calculation 3
Overcurrent protective device (OCPD)
630.12(A)
  Max. OCPD = RPC × 200%
            = 38 × 2.00
            = 76 A
Section 630.12, Section 240.6
  76 A is not a standard rating
  Next larger standard size = 80 A
While an 80A OCPD is suitable for protection of the welder in accordance with 630.12(A), as the welder is supplied with 10 AWG THWN, 630.12(B) requires the conductors to be protected by an OCPD rated at not more 200% of the ampacity of the conductors
  200% of 35 A (ampacity of 10 AWG THWN) results in an OCPD of 70 A
Answer: 70A maximum circuit breaker

PROBLEM 12-3

Calculate the ampacity of the circuit conductors for two welders to be installed on the same branch circuit when the welders are AC transformer and DC rectifier arc welders with the following rated primary current ratings and duty cycles:

| Welder No. 1 | 28 A | 30% duty cycle |
| Welder No. 2 | 18 A | 80% duty cycle |

Solution

Ampacity of welders

Welder No. 1
Table 630.11(A)
  Nonmotor generator column; duty cycle of 30%
  Multiplier = 0.55
  I = RPC × multiplier
     = 28 × 0.55
     = 15.4 A
Answer: 15.4 A

Welder No. 2
Table 630.11(A)
  Nonmotor generator column; duty cycle of 80%
  Multiplier = 0.89
  I = RPC × multiplier
     = 18 × 0.89
     = 16.02 A
Answer: 16.02 A

Calculation
630.11(B)

Welder No. 2, largest	16.02 × 100%	16.02
Welder No. 1, 2nd largest	15.40 × 100%	15.40
Total		31.42

Answer: 31.42 A

PROBLEM 12-4

Calculate the circuit conductor ampacity, the minimum size circuit conductors, and the maximum size overcurrent protection of the circuit conductors when three AC transformer and DC rectifier arc welders are to be installed on the same welder feeder circuit, with the following rated primary current ratings and duty cycles:

Welder No. 1	14 A	20% duty cycle
Welder No. 2	24 A	90% duty cycle
Welder No. 3	32 A	60% duty cycle

Solution

Calculation 1
Ampacity of welders
Welder No. 1
Table 630.11(A)
  Nonmotor generator column; duty cycle of 20%
  Multiplier = 0.45
  I = RPC × multiplier
     = 14 × 0.45
     = 6.3 A
Answer: 6.3 A
Welder No. 2
Table 630.11(A)
  Nonmotor generator column; duty cycle of 90%
  Multiplier = 0.95
  I = RPC × multiplier
     = 24 × 0.95
     = 22.8 A
Answer: 22.8 A
Welder No. 3
Table 630.11(A)
  Nonmotor generator column; duty cycle of 60%
  Multiplier = 0.78
  I = RPC × multiplier
     = 32 × 0.78
     = 24.96 A
Answer: 24.96 A
Calculation
630.11(B)

Welder No. 3, largest	24.96 × 100%	24.96
Welder No. 2, 2nd largest	22.80 × 100%	22.80
Welder No. 1, 3rd largest	6.30 × 85%	5.36
Total		53.12

Answer: 53.12 A

Calculation 2
Circuit conductors
Table 310.16
  75°C copper column
  53.12 A = 6 AWG THWN
  The asterisk note does not apply
Answer: 6 AWG THWN

Calculation 3
Overcurrent protective device (OCPD)
630.12(A)
Table 310.16 Ampacity
  75°C copper column
  6 AWG THWN = 65 A
  Max. OCPD = conductor ampacity × 200%
            = 65 × 2.00
            = 130 A
Section 630.12, Section 240.6
  130 A not a standard rating
  Next larger standard size = 150 A
Answer: 150A maximum fuse or circuit breaker

PROBLEM 12-5

Calculate the ampacity of the circuit conductors for four AC transformer and DC rectifier arc welders to be installed on the same circuit with the following rated primary current ratings and duty cycles:

Welder No. 1	40 A	20% duty cycle
Welder No. 2	28 A	70% duty cycle
Welder No. 3	24 A	50% duty cycle
Welder No. 4	16 A	40% duty cycle

Solution

Welder No. 1
Table 630.11(A)
 Nonmotor generator column; duty cycle of 20%
 Multiplier = 0.45
 I = RPC × multiplier
   = 40 × 0.45
   = 18 A
Answer: 18 A

Welder No. 2
Table 630.11(A)
 Nonmotor generator column; duty cycle of 70%
 Multiplier = 0.84
 I = RPC × multiplier
   = 28 × 0.84
   = 23.52 A
Answer: 23.52 A

Welder No. 3
Table 630.11(A)
 Nonmotor generator column; duty cycle of 50%
 Multiplier = 0.71
 I = RPC × multiplier
   = 24 × 0.71
   = 17.04 A
Answer: 17.04 A

Welder No. 4
Table 630.11(A)
 Nonmotor generator column; duty cycle of 40%
 Multiplier = 0.63
 I = RPC × multiplier
   = 16 × 0.63
   = 10.08 A
Answer: 10.08 A

Calculation
630.11(B)

Welder No. 2, largest	23.52 × 100%	23.52
Welder No. 1, 2nd largest	18.00 × 100%	18.00
Welder No. 3, 3rd largest	17.04 × 85%	14.48
Welder No. 4, 4th largest	10.08 × 70%	7.06
Total		63.06

Answer: 63.06 A

PROBLEM 12-6

Calculate the ampacity of the circuit conductors for five AC transformer and DC rectifier arc welders to be installed on the same circuit with the following rated primary current ratings and duty cycles:

Welder No. 1	40 A	50% duty cycle
Welder No. 2	12 A	40% duty cycle
Welder No. 3	24 A	80% duty cycle
Welder No. 4	20 A	30% duty cycle
Welder No. 5	24 A	90% duty cycle

RPC 40 A Duty cycle 50% No. 1
RPC 12 A Duty cycle 40% No. 2
RPC 24 A Duty cycle 80% No. 3
RPC 20 A Duty cycle 30% No. 4
RPC 24 A Duty cycle 90% No. 5

Solution

Welder No. 1
Table 630.11(A)
 Nonmotor generator column; duty cycle of 50%
 Multiplier = 0.71
 I = RPC × multiplier
   = 40 × 0.71
   = 28.4 A
Answer: 28.4 A

Welder No. 2
Table 630.11(A)
 Nonmotor generator column; duty cycle of 40%
 Multiplier = 0.63
 I = RPC × multiplier
   = 12 × 0.63
   = 7.56 A
Answer: 7.56 A

Welder No. 3
Table 630.11(A)
 Nonmotor generator column; duty cycle of 80%
 Multiplier = 0.89
 I = RPC × multiplier
   = 24 × 0.89
   = 21.36 A
Answer: 21.36 A

Welder No. 4
Table 630.11(A)
 Nonmotor generator column; duty cycle of 30%
 Multiplier = 0.55
 I = RPC × multiplier
   = 20 × 0.55
   = 11 A
Answer: 11 A

Welder No. 5
Table 630.11(A)
 Nonmotor generator column; duty cycle of 90%
 Multiplier = 0.95
 I = RPC × multiplier
   = 24 × 0.95
   = 22.8 A
Answer: 22.8 A

Calculation
630.11(B)

Welder No. 1, largest	28.40 × 100%	28.40
Welder No. 5, 2nd largest	22.80 × 100%	22.80
Welder No. 3, 3rd largest	21.36 × 85%	18.16
Welder No. 4, 4th largest	11.00 × 70%	7.70
Welder No. 2, 5th largest	7.56 × 60%	4.54
Total		81.60

Answer: 81.6 A

For additional information, visit qr.njatcdb.org Item #2555

Section 630.13 requires a disconnecting means to be installed in the supply circuit for each arc welder that is not equipped with a disconnect mounted as an integral part of the welder. The disconnecting means identity is required to be marked in compliance with NEC **110.22(A)**.

12.2.2 Motor Generator Type

The motor generator arc welder uses an electrical motor physically coupled to an electrical generator. The electrical generator delivers the low voltage and adjustable welding current necessary to weld. In many ways, a stand-alone fossil-fuel engine-driven generator (welder) is similar to an electrical motor-driven generator (welder), except that the motor-driven generator is powered by electricity as opposed to the fossil-fuel power of the engine generator.

Motor generator arc welders are less efficient than box-type arc welders because of the additional electrical motor, so motor generator welders naturally require a slightly larger set of supply conductors. Therefore, when sizing conductors for motor generators, the third column of **Table 630.11(A)** must be used to size these conductors.

12.2.2.1 Load Calculation for Individual Welders
NEC **630.11(A)** is used to determine the ampacity of the circuit conductors supplying a motor generator arc welder, which is similar to other arc welders. However, when using **Table 630.11(A)** to find the multiplier from the given duty cycle, the third column, entitled "Motor Generator," must be used. **See Problems 12-7 and 12-8.**

12.2.2.2 Load Calculation for Multiple Welders
The calculation for a group of motor generator arc welders is identical to the AC transformer and DC rectifier arc welders:

1. Calculate each welder using the multiplier listed in **Table 630.11(A)**.
2. Each welder is considered for its particular duty.
3. The total load is not the sum of the calculated individual currents.
4. All welders are not considered to be operating at the same time.
5. The ampacity of the circuit conductors is permitted to be a percentage of the total calculated duty load.

PROBLEM 12-7

Calculate the ampacity of the circuit conductors for a motor generator arc welder with a nameplate current of 60 amperes and a duty cycle of 80%.

Solution
Table 630.11(A)
 Motor generator column; duty cycle of 80%
 Multiplier = 0.91
 I = RPC × multiplier
   = 60 × 0.91
   = 54.6 A
Answer: 54.6 A

PROBLEM 12-8

Calculate the ampacity of the circuit conductors for a motor generator arc welder with a duty cycle of 60% and a rated primary current of 36 amperes.

Solution
Table 630.11(A)
 Motor generator column; duty cycle of 60%
 Multiplier = 0.81
 I = RPC × multiplier
   = 36 × 0.81
   = 29.16 A
Answer: 29.16 A

6. The percentage of calculated current varies for each welder in the group. **See Figure 12-3.**

See **Problem 12-9**.

Number of Welders	% of Calculated Current
Largest	100%
2nd Largest	100%
3rd Largest	85%
4th Largest	70%
5th Largest and More	60%

Figure 12-3. 630.11(B) Summary. *A motor generator arc welder often utilizes a 3-phase motor to spin a DC generator to produce direct current that is more desirable to weld with than DC power rectified from an AC source.*

PROBLEM 12-9

Calculate the ampacity of the branch-circuit conductors for six motor generator arc welders, when all six welders have a rated primary current rating of 21 amperes and a 60% duty cycle.

Solution

Ampacity for all 6 welders
Table 630.11(A)
  Motor generator column; duty cycle of 60%
  Multiplier = 0.81
  I = RPC × multiplier
    = 21 × 0.81
    = 17.01 A
Answer: 17.01 A

Calculation
630.11(B)

Largest	17.01 × 100%	17.01
2nd largest	17.01 × 100%	17.01
3rd largest	17.01 × 85%	14.46
4th largest	17.01 × 70%	11.91
5th largest	17.01 × 60%	10.21
6th largest	17.01 × 60%	10.21
Total		80.81

Answer: 80.81 A

12.3 RESISTANCE WELDERS

The next type of welder is the resistance welder, which is used for spot welding and seam welding and can be operated automatically or manually. According to **Article 630, Part III**, resistance welders can be operated at different timing cycles and less than their rated primary current, resulting in various calculations.

The following *Code* terms and symbols are applicable to resistance welders:

- **Nameplate** - For resistance welders, the required input marking includes voltage, phase, frequency, and rated kilovolt-amperes (kVA) at a 50% duty cycle.
- **Rated primary current** - The rated kilovolt-amperes (kVA) is multiplied by 1,000 and divided by the rated primary voltage using the values given on the nameplate. This rated primary current is expressed in the following formula:

$$I_{pri} = \frac{kVA \times 1{,}000}{E_{pri}}$$

- **Actual primary current** - The actual primary current is the current drawn from the supply circuit during each welder operation at the particular heat tap and control setting used.
- **Duty cycle** - The duty cycle is the percentage of time during which the resistance welder is loaded.

12.3.1 Load Calculation for Individual Welders

The primary current can be found using the following equation:

$$I_{pri} = \frac{kVA \times 1{,}000}{E_{pri}}$$

According to **630.31(A)(1)**, calculations depend on the duty cycle, known or unknown, and whether the welder is manually or automatically operated.

Automatic operation:

$$I_{pri} \times 70\%$$

Manual operation:

$$I_{pri} \times 50\%$$

See Problem 12-10.

PROBLEM 12-10

Calculate the ampacity of the circuit conductors for a 15 kVA resistance welder operated on a 220-volt, single-phase circuit. The duty cycle or operating time is not known and the welder is operated both automatically and manually.

Solution

Calculation 1
Automatic operation

$$I_{pri} = \frac{kVA \times 1{,}000}{E_{pri}}$$
$$= \frac{15 \times 1{,}000}{220}$$
$$= 68.18 \text{ A}$$

630.31(A)(1)

$$\text{Conductor } I = I_{pri} \times 70\%$$
$$= 68.18 \times 0.70$$
$$= 47.72 \text{ A}$$

Answer: 47.72 A

Calculation 2
Manual operation

$$I_{pri} = \frac{kVA \times 1{,}000}{E_{pri}}$$
$$= \frac{15 \times 1{,}000}{220}$$
$$= 68.18 \text{ A}$$

630.31(A)(1)

$$\text{Conductor } I = I_{pri} \times 50\%$$
$$= 68.18 \times 0.50$$
$$= 34.09 \text{ A}$$

Answer: 34.09 A

Reproduced with permission of NFPA from NFPA 70®, *National Electrical Code*® (NEC®), 2020 edition. Copyright© 2019, National Fire Protection Association. For a full copy of the NEC®, please go to www.nfpa.org.

Where a resistance welder is designated for a specific operation, each of the following values must be known before ampacity and overcurrent calculations can be completed:

1. The actual primary current, or the actual current the primary will draw at a particular heat tap and control setting
2. The duty cycle
3. The multiplier from **Table 630.31(A)**; **See Figure 12-4**.

Table 630.31(A) Duty Cycle Multiplication Factors for Resistance Welders

Duty Cycle (%)	Multiplier
50	0.71
40	0.63
30	0.55
25	0.50
20	0.45
15	0.39
10	0.32
7.5	0.27
5 or less	0.22

Figure 12-4. Table 630.31(A). Duty cycle multiplication factors are limited to resistance welders.

12.3.2 Load Calculation for Multiple Welders

When a group of resistance welders is supplied by the same circuit conductors, the ampacity of the circuit conductors is based on the calculated conductor current in accordance with **630.31(A)** for automatic or manual operation. According to **630.31(B)**, the first welder is at 100%, and all others are at 60%.

For the largest welder:

$$\text{Ampacity} = \text{Conductor } I \times 100\%$$

All other welders:

$$\text{Ampacity} = \text{Conductor } I \times 60\%$$

See Problems 12-11 and 12-12.

An example of a resistance-type welder is a 225-ampere tungsten inert gas (TIG) electric welder. Courtesy of the Lincoln Electric Company

12.3.3 Calculating Duty Cycle

Informational Note No. 3 to **630.31(B)** illustrates how to calculate the duty cycle. **See Problems 12-13 and 12-14.**

PROBLEM 12-11

Spot Welder
I Primary 40 A
Duty Cycle 40%

Calculate the ampacity of the circuit conductors for a resistance-type spot welder when the actual primary current is 40 amperes and the duty cycle is 40%.

Solution

630.31(A)(2)

Multiplier for 40% duty cycle = 0.63

$$I = I_{pri} \times \text{multiplier}$$
$$= 40 \times 0.63$$
$$= 25.2 \text{ A}$$

Answer: 25.2 A

PROBLEM 12-12

Calculate the ampacity of the circuit conductors for two resistance welders rated 20kVA, 240-volt, single-phase and installed on the same circuit, when no duty cycle is indicated and the welders are either automatically operated or manually operated.

Solution

Calculation 1
Automatic operation

$$I_{\text{pri}} = \frac{\text{kVA} \times 1{,}000}{E_{\text{pri}}}$$
$$= \frac{20 \times 1{,}000}{240}$$
$$= 83.33 \text{ A}$$

630.31(A)(1)

Conductor $I = I_{\text{pri}} \times 70\%$
$= 83.33 \times 0.70$
$= 58.33 \text{ A}$

Welder No. 1
630.31(B)
$I = \text{Conductor } I \times 100\%$
$= 58.33 \times 1.00$
$= 58.33 \text{ A}$
Answer: 58.33 A

Welder No. 2
630.31(B)
$I = \text{Conductor } I \times 60\%$
$= 58.33 \times 0.60$
$= 35 \text{ A}$
Answer: 35 A

Calculation
$I_{\text{total}} = \text{largest} + \text{others}$
$= 58.33 + 35$
$= 93.33 \text{ A}$
Answer: 93.33 A

Calculation 2
Manual operation

$$I_{\text{pri}} = \frac{\text{kVA} \times 1{,}000}{E_{\text{pri}}}$$
$$= \frac{20 \times 1{,}000}{240}$$
$$= 83.33 \text{ A}$$

630.31(A)(1)

Conductor $I = I_{\text{pri}} \times 50\%$
$= 83.33 \times 0.50$
$= 41.67 \text{ A}$

Welder No. 1
630.31(B)
$I = \text{Conductor } I \times 100\%$
$= 41.67 \times 100$
$= 41.67 \text{ A}$
Answer: 41.67 A

Welder No. 2
630.31(B)
$I = \text{Conductor } I \times 60\%$
$= 41.67 \times 0.60$
$= 25 \text{ A}$
Answer: 25 A

Calculation
$I_{\text{total}} = \text{largest} + \text{others}$
$= 41.67 + 25$
$= 66.67 \text{ A}$
Answer: 66.67 A

PROBLEM 12-13

A resistance-type spot welder makes 500 welds per hour on a 60-cycle AC circuit. It takes 18 cycles to make each weld. What is the duty cycle?

Solution

Number of cycles in one hour:
60 cycles × 60 sec/min × 60 min/hr = 216,000 cycles
Time or number of cycles current drawn in one hour:
18 cycles × 500 welds = 9,000 cycles

$$\text{Duty cycle} = \frac{\text{time of use}}{\text{time available}}$$
$$= \frac{9{,}000}{216{,}000}$$
$$= 0.041 \text{ or } 4.1\%$$

Answer: 4.1%

PROBLEM 12-14

A resistance-type spot welder is timed to be ON 6 cycles and OFF 9 cycles. What is the duty cycle?

Solution

$$\text{Duty cycle} = \frac{\text{time on}}{\text{time on} + \text{time off}}$$
$$= \frac{6 \text{ cycles}}{6 \text{ cycles} + 9 \text{ cycles}}$$
$$= 0.40 \text{ or } 40\%$$

Answer: 40%

DEFINITIONS AND TERMS

Rating Plate - The general term for a welder nameplate used in the welding industry.

Duty Cycle - The percentage of a (10-minute) cycle during which the welder is loaded, or the length of time there will be a demand for current flow in the circuit compared to the length of the time the circuit will be at rest.

I_{1max} - The maximum value of the rated supply current at maximum rated output.

I_{1eff} - The effective input current required by the welder that considers both welding and idle current.

SUMMARY

Welders are frequently encountered on construction sites and fabrication shops. The two basic types of welders addressed by the *National Electrical Code* are arc welders and resistance welders. The *Code* allows the use of duty cycles and demand factors for multiple motors to be applied to correctly size supply conductors. Proper application of **Article 630** will ensure a safe and reliable installation for electric welders.

REVIEW QUESTIONS

1. The duty cycle of a welder is best defined as __?__.
   a. the percentage of time the welder is not operated
   b. the percentage of time the welder is operated
   c. the percentage of time the welder is operated above its current rating
   d. the percentage of time the welder is operated below its current rating

2. A nonmotor generator arc welder is best defined as __?__.
   a. a spot welding machine
   b. a transformer to step down the voltage and an AC-to-DC rectifier
   c. an AC motor which drives a DC generator
   d. two electrodes that clamp the material and provide a high current

3. If five or more welders are to be supplied by the same branch-circuit conductors, what is the demand factor percentage required for the largest welder?
   a. 60%
   b. 70%
   c. 85%
   d. 100%

4. For determination of overcurrent protection of an arc welder, the overcurrent protective device shall be rated not more than 200% of which current rating of the welder?
   a. I_{1eff}
   b. I_{1max}
   c. $I_{duty\ cycle}$
   d. I_{sec}

5. If the I_{1eff} value or I_{1max} value is not provided on the arc welder, which value as marked on the welder is required to be used for sizing conductors and overcurrent protection?
   a. The duty current
   b. The power rating divided by the voltage
   c. The rated primary current
   d. The secondary current

6. If an arc welder has a marked overcurrent protective device of 60 amperes maximum, and 200% of the I_{1max} value results in an overcurrent protective device of 80 amperes, what is the maximum permitted overcurrent protective device for the arc welder?
   a. 60 A
   b. 80 A
   c. 80 A, provided the authority having jurisdiction accepts the installation
   d. Both 60 A and 80 A are correct

7. When sizing the branch-circuit conductors for an individual arc welder, which is the correct formula to use?
   a. I (ampacity) = I_{1eff}
   b. I (ampacity) = I_{1eff} × multiplier from **Table 630.11(A)** based on duty cycle
   c. I (ampacity) = rated primary current × multiplier from **Table 630.11(A)** based on duty cycle
   d. Either a. or c.

8. Four welders are installed and supplied by the same branch-circuit conductors and each has an I_{1eff} of 20 amperes. What is the minimum required ampacity of the branch-circuit conductors?
   a. 56 A
   b. 71 A
   c. 80 A
   d. 100 A

9. An arc welder has an I_{1max} current rating of 42 amperes. What is the maximum standard size overcurrent protective device to supply the welder?
   a. 50 A
   b. 60 A
   c. 80 A
   d. 90 A

10. Six arc welders are supplied with 1/0 AWG THWN copper conductors. What is the maximum standard size overcurrent protective device to supply the welders?
    a. 150 A
    b. 250 A
    c. 300 A
    d. 350 A